THE CAMBRIDGE COMPANION TO LITERATURE AND ANIMALS

The Cambridge Companion to Literature and Animals surveys the role of animals across literary history and opens conversations on what literature can teach us about more-than-human life. Leading international scholars comprehensively explore how engaging with creatures of various kinds alters our understanding of what it means to write and read, and why this is important for thinking about a series of cultural, ethical, political, and scientific developments and controversies. The first part of the book offers historically rooted arguments about medieval metamorphosis, early modern fleshiness, eighteenth-century imperialism, Romantic sympathy, Victorian racial politics, modernist otherness, and contemporary forms. The second part poses questions that cut across periods, concerning habitat and extinction, captivity and spectatorship, race and (post-)coloniality, sexuality and gender, religion and law, health and wealth. In doing so, this companion places animals at the center of literary studies and literature at the heart of urgent debates in the growing field of animal studies.

DEREK RYAN is Senior Lecturer in Modernist Literature at the University of Kent. His previous books include *Bloomsbury, Beasts and British Modernist Literature* (Cambridge University Press, 2022), *Animal Theory: A Critical Introduction* (Edinburgh University Press, 2015), and the coedited volume *Reading Literary Animals: Medieval to Modern* (Routledge, 2019).

A complete list of books in the series is at the back of the book.

T0381671

THE CAMBRIDGE COMPANION TO LITERATURE AND ANIMALS

EDITED BY

DEREK RYAN

University of Kent

CAMBRIDGE
UNIVERSITY PRESS

CAMBRIDGE
UNIVERSITY PRESS

Shaftesbury Road, Cambridge CB2 8EA, United Kingdom

One Liberty Plaza, 20th Floor, New York, NY 10006, USA

477 Williamstown Road, Port Melbourne, VIC 3207, Australia

314–321, 3rd Floor, Plot 3, Splendor Forum, Jasola District Centre, New Delhi – 110025, India

103 Penang Road, #05–06/07, Visioncrest Commercial, Singapore 238467

Cambridge University Press is part of Cambridge University Press & Assessment, a department of the University of Cambridge.

We share the University's mission to contribute to society through the pursuit of education, learning and research at the highest international levels of excellence.

www.cambridge.org
Information on this title: www.cambridge.org/9781009300056

DOI: 10.1017/9781009300032

First published 2023

A catalogue record for this publication is available from the British Library

Library of Congress Cataloging-in-Publication Data
NAMES: Ryan, Derek, editor.
TITLE: The Cambridge companion to literature and animals / edited by Derek Ryan.
DESCRIPTION: Cambridge, United Kingdom ; New York, New York : Cambridge University Press, 2023. | Series: Cambridge companions to literature. | Includes bibliographical references and index.
IDENTIFIERS: LCCN 2022061148 (print) | LCCN 2022061149 (ebook) | ISBN 9781009300056 (hardback) | ISBN 9781009300049 (paperback) | ISBN 9781009300032 (epub)
SUBJECTS: LCSH: Animals in literature. | Human-animal relationships in literature. | Animal welfare in literature. | Literature–History and criticism. | LCGFT: Literary criticism.
CLASSIFICATION: LCC PN56.A64 C36 2023 (print) | LCC PN56.A64 (ebook) | DDC 809/.93362–dc23/eng/20230216
LC record available at https://lccn.loc.gov/2022061148
LC ebook record available at https://lccn.loc.gov/2022061149

ISBN 978-1-009-30005-6 Hardback
ISBN 978-1-009-30004-9 Paperback

Contents

Figures

Contributors

LUCINDA COLE, University of Illinois

KAREN L. EDWARDS, University of Exeter

ANNA FEUERSTEIN, University of Hawai'i-Mānoa

MONICA FLEGEL, Lakehead University

ERICA FUDGE, University of Strathclyde, Glasgow

SARAH KAY, New York University

DONNA LANDRY, University of Kent

ROBERT MCKAY, University of Sheffield

TOBIAS MENELY, University of California

DEREK RYAN, University of Kent

PAUL SHEEHAN, Macquarie University

NATHAN SNAZA, University of Richmond

JANE SPENCER, University of Exeter

MELANIE BENSON TAYLOR, Dartmouth College

ANTOINE TRAISNEL, University of Michigan

Introduction

Derek Ryan

In the 2018 short story "Issue," by Irish writer Cormac James, the narrator asks readers to close their eyes and imagine looking down on a scene, gradually revealed to be an industrial-scale fish farm where roe is extracted to make caviar:

> it's all coming into focus now, as in a particularly vivid dream – it's a huge tank filled with water, and full of huge fish, all the same colour, shape and size. *The same* does not mean similar. It does not mean merely of common species. These fish are all replicas, down to the last detail. Do you understand? [...] I want you to look up and see dozens and dozens of identical tubs laid out in perfectly spaced rows in every direction, almost as far as the eye can see. It's some kind of laboratory fish farm on a scale beyond anything you've ever imagined. [...] Looking directly down again, you see no bottom to the well, if you can think of it as a kind of well, the light can't penetrate so much living flesh, it's so tightly packed [.] [...] They are sturgeon.[1]

The story is an ironic experiment in cross-species recognition: the more the plight of these fish comes into view, the more apparent is humanity's short-sightedness. In asking us to close our eyes, the narrator is aware that we must keep them open to continue the story. But open eyes do not always see – have not always seen – clearly. If "[a]lmost everything unpleasant happens out of sight," what can literature bring back into our line of vision?[2] If from our vantage point of "great height" we find "fish beyond number, or more precisely of a number the human mind can reach for but never grasp," what might words reach for, and how far does their meaning escape our grasp?[3]

Included in an issue of *Granta* magazine titled *Animalia*, "Issue" is one of several stories that play on the proximity and distance of human and nonhuman animals, along with associated tensions between recognition and alienation, empathy and exploitation. In Steven Dunn's "The Taxidermy Museum," where dead soldiers are mounted for display, we read that "lots of parallels can be drawn between performing taxidermy on the other Great Apes and Humans." The word "other" is carefully positioned; instead of animals considered the human's extreme other, here the human is treated as simply another animal.[4] In Christina Wood Martinez's "The Astronaut," the titular character (whose existence we are never quite sure is real or imagined) becomes a bemused witness to a discontented married couple and their dog as he is welcomed into their 1960s American household. The narrator describes looking into her dog's eyes and finding "wild excitement so close to a look of terror, or perhaps it was unconditional love"; her husband, meanwhile, enjoys pheasant hunting and, on one occasion, is found drowning newborn opossums whose mother was judged to be "rabid" and so "they were probably too small to make it on their own."[5] Yoko Tawada's "The Last Children of Tokyo" imagines a future in which a child is so far removed from animals that words are, poignantly, the closest he will get to them: "To Mumei, the words themselves were an animal that would start moving if only he stared at it long enough. [. . .] When he heard or saw the word heron, for instance, or sea turtle, he became obsessed, unable to take his eyes off the name from which he believed a living creature might emerge."[6] And Ben Lasman's "The Rat Snipers" homes in on the narrator and his colleague (as well as sometime lover) Nikki, whose job it was "to go shoot rats [. . .] from the roof of the Marriott downtown," even though these rats are seen as having a "human element," "a beguiling sort of personhood [. . .] an intelligence, a sensitivity."[7] Any empathy for these rats dissipates upon their killing (a point reinforced later, when a group of colleagues crowd round a smartphone to compare photos of dead rats for entertainment).[8] For all their inventive conceit and stylistic verve, these stories are most striking for the matter-of-factness with which they explore very different contexts – home or work, inner city or outer sea – in which humans meet, miss, and (mis)treat animals.

Other stories experiment with anthropomorphic voice, both to revel in the capacious worlds that animal life in its sheer variety invites us to imagine and to expose human cruelty toward those worlds and lives. In Nell Zink's "The Kabul Markhor," a goat-antelope who has been driving while drunk protests that he wants to leave the hospital he has been taken to, only to discover that he is now in debt to the zoo, which has been paying for his treatment, and is to be put to work "in the exhibition area." In response to his request to speak to his lawyer, he is told, "'I assume you know your rights,'" which the narrator informs us "was a standard phrase people used before giving animals the shaft" (these ominous words are followed by the doctor pulling out a cattle prod and revolver).[9] In "Web," Joy Williams assembles a speaking rat, horse, pig, sheep, goose, several spiders, and "silent calves who had been cloned from the meat of their butchered mothers."[10] In the tradition of Anna Sewell's *Black Beauty* (1877) – described by the horse in Williams's story as a "wonderful book" that "promoted kindness and sympathy and the worth of all creatures" – these talking animals explain how, at the same time as they have been honored "symbolically" by humans, their "creaturely kingdom is being slaughtered daily, hourly, without a qualm" as a result of "the terrible ways of men."[11] In these instances, disregarding the notion that speech belongs only to humans allows for a speculative anthropomorphism that critiques rather than colludes with anthropocentrism. Allegorical readings of the aforementioned stories – about *human* rights, alienation, incarceration, illness – are undoubtedly possible, but even such readings gain their potency via the shared vulnerability of more-than-human life. Williams's mention of *Black Beauty* is significant, too, in reminding us that the animals we encounter on the page are always already intertextual beasts with, as the essays collected in the current volume detail, their own long and complicated histories of representation and reception.

The different ways of seeing and unseeing animals, of speaking as or in place of other species, bring these stories of animalia into dialogue with John Berger's argument in "Why Look at Animals?" (1980). In this influential essay, Berger charts a broad historical movement in human-animal relations. After entering the human imaginary as metaphorical, mystical creatures and then securing their roles providing material necessities of "food, work, transport, clothing," animals in capitalist modernity increasingly become, in his view, physically marginalized and psychically co-opted.[12] In the late twentieth-century world Berger is concerned about, the slaughter of animals in factory farms happens (conveniently) out of sight; zoos "constitute the living monument to their own disappearance"; the picture-books and cartoons that fuel childhood imagination stand in for cross-species contact; and pets reveal a "withdrawal" into a private familial sphere and provide cover for our complicity in systemic exploitation.[13] It is within this (predominantly Western) context – one in which "animals have gradually disappeared" and humans have found a "new solitude" – that we have become "doubly uneasy" about an anthropomorphism that was once "integral to the relation between man and animal and was an expression of their proximity."[14] In addition, the words used to explore this complex dynamic of marginalization point in the direction of another cornerstone of contemporary thought on animals, namely, Jacques Derrida's *The Animal That Therefore I Am* (2008), which takes aim at the homogenizing function of the word "animal." "The confusion of all nonhuman living creatures within the general and common category of the animal," he writes, "is not simply a sin against rigorous thinking, vigilance, lucidity, or empirical authority, it is also a crime" – the same word is used by James in "Issue" about terms that obscure the realities of pisciculture ("*Benthic*," "*Infestation*," "*Faecal*," "*Algal*," "*Bloom*").[15] Derrida makes his own transgressive move by inventing the neologism "*animot*," a "monstrous hybrid, a chimera" that "contravene[s] the laws of the French language," thereby calling attention to the plural within the singular ("animot" as a homonym of the French plural "animaux"), as well as to the fact that such naming of the word (or "mot") is always and only a human construction.[16] Even if we continue, for the time being at least, to use the word "animal" or "animals" (we might add others, including "beast," "nonhuman," "creature," and indeed "human," similarly scrutinized in recent years),[17] he urges us "to silently substitute *animot* for what you hear."[18] This is not mere wordplay. At stake is the shedding of light on animals who have been undervalued or overlooked, redressing a situation whereby, as James writes in his story, "[t]o everyone but themselves, they are not worth the trouble."[19]

The Cambridge Companion to Literature and Animals demonstrates that consideration of how language can be used to engage with the material lives of animals runs deep through literary history. This book presents stories of medieval metamorphosis, early modern fleshiness, eighteenth-century imperialism, Romantic sympathy, Victorian racial politics, modernist otherness, and contemporary forms. It poses questions, too, that cut across periods, concerning habitat and extinction, captivity and spectatorship, race and (post-)coloniality, sexuality and gender, religion and law, health and wealth. Nonhuman creatures, as the following chapters illustrate, are to be found in any number of genres, whether fable or tragedy, realist novel or experimental poetry. They make us look anew at the writing of towering literary figures, from William Shakespeare to Virginia Woolf, while also shepherding us toward less familiar voices, like short story writer Ted Chiang or poets Tommy Pico and Janet McAdams. I began this introduction with a set of recently published stories not, then, to suggest that writing about animals is itself a new phenomenon. But if it would now require a feat of willful ignorance to imagine literature of any period or genre without animals, this is largely because of the work of scholars who have traced their multifaceted significance and shown that they have, in fact, been hidden in plain sight all along.[20] Throughout this volume, readers will encounter albatrosses, apes, axolotls, badgers, bears, caterpillars, cats, chickens, cows, deer, dogs, donkeys, elephants, falcons, flies, horses, leopards, lions, locusts, panthers, pigs, rats, sharks, whales, worms, wolves, and more. These literary animals, we will see repeatedly, challenge us to think again about the multiple ways in which the nonhuman is entangled with the human, and about how these entanglements inform our understanding of the relationship between literary creation and life itself.

Throughout the volume, emphasis is placed on tools, techniques, and topics that are of special importance to literary animal studies. The necessary centrality of human language to any reading of literature leads to sometimes paradoxical, often complicated, and frequently asymmetrical encounters. Linguistic devices help us to navigate multispecies relations and conceptualize animal worlds, yet they have also been celebrated as a marker of our exceptional status. Chapters therefore attend to the imaginative constructions of human-animal relationships found in literary texts, assessing what they reveal about animals and what they betray about the limits of human knowledge. The modeling of different kinds of subjectivity and agency; the role played by metaphor, simile, symbolism, and allegory in shaping our thoughts about nonhuman life; the different narrative techniques used to shift between human and nonhuman perspectives; the ambiguities of syntax and diction – all of these and more are crucial to the discussion of how animals figure in meaning-making. An analysis of "literature and animals" therefore requires not just close reading but *careful* reading in the two main senses of that word, which is to say being *concerned for* animals as well as *circumspect about* the assumptions we hold regarding them. In our careful but, it must be acknowledged, belated readings of animals there may even be a trace of the oldest, now obsolete meaning of the word "careful" dating back to the Middle Ages: "[f]ull of grief; mournful, sorrowful; also (of cries, etc.), expressing sorrow."[21] A careful approach to animals also guards against close reading becoming closed reading. In exploring animals in literature, the essays collected here are attuned to how writing about animals is shaped by, and can itself shape, historical events and evolving attitudes, to how textual and intertextual animals are connected to extratextual concerns of flesh, faith, and feeling.

This presence of and intensified focus on creaturely life in literature has become more apparent with the emergence of "animal studies" alongside animal rights activism against the use and abuse of animals in the global agricultural industry, medical and cosmetic research, hunting and captivity, the destruction of natural habitats, and processes of domestication. The work of numerous disciplines has defined the field since its inception in the latter decades of the twentieth century and rapid growth in more recent years. Ground-breaking interventions in analytic philosophy – most notably Peter Singer's utilitarian approach in *Animal Liberation* (1975), which popularized the term "speciesism,"[22] and Tom Regan's rights-based argument in *The Case for Animal Rights* (1983) – were crucial to the rise of the field, albeit literary critics are now more commonly drawn to the probing of species barriers in the continental tradition, of which Derrida's aforementioned book sits alongside *The Beast and the Sovereign* (2009/2011) as perhaps the most prevalent example.[23] Meanwhile, when accounting for the field's emergence and evolution it would be difficult to overstate the importance of advances in animal science – from comparative psychology to cognitive ethology – that continue to open up what philosopher and anthropologist Bruno Latour describes as "an entirely new world of capacities" beyond anything considered possible only a few decades ago.[24] Such developments have not provided definitive answers about animal life, but they have brought us closer to, in the spirit of philosopher of science Vinciane Despret's work, asking the right questions.[25] This has included returning to long-held assumptions about the animal part of the human, viewed over millennia as a threat that must be tamed or even shed. To be sure, what I am referring to as "animal studies" is subject to debates over competing terminology ("human-animal studies," "animality studies," "posthumanism") and different priorities (the relationality of species, the animal in human culture, or the dismantling of human/nonhuman binaries) that are often dependent on specific disciplinary emphases.[26] Nonetheless, the work contained in this volume, which builds directly or indirectly on various philosophical and scientific insights, suggests that the field's broad influence on literary studies has been profound and will, surely, be lasting.

The book's structure is designed to capture the field's key concerns in an informative and accessible manner for students, teachers, and researchers who may be engaging with literary animal studies for the first time. Its combination of period-based and thematic essays should provide a firm grounding for those who are keen to learn about historical continuities and shifts, while also serving those who are eager to discover how animal literature participates in wider critical debates. The fourteen chapters are split into two parts to reflect the significance of animals within the discipline of literary studies and broader terrain of animal studies: Part I, "Literary Periods," offers chapters on each of the discipline's widely recognized periods, from the medieval to contemporary;[27] Part II, "Contexts and Controversies," deepens and extends understandings of what we might, following Donna Haraway, call the "naturalcultural contact zones" literature puts us in touch with.[28] As such, it is hoped the volume will prepare new scholars of literary animal studies for the *intra*disciplinary interventions the subject demands and offer entryways into the *trans*disciplinary practice that captures theorist Cary Wolfe's idea of "distributed reflexivity," reminding us that individual disciplines can never straightforwardly reveal truths about their object of study, whether human or nonhuman.[29] Intradisciplinary and transdisciplinary work is in dynamic interaction throughout, where insights and methodologies in literary studies and animal studies are mutually informing and enriching, with the shared purpose of challenging anthropocentric orthodoxy and speciesist bias. This *Companion* works, then, as an introduction to other available resources on animals across the span of the literary tradition, encompassing book series and journal special issues,[30] as well as agenda-setting publications in animal studies more broadly conceived.[31]

Part I opens with chapters that examine matters of embodiment and flesh. Sarah Kay takes us back to the Middle Ages, where among philosophers and theologians the word *animalia* defined both human and nonhuman animals as living creatures; it was the immortal soul and perceptual apparatus that divided what in vernacular languages would be thought of as man and beast – terms that were, from their early usage, filled with ambiguity and a multiplicity of meaning. Kay explains the importance of retaining a distinction between "animals" and "beasts" in our thinking of medieval times, as doing so allows us to move from the realm of abstract ideas to concrete practices; that is, to attend to earthly entanglements associated with livestock, which provided materials for food, clothing, armor, lighting, transportation, and tools, among other things. Discussing the story of William of Palermo, snatched as a child by a wolf (who turns out to be the Spanish king's oldest son) and brought up by a cowhand, Kay is attentive to the use of coded figurative language while explaining that the text's human characters are identified as beasts in a remarkably literal manner. The chapter goes on to show that such interplay on the flesh of animalia finds its counterpart in the materiality of the story's manuscripts (one extant in French and one in English). After all, it becomes problematic if not impossible to divide culture from agriculture when writing materials and bookbinding depended on animal products, from quills and parchment to leather and glue. Fleshiness is then taken up by Erica Fudge in her exploration of early modern literature.

While encounters with living beasts in the period were various, from bear baiting and horse training to farm animals and exotic pets, the chapter locates a durable connection between man and beast in the consumption of meat. She argues that rather than straightforwardly signaling man's dominion, certain beliefs – for example, that meat from those animals deemed most similar to humans provides the best sustenance – create points of connection even amid species distinction. In particular, the question of mortality and immortality looks different from the perspective of decaying flesh as opposed to eternal afterlife, which in turn invites a different reading of a classic work such as Shakespeare's *Hamlet* (c. 1601). Picking out key scenes in which fleshiness is exposed, the perishability (and, from the point of view of worms, edibility) of the human body becomes part of our ontological condition. Like Kay, Fudge shows how turning to materiality and the body, rather than abstraction and the soul, undermines the human/animal binary.

The rise in animal welfare and feeling for animals takes center-stage in the following two chapters, which move into the eighteenth and early nineteenth centuries. Donna Landry explains that one major source of compassion for animals was found in the Oriental fictions that were popular during the European Enlightenment, a period in which natural history and fable, with its Eastern roots, intersected in fascinating ways. One work of seventeenth-century Ottoman literature by Evliya Çelebi, which combines scientific observations of animals with fiction and fantasy, is compared to a selection of eighteenth-century Anglophone writers who are, to different extents, attentive to natural history: Alexander Pope's epic poem *Windsor-Forest* (1713) imagines a bird's perspective and explores shared environments; James Thomson's *The Seasons* (1730) sees animals as fellow sensible subjects in its depiction of cross-species relations; while Jonathan Swift's *Gulliver's Travels* (1726) satirizes human exceptionalism. The Eastern influences in this latter text include knowledge about the importation of Ottoman blood horses and the compassionate way they had been looked after in their homeland. Finally, Gilbert White's *The Natural History of Selborne* (1789), full of local detail and at the same time highly aware of Britain's global commercial interests, can additionally be read, Landry points out, as a warning about the effects of climate some two centuries before the Anthropocene era was named. Turning to the tradition of Romanticism, Jane Spencer considers a series of poems that, in reckoning with animal death, challenge human superiority and blur the lines of species distinction. Her chapter ranges from the glimpses of human-animal connection we find in Samuel Taylor Coleridge's *The Rime of the Ancient Mariner* (1798) to empathy for animal bodily pain and mental torment in William Wordsworth's *Hart-Leap Well* (1800); from the bond between human and horse in Lord Byron's *Mazeppa* (1819) to the equivalence drawn between man and insect in William Blake's enigmatic poem "The Fly" (1794). Interestingly, these works echo children's literature in avowing care for animals, even if, as Spencer notes, Romantic poets have varying degrees of optimism and skepticism about transformation of the human vis-à-vis the animal. Sympathy for animals is, however, nowhere more compellingly expressed than in John Clare's poetry, attuned as it is to a wide range of species (including, as Spencer shows, badgers).

Matters of animal representation are heightened in both political and aesthetic terms in chapters on Victorian and modernist literature. The nineteenth century was the era of Martin's Act (1822), the Society for the Prevention of Cruelty to Animals (founded 1824), and the Vegetarian Society (founded 1847) – and, by the end of the period, laws would be passed to regulate slaughterhouses. It was also the epoch of Charles Darwin and new scientific texts on animal intelligence. Anna Feuerstein's chapter importantly shows, however, that human-animal relations in the period cannot be properly understood without due attention to the politics of colonial expansion and the commodification of exotic beasts through hunting and commerce. Looking at animals as characters in realist novels by Charles Dickens and Thomas Hardy, she argues that writers created a kind of racialized taxonomy under which species were brought together. Such representations of animals often went hand-in-hand with the manipulation of human characters along racialized and gendered grounds, as seen in Olive Schreiner's *The Story of an African Farm* (1883), where the farm is a space of colonial control of Indigenous peoples, animals, and land. Such racialization is rife across adventure novels, hunting and travel narratives, and colonial memoirs; it occurs in novels set in England, too, most famously in Charlotte Brontë's depiction of Bertha Mason as savage beast in *Jane Eyre* (1847). In his chapter, Paul Sheehan explores how modernist literature grapples with its nineteenth-century heritage in animal aesthetics to push alterity to its limits. He begins with one of the most conspicuous animal subjects of American literature, the giant white whale in Herman Melville's *Moby-Dick* (1851), a novel that gained belated appreciation in the early twentieth century. Modernism picks up Melville's fascination with fantastic, almost monstrous beasts and runs with it in its avowal of otherness. We are shown how hybridity is found in the poetry of W. B. Yeats, especially the cryptid beast in "The Second Coming" (1919), and how Djuna Barnes sends up species hierarchies and classification in her genre-bending bestiary *Creatures in an Alphabet* (1982) and experimental novels *Ryder* (1928) and *Nightwood* (1936). Sheehan switches focus in the second half of his chapter to domesticated animals. In Virginia Woolf's fictional biography of Elizabeth Barrett Browning's cocker spaniel, *Flush: A Biography* (1933), a canine-centered perspective sneaks through via her use of free indirect discourse – and a host of other devices – to disrupt anthropocentrism even within a human-controlled setting. In T. S. Eliot's "The Love Song of J. Alfred Prufrock" (1915) and James Joyce's *Ulysses* (1922), on the other hand, a feline aesthetic steals the show. In all instances, we find examples of modernists seeking that which escapes or exceeds the conventions of representation and identification.

To conclude the first part of the book, Robert McKay takes up the period from the end of World War II onward to chart critical approaches to contemporary literary animals – those that have emerged at the same time as the rise of animal studies as a discipline. His case study is George Orwell's *Animal Farm* (1945), a book that has influenced strands of contemporary literature including animal satire, the talking animal tale, and critical agricultural fictions, but which has also elicited some of the most fraught critical responses about the reach and limits of reading animals. McKay's central argument concerns the need to dispose, or at least become more critically aware of, the constructed nature of normative quasi-zoological knowledge about animal being – the idea, present even in many sympathetic accounts of animals, that there is a recognizable and generalizable animal form to which texts refer (or fail to). In fact, a successful reading of literary animals is one in which it becomes impossible to distinguish between the notion of a preexisting, extratextual embodied animal of "nature" and the invented and malleable animal of "culture." Orwell's text, and its critical reception, is instructive in this respect: we need not determine that Orwell is concerned with real animals, but rather recognize that his work displays a "literary zoontology" in which linguistic tools play their part in constructing significant cross-species encounters. One primary implication for our reading of literature concerns metaphor, which can reorient us toward animality rather than necessarily being a rejection of it. McKay shows us how fruitful it is to think *with* the uncertainty and blurred boundaries of animal metaphors in a more-than-human context. Indeed this is a timely reminder of something that has been evident across Part I: the difficulty of either wholly condemning literary devices as anthropocentric or wholeheartedly celebrating them as anti-anthropocentric. More often than not, animals are meaningfully if messily involved in questions that also speak to human concerns.

Part II begins with chapters that contextualize the use and significance of animal figurations in political and moral debates. Karen Edwards shows how animal names were frequently weaponized in polemical writing in Britain during and after the Protestant Reformation. She examines how and why animal epithets were used, and their political and religious ramifications, by sampling controversial pamphlets from the period of Henry VIII's reign up to the early Stuart era. Edwards locates examples of beastly rhetoric in Simon Fish's complaints about a hypocritical clergy in the early years of the Reformation; in the notorious polemical writings of puritan "Martin Marprelate" about the ignorance of clerics in the reign of Elizabeth I; and in radical Scottish reformer Alexander Leighton's attack on Arminian bishops when Charles I was on the throne. At the root of these beastly insults was the Bible, and Edwards explains how such slurs (including those returned by the establishment) would have been immediately recognizable due to the Bible's popularity, combined with influential texts from late antiquity, namely the *Physiologus* (composed sometime between the second and fourth centuries) and the *Etymologies* of Isidore, Bishop of Seville (dating to the early seventh century). Weighing up the relative safety or violence of metaphorical rhetoric in a very different sociopolitical climate, Monica Flegel assesses the perils and potential of anthropomorphism as means of persuasion by looking at two works of children's literature: Alfred Elwes's *The Adventures of a Bear, and a Great Bear Too!* (1853) and *The Adventures of a Dog, and a Good Dog Too!* (1854). Contextualizing nineteenth-century attitudes toward violent crime and anxieties about the lower classes, but also ways in which these narratives expose tensions between instinct and discipline in their animal protagonists, Flegel interrogates how an anthropomorphized world is created to teach child readers about standards of law and order. Elwes predominantly works within a framework in which character and moral flaws, rather than structural issues, are given as reasons for crime, but the chapter points to moments in these texts when the flat, allegorical use of animal characters gives way to comments that mark their species and, in the process, complicate the moral purpose of the narratives. As Flegel shows, animality as a metaphor for criminality haunted early nineteenth-century concepts of lawfulness, but in these stories embodied animals may signal to children that overcoming instinct and passion is neither entirely possible nor desirable.

The transition from rhetorical animals utilized in the fight over how humans should behave to interest in the ways in which both wild and captive animals themselves live is central to the following two chapters.

Tobias Menely reflects on the concept of habitat, which has, he notes, tended to be sidelined in favor of domesticated animals (including pets, working beasts, and those farmed for meat). Habitat is especially crucial when countering speciesist discourses and grappling with the effects of the Anthropocene precisely because it requires asking questions about how animals experience their worlds – or what biologist Jacob von Uexküll calls *Umwelten* – outside the human realm. While literary experiments with animal voice and point of view facilitate speculation about life beyond the human, Menely argues that critics have nonetheless remained wedded to characterization, plot, and perspective, and have been less rigorous in examining setting or territory. In turning to John Clare's poetry, the essay further contextualizes material explored in Spencer's chapter by attending to Clare's emphasis on synonyms for habitat and the threat of human encroachment. Its sweeping historical span also considers J. A. Baker's work of literary natural history, *The Peregrine* (1967), about the impact of industrial agriculture and toxic pesticides; Barbara Gowdy's novel, *The White Bone* (1998), which employs an extravagant anthropomorphism but does so to create sympathy around the traumas caused by habitat loss and poaching; and Ted Chiang's short story, "The Great Silence" (2016), in which a parrot narrator living on the north coast of Puerto Rico exposes human disregard for animals. Antoine Traisnel then asks in his chapter what happens to animals uprooted from their habitats and put on display in zoos. Gathering a series of texts all inspired by the zoological gardens at the Jardin des Plantes in Paris, he reflects on what kinds of encounters humans have with captive animals when those meetings are focused less on embodied or visual contact and more on detachment and alienation. If such animals are in a sense lost to their habitat and to the possibility of ethical encounter, Traisnel shows how literary texts record not only that loss but the material and epistemological conditions under which human-ity comes to terms with it. In his reading, Rainer Maria Rilke's poem "The Panther" (1902/3) – a poem Uexküll felt illustrated his theory – offers insight into the panther's caged experience and invites us to reflect on ways in which our own gaze is captive to technologies of modernity; Julio Cortázar's short story "Axolotl" (1957) presents exotic creaturely life used by Europeans for entertainment and spectacle; and Marie NDiaye's *La Naufragée* (1999) exposes links between the colonial capture of animals and the subjugation and enslavement of African peoples.

The gaze is returned to the (decentered) human in chapters that explore how understanding animality demands thinking beyond essentializing approaches to identity. In her essay on Indigeneity, Melanie Benson

Taylor looks at writing that offers epistemological alternatives to mainstream discourse around animality and the Anthropocene. Although many Indigenous writers support cross-species kinship and solidarity, all too often their insights are appropriated or affirmed in a way that reinforces a simplified idea of Indigenous people as having privileged access to nonhuman life. Taylor instead proposes "Weird Indigeneity" as a concept that builds on the work of Timothy Morton and others to emphasize the expansiveness and mutability of Indigenous writing. She samples the work of two poets: Tommy Pico, a Kumeyaay poet from the Viejas reservation near San Diego, California, whose 2017 *Nature Poem* radically disrupts any sense of stable racial or species identity; and Alabama Creek poet Janet McAdams, whose collections, including *Feral* (2007) and *Seven Boxes for the Country After* (2016), poignantly explore porous boundaries between human cultures and nonhuman environments. In the following chapter, Nathan Snaza reflects on the inseparability of discourses of sexuality, species, and coloniality by assessing the evolving and competing understandings of "biocentrism." Snaza delineates two key definitions of the term: first, Margot Norris's concept of an antirepresentational biocentric tradition, where animality is at the heart of an aesthetic promoted by mostly white, Western writers and artists; second, Sylvia Wynter's more critical use of the term to uncover a racializing process enacted by that Western culture; for her, biocentrism expresses rather than disrupts Western imperialist humanism. Nonetheless, Snaza argues, both help us to think of modes of more-than-human storytelling from which the idea of the human and of literature itself emerges.

The volume ends with Lucinda Cole's consideration of more-than-human stories of health – a subject all the more relevant in light of the Covid-19 pandemic, during which much of the work in this *Companion* was completed. If the disastrous effects of smallpox on Indigenous populations is a broadly understood part of the history of colonialism, the hitherto untold histories of zoonotic diseases such as yellow fever, Ebola, Spanish flu, and anthrax are now attracting further research. Cole looks at early modern understandings of cross-species infection, the most notorious example of which in the sixteenth and seventeenth centuries was rabies. While there was a recognition that certain animals could carry and transmit diseases (even before the term "zoonotic" was coined in the nineteenth century), theories of how diseases spread across borders often made use of theology – and, particularly, biblical stories like the ten plagues of Egypt – rather than science. To understand closely related fears of infestation and infection in these contexts, and the roles animals played in disease transmission across continents, Cole turns to swarming locusts, shipboard rats, and domesticated livestock. She starts with the belief expressed in early modern texts, and notably in George Wither's *Britain's Remembrancer* (1628), that the Christian faith offered protection against such ills. She then critiques Daniel Defoe for writing rats largely out of his novel *Robinson Crusoe* (1719) to create the illusion of imperial order and control. Defoe's *Journal of the Plague Year* (1722) repeats this pattern of erasure where the 1665 outbreak of bubonic plague is centered only on humans. Shakespeare, however, writing in the wake of at least nine cattle plagues over the preceding century or so, uses imagery replete with the language of multispecies disease in *Troilus and Cressida* (1609) and *The Merchant of Venice* (1600), in the process reminding us of the fleshiness of his beasts and humans as scrutinized by Fudge in her chapter. Attending to the presence of animals as victims and transmitters of disease is, Cole shows, a crucial part of a medical *post*humanities that seeks to correct the anthropocentrism that remains prevalent across the history of medicine and the literary criticism that depends so much on that history.

Read together, these essays illustrate how profoundly animal life is bound up with ideas of humanist doctrine and posthumanist disease, racialized people and sexualized bodies, religious fervor and political insta-bility, romanticized souls and decaying flesh. They aim not to offer definitive statements on their periods, texts, or topics but to further the long-overdue debates that are now taking hold of literary studies and what we might think of as the *animal* humanities. Far from offering the last word, each contributor asks us to think differently about the words that are used, at turns, to obscure and express animal life, and the contexts in which these words appear. But what is evident, too, is that no single point of focus will reveal the truth about animals (or *animots*, or creatures, or beasts) in all their variety, nor capture human-animal relations in all their complexity. If, to return to the questions I opened with, literature can help us to see animals, it is because of the multiple and ever-changing capacities of words to make us feel, think, imagine, and act differently. The following essays ask us to open our eyes. Animals are good to read.

Notes

1 Cormac James, "Issue," *Granta*, no. 142 (Winter 2018), 51–63, 52.
2 Ibid., 54.
3 Ibid., 52.

4 Steven Dunn, "The Taxidermy Museum," *Granta*, no. 142 (Winter 2018), 13–24, 16.

5 Christina Wood Martinez, "The Astronaut," *Granta*, no. 142 (Winter 2018), 25–42, 28, 35, 38.

6 Yoko Tawada, "The Last Children of Tokyo," *Granta*, no. 142 (Winter 2018), 43–50, 45–6.

7 Ben Lasman, "The Rat Snipers," *Granta*, no. 142 (Winter 2018), 111–28, 112, 115.

8 Ibid., 123.

9 Nell Zink, "The Kabul Markhor," *Granta*, no. 142 (Winter 2018), 129–34, 131.

10 Joy Williams, "Web," *Granta*, no. 142 (Winter 2018), 241–5, 243.

11 Ibid., 244–5.

12 John Berger, "Why Look at Animals?," in *About Looking* (London: Bloomsbury, 2009), 3–28, 1–2, 7–9. On the speculative nature of Berger's essay, which was first published in 1977, see Jonathan Burt, "John Berger's 'Why Look at Animals?': A Close Reading," *Worldviews* 9.2 (2005), 203–18.

13 Berger, "Why Look," 19–24.

14 Ibid., 9.

15 Jacques Derrida, *The Animal That Therefore I Am*, trans. David Wills (New York: Fordham University Press, 2008), 48. James, "Issue," 54. The point is reinforced by Arnon Grunberg's essay "Slaughterhouse," which draws attention to the language of "declared fit" (for slaughter), "stunned" ("rendered brain-dead"), and "been taken care of" (killed) (79). See also the "Words/ Meaning" chapter of Jonathan Safran Foer's *Eating Animals* (London: Penguin, 2009), 43–77.

16 Derrida, *Animal*, 41.

17 For a recent consideration of these terms, see Peter Adkins, *The Modernist Anthropocene: Nonhuman Life and Planetary Change in James Joyce, Virginia Woolf and Djuna Barnes* (Edinburgh: Edinburgh University Press, 2022), 97–8. See also Mariane DeKoven's discussion of the problem of negation in the use of "nonhuman" in "Why Animals Now?," *PMLA* 124.2 (2009), 361–9, 363, and Sherryl Vint's reminder that "'the human' has never been a neutral term – it is coproduced with racism, ableism, sexism, and classism, and the like," in "Introduction," in *After the Human: Culture, Theory, and Criticism in the 21st Century* (Cambridge: Cambridge University Press, 2020), 7.

18 Derrida, *Animal*, 47.

19 James, "Issue," 63.

20 See Susan McHugh, Robert McKay, and John Miller, "Introduction: Towards an Animal-Centred Literary History," in *The Palgrave Handbook of Animals and Literature* (Cham: Palgrave Macmillan, 2021), 1–11, 7; Karen L. Edwards, Derek Ryan, and Jane Spencer, "Introduction," in *Reading Literary Animals: Medieval to Modern* (London: Routledge, 2019), 1–10, 1.

21 See *OED*, "careful." For a discussion of careful reading in relation to modernist animals, see Derek Ryan, *Bloomsbury, Beasts and British Modernist Literature* (Cambridge: Cambridge University Press, 2022), 6–7.

22 Popularized by Peter Singer after being coined by Richard Ryder in the early 1970s, and most commonly used to denote bias for the human species over other animals, the term has recently come under scrutiny from critics warning against usages that imply that racism is equivalent to, or a consequence of, speciesism. See Bénédicte Boisseron, *Afro-Dog: Blackness and the Animal Question* (New York: Columbia University Press, 2018), and Zakiyyah Iman Jackson, *Becoming Human: Matter and Meaning in an Antiblack World* (New York: New York University Press, 2020).

23 For an overview of philosophical and theoretical approaches to animals, see Derek Ryan, *Animal Theory: A Critical Introduction* (Edinburgh: Edinburgh University Press, 2015).

24 Bruno Latour, "Foreword: The Scientific Fables of an Empirical La Fontaine," in Vinciane Despret, *What Would Animals Say If We Asked the Right Questions?*, trans. Brett Buchanan (Minneapolis: University of Minnesota Press, 2016), xiii.

25 See Despret, *What Would Animals Say*. For a concise overview of some major developments spanning a "2,500-year tradition of Western literary activity in support of the various propositions and commitments informing the modern animal rights movement," see Bruce Boehrer and Molly Hand, "Introduction: Beasts in the Republic of Letters," in Bruce Boehrer, Molly Hand, and Brian Massumi (eds.), *Animals, Animality, and Literature* (Cambridge: Cambridge University Press, 2018), 5–7.

26 See Michael Lundblad, "Introduction: The End of the Animal – Literary and Cultural Animalities," in *Animalities: Literary and Cultural Studies beyond the Human* (Edinburgh: Edinburgh University Press, 2017), 2–3.

27 While themselves following a similar historical organization, Susan McHugh, Robert McKay, and John Miller raise an important point in relation to whether these periods matter at all to animals, given that they "function through a humanist framework that conveys a partisan and exclusionary conception of textual production." This "conventional view of literary history privileges particular forms of life and marginalises others (and, as well as being a humanist tradition, a canonical conception of literary history is also patriarchal and Eurocentric). [. . .] Behind the grand march of literature from the medieval to the present, certainly, there are countless other directions of travel taking place." See "Towards an Animal-Centred Literary History," 9–10.

28 Donna Haraway, *When Species Meet* (Minneapolis: University of Minnesota Press, 2008), 7.

29 Cary Wolfe, *What Is Posthumanism?* (Minneapolis: University of Minnesota Press, 2010), 116.

30 For major book series, see "Palgrave Studies in Animals and Literature," "Routledge Perspectives on the Non-Human in Literature and Culture," and Penn State University Press's "Animalibus: Of Animals and Cultures";

for special issues, see "Animal Worlds" in *Modern Fiction Studies* (2004), the double special issue of *Mosaic* on "The Animal" (2006/2007), and the *PMLA* "Theories and Methodologies" cluster on "Animal Studies" (2009).

31 See, for example, Linda Kalof (ed.), *The Oxford Handbook of Animal Studies* (Oxford: Oxford University Press, 2017); Lynn Turner, Undine Sellbach, and Ron Broglio (eds.), *The Edinburgh Companion to Animal Studies* (Edinburgh: Edinburgh University Press, 2020); and Garry Marvin and Susan McHugh, *Routledge Handbook of Human-Animal Studies* (London: Routledge, 2014).

PART I

Literary Periods

CHAPTER I

Middle Ages
Chivalry and the Beast

Sarah Kay

Animals, in Claude Lévi-Strauss's well-worn dictum, are good to think with;[1] but the thinking they provoke is full of contradictions. Medieval philosophers and theologians viewed humans as animals, a word that in Latin, the language of intellectuals, meant "living creatures": insofar as humans were alive and able to move in quest of things, they were by definition *animalia*. Animals were, it was agreed, so called because they were *animated* by a life principle or "soul" (Latin *anima*). At that point, however, consensus frayed. Few medieval thinkers believed the souls of nonhuman animals to be immortal; and most thought the perceptual apparatus (known to medieval scholastics as the "animal" or "sensible" soul) varied from species to species, perhaps operating differently in humans, the only animals to have a "rational" soul. In short, the unique status of the human animal was both an underlying tenet and a matter of endless controversy, much as it has remained to this day, though the lines of disagreement have changed.[2]

The vernacular languages that laypeople spoke and in which most literary authors wrote lacked a generic word equivalent to *animal* and thereby sidestepped the Latin problematic of "the animal."[3] Instead, they distinguished between "men" (humans) and "beasts"; but this latter term was multiply ambiguous, sometimes meaning "wild carnivore," or more broadly "non-rational land animal" (as opposed to humans and birds), and at others becoming so capacious as to include humans too.[4] Consequently, although the effects of relating humans to beasts rather than *animalia* were just as contradictory, they had different connotations. Whereas *animalia* were living, mobile, and appetitive, beasts were potentially ferocious, earthbound, and dumb. They were less a biological or ontological category than active participants in the teeming, shared reality of "nature." Insofar as humans were related to beasts, they were also situated relative to nature, both included within it and, when contrasted with beasts, somewhat outside it too.

One consequence of thinking the human in relation to beasts rather than the animal is that the ground of discussion shifts from ideas to multiple, often conflicting practices. Instead of arguing over the nature of souls, vernacular authors and their audiences or readers were more concerned with behaviors, interactions, and other entanglements. Human dependence on beasts was extensive and multifaceted.[5] Livestock rearing was a major source not only of food but also of clothing (wool and leather), protective armor (leather), lighting (tallow and beeswax), labor and transportation (horses, oxen, donkeys), and tools and artifacts (bone, horn, glue). One could not easily draw a line between culture and agriculture when the primary materials of writing (quills, parchment, and wax tablets) and bookbinding (leather, gut, glue) were all directly derived from nonhuman animals. The medieval period is unique in relying on parchment as a textual support, thereby forging a material relationship between literature and animals different from that of any other period. The final section of this chapter will explore specifically medieval interactions between a story involving beasts and the physical pages that transmit it.

In the stew of material practices and ideological assumptions that make up daily life, noble identity in particular is complexly entangled with that of beasts. A medieval knight's horse mattered more to him than his peasants; his bond with it was intimate and enduring. Lancelot, who rides his horses to death in his zeal to rescue Guinevere, is exceptional in sacrificing his mounts to his beloved; literary horses often have names and personalities where wives or fiancées go without. Pedigrees and blood-lines characterize both aristocrats and their companion beasts, as they do still. Medieval laws meant that only the nobility were entitled to wear fine furs, like ermine, or hunt quarry considered noble like themselves, such as deer and boar. Princely houses saw their distinction reflected in menageries that included, alongside beasts destined for the table, "princely" (and not obviously edible) creatures, the beasts of choice veering in the twelfth century from bears and boars in favor of lions.[6] From the later twelfth century on, aristocratic and royal houses identified themselves by coats of arms that overwhelmingly featured beasts, especially lions. Not content with symbolic identification, some lineages even claimed to be literally descended from beasts, like the house of Lusignan that promoted the legend of their descent from the half-human, half-serpent Mélusine.

Thematically speaking, then, the literature of the Middle Ages has to negotiate both human exceptionalism, which purports to differentiate human from nonhuman animals, *and* what we might call "chivalric" exceptionalism, which, on the contrary, is grounded in rapprochements of various kinds between the aristocracy, exclusively, and beasts. The complexities of humans' relationship with beasts are often bound up with practices, including those involved in book production, and thus the transmission of that literature in the first place.

The Romances of William of Palermo

Most of the surviving literary production of the Middle Ages concerns people of noble rank, and beasts too. Although taking a single narrative as representative of such a long and complex period risks partiality, a story known by the name of its protagonist William of Palermo has at least the advantage of resonating across several centuries, languages, and genres, and of manifesting typically medieval ways of thinking and interacting with beasts. First known in the late twelfth- or early thirteenth-century French verse romance *Guillaume de Palerne*, the story was recast in Middle English as the mid-fourteenth-century *William of Palerne*, composed in the rougher medium of alliterative verse.[7] The French text posits an earlier Latin source and gives rise to later French prose versions, while the English one has an Irish prose spin-off; in short, "[t]he story of William of Palerne appealed to audience and patrons in various countries of Western Europe from the 13th to the 17th century."[8] Although only surviving in the cultures of northwest Europe, the tale is set in the Mediterranean south. The main action takes place in Sicily and southern Italy, with an important Spanish plotline and bit parts for the Byzantine emperor and the Saxon enemies of Rome. In addition to having a trans-European reach, the story is an amalgam of widely attested motifs from a range of genres;[9] the French romance's connections to other works are so numerous that it has even been considered parodic.[10]

Despite these broad literary resonances, the story of William of Palermo is the opposite of banal. I shall be focusing on the French and English verse redactions, which despite local differences resemble one another sufficiently closely for the following summary to serve for both.[11]

The king of Sicily's brother covets the throne and plans to kill both the king and his infant heir, William. A wolf appears and snatches up the little boy, carrying him across the straits of Messina into southern Italy. There the child is found by a cowherd, who brings him up as his own son. The Holy Roman emperor is hunting nearby and, thanks to the same wolf driving a stag in his direction, comes across William now grown into a handsome young man. Impressed, the emperor takes him back to his court where William becomes a redoubtable knight and successfully puts down a rebellion by the Saxons. He also falls in love with the emperor's daughter, Melior, and she with him. The social gulf between imperial princess and cowhand's son is, however, an insurmountable obstacle in love's path; to make matters worse, the emperor decides to marry Melior to the son of the Byzantine emperor. Notwithstanding, Melior contrives the young lovers' escape disguised as white bears, using freshly flayed bear pelts purloined from the imperial kitchens by her attendant, Alexandrine. (The bears themselves have seemingly become food for the household, although bear is an unusual menu item, to say the least.) Alexandrine skillfully sews Melior and William into their new skins and they lope off on all fours into the forest. At once, the practical difficulties of survival set in. Fortunately, the faithful wolf reappears, providing them with human food and generally serving as their factotum in the wilderness. It does not take long for the means of the lovers' escape to be discovered, however, and a hue and cry is raised for the capture of the white bears. Townspeople come close to seizing them, but the wolf again comes to their rescue. Quickly he kills two deer, enabling the lovers to abandon their bearskins for those of a stag and doe; under this cover, he takes them back to Sicily. There the queen of Palermo is under attack by the king of Spain, whose son wants forcibly to abduct her daughter.

The reader has known from the outset that the wolf is actually a prince named Alphonse. He is the Spanish king's oldest son, whose mother died; the king's second wife magically changed him into a werewolf so her own son would take his place as heir apparent. Thus the Spaniards responsible for this unjust war are the werewolf's own father and half-brother. William, meanwhile, still sees himself as a cowhand's son. Neither he nor Melior knows that the queen of Palermo is his mother and her threatened daughter his sister.

The Sicilian queen has had a cryptic dream telling her that a wolf and other beasts are coming to her aid. When she sees the wolf approaching her palace with the two deer, she recognizes them as the promised assistance. Indeed, she can tell the deer are really humans because the original deerskins have shrunk, exposing the lovers' limbs and clothing. Anxious not to frighten them but to persuade them to come to her palace, she dresses in a deerskin too and approaches them on all fours. Bizarre as this plan may sound, it succeeds, and the whole troupe of "beasts" returns to the palace. At a sign from the werewolf, the lovers abandon their deerskins. Now revealed as a knight, William leads ferocious assaults against the Spanish invaders, routing them as definitively he had earlier done the Saxons. Between battles, the werewolf appears at court and elaborately mimes his submission. When the Spanish king has acknowledged defeat, the wolf's bids for recognition are rewarded and the sorceress queen who had contrived his metamorphosis into a beast is summoned to work her magic in reverse. Restored to princely form, Alphonse reveals that William is likewise a long-lost son, at last reunited with his mother and sister. Melior's problem is now solved: no longer facing down a *mésalliance*, she can wed the queen of Palermo's son and heir. They duly marry, the other single characters are vacuumed up into suitable marriages, William and Melior's sons become emperor of Rome and king of Sicily, and that is the end.

This summary makes clear that unwinding this plot relies on humans passing as nonhuman animals, involuntarily in the case of Alphonse the werewolf, or as a deliberate ruse by the lovers and the Sicilian queen. These alternatives raise questions about identity by positing different degrees of transformation and by focusing attention on the relationship between skin and that which it encloses. The discussion that follows will pursue three lines of inquiry. First, I consider how living as nonhuman animals between the collapse and restoration of human society can be read as serving certain ideas of human exceptionalism. Second, I explore the chivalric exception that, in its practices, relishes and exploits the bestiality of nobility. And finally, I reflect on the beastly nature of the books that transmit these tales to the reader. A brief conclusion observes how the realities of human and nonhuman are less categories in opposition than a lived continuum.

Social Dysfunction as Animal: The Human Exception

A clear, overall arc of this narrative is that of the rightful heir restored.[12] That is, the story is a politically specific form of the family romance where at stake is not just returning a lost child to its true parents (as in the Freudian model) but defending the legitimacy of the one true heir against the claims of contenders from the same bloodline.[13] At the outset, the royal houses of both Spain and Sicily are menaced by usurpers, who use necromancy (in Alphonse's case) or who plot regicide and infanticide (in William's), in a bid to stymie the legitimate claims of an older son in favor of a cadet (Alphonse is older than his half-brother, William's father is older than his fratricidal brother). The resulting social dystopia is expressed as a period of animalization, with the Spanish heir immediately transformed into a werewolf and the Sicilian one seized and protected by this same wolf, then successively misrecognized as a cowherd, a bear, and a stag. In either case, animal coverings shield the princes' human identity, and their uncovering allows not only that identity to be revealed, but the rightful dynastic line to be restored. As a framework, it is, as Randy P. Schiff argues, essentially conservative of the old order.[14]

Defending patriliny as primogeniture is only one reason for this passage through the animal, however. Relatively unremarked by previous scholarship on these texts is their concomitant defense of women's right to consent, which, like heirship, is presented as unjustly assailed. If, for men, the problem is to safeguard the one true heir, for women it is to marry their one true love.[15] Melior's father wants to give her against her will to the Greek emperor; this is what determines her to run away with William. The entire subterfuge of the bear pelts is dreamed up and executed by her in cahoots with Alexandrine. The fact that both lovers wear identical bearskins confirms them as perfectly matched despite the apparent disparity in their ranks; their subsequent disguise as stag and doe implies the appropriateness of their eventual marriage. When the Sicilian queen likewise dresses in a doeskin, she does so in order to save her daughter from an unwanted union. The assault on a woman's right to consent is exacerbated, in this case, by the Spanish pretender resorting to armed force. As in the early modern fairy tale *Peau d'âne*, in which a princess disguises herself in a donkey skin to escape her incestuous father, animalization guarantees a woman's body against its would-be abusers. The Sicilian princess's right not to be forced into an unwelcome marriage is voiced particularly explicitly in the French text when the king of Spain decries his own son's behavior: "A curse on anyone who wants to take a wife against her will" (*Guillaume*, 7175–6, "Moilliers a prendre ait mal dehé | c'on fait outre sa volenté"). In the English romance, although the king's rebuke is milder, his son candidly admits, "Truly, sire, you know we have acted wrongly" (*William*, 3886–7, "Forsoþe sire, ȝe knowe | þat we have wrongli wrouȝt").

In the case of both princes and princesses, then, human injustice and social dysfunction result in a period of animality that provides a temporary escape until ultimately wrongs are righted and human order restored. This is an arc that casts animalization as loss: to be outlawed and deprived of one's just rights is to be cast out of human society into the wild. As such, it is an expression of human exceptionalism, which constructs the nonhuman animal retroactively as deficiency; and it is not without the contradictions that always accompany such a move, which in this case arise from sexual difference. On one side is automatic succession from father to eldest son; on the other, transmission from the mother. Her quality or taint is clearest in the Spanish branch of the story where, since Alphonse and his half-brother share the same father, the difference in their characters can derive only from their respective mothers, the first wife producing the upstanding firstborn and the second, spell-weaving wife responsible for the war-mongering, would-be rapist younger son. If father-son succession is ineluctable, the identity of the mother and her impact on her child are contingent, since she becomes a mother only by exercising her right to consent to union with the father. The deficiency that animalization represents in this story can be understood both as a failure of necessity (for a man) and as the failure of its opposite (for a woman). At the end, William leaves his life as nonhuman animal in order to assume his inevitable position as heir to the throne of Sicily; but Melior leaves hers because she has chosen to be with him and become the eventual mother of future kings.

Nobility as Bestial: The Chivalric Exception

Alphonse-as-werewolf and the lovers-as-bears are outlaws, Alphonse because his lupine characteristics remove him from the law's remit, and the lovers in consequence of the emperor's hue and cry, a proclamation that legally obliged all those who heard it to hunt down like outcasts those against whom it was issued. Rather than seeing their outlawry in terms of animal deficiency vis-à-vis human community, however, some critics of these romances have instead interpreted it in light of Giorgio Agamben's account of the "state of exception." In *Homo Sacer*, Agamben contends that the werewolf protagonist of the medieval lay "Bisclavret" occupies, as a hybrid beast or liminal man, a similar position on one edge of the law to the king on the other. Neither beast nor sovereign falls properly under law's rule, their shared position of exclusion from it being what grounds the inclusion of others.[16] This founding of inclusion on exclusion is what enables the sovereign to claim jurisdiction over nature as well as over society; as Schiff puts it with reference to the medieval world, "aristocratic privilege straddle[s] the natural and cultural worlds."[17] Both Alphonse and William, he and others have argued, are singled out by their very beastliness as being qualified to rule: the beast *is* the sovereign.[18]

The approximation to beasts of both princes certainly manifests the same liminality that Agamben discerns in the werewolf in the tale "Bisclavret," who is simultaneously human and beast. Throughout his transformation into a wolf, Alphonse somehow continues to function as a recognizably rational being. His bodily movements and capacities are those of a beast – he hunts and eats like a wolf, he cannot speak – and yet they are also eloquent toward humans. In particular, he twice seizes human children only in order to save them, as he does the infant William at the start of the romance; and we only ever see him catch prey in order to help his human charges. Even though he cannot speak, William and Melior defer to his judgment and obey his signals; at the court of Palermo, he communicates so effectively that he brings about his own return to human form.

The persistence of William and Melior as humans inside their animal skins is also palpable, in their case physically. When they first make their escape, Alexandrine sews them into the bear pelts so that only their hands and faces are accessible under the white fur. Peggy McCracken writes entrancingly about the delightful scene in the French romance where the hungry lovers delicately feed one another, each poking their little human hands out of the enveloping bearskins to convey morsels of food to the other's mouth.[19] The scene focuses attention on bodies deliberately occluded inside a bestial covering and visible only, as if in concentrated form, in the extremities of hand and mouth, prompting the reader to reflect on the human specificity of these body parts in particular.[20] There is something Edenic about this distillation of the human into hand and mouth, as if the very beastliness of the young lovers' life in the forest was an opening onto an alternative idyll.[21] Their identity as beasts seems especially appropriate to them as noble children. The narrators of both texts insist how comfortable and secure they feel in their new skins; it is only under duress, or after much hesitation, that they relinquish their identity as bears or deer. And when they restyle themselves in human dress at the court of Palermo, it is in garments trimmed with fine furs.

The form liminality and sovereignty take in the William of Palermo narratives is somewhat unusual. Werewolves appear in many medieval narratives; the late twelfth century is practically a time of werewolf fever.[22] But if these romances conform to their period in this respect, they are quite exceptional in having characters that pass as bear or deer. Why these beasts, specifically? Perhaps, as McCracken has suggested, the association of white, wild animals with fairies and the Celtic Other World was a reason for choosing the white bears, their otherworldly qualities suffusing the wood-land idyll with a sense of enchantment.[23]

Or maybe it is because white bears also belong among the beasts used in chivalric society as heraldic emblems, by women as well as men? A wolf, a bear, a hart, and hind (as a stag and doe are termed in the language of heraldry) were all familiar sights on family crests, knights' shields, and other trappings of nobility. In heraldry, white (*argent*) is one of the two metals used alongside gold (*or*). When a creature figures as a heraldic device (a *charge*), depicting it in the color it has in day-to-day reality is sufficiently unusual to be referred to by a technical term (*proper*); beasts as *charges* were more likely to be *argent* or *or* than *proper*. Both the French and English narrations of the story of William of Palermo were composed in a period when heraldry had already been elaborated as a chivalric code, and so the lovers could be seen as signaling their specifically noble identity through their association with these beasts. Identification of warriors with fierce bears has a longer history again, as McCracken shows.[24]

In the romances themselves, however, the only beast that explicitly becomes a heraldic device is the wolf.[25] This occurs toward the end of the story when William, his identity not yet revealed, tells the Sicilian queen that he will bear the arms of a wolf (*Guillaume*, 5396) or a werewolf (*William*, 3218) on his shield in the war against the Spaniards. He is such a ferocious fighter that a wolf is how he seems to the Spanish forces, who scatter in terror before his onslaught; they go from calling him "the man with the wolf shield" to simply "the wolf" (*Guillaume*, 6583; *William*, 3832). The choice of device perfectly reflects William's experience of Alphonse-werewolf who, intrepid against his enemies and always gentle and protective toward his friends, is indeed a figure of perfect chivalry. William's identification *as* beast is paralleled by his identification *by* beasts, since although various human characters vaguely intuit his nobility, the only creatures to know who he is are the wolf and, as he prepares for battle in Palermo, his dead father's warhorse. This horse displays quite as much character as the queen, William's mother. It prances for joy on first seeing him (*Guillaume*, 5502–4; *William*, 3283–6), bowing or even, in the English redaction, kneeling, and of course carrying him in battle. His chivalry located between horse and wolf, William the knight effectively occupies the role of hyphen in a terrifying wolf-horse hybrid.

In addition to heraldry, aristocratic identification with beasts is supported elsewhere in the French text by epic similes (for example, when William fights the Saxons his eyes burn scarlet like a dragon's and his expression is as fierce as a lion's; *Guillaume*, 2037–8), and in both texts by elaborately coded dreams. The most complex of these beast-dreams is the one, already mentioned, that is dreamed by the queen of Sicily. In it, she experiences herself as surrounded by hundreds of thousands of fierce beasts – bears, lions, and leopards – all with their mouths wide open, ready to devour her, when help arrives in the form of "a single white wolf and two white bears" (*Guillaume*, 4731; *William*, 2878). Then, as the dream continues, the bears mysteriously take on the appearance of two deer surmounted by the faces of young humans wearing golden crowns (*Guillaume*, 4734–8; *William*, 2880–8); the larger one reminds the queen of her lost son. As Alain Corbellari observes, this dream is not prophetic in the way such dreams usually are in medieval texts; rather, it manifests the plot that is unfolding around her at that very moment. The open-mouthed beasts assailing the dreamer may be understood as metaphors, but the core of the dream is not only literally true, it is, in Corbellari's phrase, "more transparent than reality itself."[26] One of the other, shorter dreams, dreamed by Melior, is equally factual: the forces massed against the lovers appear to her as wild beasts from which they are rescued by "nostre beste" (*Guillaume*, 4014, "our beast"), "our wurþi werwolf" (*William*, 2306, "our worthy werewolf").

I began this section by recording how the liminality of the outlaws in the William of Palermo narratives can be put in conversation with Agamben's werewolf commentary. Although the lovers are not transformed into beasts to the extent that Alphonse is, I want to end it by stressing the literalness with which all the principal characters, despite the persistence in them of humanity, are identified as "beasts." The narrator of the Middle English romance regularly refers to the lovers as "þe beres" or "þe hert and þe hinde" ("the bears," "the stag and the doe").[27] It is also as beasts that the characters, on occasion, see themselves. A twice-repeated line in the French text locates beastliness not in the envelope of animal skin but in the being it encloses. Threatened with capture in the forest, William wishes that he had his horse or arms so that his attackers might know "quel beste ceste piax acuevre" ("what kind of beast this skin covers," *Guillaume*, 4054). The identical words are spoken by Alphonse's stepmother, as she begins to work the magic that will undo his appearance as a werewolf. "Let us see," she says, "what kind of beast this skin covers" (*Guillaume*, 7690–1). In both cases the removal of an animal exterior will reveal the bestial character of the being inside it. Neither iteration of this line is retained in the English *William*, but both versions of the romance agree on another passage involving self-identification as "beast." When the queen of Sicily conceals herself in a deerskin in order to avoid alarming the similarly disguised lovers, her words to them are, in French, "Je sui tex beste comme vos," and in English, "I am swiche a best as ȝe ben" ("I am just such a beast as you are," *Guillaume*, 5334; *William*, 3132).

In her sparkling study of the French romance, Miranda Griffin pushes back against any suggestion that its treatment of skin is in any sense superficial. On the contrary, "Alphonse, Guillaume, and Melior may be 'overclothed' in skins taken from nonhuman animals, but that does not mean that this skin does not reveal a profound identity."[28] The constant interplay of inside and outside, self and skin, Griffin insists, is precisely what characterizes "the animality which is both the ground and foil to chivalric identity."[29] I completely endorse this last formulation provided we replace "animality" (having the status and qualities of an animal) with "bestiality" (having those of a beast).[30] Given the constant equivocation between the separability and inseparability of beastly insides and outsides, it is bestiality specifically that serves as "ground and foil to chivalric identity" in the William of Palermo romances. The play of inner and outer operates differently for Alphonse than for William and Melior, and differently again for beasts that are flayed, like the unfortunate white bears that once inhabited the bearskins only to end up in the Roman emperor's kitchens. A shield with a wolf on, a deerskin, a wolf's body, a bear's skin are all shown to be removable – in different ways – from an underlying "self." Skinning a bear will kill it if it is not already dead, and there are plenty of dead beasts in these romances to remind us of that grisly fact. Not so with princes, whose coverings can alternate. And yet, although you can take the aristocrat out of the beast, you cannot take the beast out of the aristocrat. Stripping away the surface only reveals an inside that both is and is not a beast as well. The difference between skinning a bear and taking off a shield is real, but the ground between them is murky, equivocal, and ultimately contradictory. Both beasts and not beasts, nobles keep demonstrating in practice their "natural" affinity with them, and explicitly embracing it too.

Beast and Book: The Medieval Exception

The interplay of skin and body in these two romances finds its material counterpart in the manuscripts that transmit them. Each work is preserved in a single witness, *Guillaume* in Bibliothèque nationale de France, MS Arsenal 6565, and *William* in King's College, Cambridge, MS 13. Both are parchment manuscripts (made, that is, from a processed form of animal skin, usually that of lambs or calves), the Arsenal manuscript dating from the thirteenth century and King's 13 from the fourteenth, neither copied more than a few decades after the text it contains was composed.

The era of the parchment book is broadly coterminous with the Middle Ages. And parchment pages typically bear traces both of their animal origins and of the processes of their manufacture. They look, feel, smell, and sound distinctively different from the papyrus they displaced and the paper to which they gave way.[31] Many of the pages of Arsenal 6565 have holes in them, caused by the way the membrane from which they were made was scraped and stretched. Take the example of Figure 1.1: the text in its left-hand column,

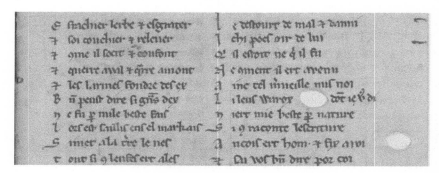

Figure 1.1.   From *Guillaume de Palerne*.
Reproduced with permission of Bibliothèque nationale de France. BnF Arsenal 6565, fol. 79r.

which starts at *Guillaume*, 239, describes the werewolf's horror when he returns
to where he left the young William and finds him gone. He howls, bites the
ground, and weeps in a human-bestial hybrid display of grief. Later in that
column, he is reassured to discover the child safe with the cowherd. The text at
the top of the second column, *Guillaume*, 269 ff., explains that Alphonse was
originally a human, thereby accounting for his hybrid nature. The first hole
occurs in the middle of line 274, which reads "Li leus warox <HOLE> dont je
vos di," "The werewolf <HOLE> of which I tell you," and continues, "was
not a beast by nature, as my source records, rather he was a man and the son of a
king." The last line of this quotation ("Ançois ert hom et fix a roi," *Guillaume*,
277) falls beside the second hole, located in the margin. The text gives a sense,
materialized by the parchment, of Alphonse's human existence punctuated by
his period as a werewolf, and of us being offered a glimpse, through the
werewolf's skin, of the man beneath. On the verso, these same holes accompany the account of how Alphonse's stepmother transformed him into a
werewolf, where the same issues of inside and outside are at stake.

Some of the larger holes in this manuscript's leaves have been stitched
closed, a feature that, as McCracken points out, resonates with the text's
repeated narrative of being sewn into animal skins. For McCracken, an
implication of the scene when the lovers feed one another through the
vents in their bear coverings, with its focus on human hand and animal
skin, is to evoke the pages on which it is inscribed. She cites folio 109r of
the Arsenal manuscript, the first line of which recapitulates how the lovers
were stitched into their bearskins, as an example of this reflexivity. On the
outer margin about halfway down are three holes, which were once all
stitched closed, though the stitching has rotted on two of them, such that
"[r]eaders would have read a work about lovers sewn into animal skins on
pages of skin stitched together in the margins."[32]

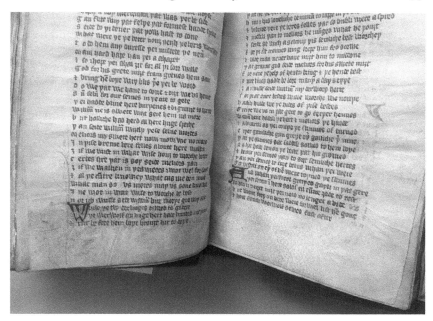

Figure 1.2. From *William of Palerne.*
Reproduced by permission of the Provost and Fellows of King's College, Cambridge. MS 13, fols. 41v–42r.

Figure 1.2 shows the rather different character of the King's manuscript, whose uneven-sized folios vary in thickness, their hair and flesh sides visibly distinct from one another. On this double page, the hair side is uppermost as is plain from the hair follicles on the lower right. Similar pores can be seen at the foot of the left-hand page, too, though it is also somewhat stained. The stain falls at the point where the werewolf comes to the lovers, still in their bearskins but already discovered and in hiding, bringing with him an enormous stag (*William*, 2569–71). The unfortunate beast will provide the first of the deer hides they exchange for the bear pelts. At the foot of the facing page 42r, just before the colored initial A that introduces line 2597, the lovers put on the deerskins, the narrator commenting that "they looked a lot more like deer than they had bears, because the skins were fitted to them so exactly" (3594–6). With the book open at this point, the uppermost leaves are smaller than those beneath, which extend beneath them and at the bottom right-hand corner, as if to confirm the different sizes of skins represented in the text, and their capacity to dry and shrink, as these deerskins eventually do. As one turns the leaves of this manuscript, the alternation of hair and flesh sides underlines the mobility as well as the bestiality of skins, the hair sides being not just differentiated by hair follicles but also looking darker and harder than the paler, more velvety flesh sides.

An episode in both the French and English versions that effectively sutures the entire content of the works to the material books that transmit them is when Alphonse's stepmother transforms him back from werewolf to prince by means of a ring and a book (*Guillaume*, 7731–51, Arsenal 6565, fol. 141r; *William*, 4424–34, King's MS 13, fol. 69v). Hers is a book of magical spells that can transform one skin into another. Just as surely, the codices containing these texts work an identical magic, turning their characters in and out of their skins. In this particular episode, Alphonse emerges naked and embarrassed, before eventually re-enveloping himself in garments given him by William. In the French text, his "human" robe is in fact lined with white ermine (*Guillaume*, 7836), provoking Christine Ferlampin-Acher wryly to observe the text's concern with getting the fur in the right place, inside the clothes and not outside the skin.[33] The same interleaving of inside and outside that we find in the story is materialized in the systematic alternation, in the book's quires, of flesh and hair sides. Human artwork or animal by-product? These medieval books are both, both support and mute commentary on the liminal, hybrid protagonists of their texts.

These discussions of the William of Palermo romances collectively show how relations between human and nonhuman animals in medieval literature are not only, as medieval theologians conceived them, categorical and abstract, but also real, practical, and variable according to context. Different degrees of gradation are upheld simultaneously; "human" and "beast" can be everything from antonyms to synonyms. From forest deer and dead bears to William's father's horse, the werewolf, the lovers in the bears' skins, the Sicilian queen strategically covered in deer hide, or William with his wolf blazon, to Alphonse's determined recovering of his princely role, lies a continuous field of likenesses, overlaps, and divergences, which manifest themselves in function of changing practical circumstances. The Middle Ages are all too often represented as treating nonhuman animals "allegorically" or "figuratively"; but the William of Palermo romances suggest that, on the contrary, the connections perceived as holding between creatures are grounded in material reality. In some situations humans are exceptional – but not always. At times, an otherwise princely knight is a beast: ferocious, dumb, and earthbound. The human-beast continuum is reduplicated by medieval books, its animal pages inscribing how, in the Middle Ages, the beast really was a sovereign, and chivalry could undoubtedly be beastly.

Notes

1 On the use and abuse by critical animal studies of Lévi-Strauss's tag from his book *Totemism*, see Scu, "Animals Are More Than Good to Think With, Part 1," Critical Animal blog, July 6, 2012, www.criticalanimal.com/2012/07/animals-are-more-than-good-to-think.html.

2 At the root of medieval disagreements lie incompatibilities between Aristotelian and Augustinian worldviews. See Ian P. Wei, *Thinking about Animals in Thirteenth-Century Paris: Theologians on the Boundary between Humans and Animals* (Cambridge: Cambridge University Press, 2020), for a close-up analysis.

3 This remained so into the Early Modern period; see Laurie Shannon, "The Eight Animals in Shakespeare; or, Before the Human," *Publications of the Modern Language Society of America* 124.2 (2009), 472–9.

4 Sarah Kay, "Before the *animot*: *Bêtise* and the Zoological Machine in Medieval Latin and French Bestiaries," *Yale French Studies* 127 (2015), 34–51.

5 See Susan Crane, *Animal Encounters: Contacts and Concepts in Medieval Britain* (Philadelphia: University of Pennsylvania Press, 2013).

6 Michel Pastoureau, "L'animal et l'historien au moyen âge," in *L'animal exemplaire au Moyen Âge Ve–XVe siècle*, ed. Jacques Berlioz, Marie Anne Polo de Beaulieu, and Pascal Collomb (Rennes: Presses de l'Université de Rennes, 1999), 13–26 (23–6).

7 The editions referenced are Alexandre Micha (ed.), *Guillaume de Palerne: Roman du XIIIe siècle* (Geneva: Droz, 1990), and G. H. V. Bunt (ed.), *William of Palerne: An Alliterative Romance* (Groningen: Bouma, 1985). Translations from both works are my own; the French text has also been translated into English by Leslie A. Sconduto, *Guillaume de Palerne: An English Translation of the 12th-Century French Verse Romance* (Jefferson, NC: McFarland, 2004). I cite each of the medieval texts by short title and line number, and the editors' introductions by the editor's name and page number. Micha dates the French version somewhere between 1194 and 1220 (Micha, 23), whereas Bunt accepts an earlier date for it of 1194–7 (Bunt, 20–1). The English text is internally dated to soon after its patron's death in 1361 (*William*, 161–9).

8 Bunt, 20–8 (quotation at 20).

9 Bunt, 99.

10 Christine Ferlampin-Acher, "*Guillaume de Palerne*: Une parodie?," *Cahiers de recherches médiévales et humanistes* 15 (2008), 59–72.

11 Differences between the French and English versions are documented by Bunt, 31–5, and interpreted by Arlyn Diamond, "Loving Beasts: The Romance of *William of Palerne*," in Jane Gilbert and Ad Putter (eds.), *The Spirit of Medieval English Popular Romance* (Harlow: Pearson, 2000), 142–56; Randy P. Schiff, "Cross-Channel Becomings-Animal: Primal Courtliness in *Guillame de Palerne* and *William of Palerne*," *Exemplaria* 21.4 (2009), 418–38; and Renée Ward, "The Politics of Translation: Sanitizing Violence in *William of Palerne*," *Studies in Philology* 112.3 (2015), 469–89, among others.

12 See excellent discussion by Diamond, "Loving Beasts," and its refinement by Angela Florschuetz, "Bad Blood: Patrilineal Inheritance and the Body of the Heir in *William of Palerne*," *Studies in the Age of Chaucer* 42 (2020), 147–82.

13 On the "family romance" in the narrative, see Bridget Behrmann, "'Quel beste ceste piax acuevre': Idyll and the Animal in *Guillaume de Palerne's* Family Romance," *Cahiers de recherches médiévales et humanistes* 24 (2012), 331–46.

14 Schiff, "Cross-Channel Becomings-Animal," 418–22.

15 The issue of consent rose to the fore in canon law in the twelfth century and dominated discussions of marriage thereafter. See Philip Lyndon Reynolds, *How Marriage Became One of the Sacraments: The Sacramental Origins of Marriage from Its Medieval Origins to the Council of Trent* (Cambridge: Cambridge University Press, 2016).

16 Giorgio Agamben, *Homo Sacer: Sovereign Power and Bare Life*, trans. Daniel Heller-Roazen (Stanford, CA: Stanford University Press, 1998), 63–6. The section is titled "The Ban and the Wolf"; a proclamation of hue and cry falls within the medieval legal concept of "ban." *Guillame de Palerne* has been read in light of Agamben by Peggy McCracken, *In the Skin of a Beast: Sovereignty and Animality in Medieval France* (Chicago: University of Chicago Press, 2017), 92–3, and both romances together by Schiff, "Cross-Channel Becomings-Animal," 421–2.

17 Schiff, "Cross-Channel Becomings-Animal," 421.

18 This last formulation is Derrida's: "There is the beast and [*et*] the sovereign, but also the beast is [*est*] the sovereign, the sovereign is [*est*] the beast." Jacques Derrida, *The Beast and the Sovereign*, trans. Geoffrey Bennington (Chicago: University of Chicago Press, 2009), vol. 1, 18; cf. McCracken, *In the Skin*, 94.

19 "Each has drawn their naked hand out of the skin they were wearing ... Through the animal mouths in the skins they feed one another morsels" ("Cascuns a traite sa main nue | fors de la pel c'avoit vestue ... Par les geules qui sont es piax | s'entrepaissoent des morrsiax," *Guillaume*, 3321–2, 3327–8). This detail is absent from the English romance, which simply describes them eating at their ease (*William*, 1881).

20 McCracken, *In the Skin*, 81–3.

21 "It is Guillaume's *animalization* that results in his regression," observes Behrmann, "'Quel beste ceste piax acuevre,'" 343.

22 Caroline Walker Bynum, *Metamorphosis and Identity* (New York: Zone, 2005), 94, speaks of a "werewolf renaissance." Miranda Griffin, *Transforming Tales: Rewriting Metamorphosis in Medieval French Literature* (Oxford: Oxford University Press, 2015), 108–25, discusses the French *Guillaume de Palerne* as exemplifying this phenomenon.

23 McCracken, *In the Skin*, 80.

24 Ibid., 68–9, including "stories of men who become like animals by wearing their skins" (69). For Alain Corbellari, both bear and stag specifically connote royalty, the bear being in his view an older, imperial beast and the stag more associated with a Christian ideal of monarchy. See his "Onirisme et

bestialité: Le roman de *Guillaume de Palerne*," *Neophilologus* 86 (2002), 353–62 (at 358–9).

25 McCracken, *In the Skin*, 87.

26 "Plus transparent que la réalité même," Corbellari, "Onirisme et bestialité," 358.

27 Bunt, 106.

28 Griffin, *Transforming Tales*, 125.

29 Ibid., 107.

30 The medieval words cognate with modern English "bestiality," such as *bestialité*, do not have the modern word's sexual meaning. Manuals for confessors designate intercourse with animals as a form of fornication or sodomy. See Joyce E. Salisbury's chapter "Bestiality" in her edited volume *Sex in the Middle Ages* (New York: Garland, 1991), 267–86.

31 Elaine Treharne, *Perceptions of Medieval Manuscripts: The Phenomenal Book* (New York: Oxford University Press, 2021), 19–25. The readings advanced here follow the model used by Sarah Kay, *Animal Skins and the Reading Self in Medieval Latin and French Bestiaries* (Chicago: University of Chicago Press, 2017).

32 McCracken, *In the Skin*, 83. The page can be seen at https://gallica.bnf.fr/ark:/12148/btv1b52513074c/f229.item.r=Asrenal%206565

33 Ferlampin-Acher, "*Guillaume de Palerne*," 70, especially n. 40.

CHAPTER 2

Early Modern
Flesh

Erica Fudge

Over the past three decades scholars in early modern human-animal studies have addressed crucial issues relating to being human and being animal. They have looked, for example, at what makes character, the polis, and reason when the nonhuman is recognized as having a role to play in discussions about those aspects of human life.[1] A body of work has thus emerged that has returned us to a past in which ideas about species difference were being negotiated in terms that might seem strange to us now, but which have been foundational to many of the ways we live and think today in the West. As Sandra Swart has written of animal history generally, these studies of our early modern past are "usefully unfamiliar" in that they ask us to recognize that conceptions of animals and of being human have not always been as they are now, and that they can, in turn, change.[2]

Humans interacted with nonhumans in numerous ways in the early modern period: from watching bear baiting to engaging in horse training, from working with agricultural animals to owning exotic pets, and more. All of these areas have been addressed in recent scholarship,[3] and almost inevitably, eating animal flesh has also been a focus of research, leading to questions about individual and species stability in the act of consuming – taking in – the flesh of another being.[4] The dead flesh of nonhumans has also been read as having a role (possessing agency) in the performance of the meal.[5] This chapter takes these arguments in a different direction and brings to the fore a particular early modern conception of flesh as transcending species: it takes seriously the period's many conceptions of the human as itself meat and as such opens up a new perspective on the relationship between species. It reads William Shakespeare's *Hamlet* (c. 1601) – a play often regarded as a beacon of modern selfhood – as offering a glimpse of a moment when a particular conception of the human was being set aside and hidden from view. By bringing that invisibilized human back into focus, by tracing the way in which early modern thought understood that meatiness was a quality shared by humans and animals, the chapter offers a revised history of our relationship with other species, and reads Hamlet's musings on edibility as offering a familiar starting point for what might be a "usefully unfamiliar" conception of the human.

My argument here is underpinned by Jacques Derrida's concept of "calculated forgetting." In *The Animal That Therefore I Am* (2008), Derrida argues that the idea of the animal as a being with a capacity for a response and not just a reaction is "something that philosophy perhaps forgets, perhaps being this calculated forgetting itself."[6] I take this to suggest that there have been calculations – willed choices – about the nature of animals that were taken up by philosophical thought and in time became the unthought (naturalized) orthodoxy. Indeed, I have traced elsewhere how this could be interpreted as what happened for the modern era with the emergence of Cartesian dualism in the mid-seventeenth century.[7] In this chapter, I wonder if rereading *Hamlet* with a focus on flesh might offer a prompt to "remember" an earlier moment when assumptions about human selfhood and human exceptionalism were being thought differently. In reading *Hamlet* in this way we can, I suggest, retrace some steps of forgetting and see humans as they were once recognized, that is, as embodied and embruted (to borrow John Milton's terms[8]) in ways that differ greatly from those that we might contemplate today – even as we are so often celebrating what Cary Wolfe has called the recontextualization of *Homo sapiens* "in terms of the entire sensorium of other living beings."[9]

Original Flesh

Hamlet's thoughts about the human, like those of so many in the early modern period, frequently take animals as the Other. Whether he is extolling humanity's powers or challenging them, they are there to clarify, but all too often serve also to undermine human superiority. Famously, he states:

> What a piece of work is a man – how noble in reason; how infinite in faculties, in form and moving; how express and admirable in action; how like an angel in apprehension; how like a god; the beauty of the world; the paragon of animals.[10]

In this moment, even while announcing his own species as the greatest of God's creation, Hamlet recognizes "man" as the paragon – the highest – among the animals: not entirely set apart, but best. Earlier, this refusal to completely separate human from animal had taken on negative meaning. In the face of his widowed mother's swift remarriage, Hamlet cries: "a beast, that wants discourse of reason, / Would have mourn'd longer" (1.2.150–1). Gertrude's failure is both inhuman (it marks her as not using the reason that humans are endowed with) and unnatural (it goes against the natural – i.e., untaught – actions of animals).

This sense of the complex link between humans and animals was there from the beginning in Judeo-Christian culture. At the end of the sixth day of the Creation, just before retiring to rest, God told Adam that "every herb bearing seed, which is upon all the earth, and every tree, wherein is the fruit of a tree bearing seed: that shall be to you for meat." The vegan directive, found in the text that was the foundation of thinking about human status in the early modern period, was also given to animals: "Likewise to every beast of the earth, and to every fowl of the heaven, and to everything that moveth upon the earth, which hath life in itself, every green herb shall be for meat, and it was so."[11] Laurie Shannon has proposed that what she terms "Genesis's first charter thus fashions plants as commodity-like consumable things." Animals, however, are placed differently: they are, she continues, "in a political relation with humans as the herb-entitled subjects of human 'rule.'"[12] From this perspective, the original distinction of "man" from "beast" was there, but it was a distinction in which a connection persisted.

The Flood was God's response to human sinfulness, and it not only destroyed all that humans had built; it also brought about a change in the dietary directive from the Almighty. In Genesis 9, on finding land after the waters have subsided, Noah is told:

> the fear of you, and the dread of you shall be upon every beast of the earth, and upon every fowl of the heaven, upon all that moveth on the earth, and upon all the fishes of the sea: into your hand are they delivered. Everything that moveth and liveth, shall be meat for you: as the green herb, have I given you all things. (9:2–3)

The consumption of animals was thus understood to be part of humanity's full and proper engagement with God's creation after this moment: it followed a divine directive. In the poet George Herbert's vision of this providential universe, "[t]he beasts say, Eat me";[13] these animals know humans have dominion, and they agree, apparently enthusiastically, that it is their role to be consumed. However, the timing of the introduction of meat eating after the flood also meant that it marked humanity's slide from perfection, and, as such, it revealed our corruption as much as our

dominion. It is wholly appropriate in response to such a paradox, therefore, that the making-commodity of animals does not serve to simply
reinforce human superiority. Far from it – the commodification of beasts
is both produced by and a reflection of human failure.

This ambiguity in human-animal relations can be traced in many
different ways in early modern culture, sometimes with negative connotations and sometimes with positive. To start with the negative: as well as
marking human failure because it is a postlapsarian addition to our diet,
and therefore a reflection of our sinfulness, writers of dietetic manuals from
the early modern period argued that meat had the capacity to act on the
eater in ways that brought to the fore not so much human dominance
(with its assumption of the power of eater over eaten) as humanity's
interconnectedness with the creatures that they consumed. As Ken
Albala has shown, "those substances most similar to the human body were
believed to be the most easily assimilated and thus the most nutritious" by
early modern authors, and so inevitably the "idea of eating human flesh
was [. . .] a perennial obsession for dietary writers" as human flesh was, in
the logic of this system, viewed as the most nutritious substance.[14]
Cannibalism was, of course, regarded as an unnatural and irreligious
act,[15] and so, to simultaneously avoid anthropophagy and maintain a
healthy diet, animal flesh was eaten – something that underlined the
closeness of humans to their nonhuman Others. As James Hart stated in
1633, pigs were believed to have a great "likenesse and resemblance [. . .] to
mans flesh,"[16] and this made them, as Albala puts it, the "next best thing
to human flesh, by universal assent."[17] As such, dietetic advice was not
only bad for pigs, but it also posited a paradoxically close connection
between them and humans.

In the humoral medicine that was dominant in the period, conceptions
of the boundary between humans and animals were even more complicated. This medical system argued that humans were made up of humors
(liquids) that needed to be kept in as balanced a state as possible, while a
preponderance of one humor – black bile, phlegm, blood, or choler –
produced a particular nature: respectively, melancholic, phlegmatic (calm),
sanguine (optimistic), or choleric (quick to anger). Each individual had a
predilection to a particular humor because, after the Fall, a perfect balance
was impossible.[18] An individual's humoral makeup was also impacted by
changes in the seasons (summer was more choleric, while autumn was
more melancholy), and by age, with old people deemed to be more moist
(phlegmatic) than children, who were believed to be cooler and so more
sanguine. Within this context, meat impacted the eater because animals,

like humans, were also made up of humors and so their natures needed to be taken into account when pondering the best diet. In his *Haven of Health* (1584), for example, Thomas Cogan argued that a "moyste and flewmatike" (phlegmatic) meat like lamb was "not convenient for aged men" as it would increase the amount of phlegm in the body, and so overbalance the humors. Likewise, particular parts of animals had particular humoral implications: "The Splene or milt, maketh ill iuice and melancholy bloud. For it is the very place where melancholy is made." And in another instance the impact of the consumed object on the consuming subject is presented in a way that highlights the strange interconnections the act of eating can produce: Cogan argues that "the braines of Chickens and Capons, is good for the memorie and comforteth the wit."[19] The operation of reason ("wit") – the very capacity of which marks humans out as distinct from animals – is in part, it seems, reliant on the consumption of a bird's brain.

Taking the interconnectedness of humans and animals in discussions of consumption in a different direction, in her reading of *Hamlet* Karen Raber thinks about humans as themselves consumable beings. The existence of parasitic creatures like tapeworms that lived within and so fed on humans leads her to contemplate what she calls "mutual cannibalism." While humans eat meat and so display their power, at the same time, as the dietetic and medical texts of the period remind us, they "physically 'house' creation in the form of worms or maggots." This leads her to ask, "do we become indistinguishable from the vermin we house – are we merely 'common' vermin as well?"[20] To add to this conundrum, the very existence of parasitic worms raised theological questions: if God created all animals on the fifth day, and "man" on the sixth, was man created with a worm already inside him? Ian MacInnes has pondered this:

> On the one hand, the tapeworm, being a creature of corruption, should emblematize the mortal taste of the fruit: Adam's worm is Adam's choice writ within. On the other hand, since worms and other invertebrates are a natural part of the created world, they might, like the serpent (which was often classed with invertebrates) be innocent victims of Adam's choice.[21]

From every angle, it seems, eating animal flesh upsets humanity's exceptional status.

But while the meaning of meat eating was so paradoxical – an act of human dominion over nonhumans that marked human failure and could undermine human status – in another context the commodification of animals that often led directly to the production of meat was felt to have the potential to breed a positive sense of interspecies community. For example, in the third sermon of his 1609 text *The House-holder*, the clergyman Edward Topsell cited Proverbs 12.10, "[a] righteous man regardeth the life of his beast," and reminded his readers that their "household" includes animals, and that the "perfect man" must "provide [. . .] Hay and Grasse" for cattle. He also noted that "our Flockes and Heards are our Families, our Cattell, our charges Pastorall and Magisteriall, kingdoms to Kings, Monarchies to Emperors."[22] While the latter statement brings in the analogical potential of dominion over animals (it symbolizes the rule of the monarch over their subjects), underpinning Topsell's words is another conception of a connection between humans and their "quick cattle" (i.e., living property) that we should take seriously.[23] Indeed, in a chapter titled "Animal Families," Helen Smith has shown how, in Topsell's and others' writings, "the animal, the household, and civil life [were] tightly interlinked." She cites Robert Cleaver's 1598 declaration that a householder should have "a christian care" over his animals, and argues that such a declaration blurs "the line between rational, contractual man and 'dumbe & insensible' beast."[24]

Amid such discussions of both the negative and the positive entanglements of humans and animals in early modern thought there remained, however, a crucial difference, a difference that underpinned all relations between the species, even the more communitarian ones. In his *Exposition of the Symbole* of 1595, the leading English Calvinist of the age, William Perkins, put it in these terms: "some creatures made before [man] were onely bodily: as beasts, fishes, fowles: some spirituall, as Angels: now man is both: spirituall in regard of his soule, corporall and sensible in regard of his bodie."[25] There is, as such, an essential, God-given difference between man and beast. And the human's possession of an immortal ("spirituall") soul was believed to have practical implications in the terrestrial realm too: it gave them the capacity to reason. On the other hand, animals' wholly mortal state meant that they lacked reason (or lacked *human* reason) and were killable in a way that humans (or those beings classed as human) could not be.[26] As such, the claim for human immortality (our possession of a soul) was inherently linked to human dominion – rule – over the natural world, and was manifested in caring for animals, as much as in eating them.

For this reason, discussions of human immortality can be found in areas of early modern culture beyond sermons or works of theology. To offer one example: in the opening chapter of his horse-training manual that was printed in the same year as Topsell's *House-holder*, Nicholas Morgan wrote that "the Creation of man" was distinct from that of animals because God,

> hauing created all other creatures with bodies and faculties of life together, yet to make the excellency and dignitie of the creation of man greater, he fashioned the body of man onely apart, to plant therein the soule by inspiration, shewing that the soule that he inspired in the body of man is not taken of the earth, or of the elements, to die as the body doth, but in his creation hee breathed in his face the breath of life, wherby ma[n] was made a liuing soule: [. . .] all other creatures were subiect to corruption, & man to a perpetuitie of felicitie to eternall life.[27]

Immortality thus places humans above animals in the Christian hierarchy, and makes us capable of training, taming, controlling nature. Indeed, performing such acts of domination become a human duty, a fulfilling of the responsibility handed down by the Almighty.

However, moving straight from thinking about life (eating, riding) to contemplating the afterlife (our species' essential immortality) when focusing on human status in early modern ideas is to miss a moment of what might be termed fleshy overlap, because a challenge to any distinctions established in the binaries human/animal, immortal/mortal can be found when our gaze is focused not on the rationally organized life, or on the eternal soul of the human, but on the body, and it is in this context that *Hamlet* can be read. What *Hamlet* draws attention to is not so much the capacity of the human to be a host to parasites as Raber argues (although it does, as she shows, suggest that), or that the human is always destined to be food for worms (it suggests that too). I want to argue here that the play challenges us to think about our distinction from animals in ways that counter Morgan's claim that the human "was made a liuing soule" while "all other creatures were subiect to corruption."

From the orthodox Christian perspective voiced by Morgan, human dominion is the crucial marker of our special status. However, because in the consumption of the human by worms and other "lower" creatures, humans cease to be the possessors of dominion, our postmortem humanity is understood to exist not in the (edible) body but beyond the realm of the physical – in the soul. Without the life force, the body is simply a kind of terrestrial residue, and so, when that body is eaten, when it rots, what is eaten and rotting is not human, as what is human has already departed into the afterlife. As such, the conception of our species as exceptional in our immortality (whether we are saved or damned) reinforces the sense of human difference in the flesh as well as in the spirit: we are always potential immortal essences. *Hamlet*, I suggest, also does something else.

It does offer the reassurance of immortality, for sure – when Horatio calls on "flights of angels" to sing Hamlet to his "rest," for example (5.2.344). But what we also encounter is the idea that the staging of that reassurance is a kind of calculated forgetting. *Hamlet*, in fact, persistently reminds its audiences that we are flesh; that is, alongside voicing a faith in human immortality, it reveals that our belief in our utter difference from animals is something that we have had to work at.

Hamlet's Flesh

In his book *Shakespeare and Ecology* (2015), Randall Martin argues that "[w]orms enable [Hamlet] to re-theorize human mortality as a transitional stage of ongoing ecological interdependency rather than physical closure."[28] For Martin, as for me, there is something other than immortality after death for humans, but he focuses on Hamlet's acknowledgment of what he terms the "biological metadrama" of decay, consumption, growth, and the way in which that allows Hamlet to see "from the viewpoint of worms" that "the relationship between death and life is not ethically fraught [. . .] that all physical matter passes through the bodies of worms to be reborn in new biodynamic relationships." Martin offers as the key illustration of this proto-Darwinian perspective in the play Hamlet's "physical interactions with Polonius's body" in Act 4. These interactions, Martin argues, "prompt him to look downward and take upon him the mystery of things from below."[29] In *Ecocriticism and Early Modern English Literature* (2011), the same moment leads Todd A. Borlik to write of "Hamlet's morbid ecology," which, he argues, "is also very much aligned with ecocriticism and its rebuke to anthropocentric assumptions promoted by Christian theology."[30] For both of these writers, *Hamlet* is best read as a text that looks forward, as preempting, current environmental thinking – whether ecological or ecocritical. My reading points in the opposite direction; it sees *Hamlet* as recognizing past ideas, while also working in the present to construct a reassuring future. But in staging the comfort to come it reminds us that there is another way of thinking. Like Martin and Borlik, I also think that Hamlet's encounter with death in Act 4 is a moment of significance and that it offers a crucial exposition of the play's conceptions of humans, animals, and the simultaneous and sometimes paradoxical connections and distinctions between them, but I read it in a different way from them. Where Martin writes of "Polonius's body," and Borlik of "Polonius's corpse," I write of Polonius.

After Hamlet has killed Polonius and has hidden his body, members of the court are searching for it, and we get this exchange:

> KING CLAUDIUS: Now, Hamlet, where's Polonius?
> HAMLET: At supper.
> KING CLAUDIUS: At supper! Where?
> HAMLET: Not where he eats, but where he is eaten   (4.3.16–19)

The soul – the immortal marker of human distinction – has gone but Polonius remains Polonius. He remains a "he" when "he is eaten" in that his body remains him. He does not become an "it," a different, emptied, thing. At this moment, for Hamlet, being a human – being Polonius – persists physically after death. Or perhaps we should say that Polonius being dead is part of an understanding of Polonius being alive. Humans here are always rotting corpses, always inevitable food for worms. And that is who they are, not what happens to their bodies.

The emphasis on human flesh and its edibility was a convention in medieval thought, as Karl Steel has shown.[31] It persisted in early modern ideas, despite the seismic shifts in religious belief of the sixteenth century, and Shakespeare's engagement with the idea in *Hamlet* represents a logical extension of what were a set of cultural commonplaces. We can return to William Perkins to find a telling illustration of the ideas that underpin Shakespeare's thinking. His 1591 *Foundation of Christian Religion* is written as a catechism; that is, in question-and-answer form:

> Q. Let us now come to ourselves, and first, tell me what is the natural estate of man?
>
> A. Every man is by nature dead in sin as a loathsome carrion, or as a dead corpse lieth rotting and stinking in the grave, having in him the seeds of all sins.[32]

This is a simile – "as a loathsome carrion," "as a dead corpse" – but its very carnal nature makes that simile feel like the dominant reality in the response. And this is a catechism, so that response was written to be learned, as Perkins put it, "without book [. . .] and in some measure felt in the heart."[33] It was to be embedded in the self.

It could, of course, be argued that if this conception of the human as loathsome carrion was familiar, then it might have become a dead metaphor rather than a living understanding, or an understanding of life. But another example from Perkins shows that he for one did not think that was the case. In his 1595 *Salve for a Sicke Man* he makes clear his belief that the simile of his catechism was the horrifying primary understanding for many, an understanding that was very difficult to displace. Proposing the idea that "death is more excellent then life," Perkins writes:

> It may be, here the mind of man vnsatisfied wil yet further reply & say, that howsoeuer in death the soules of men enter into heauen, yet their bodies, though they haue bin tenderly kept for meat, drink, & apparel; and haue slept many a night in beds of doune, must lie in dark & loathsome graues, & there be wasted & consumed with worms. Ans. All this is true indeede, but all is nothing: if so be it we will but consider aright of our graues as we ought. We must not iudge of our graues, as they appeare to the bodily eye, but we must looke vpon them by the eye of faith.³⁴

For Perkins, then, even though the focus on the physical conception of the grave is the wrong one for a good Christian, because humans are fallen, all are most likely to judge first with a "bodily eye" and so to dwell on this earthly place of corporeal decay and consumption rather than on an incorporeal ever after. Such is our nature. We must learn to look beyond the physical and use what Perkins calls the "eye of faith," to focus on the inorganic, spiritual being that is also part of us. Thus, the early modern vision of human fleshiness is, for Perkins, very much at the forefront of human understanding and is very different from the idea of human embodiedness that we are more familiar with in current antihumanist and posthumanist engagements with human-animal relations. To offer just one example, when Anat Pick advocates a focus on the "corporeal reality of living bodies" her examination of vulnerability calls up positive conceptions of species weakness and mutuality.³⁵ In distinction, the early modern vision is of a nauseating meatiness – a being acknowledged by Hamlet in his description of Polonius "being eaten."

When critics have recognized eating and rotting flesh in *Hamlet*, they have mostly used it to point to other than fleshy issues. John Hunt, for example, sees the emblematic value of human flesh, writing that its potential to decay reveals that the "body personal and politic is a provisional structure."³⁶ Richard Fly, likewise, reads for political ideas when he links the idea that "a rank corruption infects all social spheres of the kingdom" with the Gravedigger's complaint that "we have many pocky corpses that will scarce hold the laying in" (5.1.155–7).³⁷ And Richard Halpern pushes the analogy in a very different direction, cleansing corruption of all but analogical meaning:

> Flesh corresponds to the play as performance: a merely momentary thing composed of speech and movement, mutating from day to day, incorporating improvisation, reacting to immediate circumstance. Bone

corresponds to the play as text: more stable and permanent, but by no
means infinitely so.[38]

Even when critical readings of *Hamlet* do not make analogy their focus,
flesh seems to disappear. Robert N. Watson argues that in the play "it is
not merely 'the dread of something after death' that robs 'enterprises of
pitch and moment' of 'the name of action' (3.1.77–87); the dread of
nothing after death can have a similar effect."[39] The play, of course, makes
clear that there is something (however bad) after death – the Ghost's
coming from Purgatory is evidence of that. But the play also thinks of
"after death" as having another meaning in that it also shows that there is
always something that happens to the human (as to the animal) after
death, when we recognize, as Hamlet so clearly does, its fleshiness.
Likewise, in his study of the connections between the theater, the scaffold,
and the animal baiting arena in what he terms "Shakespeare's explorations
into the nature and workings of humanness as a psychological, ethical and
political category," Andreas Höfele marginalizes questions of human and
animal flesh, even while arguing that "flesh is the obsessive focus of
[Hamlet's] thinking" as, within pages, he looks at something else, writing
of humans as "dust," noting that "the earth disgorges skulls and bones in
the graveyard scene."[40] Once again, we have a critical text that erases the
presence of rotting human meat.

Polonius's death is central to all the readings that recognize the play's
"obsession" with flesh and decay, and yet Hamlet's continuing to view
Polonius as "he" after his demise is made invisible. The readings think
instead about Polonius's body (it) and not about the implications of the
persistence of Polonius as Polonius once his spiritual essence has departed.
Such readings therefore push to the side an aspect of the human that places
us not only among the animals, but also – worse even than that – as food
for them. They collude, you might say, with the orthodox Christian idea
that the human ceases to be a terrestrial being once breathing stops, and as
such are doing the important work of "calculated forgetting" that Derrida
warned us about. For, although writing in the secular field of literary
criticism, these critics have, like William Perkins, asked us to take on faith
that humans are special, that we are the ones who die rational, inorganic
deaths. That Polonius's corpse is not Polonius, that we are not animals.

Hamlet is, of course, stuffed full of metaphorical human edibility that
would seem to offer good evidence as to why the reality of our edibility
should not be the focus in our interpretations. Fortinbras has "Sharked up
a list of lawless resolutes / For food and diet to some enterprise"

(1.1.97–8); while Marcellus and Barnardo are "distilled / Almost to jelly" by the sight of the Ghost (1.2.203–4). In the speech Hamlet recites to the players, Pyrrhus is *"Baked and impasted* [put in pastry] *// [...] roasted in wrath and fire"* (2.2.397 and 399); and in the Player's continuation of it, Hecuba sees Pyrrhus *"mincing with his sword her husband's limbs"* (2.2.452). Following this speech Hamlet berates himself that he should by this time "ha' fatted all the region's kites" with his Uncle's "offal" (2.2.514–15), and this vision of Claudius's edibility is taken up again later when Guildenstern speaks of "those many many bodies" that "live and feed upon your majesty" (3.3.9–10); and when Hamlet accuses Gertrude of leaving the "fair mountain" of his father "to feed / And batten on this moor" (3.4.64–5). Metaphorically made into a corrupted landscape here – the "thing" that is "rotten in the state of Denmark" perhaps? (1.4.90) – Claudius remains edible. As such, the critics who absent the reality of human edibility are working within the rules that the play also accepts. But the metaphorical use of ideas of eating and being edible ceases at some moments. I have already discussed how Hamlet's statement that Polonius "is being eaten" in Act 4, scene 3, focuses on the terrestrial continuity of the old man after his death rather than on his postmortem persistence only as immortal soul, and this presence of the human as flesh is the focus once again at the start of the final act when Hamlet draws our attention to its inevitable rottenness in the graveyard when he has a very close encounter with some of what Perkins had called loathsome carrion.

"Pah!"

Borlik says of the graveyard scene that in it Hamlet "arrives at a stoic acceptance of carnality," that he has by this time rejected "a fantasy of a transcendent subjectivity."[41] I suggest that something very different happens in the scene. Contemplating Yorick's skull, Hamlet ponders:

HAMLET: Prithee, Horatio, tell me one thing.
HORATIO: What's that, my lord?
HAMLET: Dost thou think Alexander looked o' this fashion i' the earth?
HORATIO: E'en so.
HAMLET: And smelt so? pah!
HORATIO: E'en so, my lord. (5.1.185–91)

David Hillman writes that Hamlet's "reactions to the body parts strewn about him are strongly visceral: his 'gorge rises at it' (5.1.181)."[42] I likewise see the "pah!" not only as an acknowledgment of the unavoidable presence of humanity's stinking fleshy persistence but also as a mark of the olfactory distress the material world causes Hamlet, and as such at this moment he can hardly be called stoical.

Indeed, the nauseating rot that is now Yorick, or that Yorick is now (questions of passive and active agency come up in this scene a lot), leads Hamlet to a moment of forgetting. Rather than dwelling on the stinking carcass, he, like so many critics of the play, offers an analysis that absents the flesh, even while persisting with his "morbid ecology." He narrates Alexander the Great's journey as being from life to death to burial to dust to earth to loam, and ultimately to that loam's role as "stopping a bung-hole" in a "beer-barrel" (5.1.200, 194 and 201). As such, at this moment Hamlet makes his (and so our) focus not Alexander's edible, stinking fleshiness but another residue of humanity. The Arden edition of the play defines loam as "clay moistened to make plaster," and so in becoming loam Alexander is made dust alone. This shift from flesh to dust illustrates what Susan Zimmerman calls Hamlet's "preoccupation with the indistinguish-able skulls" in the graveyard scene, which, she argues, serve "to deflect a still more horrifying recognition of their prior process of decomposition." Citing George Bataille's ideas, she proposes that "bones are emblems of death which bear no trace of nature's cannibalism; they are the hard, clean, sanitised remnants of putrefaction."[43] To turn from "pah!" to loam as Hamlet does is thus to cleanse human death of its meatiness; it is to forget what has been. And the forgetting becomes more calculated when it is (too) neatly wrapped up in a rhyme:

> Imperious Caesar, dead and turned to clay,
> Might stop a hole to keep the wind away.
> O, that that earth which kept the world in awe
> Should patch a wall t'expel the water's flaw. (5.1.202–5)

The shift from prose to perfect iambic couplets, from "pah!" to wit, marks the move from flesh to bone; from death revealing the human as decaying meat to death as encountered in religious ritual: "earth, to earth, asshes, to asshes, dust to dust."[44] It is notable, as well, that in Hamlet's biographies of Alexander and Caesar he has them both as active agents of the gram-mar – they stop the holes; they are not passively being eaten.[45]

Hamlet's shift of emphasis from flesh to "loam" can be read as doing important work for him and for his audience. It is an act of calculated forgetting, a moment in which the similarity of human and animal flesh that haunts the play, as it haunts the culture that it existed in, is made invisible. For Perkins this is an appropriate shift. It takes Hamlet from the focus on "our graues, as they appeare to the bodily eye," to a vision of the human as seen "by the eye of faith." It returns man to his special status as the possessor of the angels' spiritual essence. But the fact of "pah!" – the inclusion of it in the text – makes that shift incomplete. Indeed, the play seems to move backward and forward between seeing with the bodily eye and seeing with the eyes of faith. This is not a single step; the play forgets and remembers, remembers and forgets.

As illustration, the fleshy human was present in the graveyard scene even before the smelly encounter with Yorick, and before Hamlet turned to contemplate clay. It was there when he asked a question that is, in this context, just as profound as "To be, or not to be" (3.1.55): "How long will a man lie i' th' earth ere he rot?" (5.1.154). Again, this is "a man," not "a body" or "a corpse": it is the individual, "he," who is i' th' earth. The answer the Gravedigger gives is:

> Faith, if 'a be not rotten before 'a die (as we have many pocky corpses that will scarce hold the laying in) 'a will last you some eight year – or nine year – a tanner will last you nine year. (5.1.155–8)

The tanner, the Gravedigger states, lasts a bit longer because his "hide is so tanned with his trade, that he will keep out water a great while" (5.1.160–1). The "he" marks, as it did with Polonius in Act 4, that the individual continues after death, and it is for this reason that I have paused over Martin's writing about "Polonius's body," and Borlik discussing "Polonius's corpse." What unthought conception of the human, and its distinction from animals, is being reinforced in such interpretive strategies? What acts of forgetting can we trace when we separate the human body from the human individual?

At the end of the play, the anxiety about human status – about our difference from animals – persists. Even after Horatio has called on "flights of angels" to sing Hamlet to his rest, thus evoking the special status of the human as the immortal earthly being (5.2.344), Fortinbras enters and speaks of the bodies he sees as "quarry" (a hunting term), asking personified Death, "What feast is toward in thine eternal cell"? (5.2.348–9). But this language of human edibility is swiftly replaced by the image that closes the play:

> Let four captains,
> Bear Hamlet like a soldier to the stage,
> For he was likely, had he been put on,
> To have proved most royal. (5.2.379–82)

The monumentalizing of Hamlet is a cover for the ambiguity of human existence: "*like* a soldier," "he was *likely, had he been* put on." Hamlet is not what he is staged to be; he has never been that thing, but he will be celebrated like this because Fortinbras sees with the eye of faith: he believes something would have happened to Hamlet in life, just as he, like Perkins, believes something will happen to Hamlet in death.

Human Meat

The naturalizing of our humanity as existing beyond – or perhaps even in spite of – our flesh has had massive impact on our relationship with animals and with our planet. This has been recognized by environmental thinking for generations: Lynn White Jr.'s influential essay "The Historical Roots of Our Ecologic Crisis" was published in 1967, and in it he argued that "by destroying pagan animism, Christianity made it possible to exploit nature in a mood of indifference to the feelings of natural objects."[46] As humans are constructed as subjects – in life and death – all else is commodified, and we are now more than ever recognizing the impact of the conception of our species as transcending the material, and as having unlimited rights to use the planet and its inhabitants. It took René Descartes to construct (calculate) a philosophy in which the ambiguous closeness of humans and animals enabled by Christian thinking was made unimportant as the human was traced only in reason, the *cogito*. What Shakespeare was showing decades before is that there was already discomfort at the connections that drew humans too close to the creatures they were meant to hold dominion over. And knowing that you yourself were edible was at the core of that discomfort.

The thoroughgoing forgetting that followed Descartes can be brilliantly traced in the ecofeminist philosopher Val Plumwood's discussion of her near-fatal encounter with a wild animal in 1985:

> It is not a minor or inessential feature of our human existence that we are food: juicy, nourishing bodies. Yet, as I looked into the eye of the crocodile, I realised that my planning for this journey upriver had given insufficient attention to this important aspect of human life, to my own vulnerability as an edible, animal being. [. . .] Of course, in some very remote and abstract way, I knew it happened, I knew that humans were animals and were sometimes – very rarely – eaten like other animals. I knew I was food for crocodiles, that my body, like theirs, was made of meat. But then again in some very important way, I did *not* know it, absolutely rejected it.[47]

For Plumwood, as for *Hamlet*, the knowledge of human fleshiness is there, but is rejected. The fact of our edibility is calculatedly forgotten, and human exceptionalism is allowed to reign supreme. She wrote of this moment: you "gasp in disbelief that some powerful creature can ignore your special status and try to eat you."[48] Who we are, or who we have been naturalized to see ourselves as being, is distinct, superior, better. We have almost forgotten, almost, our other self. But that other self comes back to catch us out – whether in the form of an animal who views us as food or in our own attempts to forget that potential. When Laertes says of Ophelia, "Lay her i' th' earth, / And from her fair and unpolluted flesh / May violets spring" (5.1.227–9), he is claiming her immortal purity in the face of institutional religion's rejection of her; but he is also – albeit accidentally – recognizing her value as fertilizer. This humiliation of the human plays a crucial role in the terrors that *Hamlet* presents, terrors that are still horrifying today. Remembering this asks us to recall that the separation of humans from animals that has been naturalized so destructively is an act of faith. But there is, to return to Perkins, another "true indeede" being that is human who we might do well to focus on a little more.

Notes

1 Respectively: Bruce Thomas Boehrer, *Animal Characters: Nonhuman Beings in Early Modern Literature* (Philadelphia: University of Pennsylvania Press, 2010); Laurie Shannon, *The Accommodated Animal: Cosmopolity in Shakespearean Locales* (Chicago: University of Chicago Press, 2013); Erica Fudge, *Brutal Reasoning: Animals, Rationality and Humanity in Early Modern England* (Ithaca, NY: Cornell University Press, 2006). For a useful overview of the range of work in the field, see Nicole Mennell, "Animal Studies and the Early Modern Period," in *Oxford Research Encyclopedias: Literature* (Oxford: Oxford University Press, 2021), https://doi.org/10.1093/acrefore/9780190201098.013.1191.
2 Sandra Swart in "Roundtable: Animal History in a Time of Crisis," *Agricultural History* 94.3 (2020), 455.
3 Respectively: Andreas Höfele, *Stake, Stage and Scaffold: Humans and Animals in Shakespeare's Theatre* (Oxford: Oxford University Press, 2011); Karen L. Raber, "'Reasonable Creatures': William Cavendish and the Art of Dressage," in Patricia Fumerton and Simon Hunt (eds.), *Renaissance Culture and the Everyday* (Philadelphia: University of Pennsylvania Press, 1999), 42–66; Erica Fudge, *Quick Cattle and Dying Wishes: People and Their Animals in Early Modern England* (Ithaca, NY: Cornell University

Press, 2018); Sarah Cockram, "Sleeve Cat and Lap Dog: Affection, Aesthetics and Proximity to Companion Animals in Renaissance Mantua," in Sarah Cockram and Andrew Wells (eds.), *Interspecies Interactions: Animals and Humans between the Middle Ages and Modernity* (London: Routledge, 2018), 34–65.

4 For example, see Erica Fudge, "Saying Nothing Concerning the Same: On Dominion, Purity and Meat in Early Modern England," in Fudge (ed.), *Renaissance Beasts: Of Animals, Humans and Other Wonderful Creatures* (Urbana: University of Illinois Press, 2004), 70–86; and Karen Raber, *Animal Bodies, Renaissance Culture* (Philadelphia: University of Pennsylvania Press, 2013), 103–25.

5 Karen Raber, "Animals at the Table: Performing Meat in Early Modern England and Europe," in Karen Raber and Monica Mattfeld (eds.), *Performing Animals: History, Agency, Theater* (University Park: Pennsylvania State University Press, 2017), 14–27.

6 Jacques Derrida, *The Animal That Therefore I Am*, trans. David Wills (New York: Fordham University Press, 2008), 11.

7 Fudge, *Brutal Reasoning*.

8 John Milton, *A Masque at Ludlow Castle* (1634), in Tony Davies (ed.), *John Milton: Selected Shorter Poems and Prose Writings* (London: Routledge, 1988), line 463.

9 Cary Wolfe, *What Is Posthumanism?* (Minneapolis: Minnesota University Press, 2010), xxv.

10 2.2.269–73. The edition used, and cited in text hereafter, is Ann Thompson and Neil Taylor (eds.), *Hamlet* (London: Arden, 2016).

11 Geneva Bible, Genesis, 1.29–30, at www.biblegateway.com/versions/1599-Geneva-Bible-GNV/ (accessed April 28, 2022)

12 Shannon, *Accommodated Animal*, 41–2.

13 George Herbert, "Providence," in John Drury and Victoria Moul (eds.), *George Herbert: The Complete Poetry* (London: Penguin, 2015), line 21.

14 Ken Albala, *Eating Right in the Renaissance* (Berkeley: University of California Press, 2002), 68.

15 The use of "mummia" (dried human flesh) in medicine was the exception to this. See Louise Noble, *Medicinal Cannibalism in Early Modern Literature and Culture* (New York: Palgrave Macmillan, 2011).

16 James Hart, *ΚΛΙΝΙΚΗ, Or The Diet of the Diseased* (London: Robert Allot, 1633), 71.

17 Albala, *Eating Right*, 70.

18 A useful overview of humoral medicine can be found in Jack Hartnell, *Medieval Bodies: Life, Death and Art in the Middle Ages* (London: Profile Books, 2018), 12–16. See also Raber, "Animals at the Table," 24.

19 Thomas Cogan, *The Haven of Health* (London: Thomas Orwin, 1589 edition), 116, 127–8 and 125.

20 Raber, *Animal Bodies*, 111.

21 Ian MacInnes, "The Politic Worm: Invertebrate Life in the Early Modern English Body," in Jean E. Feerik and Vin Nardizzi (eds.), *The Indistinct Human in Renaissance Literature* (Basingstoke: Palgrave Macmillan, 2012), 253–74, quotation 259–60.

22 Edward Topsell, *The House-holder* (London: Henry Rockyt, 1609), 100 and 123.

23 See Fudge, *Quick Cattle*, 28–9.

24 Helen Smith, "Animal Families," in Hannah Crawforth and Sarah Lewis (eds.), *Family Politics in Early Modern Literature* (Basingstoke: Palgrave Macmillan, 2017), 76.

25 William Perkins, *Exposition of the Symbole* (1595), in *The Workes of that Famous and Worthy Minister of Christ* (London: John Legatt, 1616–18), I, 152.

26 The issues in the parentheses in this sentence clearly point to the very problematic nature of the orthodox conception of both reason and the human in the period. Both issues are explored in Fudge, *Brutal Reasoning*.

27 Nicholas Morgan, *The Perfection of Horse-manship, drawne from Nature; Arte, and Practise* (London: Edward White, 1609), 1–2.

28 Randall Martin, *Shakespeare and Ecology* (Oxford: Oxford University Press, 2015), 144.

29 Ibid., 144.

30 Todd A. Borlik, *Ecocriticism and Early Modern English Literature: Green Pastures* (London: Routledge, 2011), 202.

31 Karl Steel, *How Not to Make a Human: Pets, Feral Children, Worms, Sky Burial, Oysters* (Minneapolis: University of Minnesota Press, 2019), 75–110.

32 Perkins, *Foundation of Christian Religion* (1591), in *Workes*, I, 1.

33 Perkins, "Epistle" to *Foundation*, n.p.

34 Perkins, *Salve for a Sicke Man* (1595), in *Workes*, I, 494.

35 Anat Pick, *Creaturely Poetics: Animality and Vulnerability in Literature and Film* (New York: Columbia University Press, 2011), 3.

36 John Hunt, "A Thing of Nothing: The Catastrophic Body in *Hamlet*," *Shakespeare Quarterly*, 39.1 (1988), 34.

37 Richard Fly, "Accommodating Death: The Ending of *Hamlet*," *Studies in English Literature 1500–1900*, 24.2 (1984), 264.

38 Richard Halpern, "Eclipse of Action: *Hamlet* and the Political Economy of Playing," *Shakespeare Quarterly*, 59.4 (2008), 480.

39 Robert N. Watson, "Giving up the Ghost in a World of Decay: *Hamlet*, Revenge and Denial," *Renaissance Drama*, 21 (1990), 218.

40 Höfele, *Stake, Stage and Scaffold*, 2, 156 and 168.

41 Borlik, *Ecocriticism*, 203.

42 David Hillman, *Shakespeare's Entrails: Belief, Scepticism and the Interior of the Body* (Basingstoke: Palgrave Macmillan, 2007), 111.

43 Susan Zimmerman, *The Early Modern Corpse and Shakespeare's Theatre* (Edinburgh: Edinburgh University Press, 2005), 190.

44 "The ordre for the Buryall of the Deade," in *The Booke of Common Prayer* (London: Johannis Cawood), 1559, sig.V.ii recto.

45 On this, see Jonathan Hope, *Shakespeare and Language: Reason, Eloquence and Artifice in the Renaissance* (London: Arden, 2010), especially 138–69.

46 Lynn White Jr., "The Historical Roots of Our Ecologic Crisis," *Science*, 155 (1967), 1205.

47 Val Plumwood, *The Eye of the Crocodile* (Canberra: Australian National University Press, 2012), 10

48 Ibid., 11.

CHAPTER 3

Eighteenth Century
Enlightenment and Empire

Donna Landry

When, on his twenty-fifth birthday, Alexander Pope published in Richard Steele's short-lived periodical *The Guardian* an essay against cruelty to animals, he observed how "[e]very one knows how remarkable the *Turks* are for their Humanity in this kind."[1] Feeling for fellow creatures was often coupled in eighteenth-century English minds with Eastern cultures. This coupling means that ideas about compassion for animals and the Oriental fictions that had become so popular with British audiences sprang from the same source. These Oriental tales were Arabic, Ottoman, Persian, and Indian, including, most famously, *The Thousand and One Nights* (*Alf Laylah wa-Laylah*), or *Arabian Nights' Entertainments*, and *The Pañcatantra*, also known as *Kalilah wa-Dimnah, Fables of Bidpai*, or *Tales of Pilpay*. "Derived from a third century CE Sanskrit original" and "even earlier Buddhist Jakata tales," this beast fable cycle "came to Europe through complex transformations via Asia and the Levant"; the tales belong to the ever-popular genre of the mirror for (or advice to) princes, as does the *Arabian Nights*: "By the late nineteenth century, it was documented that the Bidpai tradition existed in 112 versions in 38 languages and 180 printed editions."[2] Alongside Eastern luxury goods and addictive commodities such as coffee and tea, Eastern beast fables circulated widely.

The taste for these exotic consumables was fueled by mercantile networks, scholarly and scientific exchanges, and travelers' tales, culminating in what Srinivas Aravamudan has called "Enlightenment Orientalism," through which "[i]maginative fiction, just as much as scholarly disquisitions, or mainstream philology," came to define European understandings of the East. This experiment in cultural openness and cosmopolitanism would come to an end later in the century, he claims, "partly out of generic exhaustion and partly as a result of a rising nationalist tide that combined self-contemplative narcissism with intense xenophobia."[3] Beginning with the Seven Years' War (1756–63) and ending in the French and Napoleonic wars (1792–1815), there arose new British nationalist and imperialist sentiments, accompanied by a triumphalist assumption of cultural superiority to the Eastern empires that had earlier been so admired and imitated. Aravamudan clarifies that "Orientalism" in Edward Said's sense of the array of institutions of knowledge employed in the "imperial management of subject peoples since the turn of the nineteenth century" still holds for later periods, and that the substance of Said's "broad historical claims" cannot be gainsaid, "a trend that continues well into contemporary Occidental geopolitics in relation to Islam."[4]

The sense of cosmopolitan buzz in early eighteenth-century London was captured well by Joseph Addison's character of Mr. Spectator in the eponymous periodical *The Spectator*, describing the Royal Exchange in 1711:

> It gives me a secret satisfaction, and, in some measure, gratifies my Vanity, as I am an *Englishman*, to see so rich an Assembly of Country-men and Foreigners consulting together upon the private Business of Mankind, and making this Metropolis a kind of *Emporium* for the whole Earth [...] Trade, without enlarging the *British* Territories, has given us a kind of additional Empire: It has multiplied the Number of the Rich, made our Landed Estates infinitely more Valuable than they were formerly, and added to them an Accession of other Estates as Valuable as the Lands themselves.[5]

Britain's international mercantile networks via monopoly companies preceded and clearly fed the desire for territorial empire. It was as if Britain already possessed an empire in the commercial sense, if not in the political one. The wealth, ingenuity, and splendor of the Eastern empires of the Ottomans, Safavids, and Mughals flowed into London on English ships, and British print culture was likewise saturated with Oriental influences.[6] In this period of "Enlightenment" Orientalism, Europeans traded commercially with Islamic imperial states but there was no presumption of European superiority – far from it; that would only come later, by the century's end.[7]

Early eighteenth-century writing about animals often breaks new ground in the light of this Orientalized and cosmopolitan milieu. Pope's *Guardian* essay and his poems *Windsor-Forest* (1713) and *An Essay on Man* (1733–4) question the barbarity lurking in traditional English human-animal relations. The Scottish poet James Thomson's *The Seasons* (1726–30) represents individual animal species as "peoples" in their own right, conjoined by social and power relations.[8] Part 4 of the Anglo-Irish writer Jonathan Swift's *Gulliver's Travels* (1726) envisages a newly discovered land in which a superior equid species, the Houyhnhnms, dominates a debased hominid, the Yahoos. All these works present different versions of nonhuman animals as coevals with humanity. These representations resonate with Islamic ideas, as interpreted by Sarra Tlili, who reads the Qur'an as a "non-anthropocentric" and even "eco-centric" text that directly counters human exceptionalism.[9] The Qur'anic verse "[t]here is not an animal in the earth nor a flying creature flying on two wings, but they are people like you" (Sura 6/al-An'ām: 38) applies equally to the vantage point of Pope, Swift, Thomson, and also to Gilbert White.[10] Even earthworms are worthy of White's close attention and have a story to tell, anticipating today's new nature writing: "Earth-worms, though in appearance a small and despicable link in the chain of Nature, yet, if lost, would make a lamentable chasm."[11] Within his closely observed parish of Selborne, White's thinking remains far from parochial. Observing birds who clean themselves by dusting, White thinks of Islamic practices in the desert: "*Query.* – Might not *Mahomet* and his followers take one method of purification from these *pulveratrices?*"[12]

Scientific observation coupled with sensibility, or sympathetic identification with other species, was a new feature of eighteenth-century Enlightenment writing about animals. New ways of conceiving of and relating to "others," new forms of alterity, relationship, and possible attachment came to the fore in this period, with resonances for today. As Laura Brown proposes, what we could classify as deriving principally from Eastern sources, the animal fable, by the later eighteenth century began "to dissolve into natural history and realist description, blending materials from contemporary experience and observation with the symbolic depiction that made it a core component of the emblematic worldview."[13] Stories about animals continued in European and English writing but they were differently framed: naturalistically, empirically, or as children's literature; or as anthropologically interesting, or as folklore, with increasingly imperialist overtones, as Kaori Nagai amply demonstrates in her study of imperial beast fables in the nineteenth and twentieth centuries.[14]

A Seventeenth-Century Ottoman Comparison: Evliya Çelebi's Elephant Watching

Although unknown to Pope and his contemporaries, there were other traditions of representing animals in the Ottoman world beyond the beast fable. Natural history and realist description, not only symbolic or allegorical depiction, formed part of the Eastern literary legacy.

Empirical, scientific observations of real animals as well as animal fictions and fantasy are present in a notable instance of seventeenth-century Ottoman literature, the ten-volume manuscript *Seyahatname* ("Book of Travels") of Evliya Çelebi (1611–c.1687). Pope draws only on the Eastern fictional repertoire, closing his *Guardian* essay against barbarity to animals with a story from the *Tales of Pilpay* (originally Indian, but known to Pope from a Persian source), as we shall see. As mentioned earlier, Pope invoked Turkish precedents for his arguments about why compassion and not cruelty should be humanity's guiding principle in relation to fellow creatures. There could be no better exemplar of Ottoman Turkish compassion for animals as fellow creatures than Evliya Çelebi.

We might compare Evliya's description of elephants when he is traveling in Upper Egypt and the Sudan with the natural history writing of the European Enlightenment, including later eighteenth-century English writers such as Gilbert White. In the final volume of his manuscript, Evliya and his soldier escorts are returning to Cairo after visiting various kingdoms and peoples in the region of the Upper Nile. Along the way they encounter elephants, and although used to hunting with hounds and shooting many kinds of game, the party opt not to kill but to observe. In fact, they attempt to rescue an elephant calf attacked by an eagle but fail to save the vulnerable creature. Despite the humans' lack of success in rescuing the young elephant, some sort of bond seems to have been established. Evliya reports:

> Eleven huge Mahmudi elephants accompanied us [. . .] They paid us little heed, sometimes walking in front of us, sometimes to our right or left, chasing one another, or playing, or fighting. This went on for seven hours. Though we were armed, we agreed not to shoot at them, but simply to watch.
>
> One of them was a very large old elephant. He did not prance around like the others, but several times came close to the soldiers in order, as it seemed, to exhibit his beauty. He was a very clever animal. His legs were like minarets, tusks like ship-masts, trunk like a chimney, belly like an Isfahan kettledrum, hide like a worn carpet, mouth like the mouth of a stokehold, eyes like gazelle eyes, tail like the staff of a dervish sheikh, anus like the Cave of Orpheus.
>
> These eleven elephants accompanied us all the way to the next stage, and no one laid a hand on them.[15]

Evliya stresses his party's peaceful approach to the elephants, apparently unusual among soldiers who were armed marksmen accustomed to field sports, and he combines naturalist description with highly literary tropes. The most senior elephant, a particularly striking figure, commands utmost respect. The prose turns lyrical and fable-like in striving to capture this elephant's beauty, cleverness, and general impressiveness – his majesty. Evliya has recourse to a rich repository of similes drawn from the many literary traditions that would have been familiar to an Ottoman audience. As a Sufi dervish, though he often traveled with the Ottoman army and was familiar with soldiers' ways, Evliya emphasizes that this episode is one of "accompaniment," of human-elephant companionship and mutual observation on the road.[16] It is instructive to remember that before the mid-eighteenth century, species other than the ape, especially the elephant, were considered comparable to humans in intelligence and thereby crucial "for defining human nature."[17] From Evliya's point of view both the elephant and the monkey are notably "clever" animals.[18]

Pope and Thomson: Animals as Fellow Peoples

Pope's *Guardian* essay, no. 61 (1713), may be the first periodical essay in English devoted to the question of animal welfare.[19] Citing Ovid, Michel de Montaigne, John Locke, Plutarch, the Bible, and "an Arabian author" (probably Ibn Tufayl [d. 1185], author of *Hayy ibn Yaqzan*, a desert-island predecessor of *Robinson Crusoe* [1719]),[20] and implicitly exploring ideas from Pythagoras[21] to which he will return twenty years later in *An Essay on Man*, Pope deplores how his fellow countrymen fail to recognize their kinship with other species, even going to great lengths to abuse, torture, kill, and consume them:

> I Cannot think it extravagant to imagine, That Mankind are no less, in Proportion, accountable for the ill Use of their Dominion over Creatures of the lower Rank of Beings, than for the Exercise of Tyranny over their own Species. The more entirely the Inferior Creation is submitted to our Power, the more answerable we should seem for our Mismanagement of it; and the rather, as the very Condition of Nature renders these Creatures incapable of receiving any Recompence in another Life, for their ill Treatment in this.
>
> [...]
>
> MONTAIGNE thinks it some Reflection upon Human Nature it self, that few People take Delight in seeing Beasts caress or play together, but almost every one is pleased to see them lacerate and worry one another. I am sorry this Temper is become almost a distinguishing Character of our own Nation, from the Observation which is made by Foreigners of our beloved Pastimes, *Bear baiting*, *Cock-fighting*, and the like. We should find it hard to vindicate the destroying of any thing that has Life, meerly out of Wantonness; yet in this Principle our Children are bred up, and one of the first Pleasures we allow them, is the Licence of inflicting Pain upon poor

> Animals: Almost as soon as we are sensible what Life is our selves, we make
> it our Sport to take it from other Creatures.[22]

The young writer proceeds to criticize many forms of excessive and
needless cruelty to animals that he finds all too commonplace in
English society.

It is not hunting with hounds per se that Pope attacks, but rather the
way that peer pressure, being at one with an exhilarated crowd, tends to
prevent those following hounds from enacting those compassionate (or
sportsmanlike) "checks" in the chase, giving the hunted animal a fair
chance of escape, or not digging out one that has gone to ground. Pope
declares that he "must have leave to be of Opinion that the Agitation of
that Exercise, with the Example and Numbers of the Chasers, not a little
contributes to resist those *Checks*, which Compassion would naturally
suggest in behalf of the Animal pursued."[23] Pope finds it especially
grotesque when ladies are invited to administer the coup de grâce in the
pursuit of deer, slitting the throat of the fallen stag. It is not meat-eating as
such he deplores but rather gluttony and the subjecting of those animals to
be eaten to needless pain and suffering before they are killed:

> *Lobsters roasted a live, Piggs whipt to Death, Fowls sewed up*, are Testimonies
> of our outragious Luxury. [. . .] I know nothing more shocking or horrid,
> than the Prospect of one of their Kitchins cover'd with Blood, and fill'd
> with the Cries of Creatures expiring in Tortures.[24]

Indeed it is the cry, the moment of animals' giving voice to their suffering,
that most inspires Pope's indignation at human indifference to or even
enjoyment of such spectacles. Surely, he speculates, the humanlike vocal-
izations with which many other species speak ought to signify kinship and
fellow-creaturely status:

> Perhaps that Voice or Cry so nearly resembling the Human, with which
> Providence has endued so many different Animals, might purposely be
> given them to move our Pity, and prevent those Cruelties we are too apt to
> inflict on our Fellow Creatures.[25]

Ideas about nonhuman animals' claims to be heard, grounded in "interspecies affiliation" between humans and other creatures through a notion
of shared "sensibility," are a feature of eighteenth-century writing, as
shown by Tobias Menely.[26] From the Earl of Shaftesbury and Pope to
later authors such as the Scottish journalist John Oswald (author of *The
Cry of Nature, or, An Appeal to Mercy and to Justice on Behalf of the
Persecuted Animals* [1791]), such appeals called on audiences' sensibilities

to act compassionately and justly, anticipating the anti-cruelty legislation of the nineteenth century.[27]

Pope derives some clear ethical principles from Eastern sources. He follows the reminder that the Turks are famous for their humanity to animals with the tale by "the Arabian author" (ibn Tufayl) of the man on a peopleless island whose "first Act of Virtue" is "to Relieve and Assist all the Animals about him in their Wants and Distresses."[28] Pope's conclusion, however, leads to a further invocation of an Eastern source that complicates any clearcut moral and ethical program:

> TO conclude, there is certainly a Degree of Gratitude owing to those Animals that serve us; for as such as are Mortal or Noxious, we have Right to destroy them; and for those that are neither of Advantage or Prejudice to us, the common Enjoyment of Life is what I cannot think we ought to deprive them of.
>
> THIS whole Matter, with regard to each of these Considerations, is set in a very agreeable light in one of the *Persian* Fables of *Pilpay*, with which I shall end this Paper.[29]

The tale from Pilpay of the Man, the Adder, and the Fox (including contributions from a Tree and a Cow) is at best ambiguous in its advice regarding humanity's place within interspecies relations and affiliations. The Man who saved the Adder from a fire, and expected gratitude, is disappointed – because the Tree and the Cow corroborate the Adder's testimony that humans do not as a species show any gratitude whatsoever to other species, and are not to be trusted. A further appeal to a Fox elicits that canny animal's momentary complicity with the Man against the Adder, who is persuaded to trust the Man against his better judgment – and is crushed to pieces as a result. As Aravamudan remarks, "Pope's fable from Pilpay is brought up to inculcate compassion toward animals, a trait associated with Indian sensibilities based on beliefs in metempsychosis and the practice of vegetarianism," but an irony lurks in the narrative function of Eastern beast fables: "The fox reveals the narrative principle of fable, whereby permutation radically changes the outcome and destabilizes the possibility of any moral takeaway."[30]

Pope's poem *Windsor-Forest*, published on March 7, 1713, not quite three months earlier than his *Guardian* essay,[31] similarly dwells in ambiguities rather than offering a clear route to any "moral takeaway." The poem celebrates in the topographical and georgic modes the Peace of Utrecht that concluded the Wars of the Spanish Succession; the reign of the last Stuart monarch, Queen Anne; and the often blood-soaked historicity and glories of the English countryside, including the pleasures of field sports.[32] However, it is also a poem that foregrounds animal sensibility, and even subjectivity, as Katherine Quinsey proposes.[33] No passage has attracted more attention, and more differing readings, than Pope's description of the shooting of a pheasant:

> See! from the Brake the whirring Pheasant springs,
> And mounts exulting on triumphant Wings;
> Short is his Joy! he feels the fiery Wound,
> Flutters in Blood, and panting beats the Ground.
> Ah! what avail his glossie, varying Dyes,
> His Purple Crest, and Scarlet-circled Eyes,
> The vivid Green his shining Plumes unfold;
> His painted Wings, and Breast that flames with Gold?[34]

Some have found political significance in the splendid plumage and death of the bird as allusions to the martyring of Charles I, in keeping with the allegory by which William I, the Norman conqueror, may also signify William III, the Protestant Dutchman who replaced Charles's Catholic son James II on the throne.[35] The command to the audience to "See!," to witness, is followed immediately by a shift to the pheasant's point of view. The "fiery Wound," the fluttering of the wings "in Blood," and the "panting" as the bird's body "beats the Ground" in his death-throes are vividly palpable. Maynard Mack observes how "Pope accentuates the pathos of the unexpected death by appropriating it to a formula of feeling" that originated in Homeric epic, "where time and again gifts that might have been expected to save a warrior's life – extreme youth, courage, goodness, high birth, great wealth, or all together – fail him."[36] This formula became commonplace in later poetry, says Mack, "[b]ut nowhere except in *Windsor-Forest*, so far as I am aware, is this particular complex of feelings applied to a bird."[37]

When Pope comes to write *An Essay on Man* in 1733, he turns again to Pythagorean ideas in order to characterize human-animal relations as they had been in Eden, before humanity's fall:

> Man walk'd with beast, joint tenant of the shade,
> The same his table, and the same his bed;
> No murder cloath'd him, and no murder fed. (*Epistle III*, 152–4)

Joint tenancy is Pope's formula for the peaceful coexistence of humankind with all other species. Walking together under the benign canopy of shady trees, making his table and bed as other (herbivorous) animals do, without the need for any bloodletting, the "Man" of Pope's essay is not yet the murderer of fellow beings he will become at the Fall. Pope here follows Pythagoras in equating vegetarianism with a paradisiacal Golden Age.

Pope was not alone among British poets of the first half of the eighteenth century in foregrounding animals as fellow sensible subjects who might rightly be regarded as "joint tenant[s]" worthy of fellow feeling: James Thomson (1700–48) in *The Seasons* follows Great Chain of Being philosophy to link humans with other species in complex hierarchies from which they emerge as fellow "peoples."[38] We might recall Tlili's reading of the Qur'anic passage "[t]here is not an animal in the earth nor a flying creature flying on two wings, but they are people like you" (Sura 6/al-An'ām: 38).[39] Sheep having their fleeces washed in *Summer* reveal a multispecies assemblage at work in the countryside:

> Urged to the giddy brink, much is the toil,
> The clamour much of men and boys and dogs
> Ere the soft, fearful people to the flood
> Commit their woolly sides. And oft the swain,
> On some impatient seizing, hurls them in.
> Emboldened then, nor hesitating more,
> Fast, fast they plunge amid the flashing wave,
> And, panting, labour to the farther shore.
> Repeated this, till deep the well-washed fleece
> Has drunk the flood [. . .] [40]

Heather Keenleyside has argued how Thomson's personifications, far from being a merely conventional use of figurative language, constitute a whole philosophy of fellow-creaturely being, an anti-anthropocentric manifesto. Thomson, according to Keenleyside, "calls sheep 'soft fearful People' and chickens 'houshold feathery People' just as he calls Greeks 'lively People' and Romans 'mighty People' (*Su*, 378; *W*, 87, 448, 498)" and he "writes of 'the Tulip-Race' in the same terms as he does of the 'human Race' (*Sp*, 539; *A*, 1021)." Thomson, in Keenleyside's terms, uses "personification to define all kinds of beings as people – a term of relation rather than being, of sociality rather than individual essence."[41] Here she reveals the possibility of ecological connectivity rather than boundary-drawing in Thomson's play with taxonomic conventions as explored by Ralph Cohen, who had suggested that Thomson employed periphrasis "to create a coherent binomial nomenclature, in which the 'personification is implicit in the substantive, and the natural description in the adjective.'"[42] But rather than emphasizing human difference and uniqueness, this "peopling" of the globe with animal and even plant socialities creates cross-species affinities.

Pope is, I think, engaging with Thomson when he describes humans learning from animals as learning from other "Peoples":

> Learn from the birds what food the thickets yield;
> Learn from the beasts the physic of the field; [. . .]
> Learn of the mole to plow, the worm to weave, [. . .]
> Learn each small People's genius, policies,
> The Ant's republic, and the Realm of Bees. (173–84)

Here Pope turns anthropocentric speciesism on its head: *Homo sapiens* should be humble, attentive, and should listen and learn from other species, not seek to dominate and exploit them.

Swift and Equicentricity

Part 4 of Jonathan Swift's *Gulliver's Travels*, "A Voyage to the Country of the Houyhnhnms," takes learning from another species to an unprecedented level. The human protagonist, Lemuel Gulliver, voyages to a land of equids so superior to the local species of hominids, the Yahoos, that Gulliver strives to become as much like a horse as possible. When he returns home to England, Gulliver spends all his time in the stables, conversing with his horses, while deploring the treatment other members of *Equus caballus* receive at the hands of his fellow countrymen. Aravamudan asks: "Is Gulliver's steady retreat into hippophilia and equitherapy insanity or a radical critique of anthropocentrism?"[43]

There is every reason to read Swift's satire as performing a critique of human arrogance and exceptionalism. Once again Eastern influences are at work in Swift's milieu, giving a material grounding to these otherwise seemingly outrageous claims of equine superiority. According to Swift's biographer, Irvin Ehrenpreis, "the delight in horses and the acute observation of them which appear in Houyhnhnmland are derived from an immense firsthand knowledge."[44] As I have argued elsewhere, Swift knew well from his friends the Harleys about the importation of Ottoman blood horses (Turks, Arabians, and Barbs) about whom so many stories of extraordinary intelligence, even rationality, were told.[45] We can track the effects of collective equine agency in the cultural work performed by these horses, transforming ideas about how they should be cared for, handled, ridden, painted, and written about.[46]

Englishmen's admiration for Ottoman horses encompassed respect for the compassionate way in which these horses had been treated in their homeland, another version of enlightened Orientalism in a comparative imperial frame. As with so many aspects of English or British sociality, there is, of course, a class hierarchy to be observed with the new ideas pertaining particularly to "blood" horses, of high birth. However, as Bryan Alkemeyer has observed, Swift's portrayal of the Houyhnhnms as noble and rational animals, grounded in eighteenth-century popular views of horses, applies to *all horses as a species*, and not simply to particular types or breeds.[47] Alkemeyer argues "that a major satiric function of part 4 of *Gulliver's Travels* is to confront readers with the incongruity between traditional beliefs about horses and their systematic exploitation; thus, Swift exposes the human/horse relationship as hypocritical, incoherent, and contradictory."[48] And yet Swift's is far from a modern approach to animal welfare. The defamiliarizing or estranging effect of Swift's satire sits uneasily in relation to the human hypocrisy, cruelty, and exploitation described by Gulliver. As Alkemeyer puts it, "[w]hile Swift's satire exposes contradictions in attitudes toward horses, it admits an ambivalent response: it is unclear whether Swift's text advocates better treatment for horses (to accord with their status as the noblest animals) or undermines idealizations of horses (to produce a more compelling rationalization for exploitation)."[49] The effect of this ambiguity and the ambivalence it arouses may cause a paradigm shift for modern readers so that, Alkemeyer argues, "the [modern] animal welfare movement's premises" – and thereby the split between those who presume that humans can understand other species' needs versus those who dismiss these claims as "anthropomorphic mystifications" – may "begin to seem strange or even suspect."[50] Swift shifts the very ground beneath our feet.

Aravamudan answers his own question about the displacement of *Anthropos* by *Equus* by dismissing the charge of Gulliver's insanity, arguing that by "attempting to pass as a Houyhnhnm, mimicking the gait, gestures, and accents of horses, and by his unshakeable identification with Houyhnhnm forms of reasoning, Gulliver demonstrates the ultimate form of xenophilia: interspecies romance." If animals *as* animals have sometimes seemed to disappear from beast fables in the interest of human concerns, in *Gulliver's Travels*, Aravamudan proposes, Swift "does the opposite by meticulously working out the corporeal effects of the sense-perception that would be needed to create knowledge of the world with the assistance of an equine body rather than a hominid one."[51] The eighteenth-century animal fable need not be merely an allegory or screen for strictly human concerns in that in Swift's hands the Houyhnhnms deal a fatal blow to ideas of human exceptionalism or superiority.[52] However, a merely anti-anthropocentric reading will not do.

In Swift's account of Gulliver's narrated exchanges with the Master Houyhnhnm, something of actual equid species-being comes across. Swift could even be said, I think, to anticipate those later intellectual currents described by Laura Brown, in which the beast fable began to "to dissolve into natural history and realist description." What happens when we must, perforce, adopt an equine interlocutor's point of view regarding the human cruelty and exploitation described by Gulliver – that the horses of "Persons of Quality" receive kind treatment only until they become lame or ill, whereupon they are sold and "used to all kind of Drudgery till they died," to be skinned and eaten by dogs and birds of prey, whereas "the common Race of Horses had not so good Fortune"?[53] English Yahoos, supposedly reasonable creatures, stand revealed as Arch Predators. Horses are prey animals, with only flight or fight at their disposal. Gulliver's tales of Houyhnhnm oppression in his own country intensify his hosts' worst fears about Yahoo capabilities. The Houyhnhnms' periodic Grand Assembly debates on "Whether the *Yahoos*"– who are not, like the Houyhnhnms, aborigines, but settlers who arrived by sea, deriving from an Adam and Eve–like duo -- "should be exterminated from the Face of the Earth" come to seem less unreasonable under Gulliver's influence than before.[54] Genocide is the standard fate of Indigenous peoples within settler colonialism, never the fate of colonial settlers themselves.[55] Swift knew this asymmetrical power dynamic well from Irish experience. In a dizzying reversal, the Houyhnhnms' stance comes to seem less like a proposed genocide of the oppressed and more like an Indigenous people's liberation struggle in their own defense. As Gulliver's tales of British and Continental European human society have starkly shown, violence meets with violence. In Gulliver's case, this means deportation from his adopted Houyhnhnm homeland, but with mitigating benefits (he is helped to build a canoe). Swift's satire radically destabilizes on all counts. No supposedly enlightened premises or orthodoxies go unquestioned. In this equicentric fable, the natural-historical and experiential become fused with satire and fantasy, creating a world apart.

Gilbert White, Natural History, Animal Stories

The clergyman Gilbert White in his parish of Selborne creates a world apart that is very different from Houyhnhnmland but no less rich in animal stories. Robert Macfarlane, for whom White is an important precursor, has described how in 1937 the artist Eric Ravilious visited Selborne and endeavored to walk "the holloways of which White had written in his third letter to Thomas Pennant," producing a haunting engraving of "a deep lane, over which the trees are leaning and locking, and the entry to which is guarded by a barn-owl in flight."[56] Introducing *The Natural History of Selborne* in the much-reprinted Penguin edition, the nature writer Richard Mabey (author of *Food for Free*, a guide to foraging, and many other works), asks:

> How was it that a collection of letters on local natural history – for that is all there is to the book – written with wilful parochialism at a time of social revolution in France and agricultural upheaval at home, could become the fourth most published book in the English language?[57]

Mabey's answer to the question is that: "More than any other single book it has shaped our everyday view of relations between man and nature" – with "everyday" here in no sense signaling a belittling of White's "scientific contributions," which were "considerable," "particularly in the area of observational method."[58]

White described his observational method as follows:

> For many months I carried a list in my pocket of the birds that were to be remarked, and, as I rode or walked about my business, I noted each day the continuance or omission of each bird's song; so that I am as sure of the certainty of my facts as a man can be of any transaction whatsoever.[59]

White's way of looking, as Raymond Williams puts it, is both "a way of looking that will come to be called scientific" and a product of "the devoted and delighted attention of a lifetime, from which anybody living in the country can still learn."[60]

> The titlark and yellowhammer breed late, the latter very late; and therefore it is no wonder that they protract their song: for I lay it down as a maxim in ornithology, that as long as there is any incubation going on there is music. As to the redbreast and wren, it is well known to the most incurious observer that they whistle the year round, hard frost excepted; especially the latter.[61]

White's writing is at once intensely local, enmeshed in European-wide intellectual networks that we could call signs of the Enlightenment, and aware of Britain's commercial and imperial aspirations around the globe:

> MY near neighbour, a young gentleman in the service of the *East-India* Company, has brought home a dog and a bitch of the *Chinese* breed from *Canton*; such as are fattened in that country for the purpose of being eaten: they are about the size of a moderate spaniel; of a pale yellow colour, with coarse bristling hairs on their backs; sharp upright ears, and peaked heads, which give them a very fox-like appearance.[62]

The axis of Britain's overseas ambitions has shifted – from Turkey, the Ottomans, and the Levant Company in Steele's, Addison's, and Pope's day to India, the East India Company, and China in White's – but the global perspective remains the same.

Alert even in deepest Hampshire to happenings abroad, White gives us early warning of the effects of climate and weather and an awareness of the interconnectedness of environments that will come to be called ecological:

> THE summer of the year 1783 was an amazing and portentous one, and full of horrible phenomena [. . .] The sun, at noon, looked as blank as a clouded moon, and shed a rust-coloured ferruginous light on the ground, and floors of rooms; but was particularly lurid and blood-coloured at rising and setting. All the time the heat was so intense that butchers' meat could hardly be eaten on the day after it was killed; and the flies swarmed so in the lanes and hedges that they rendered the horses half frantic, and riding irksome. [. . .] [I]ndeed there was reason for the most enlightened person to be apprehensive; for, all the while, *Calabria* and part of the isle of *Sicily*, were torn and convulsed with earthquakes; and about that juncture a *volcano* sprung out of the sea on the coast of *Norway*.[63]

Here we have an instance of climate awareness and proto-geological or earth-science consciousness that anticipates the most recent environmentalist thinking.[64] This new alertness to natural forces accompanies a continuing recognition of the mutual imbrication of humans and other species – butchered livestock, flies, horses.

Conclusion

Animal stories abounded in early and mid-eighteenth-century British writing, often derived from Eastern sources. These Oriental fictions served as conduits for intellectual and aesthetic engagement with the great Muslim empires of the day. In some sense part and parcel of the trade in exotic Eastern consumables and luxury goods, animal fables enabled a newly enlightened view of fellow creatures and possibilities for kindness and sympathy. These new trans-species and fellow-creaturely feelings, products of an experience of comparative imperialisms, will in turn lead to greater awareness of the need for improvements in animal welfare at home. From Pope's stinging criticism of human barbarity to nonhuman animals in 1713 to Gilbert White's affectionate account of the birds and animals around him in 1789, natural history and fable were often conjoined in this period of literary history. In seventeenth-century Ottoman literature, Evliya Çelebi produced a distinctive combination of natural historical awareness and fabulist impulse. James Thomson's panoply of animal species apprehended as peoples in their own right and Swift's equicentric turning of the world upside down both showed the way to alternative understandings of human and nonhuman animals as sharing common ground. In this period of literary cosmopolitanism, questions of enlightenment were largely inseparable from imperial ambitions. Yet it was also possible to entertain the prospect of living as "joint tenant[s] of the shade" with fellow creatures.

Notes

1 [Alexander Pope], *The Guardian*, no. 61, May 21, 1713, 2 vols. (London: Printed for J. Tonson, 1714), I, 256–61.

2 Srinivas Aravamudan, *Enlightenment Orientalism: Resisting the Rise of the Novel* (Chicago: University of Chicago Press, 2012), 129–30. See also Ros Ballaster, *Fabulous Orients: Fictions of the East in England 1662–1785* (Oxford: Oxford University Press, 2005), 343–59.

3 Aravamudan, *Enlightenment*, 4.

4 Ibid., 2.

5 [Joseph Addison], *The Spectator*, no. 69, ["The Royal Exchange"], May 19, 1711.

6 See Gerald MacLean and Nabil Matar, *Britain and the Islamic World, 1558–1713* (Oxford: Oxford University Press, 2011), 198–238.

7 Said dated the discourse of Western superiority and colonial domination, the object of his study, from Bonaparte's invasion of Egypt in 1798 onward; *Orientalism* (New York: Vintage, 1978; 25th anniversary edition, 2003), 17, 87–9.

8 Inspired by Thomson, Heather Keenleyside recaptures the purchase of personification for thinking about animals in a number of eighteenth-century writers: *Animals and Other People: Literary Forms and Living Beings in the Long Eighteenth Century* (Philadelphia: University of Pennsylvania Press, 2016). For an earlier instance of the anti-anthropocentric usefulness of the category of "animal people," see Donna Landry and Gerald MacLean, *Materialist Feminisms* (Cambridge, MA: Blackwell, 1993), 214–17.

9 Sarra Tlili, *Animals in the Qur'an* (Cambridge: Cambridge University Press, 2012), ix–xii, 252–6.

10 Ibid., 10–11.

11 Gilbert White, *The Natural History and Antiquities of Selborne, in the County of Southampton* [1789] (Menston: Scolar Press, 1970), 216.

12 Ibid., 133.

13 Laura Brown, *Homeless Dogs and Melancholy Apes: Humans and Other Animals in the Modern Literary Imagination* (Ithaca, NY: Cornell University Press, 2010), 22.

14 Kaori Nagai, *Imperial Beast Fables: Animals, Cosmopolitanism, and the British Empire* (Cham: Palgrave Macmillan/Springer Nature, 2020), 7–75.

15 Evliya Çelebi, *An Ottoman Traveller: Selections from the Book of Travels of Evliya Çelebi*, ed., and trans. Robert Dankoff and Sooyong Kim (London: Eland, 2010), 448. The manuscript was composed in Cairo, where Evliya settled after making the pilgrimage to Mecca in 1671–2, and it was disseminated by the chief eunuch El-Hajj Beshir Agha (c.1657–1746), who, having received the original from Cairo in 1742, had it copied in Istanbul; Jane Hathaway, *The Chief Eunuch of the Ottoman Harem: From African Slave to Power Broker* (Cambridge: Cambridge University Press, 2018), 209–10. Apart from this recognition by an important Ottoman court intellectual, there is no evidence of the text's original reception because the manuscript did not come to public attention until the early nineteenth century. See Caroline Finkel, "Joseph von Hammer-Purgstall's English Translation of the First Books of Evliya Çelebi's *Seyahatname* (Book of Travels)," *Journal of the Royal Asiatic Society*, 3rd, series, 25.1 (January 2015), 41–55 (41–2).

16 For more on Evliya, see Robert Dankoff, *An Ottoman Mentality: The World of Evliya Çelebi* (Leiden: Brill, 2004), and Landry, "Evliya Çelebi, Explorer on Horseback: Knowledge Gathering by a Seventeenth-Century Ottoman," in Adriana Craciun and Mary Terrell (eds.), *Curious Encounters: Voyaging, Collecting, and Making Knowledge in the Long Eighteenth Century* (Toronto: University of Toronto Press, 2018), 43–70. See also Alan Mikhail, *The Animal in Ottoman Egypt* (Oxford: Oxford University Press, 2013).

17 Laura Brown and Bryan Alkemeyer, "Rational Elephants or Hominoid Apes: Which Is Early Modern?," *Journal for Early Modern Cultural Studies* 13.4 (Fall 2013), 61–8 (62).

18 Evliya, *Traveller*, 450.

19 Tobias Menely, "Zoophilpsychosis: Why Animals Are What's Wrong with Sentimentality," *Symploke* 15.1–2 (2017), 244–67 (252).

20 Aravamudan, *Enlightenment*, 15–17, 136.

21 The Pythagorean tradition is particularly well explicated by Menely in *The Animal Claim: Sensibility and the Creaturely Voice* (Chicago: University of Chicago Press, 2015), 83–95.

22 Pope, *Guardian*, 256.

23 Ibid., 258.

24 Ibid.

25 Ibid., 260.

26 Menely, *Claim*, 1–2, 7, 80–105.

27 Ibid., 164–82, 202–5. See also Harriet Ritvo, *The Animal Estate: The English and Other Creatures in the Victorian Age* (Cambridge, MA: Harvard University Press, 1987).

28 Pope, *Guardian*, 259.

29 Ibid., 260.

30 Aravamudan, *Enlightenment*, 135, 137.

31 Maynard Mack, *Alexander Pope: A Life* (New York: W. W. Norton; New Haven, CT: Yale University Press, 1985), 199.

32 On the poem as topographical, see Landry, "Poems on Place," in Jack Lynch (ed.), *The Oxford Handbook to Eighteenth-Century English Poetry* (Oxford: Oxford University Press, 2016), 335–55. On the georgic, see Karen O'Brien, "Imperial Georgic, 1660–1789," in Gerald MacLean, Donna Landry, and Joseph P. Ward (eds.), *The Country and the City Revisited: England and the Politics of Culture, 1550–1850* (Cambridge: Cambridge University Press, 1999), 160–79.

33 Katherine M. Quinsey, "'Little Lives in Air': Animal Sentience and Sensibility in Pope," in Quinsey (ed.), *Animals and Humans: Sensibility and Representation, 1650–1820* (Oxford: Voltaire Foundation, 2017), 141–72 (142).

34 Pope, *Windsor-Forest*, in John Butt (ed.), *The Poems of Alexander Pope: A One-Volume Edition of the Twickenham Text with Selected Annotations* (London: Methuen, 1963), 195–210; lines 111–18. Further references to Pope's poetry are to this edition by line numbers.

35 The *locus classicus* for a political reading (stressing *Concordia discors*) is Earl R. Wasserman, *The Subtler Language* (Baltimore, MD: Johns Hopkins University Press, 1959), 101–68.

36 Mack, *Pope*, 74.

37 Ibid., 75.

38 On continuity between species, see Denys Van Renen, "'A hollow Moan': The Contours of the Non-Human World in James Thomson's *The Seasons*," 75–98; on the Great Chain of Being, see James P. Carson, "The Great Chain of Being as an Ecological Idea," 99–118, both in Quinsey (ed.), *Animals and Humans*.

39 Tlili, *Animals in the Qur'an*, 10.

40 Thomson, *Summer*, in *The Seasons*, in J. Logie Robertson (ed.), *The Complete Poetical Works of James Thomson* (Oxford: Henry Frowde/Oxford University Press, 1908), 52–132 (67), lines 377–85.

41 Keenleyside, *Animals*, 30.

42 Ibid., 30; Ralph Cohen, *The Unfolding of "The Seasons"* (Baltimore, MD: Johns Hopkins University Press, 1970), 23.

43 Aravamudan, *Enlightenment*, 143.

44 Swift was also "a sharp-eyed, if appreciative (and generous) master" to his servants, particularly his grooms; Irvin Ehrenpreis, *Swift: The Man, His Works, and the Age, vol. 3: Dean Swift* (Cambridge, MA: Harvard University Press, 1983), 432. On Swift and equine companionship, see Ann Cline Kelly, "Gulliver as Pet and Pet Keeper: Talking Animals in Book 4," *English Literary History* [ELH] 74.2 (Summer 2007), 323–49 (343–5), and Michael DePorte, "Swift's Horses of Instruction," in *Reading Swift: Papers from the Second Munster Symposium on Jonathan Swift*, ed. Richard Rodino and Hermann Real (Munchen: Wilhem Fink, 1993), 199–211.

45 Landry, *Noble Brutes: How Eastern Horses Transformed English Culture* (Baltimore, MD: Johns Hopkins University Press, 2008), 123–5, 126–36.

46 Ibid., 8–10, 13–14, 142–6, 148–61, 167–75.

47 Bryan Alkemeyer, "The Natural History of the Houyhnhnms: Noble Horses in *Gulliver's Travels*," *The Eighteenth Century* 57.1 (Spring 2016), 23–37 (24).

48 Alkemeyer, "Houyhnhnms," 24.

49 Ibid., 25.

50 Ibid., 35.

51 Aravamudan, *Enlightenment,* 146.

52 Ibid., 147.

53 Jonathan Swift, *Gulliver's Travels* [1726, 1735], edited by Claude Rawson and Ian Higgins (Oxford: Oxford University Press, 2005), 224.

54 Ibid., 253.

55 Patrick Wolfe, "Settler Colonialism and the Elimination of the Native," *Journal of Genocide Research* 8.4 (2006), 287–409.

56 Robert Macfarlane, *The Old Ways: A Journey on Foot* (London: Hamish Hamilton, 2012), 296–7.

57 Mabey, "Introduction," in Gilbert White, *The Natural History of Selborne* (Harmondsworth: Penguin, 1977), vii–xxii (viii). The top three are the Bible, the works of Shakespeare, and John Bunyan's *The Pilgrim's Progress*. Richard Mabey, *Food for Free* (1972, 1989; London: Harper Collins, 1992). Mabey has also written a biography of White, *Gilbert White* (1986; London: Profile Books, 2006).

58 Mabey, "Introduction," viii.

59 White, *Selborne,* 123.

60 Raymond Williams, *The Country and the City* (Oxford: Oxford University Press, 1973), 118–19. See also Sam Lee, *The Nightingale: Notes on a Songbird* (London: Century, 2020), 70–2.

61 White, *Selborne,* 113.

62 Ibid., 279.

63 Ibid., 301–2.

64 See Jeremy Davies, *The Birth of the Anthropocene* (Oakland: University of California Press, 2016), and Tobias Menely, *Climate and the Making of Worlds: Toward a Geohistorical Poetics* (Chicago: University of Chicago Press, 2021).

CHAPTER 4

Romantic
Animal Bonds and Animal Death

Jane Spencer

Romantic poetry's concern with the relationship between humanity and nonhuman nature made it central to the wave of ecocriticism that began in the 1990s. It was seen as a means of registering, even of healing, humanity's growing alienation from the natural: for the Romantics, "poetry is to be found not only in language but in nature; it is not only a means of verbal expression, it is also a means of emotional communication between man and the natural world."[1] The critical animal studies emerging in the same decade were skeptical about the value of communication that seemed to be between "man" and a landscape made in his image, rather than between a human being and a nonhuman animal with its own existence. "In its religious and supernatural mode," warned Marian Scholtmeijer, "the Romantic imagination was inclined to jump from the individual person to the panorama of nature, overleaping the animal in the process."[2] Those Romantic poems that stay with the animal, however, have been a focus for literary animal criticism over the last three decades or more, Scholtmeijer herself praising Samuel Coleridge's *Rime of the Ancient Mariner* (1798) as an early apprehension of the "animal victim" and its significance.[3] David Perkins has examined the concern for animal rights among eighteenth-century and Romantic writers, preferring literal approaches to animals that show "a sympathetic interest in the creatures they naturally are" over allegory.[4] He especially criticizes bird lyrics such as Percy Bysshe Shelley's "To a Skylark" and John Keats's "Ode to a Nightingale" for their appropriation of living creatures: "The poet perceives only himself, and taking the bird as other, he bestows on it whatever he himself lacks and deeply desires. [. . .] This is the poets' way of exploiting animals."[5] Other animal critics look more favorably on the Romantics' intensive exploration of the ancient identification between poet and singing bird. For Onno Oerlemans, Coleridge's and Keats's nightingale poems express a desire to apprehend and translate the bird's song and to cross the division between bird and poet, while at the same time acknowledging the impossibility of so doing.[6] Paying tribute to animal life yet using it to signify the unknowable, they exemplify a poetry that "incorporates and mimics the otherness of animal being, even as it reveals and shares it."[7]

The increasing number of animal poems is one sign of the "expansion of the boundaries of concern and community" in this period.[8] Inheriting from the eighteenth-century culture of sensibility an interest in living beings' shared capacity for feeling – what Anna Letitia Barbauld called the "fellowship of sense with all that breathes" – Romantic-era writing affirmed the idea of a bond between human and nonhuman animals.[9] Such affirmation did not necessarily challenge age-old notions of humanity's categorical difference from animal life. Christian thinkers characterized both humans and animals as God's creatures under his care, while emphasizing humanity's divinely ordained dominance over all the species entrusted to its stewardship. However, some Romantic poets did pursue the human-animal bond into disturbing new territory, questioning the sacred human distinction and suggesting a degree of leveling between species. In this essay I consider a range of poems – Coleridge's *Rime of the Ancient Mariner*, William Wordsworth's *Hart-Leap Well* (1800), Lord Byron's *Mazeppa* (1819), William Blake's "The Fly" (1794), and John Clare's badger poems (composed 1832–7) and "To the Snipe" (composed 1832) – which in various ways put human distinction and superiority into question.

Most of these poems turn on the death of their central nonhuman figure, leaving the human protagonists alive to explain what they have learned from their encounter with the animal or its story. In Coleridge's *Rime*, published in the 1798 *Lyrical Ballads*, the mariner's motiveless slaying of the albatross brings death to his crewmates and an ordeal of guilt to himself, turning him into the driven speaker whose tale compels the wedding-guest's attention. Wordsworth's *Hart-Leap Well*, appearing in the 1800 *Lyrical Ballads* and also exploring the bond between human and nonhuman, reflects on the long-ago death of a hunted deer and envisages a future of interspecies harmony. In Byron's *Mazeppa*, man and horse are both victims of human violence, but while the horse dies, the man lives to tell the tale. In Blake's "The Fly," one of the *Songs of Experience*, the speaker's casual killing of an insect prompts dizzying questions about life and death. Although the animal's death may be mourned, or its killing condemned, we can see a sacrificial logic at work within these poems, according to which animal death creates the occasion for the speaker's poetic authority.

Mark Payne describes a humanizing process that can fruitfully be compared with but also contrasted to the way Coleridge, Wordsworth,

Byron, and Blake treat the same subject. He discusses a hunting incident in Aldo Leopold's *A Sand County Almanac* (1949), in which Leopold, looking into a dying wolf's eyes, understands that she has her own perspective; a realization that precipitates his own "emergence from background awareness into conscious imagining, a life of writing."[10] In this way the sacrifice of the wolf aids the development of a fully human subject, who appreciates the life he has taken. Apart from Clare's, the Romantic poems considered here also found their writers' authority on the animal deaths that they recount; but they show a marked hesitation about the kind of "conversion" described by Payne, in which animal death enables growth and change in the human self.[11] They are too troubled by animal death, too uncertain about the efficacy of the message they attempt to draw from it, or, in Blake's case, too wedded to the radical equivalence of all beings to be fully committed to a story of progress through sacrifice. The bond to the animal remains a source variously of trauma, hope, uneasiness, happiness, and ambivalence.

The Rime of the Ancient Mariner, like *A Sand County Almanac*, features the protagonist's killing of an animal, but unlike Leopold, the mariner never comes to terms with his action; without rest or resolution, he relives his ordeal each time he recounts it. Coleridge's haunting lyrical ballad of crime and punishment in a sea peopled by mysterious supernatural forces has become central to a green and animal-centered Romantic criticism. The mariner's unmotivated killing of the albatross, previously considered inadequate grounds for his torment at sea, his companions' deaths, and the guilt that spurs him to tell his tale, takes on new significance when the poem is read as "a parable of ecological transgression," in which it is "as if the destruction of a single creature had disrupted the whole economy of nature."[12] Based on a story in Shelvocke's *Voyages Round the World by the Way of the Great South Sea* (1726), where an albatross following a ship is shot by a sailor who believes it to be an ill omen, this tale of senseless slaughter reflects the destruction that was visited on newly discovered natural habitats in the age of European exploration and colonization and has only intensified since. The poem stresses the innocence and benignity of the albatross, which appears out of the fog as the ship plows through ice-laden Antarctic waters and is greeted with a recognition of likeness between human and bird:

> And an it were a Christian Soul,
> We hail'd it in God's name.[13]

Coming "for food or play" when the sailors call (71), the albatross forges a human-animal bond. Breaking that bond by shooting the bird, the mariner exemplifies the human alienation from the natural world that so much Romantic writing laments.

Critics have suggested that it is the mariner's later blessing of the watersnakes that reconnects him to the natural world he has violated and leads to his partial rehabilitation: "the mariner has learned [...] that he must cross the boundaries that divide him from the natural world."[14] However, the mariner identifies himself throughout with the world around him, experiencing it according to his shifting subjective state. Becalmed after the albatross's death, the mariner understands sea life in terms of abjection:

> Yea, slimy things did crawl with legs
> Upon the slimy Sea. (121–2)

That his self-disgust conditions this response to living creatures is underlined by a later verse placing himself with them as against his dead shipmates:

> The many men so beautiful,
>   And they all dead did lie!
> And a million million slimy things
>   Liv'd on – and so did I. (228–31)

His change in perception happens under the light of the "moving Moon," which renders the slimy things lovely water-snakes:

> They mov'd in tracks of shining white;
>   And when they rear'd, the elfish light
> Fell off in hoary flakes. (266–8)

While the reliance on moonlight suggests the necessity of external grace to the mariner's new vision, equally important is his internal response, as indicated when the water-snakes' beauty becomes apparent outside the moon's reach, in the "awful red" shadow cast by the ship:

> Blue, glossy green, and velvet black
> They coil'd and swam; and every track
>   Was a flash of golden fire. (271–3)

The water-snakes' blue and green hues, repeating the reflected colors of the "Death-fires" of his earlier nightmare vision (124), underscore the identity between the disgusting "slimy things" of the poem's second section and the "happy living things" (274) of its fourth. Coleridge is famous for maintaining, in his dialogues with Wordsworth, the inadequacy of impressions from external nature to the task of healing the soul: "I may not hope from outward forms to win / The passion and the life, whose fountains are within."[15] In the *Rime* the internal fountain is vital, but so is the external spiritual force that allows it to rise:

> A spring of love gusht from my heart,
> And I bless'd them unaware!
> Sure my kind saint took pity on me,
> And I bless'd them unaware. (276–9)

Is the mariner, freed from his abject identification with disgusting slime, able to share the water-snakes' new beauty and happiness? The poem does not take his redemption so far, remaining what Kurt Fosso calls a "eucharistic and guilt-ridden" narrative, based on "a sacrificial, originary *before* whose knot of sin cannot be undone but whose irredeemable violence makes atonement and its totemic human-animal wisdom possible."[16] By blessing the water-snakes, by repeating his story of crime and punishment, the mariner can only partially repair the human-animal bond.

The didacticism of the mariner's conclusion has been a source of embarrassment, not least to the poet himself, who later criticized his own poem for "*too much*" moral.[17]

> He prayeth best who loveth best,
> All things both great and small:
> For the dear God, who loveth us,
> He made and loveth all. (647–50)

The lines would fit into any number of children's stories from Coleridge's time, with their lessons about kindness to animals. Peter Mortensen, finding "the simplicity of these lines both moving and profound," clearly feels himself to be in a minority.[18] More suspicious readers find the message of the poem elsewhere. Peter Heymans reads the mariner's recognition of the water-snakes' beauty not as a gush of love but "a barely covert attempt to save himself" by assigning "a meaningful teleology to nature." He adds that because it is the albatross's apparent familiarity that breeds the contempt shown in its slaughter, the poem is not so much lamenting human estrangement from nature as pointing "to the beneficial ecological effects of alienation and to the moral risk of too much sympathy or environmental identification."[19] I agree that we can find a warning against the kind of identification found in anthropocentric readings such as those of the sailors, whose view of the albatross changes with the weather they imagine it controls. But I think that the *Rime* treats as real and valuable a human impulse to connect with other animals, and in expressing such a message in the embarrassingly simple diction of a child's tale it partakes of a Romantic willingness to risk absurdity in the pursuit of that connection.

Wordsworth's *Hart-Leap Well*, like the *Rime*, explores the implications of human violence for human-animal bonds.[20] Influentially read by Perkins as part of an eighteenth-century and Romantic critique of hunting,[21] it is in two parts: the first describing Sir Walter's long-ago pursuit of the hart, the fatal leap commemorated in the well's name, and the huntsman's erection of a "Pleasure-house" (57) where the animal died; the second telling of the present-day speaker's chance discovery of the well, the remains of Sir Walter's bower, and the site of the now lost "Mansion" (123). Encountering a shepherd who claims that nature mourns the deer's cruel death and has effaced Sir Walter's celebration of his victory, the speaker offers his own version of nature's actions, and concludes on a moral note that echoes the *Rime*'s message:

> One lesson, Shepherd, let us two divide,
> Taught both by what [Nature] shews, and what conceals,
> Never to blend our pleasure or our pride
> With sorrow of the meanest thing that feels. (173–6)

The advice is to become the opposite of Sir Walter, described in the first part of the poem as deriving excited joy from finding the hart dead:

> And now, too happy for repose or rest,
> Was never man in such a joyful case,
> Sir Walter walked all around, north, south and west,
> And gazed, and gazed upon that darling place. (45–8)

The knight's single-minded pursuit – riding three horses to the point of collapse and overtaking the exhausted dogs – and the sexually tinged pleasure suggested by transforming the animal's death-scene into a place for "merriment" with his "paramour" (92, 90) are implicitly criticized, but the criticism is half-hidden within the naïve ballad-maker's voice adopted in this part of the poem. Critics have concluded that Wordsworth expresses some collusion with the hunter's mentality. Perkins suggests that the poet remains ambivalent, partly attracted to the violent world he wants to consign to history.[22] David Chandler links the poem's aggressive knight to Wordsworth's sense of his own revolutionary self, a self that at the time of writing he was attempting both to move beyond and to incorporate into

a benign story of lessons learned and progress made.[23] Both readings fit
with the view expressed by Kurt Fosso, that in *Hart-Leap Well* and its near-
contemporary *Home at Grasmere* the poet is building a vision of a new life
of human-animal harmony that depends on the prior, sacrificial death of
animals.[24]

The second part of *Hart-Leap Well* develops a dialogue about the
meaning of the hart's death and nature's response to it. The shepherd's
view, presented as coming from the self-acknowledged "simple mind"
(142) of a "Gray-headed" rustic (157), in fact articulates some of the most
up-to-date thinking on animal minds at the turn of the nineteenth
century. Evidently steeped in the contemporary culture of sensibility and
the literature of animal rights, the shepherd insists on the significance of
the hart's death. The well's water periodically groans, and no animal will
now drink from it, because nature has responded not to the fate of a
human murder victim but to a deer's: "it was all for that unhappy Hart"
(136). The shepherd evokes sympathy, as so many pro-animal writings of
the time did, by imagining what it would be like to be the suffering creature,
his emphasis not on the physical pain generally understood as an animal
sensation but on the mental torment endured in a thirteen-hour "desperate
race" (141): "What thoughts must through the creature's brain have passed!"
(137). Like the philosopher David Hume, and animal-rights campaigners
such as John Oswald and Joseph Ritson, the shepherd believes that other
animals have the capacity for interior mental states traditionally understood
as human only.[25] His speculation about the hart's thought-processes follows
the example of contemporary children's stories, which were foremost in
popularizing belief in animal mind through their animal characters' reflections and memories.[26] The hart of the shepherd's tale chooses the well for
his death scene because it recalls his earliest moments:

> Here on the grass perhaps asleep he sank,
> Lulled by this fountain in the summer-tide;
> This water was perhaps the first he drank
> When he had wandered from his mother's side. (145–9)

While the shepherd's repeated "perhaps," along with the disclaimer "we
cannot tell / What cause the Hart might have to love this place" (142–3),
disavows certain knowledge of the deer's mind, he imaginatively attributes
to the animal memories of early life and an attachment to birthplace: "he,
perhaps, for aught we know, was born / Not half a furlong from that self-
same spring" (151–2). In his version of the tale, Hart-Leap Well is
significant for what it meant to the hart, not to the hunter.

The device of the shepherd allows Wordsworth to give voice to a potentially embarrassing sentimental anthropomorphism without committing himself to it. Whereas in Coleridge's poem the albatross's death authorizes the mariner as compelling spokesman for human guilt, in Wordsworth's two figures compete to interpret the death of the hart, with the Wordsworthian speaker given the final say. The shepherd's words receive only carefully qualified agreement. He believes that in response to the hart's agony, Nature will keep the well desolate into the indefinite future, but the speaker merely acknowledges, in a somewhat grudging double negative, that "This beast not unobserved by Nature fell" (159). Speculation about the hart's mind is replaced by a Wordsworthian pantheism focused on a nature-spirit's concern about animals:

> The Being, that is in the clouds and air,
> That is in the green leaves among the groves,
> Maintains a deep and reverential care
> For them the quiet creatures whom he loves. (161–4)

This "Small difference" between the creeds of shepherd and speaker (158) distances us from the former's sharply felt, personal investment in the hart's suffering, and leads to the latter's more optimistic, and more anthropocentric, view. Nature stages the well's desolate scene as a reminder to human beings of "what we are, and have been" – cruel beings like Sir Walter, taking joy in the hunted animal's death (170); but we can look forward to a "milder day" (171) free from such sensations, when the monuments to the hart's suffering will be overgrown as nature resumes "her beauty and her bloom" (168). The "milder day" of human improvement is vaguely conjured; the implication is that it will arise naturally with the passing of time. With the animal's sacrificial death receding into the background, mourned and accepted, the final verses express Wordsworth's hope for a new social dawn coming about through nature's ministrations instead of human action. Troubling that conclusion is the shepherd's insistence, memorable for its very excess, on the mental suffering of an animal dead for hundreds of years, a response that refuses to absorb the hart's experience into the logic of animal sacrifice and human survival.

Like Coleridge and Wordsworth, Byron engages with contemporary debates about animal mind and animal rights. In *Mazeppa* he literalizes the concept of a human-animal bond by having his protagonist tied, naked, back-to-back to a horse and driven out from human society.[27] This central situation – focus of many contemporary illustrations – was based, as Byron's headnote explained, on a story recounted in Voltaire's

Histoire de Charles XII (1731) about the aftermath of Sweden's defeat by Russia in the 1709 battle of Poltova. Voltaire's story would seem to celebrate the resilience of a flawed but mighty hero. Mazeppa, a Polish-born Ukrainian military leader, has changed sides to join the Swedish king Charles, and after the lost battle tells the tale of being carried to Ukraine in his youth, bound to the horse as a punishment for an affair with another man's wife. Byron, predictably enough, adds detail about Mazeppa's adulterous love, a prominent theme in his *The Giaour* (1813), as well as in *Don Juan* (1819–24), the great comic epic he began while writing *Mazeppa*; but a more significant addition is his focus on the experience and meaning of being tied to a horse. Mazeppa's love for and loss of his Theresa fade from sight as he unfolds his story of animal encounter. Nor is any relationship developed with the "slender girl" (806) who, foreshadowing Haidee's rescue of the hero in *Don Juan*, eventually finds Mazeppa and is instrumental in returning him to human society. Reflecting Byron's theriophilic belief in animal rather than human virtue, human bonds have been replaced by a human-animal one.[28]

Mazeppa's tale is framed by a description of the aftermath of battle that takes less notice of the defeated soldiers than of the protagonist's affection for the horse he now rides. Unlike the Swedish king, who has lost two horses that day, Mazeppa has brought his mount uninjured from the field, and now looks after its needs before his own. Both "spirited and docile" (68), the battle-horse knows Mazeppa and would follow him "like a fawn" (77). The "calm and bold" old soldier shows emotion only for his horse: he

> joy'd to hear how well he fed;
> For until now he had the dread
> His wearied courser might refuse
> To browse beneath the midnight dews. (62–5)

Charles's comment on the bond between Mazeppa and his horse prompts the telling of his tale. Unlike his present mount, the horse to which Mazeppa was once bound was:

> Wild as the wild deer, and untaught,
> With spur and bridle undefiled –
> 'Twas but a day he had been caught (363–5)

Violently joined together, horse and man are initially aliens, each the cause of the other's torment. Mazeppa is mentally separate from the horse to which he is physically tied: "I saw not where he hurried on," he explains (376); but later, a shift of pronouns indicates the beginnings of a bond of feeling as Mazeppa refers to "my steed and I" (423,) and recounts that "We sped like meteors through the sky" (426). As they leave "all human dwellings" behind (425), and gallop over plains bounded by forests with – apart from distant strongholds – "No trace of man" (435), they gradually come together. Mazeppa tries to speak to the horse, only to find it swerves from his voice, and when they are chased by wolves he doubts it can outrun them; but he soon acknowledges his mistake: "Vain doubt! His swift and savage breed / Had nerved him like the mountain roe" (510–11). In a misogynistic aside that perhaps suggests how his interest has switched from lost lover to equine companion, he describes the horse as

> Untired, untamed, and worse than wild;
> All furious as a favour'd child
> Balk'd of its wish; or fiercer still—
> A woman piqued – who has her will. (517–20)

Fainting, apparent death, and revival follow, and in rebirth Mazeppa not only thinks of the horse as "My courser" (590), with whom the terrible journey is now shared – "And onward we advance!" (592) – but records the near loss of his own species identity: "I scarcely knew / If this were human breath I drew" (599–600).

At this turning point, horse and man together are exiled not just from human civilization but from all other animal life; in a world devoid of brute, bird, or insect, "we were – or seem'd – alone" (667). Then a troop of wild horses approach the pair. With their

> Wide nostrils never stretch'd by pain,
> Mouths bloodless to the bit or rein,
> And feet that iron never shod,
> And flanks unscarr'd by spur or rod, (681–3)

they represent "the wild, the free" (684). Mazeppa's encounter with animal life untainted by humanity is marked by the breaking of the bond between him and his courser, who neighs to his conspecifics and then falls dead from exhaustion. The wild horses "fly / By instinct, from a human eye" (707–8), their fear thrusting Mazeppa's human identity back at him. From now on, though apparently dying bound to a dead horse, he suffers as a human being. Having managed to scare off the raven circling in hope of carrion, he falls asleep and wakens restored to human life. The girl who has rescued him has "wild and free" eyes recalling the wild horses (812), but her "pitying glance" (811) bespeaks humanity – a new humanity, based on compassion instead of warfare and cruelty. The reborn Mazeppa shows a strictly limited allegiance to such sentiments, the humane ideals of Byron's time. Though, in his treatment of his battle-horse, he conspicuously practices the "humanity to animals" that was recommended by a host of pamphleteers, his revenge on his tormentors is pitiless.[29] Taking "twice five thousand horse" (411), many times the "thousand" wild ones whose freedom from man he had admired (678), he burns his enemies' castle and rejoices in their "day of pain" (407).

At its end Mazeppa's story is "mockingly undercut by a narrative frame which draws attention to boredom in the audience": the king has been asleep for an hour.[30] This wry twist marks a difference from Byron's earlier tales of guilt, exile, and revenge. *Mazeppa* has been seen as a kind of bridge between the gloomy misanthropy of Byron's "Turkish tales" and the multifaceted *Don Juan*, with its detached amusement about life and love and its sardonic anger about war. Yet whereas *Don Juan* remains a poem committed to bonds between human beings, *Mazeppa* refuses fully to restore its protagonist to human community. As Mazeppa fails to communicate his experience of dehumanization and alienation, the king misses the answer to his question about horsemanship: that shared suffering created Mazeppa's sympathetic care for his current mount. He also misses the tale's development of the moral offered by the frame narrator in the opening section: "danger levels man and brute, / And all are fellows in their need" (51–2). If in relation to horses Mazeppa has learned the compassion that Byron's age labels "humanity," to his human enemies he shows the unrepentant cruelty that is called "brutal."

The Rime of the Ancient Mariner, Hart-Leap Well, and *Mazeppa* all chart the inception of a new understanding of human-animal relationship. All attempt to communicate their insights in words and actions that echo commonplaces from moral pamphlets and children's stories: love God's creatures, do not take pleasure in animals' pain, be kind to your horse. But the transformative power that Coleridge attributes to his protagonists' words and Wordsworth to nature's teaching is absent from Byron's poem. The mariner, for all his continuing torment, succeeds in arresting the wedding-guest's attention, casting the spell of his words over him, changing him into a "sadder and a wiser man" (657). Wordsworth's speaker shares nature's lesson with the shepherd and the reader. Byron, skeptical about the hopes of widespread human reform nurtured by Wordsworth and Coleridge in the 1790s, leaves his Mazeppa incompletely changed and largely unheard.

Blake's "The Fly" is perhaps the most enigmatic of the Romantic poems of animal death. Five deceptively simple verses muse on the swatting of an insect.

Little fly,
Thy summer's play
My thoughtless hand
Has brushed away.

Am not I
A fly like thee?
Or art not thou
A man like me?

For I dance
And drink and sing,
Till some blind hand
Shall brush my wing.

If thought is life
And strength and breath,
And the want
Of thought is death;

Then am I
A happy fly,
if I live,
Or if I die.[31]

The poem has been interpreted in wildly different ways. The fly's death itself, never unequivocally announced, has been doubted in readings that see it as only having its summer's play interrupted, as harmed by the speaker but surviving to chide him, and even, by syntactic inversion, as itself brushing away the speaker's hand.[32] The majority view that the fly dies, however, makes more sense of the speaker's reflection on the "blind hand" that will one day destroy him, and of his apprehension that the "want of thought" is death. The poem belongs to a tradition in which man is like a fly in his short life and vulnerability, but Blake's speaker goes further than others in his insistence on equivalence between man and fly.[33] It used to be argued that Blake opposes such equivalence, ironizing the speaker as "imaginatively dead [. . .] indeed like a fly, mindlessly content to be buffeted about by fate,"[34] and replacing his "sentimental" mood with "a saner one, that differentiates between insentient nonman and sentient man,"[35] but more recent readers tend to agree with John E. Grant, who already in the 1960s argued for the importance of the fly to Blake, citing his words in *Milton* (1810):

Seest thou the little winged fly, smaller than a grain of sand?
It has a heart like thee, a brain open to Heaven & Hell[36]

As John Keir concludes, to insist on the difference between man and fly seems "to resist the poem's vision," while the equivalence of the two recalls "Blake's oft-repeated precept that everything that lives is holy."[37]

The enigma of "The Fly" lies in the turn from fourth to fifth verse, in which a logical argument following from "If thought is life," seeming to unite a Cartesian understanding of being with an admonition against the thoughtless killing of flies, is apparently derailed by an illogical leap into identification with a creature to whom being and unbeing are equally welcome: "Then am I / A happy fly." "Instead of a moral, we have a non sequitur that becomes more absurd the more one considers it."[38] To solve the problem, some critics have postulated a second speaker in the poem. G. S. Morris suggests that the fourth and fifth verses are spoken by the fly itself, who represents a better-than-human viewpoint, valuing happiness over thought and scornfully denying the first speaker's claim of likeness between man and fly.[39] John Keir uses the poem's illustrative plate, featuring a girl playing shuttlecock and a toddler with a nurse, to suggest that the first three stanzas are spoken by a maturing child who is leaving her earlier "inconsiderate, thoughtless life" behind, while the final two come from the younger child, rejecting logic.[40] I question whether the logical problem exists in the first place. The last two verses seem to me fitting as the further reflections of the same speaker who has brushed the fly away. The fourth verse can be read not as pitting thought and life as opponents against thoughtlessness and death but as the start of an even-handed meditation on the advantages of either pairing: thought and life have the attraction of "strength, and breath," but death, taking fly or human being beyond thought and suffering, may also be read, as the fifth verse suggests, as "happy." If both life and death have something to be said for them, then the speaker's contented conclusion is not illogical, but expressive of a strange and rare equanimity in the face of mortality.

Turning to John Clare's poetry, we leave behind the sacrificial animal whose death in Coleridge, Wordsworth, Byron, and Blake is associated, however ambivalently and critically, with a human gain in understanding and poetic authority. Clare's steadily growing reputation as the Romantic period's most distinctive animal poet rests on his fresh and delicately precise observation of an abundance of species ranging far beyond the usual poetic subjects, coupled with his unusual reticence about drawing moral conclusions or highlighting symbolic connections between human and animal life. This is not to say that he is a poet of simple description, or that symbolism and poetic identification with animal figures are not present in his work: critics have remarked on his treatment of birds as metaphors for the human soul, and on his strong sense of sharing his wild creatures' alienation from human society and vulnerability to human attack.[41] But his animals (and indeed his plants), first and foremost imagined in their independent being, can have, in Simon Kövesi's striking phrase, "a song without the poet's presence," in a poetic treatment that "questions the placing of humanity in a hierarchy above all other beings and natural processes."[42] Here I examine two works from the 1830s, the sequence of badger sonnets and "To the Snipe," in an attempt to elucidate something of the difference Clare brings to Romantic animal poetry.

The badger poems are some of Clare's bleakest. Four sonnets form an untitled sequence (here for convenience referred to as "The Badger") about the baiting of a badger, the final one cut off after twelve lines as the animal dies. A separate sonnet, "Some keep a baited badger tame as hog," further develops the theme.[43] "The Badger" begins with close focus on the animal as it goes about its life, "grunting on the woodland track" (1), describing its "shaggy hide & sharp nose scrowed with black" (2), and its rooting and burrowing activities. This careful observation is made, as it were, from the badger's own level and without comment. At the fifth line an element of commentary appears: the badger's running with "nose on ground" is judged "a awkard pace" (5), and this awkwardness, referred to again in line 45, signals the badger's vulnerability: "anything will beat him in the race" (6). At this point the dogs and men who will track and bait the badger are introduced, and their persecution of the animal builds up throughout the sequence. They do not have everything their own way: the wood man "tumbles headlong" into old badger holes (14), and the badger, turning on its attackers, injures the dogs (36) and bites peoples' heels (41); but the tetrameter lines, recording action after action in steady beat, create a sense of the assault's relentlessness and the inevitability of its ending:

> They get a forked stick to bear him down
> & clapt the dogs & bore him to the town
> & bait him all the day with many dogs
> & laugh & shout & fright the scampering hogs (23–6)

There is no overt condemnation of the baiters, no comment on the badger's pain, nor any speculation about what is going through its mind, but the narrative sympathy is with the beleaguered animal, fighting off the dogs despite being "scar[c]ely half as big dimute & small" (35), failing to get away, turning again and again to fight but finally defeated:

> He falls as dead & kicked by boys & men
> Then starts & grins & drives the crowd agen
> Till kicked & torn & beaten out he lies
> & leaves his hold & cackles groans & dies (51–4)

"Some keep a baited badger tame as hog" admits more pathos into the scene; the lamed badger, following men "like the dog" (2), repeatedly allowed to escape the dogs and fight another day, is robbed of the defiance shown by the badger in the longer sequence:

> He licks the patting hand & tries to play
> & never trys to bite or run away (11–12)

The sonnet ends on an ambiguous note: the badger that never tries to run away suddenly does exactly that in the following line: "& runs away from noise in hollow tree[s]" (13) – perhaps an escape, though the last line, describing the trees as "Burnt by the boys to get a swarm of bees" (14), returns to the theme of human attack on wild creatures. Clare's critics are no doubt right to read in the badger poems an expression of the poet's own feelings of alienation and persecution after leaving his home in Helpston for Northborough, only three miles away but to him a strange land. He "can speak for the badger because by now he feels kicked and torn and beaten himself."[44] But he leaves it to the reader to make the connection, drawing no explicit parallels and offering no reflections. Above all, he attaches no sacrificial meaning to the badger's death. There are no spirits to enforce a penance for killing the animal; there is no purposeful Nature turning the scene into a lesson for humanity; the animal's death does not return a human being to the world with new understanding, or prompt contemplation of mortality. In a refusal of sacrificial logic, the reader is confronted with the stark chaos and ugliness of the badger's end.

The badger sonnets are unusual among Clare's poems for dealing with the animal's death; much more frequently, he writes about living creatures in danger. His poems about birds and birds' nests are unparalleled in their evocation of the vulnerability of wild lives. "To the

Snipe" enters a remote marshy world where human intrusion is a
constant source of fear: there are "fowl that dread / The very breath
of man," who avoid "mans dreaded sight" and "dread mans sight"; even
the "trembling grass / Quakes from the human foot," and the "trepid
air" is startled by gunshot.[45] As in other Clare poems, the speaker's
presence paradoxically brings humanity into the "untrodden" place he
celebrates (34), but he minimizes the disturbance by the practice of
what has been called Clare's "non-intrusive observation,"[46] carefully
registering minute details of the swampy terrain such as the "tiney
island[s]" (14), "Just hilling from the mud & rancid streams" (15).
His original stanza form of uneven beats (2, 3, 5, 3) offers a slightly
jerky, stop-start rhythm, as if he hesitates to break the silence; and he
attempts to warn the snipe of dangers to avoid, for the timid wild
creatures are never fearful enough:

> Yet instinct knows
> Not safetys bounds – to shun
> The firmer ground where stalking fowler goes
> With searching dogs & gun
> By tepid springs
> Scarcely one stride across
> Though brambles from its edge a shelter flings
> Thy safety is at loss
> & never chuse
> The little sinky foss (53–62)

The poet's own sense of alienation from human society pervades the poem,
creating that "sense of mutuality felt between poet and solitary bird,"
which is one of Clare's signature notes.[47] The final verses reflect on the
hidden places where snipe and speaker can both find safety. Clare moves as
many Romantic poets do from the natural world to its lessons for the
human mind, but without magnifying the mind's powers; rather, the
emphasis is on human-animal sharing:

> I see the sky
> Smile on the meanest spot
> Giving to all that creep or walk or flye
> A calm & cordial lot
> Thine teaches me
> Right feelings to employ
> That in the dreariest places peace will be
> A dweller & a joy (81–8)

At the very end this poem of wilderness and trepidation reaches the "joy" that for Clare is the state reached through poesy.[48] Whereas Wordsworth and Coleridge, Blake and Byron circle around, affirming or ironizing, a bardic authority that comes through reflecting on animal death, Clare pursues a poesy that unites him with nonhuman creatures, who express in their being what he expresses in human language.

Notes

1 Jonathan Bate, *Romantic Ecology: Wordsworth and the Environmental Tradition* (1991; rpt. London: Routledge, 2013), 17.
2 Marian Scholtmeijer, *Animal Victims in Modern Fiction: From Sanctity to Sacrifice* (Toronto: University of Toronto Press, 1993), 25.
3 Ibid., 28.
4 David Perkins, *Romanticism and Animal Rights* (Cambridge: Cambridge University Press, 1993), 47–8.
5 Ibid., 142.
6 Onno Oerlemans, *Poetry and Animals: Blurring the Boundaries of the Human* (New York: Columbia University, 2018), 94–8.
7 Ibid., 89.
8 Ibid., 90.
9 Anna Letitia Barbauld, "The Caterpillar," in William McCarthy and Elizabeth Kraft (eds.), *The Poems of Anna Letitia Barbauld* (Athens: University of Georgia Press, 1994), 172–3, line 27.
10 Mark Payne, *The Animal Part: Human and Other Animals in the Poetic Imagination* (Oxford: Oxford University Press, 2010), 4.
11 Ibid., 4.
12 James McKusick, *Green Writing: Romanticism and Ecology* (2000; rpt. New York: Palgrave Macmillan, 2010), 44, 45.
13 S. T. Coleridge, *The Rime of the Ancyent Marinere*, lines 63–4, in Wordsworth and Coleridge, *Lyrical Ballads*, ed. R. L. Brett and A. R. Jones (London: Methuen, 1968), 9–35, 12. Cited hereafter in text by line number.
14 McKusick, *Green Writing*, 47.
15 S. T. Coleridge, "Dejection: An Ode," lines 45–6, in Coleridge, *The Major Works*, ed. H. J. Jackson (Oxford: Oxford University Press, 1985), 114–18, 115.
16 Kurt Fosso, "'Sweet Influences': Animals and Social Cohesion in Wordsworth and Coleridge, 1794–1800," *ISLE: Interdisciplinary Studies in Literature and Environment* 6 (1999), 1–20, 11.
17 Henry Nelson Coleridge reported in an 1834 review that "Mrs. Barbauld [. . .] told our poet, that she thought the 'Ancient Mariner' very beautiful, but that it had the fault of containing no moral. 'Nay, Madam,' replied the poet, '[. . .] there is *too much*. In a work of such pure imagination I ought not to have stopped to give reasons for things, or inculcate humanity to beasts.'" A similar

conversation is reported in *Table Talk* in 1830. See Thomas M. Raysor, "Coleridge's Comment on the Moral of 'The Ancient Mariner,'" *Philological Quarterly* 31 (1952), 88–91, 88.

18 Peter Mortensen, "Taking Animals Seriously: William Wordsworth and the Claims of Ecological Romanticism," *Orbis Litterarum* 55 (2000), 296–311, 305.

19 Peter Heymans, *Animality in British Romanticism: The Aesthetic of Species* (New York: Routledge, 2012), 57, 59.

20 Wordsworth, "Hart-Leap Well," in *William Wordsworth: The Major Works*, ed. Stephen Gill, rev. ed. (Oxford: Oxford University Press, 2008), 168–73. Cited hereafter in text by line number.

21 Perkins, *Romanticism*, 77–88.

22 Ibid., 78.

23 David Chandler, "The Politics of Hart-Leap Well," *The Charles Lamb Bulletin* NS 11 (2000), 109–19.

24 Fosso, "'Sweet Influences,'" 11–12.

25 See my discussion of Hume on animal mind and of Oswald and Ritson in Jane Spencer, *Writing about Animals in the Age of Revolution* (Oxford: Oxford University Press, 2020), 21–4, 206–15.

26 Ibid., 93–108.

27 Byron, "Mazeppa," in *Byron: Poetical Works*, ed. Frederick Page, corr. John Jump (London: Oxford University Press, 1970), 341–8. Cited hereafter in text by line number.

28 On Byron and the Renaissance tradition of theriophily, see Christine Kenyon-Jones, *Kindred Brutes: Animals in Romantic-Period Writing* (Aldershot: Ashgate, 2001), 12–16.

29 See, e.g., Thomas Young, *An Essay on Humanity to Animals* (London: T. Cadell jun. and W. Davies, 1798).

30 Jane Stabler, "Byron, Postmodernism, and Intertextuality," in Drummond Bone (ed.), *The Cambridge Companion to Byron* (Cambridge: Cambridge University Press, 2004), 265–85, 265.

31 William Blake, "The Fly," in *Blake: The Complete Poems*, ed. W. H. Stevenson and David V. Erdman (New York: Longman, 1971), 220–1.

32 Leo Kirschbaum, "Blake's 'The Fly,'" *Essays in Criticism* 11 (1961), 154–62; Jon Saklofske, "A Fly in the Ointment: Exploring the Creative Relationship between William Blake and Thomas Gray," *Word and Image: A Journal of Verbal/Visual Enquiry* 19 (2003), 166–79; Michael Simpson, "Who Didn't Kill Blake's Fly: Moral Law and the Rule of Grammar in *Songs of Experience*," *Style* 30 (1996), 220–40.

33 See Steven Connor, *Fly* (London: Reaktion, 2006), 19, 26–31. Famous among human-fly comparisons is Gloucester's lament: "As flies to wanton boys, are we to th'Gods; /They kill us for their sport." William Shakespeare, *King Lear*, ed. Kenneth Muir (London: Methuen, 1978), 4.1.36–7.

34 Warren Stevenson, "Artful Irony in Blake's 'The Fly,'" *Texas Studies in Literature and Language* 10 (1968), 77–82, 80–1.

35 Kirschbaum, "Blake's 'The Fly,'" 161.

36 Blake, *Milton*, pl. 20, ll. 27–9, in *Blake: The Complete Poems*, 516; John E. Grant, "Misreadings of 'The Fly,'" *Essays in Criticism* 11 (1961), 481–7.

37 John Keir, "The Grasshopper and the Ant in Blake's 'The Fly,'" *English Language Notes* 38 (2001), 56–68, 62, 63.

38 G. S. Morris, "Blake's 'The Fly,'" *The Explicator* 65 (2006), 16–18, 16.

39 Morris, "Blake's 'The Fly,'" 17.

40 Keir, "The Grasshopper," 63.

41 See Johanne Clare, *John Clare and the Bounds of Circumstance* (Kingston: McGill-Queen's University Press, 1987), 173; Mina Gorgi, *John Clare and the Place of Poetry* (Liverpool: Liverpool University Press, 2009), 109; John Goodridge, *John Clare and Community* (Cambridge: Cambridge University Press, 2012), 131, 143; Cassandra Falke, "Thinking with Birds: John Clare and the Phenomenology of Perception," *Romanticism* 26 (2020), 180–90, 180.

42 Simon Kövesi, *John Clare: Nature, Criticism and History* (London: Palgrave Macmillan, 2017), 94.

43 John Clare, "The Badger" and "Some keep a baited badger tame as hog," in *John Clare: Poems of the Middle Period, 1822–1837*, vol. V, ed. Eric Robinson, David Powell and P. M. S. Dawson (Oxford: Clarendon, 2003), 360–2. Cited hereafter in text by line number.

44 Jonathan Bate, *John Clare: A Biography* (London: Picador, 2003), 405.

45 John Clare, "To the Snipe," in *John Clare: Poems of the Middle Period, 1822–1837*, vol. IV, ed. Eric Robinson, David Powell and P. M. S. Dawson (Oxford: Clarendon, 1998), 574–7, lines 36–7, 43, 47, 5–6, 67. Cited hereafter in text by line number.

46 Sehjae Chun, "'An Undiscovered Song': John Clare's Bird Poems," *Interdisciplinary Literary Studies* 6 (2005), 47–65, 53.

47 Johanne Clare, *John Clare*, 173.

48 Adam White, *John Clare's Romanticism* (London: Palgrave Macmillan, 2017), 241–57.

CHAPTER 5

Victorian

Character, Politics, and Racialization

Anna Feuerstein

In the Victorian era, relationships with animals were wide-ranging and at times contradictory, and this multiplicity and its attendant tensions are reflected in the diverse body of literature produced throughout the period. Even with this diversity, animals in Victorian literature often relate to two overarching themes that structured much of the Victorian era itself: shifting definitions of the animal and the human, especially in relationship to racialization and empire, and the expansion of liberal politics to bring more subjects into its fold and regulate more aspects of daily life. In this chapter, I discuss how Victorian literature reflects the incorporation of animals into the political sphere through animal welfare, and how animality demarcated racial categories and structured the borders of the human. Both topics offer a productive and foundational lens to analyze the vast representations of animals in Victorian literature, and relate to a variety of other themes such as care and control, domesticity and the family, scientific classification, class, and gender.

By the beginning of the Victorian era, the Society for the Prevention of Cruelty to Animals, formed in 1824, had become an influential organization. It received its "Royal" designation in 1840, linking the welfare of animals directly to the state. In 1835, Parliament expanded the original 1822 Martin's Act – aimed at bettering the lives of mostly working animals labeled as "cattle" – to cover "wanton cruelty," and banned bear and bull-baiting. In the years following, dog carts were banned in certain parts of England, more protections were laid out for domestic animals, and Parliament debated regulating cattle slaughter. By the end of the century, Parliament would pass laws regulating slaughterhouses and the importation of cattle, the shooting of birds, and the captivity of wild animals. The RSPCA was foundational to this legislation. It not only lobbied for anti-cruelty laws and regulations, but published two popular periodicals, sponsored essay contests for school children, sent its team of inspectors into the streets to monitor people for breaking anti-cruelty laws, and expanded its reach to the British colonies.[1] Alongside the more liberal and reform-minded RSPCA, the London Vegetarian Society, which broke away from the Vegetarian Society in 1888, sought a radical shift of our relationships not only with animals but with women, the working class, and the colonies, aligning a vegetarian diet with a socialist agenda.[2] As I have argued elsewhere, this new incorporation of animals into the state worked in tandem with the proliferation of animals in literature, shifting how Victorians saw and represented animals.[3] To encourage better treatment, mostly domestic animals were often represented as liberal subjects with good character who accepted an human-animal hierarchy in return for kind treatment.

At the same time that animals were increasingly incorporated into the political sphere, the British empire was expanding across the world, resulting in a plethora of literature that reinforced British power and solidified its categorizing impulse. Alongside the colonization of non-Western peoples and their land, a wide range of "exotic" animals were commodified, hunted, displayed, and domesticated. While hunting became an excessive display of British masculinity, animal products such as ivory and ostrich feathers boosted the British economy and inspired citizens to pull up their bootstraps and set up farms in places like South Africa.[4] Throughout the empire, animals and humans were brought together in a racialized taxonomy that was especially prominent within travel literature, Victorian anthropological discourses, and debates over evolution and species divisions, and was reflected in adventure fiction and colonial memoirs. Animals thus became an important tool mediating understandings not only of non-Western countries and cultures but of the human itself, structuring ideas of race and strategies of racialization.

Animal Character

Given the many ways animals existed in daily life, it is no surprise they would appear prominently throughout realist novels, a body of work committed to representing the life of average individuals while reinforcing bourgeois subjectivity and culture. From Barnaby Rudge's chatty pet raven Grip and Adam Bede's anxious dog Gyp to Olive Schreiner's ostrich Hans, animals frequently appear throughout Victorian novels with names, sub-jectivities, and roles in the plot. Building on Alex Woloch's formulation of the "minor character," Ivan Kreilkamp has labeled such animals *semi*char-acters: "animals, or certain privileged domesticated animals," who "are given names and invested with personality and individual identity but

[. . .] this status is unreliable and subject to sudden abrogation."[5] Building on Woloch's claim that the mass incorporation of characters into the realist novel represents a burgeoning form of democracy, I suggest that the simultaneous incorporation of animals into the novel as minor or semi-characters worked as a form of political representation for animals. This representation was mirrored in other texts throughout the period that aimed to show the "real lives" of animals: animal welfare texts such as John Styles's *The Animal Creation* (1839) and William Drummond's *The Rights of Animals* (1838), and later in the period scientific texts on animal intelligence such as Darwin's *The Expression of the Emotions in Man and Animal* (1872) and George Romanes's *Animal Intelligence* (1878).[6] These texts represent animals as emotional and intelligent beings, at times with more loyalty and character than humans. Often the representations of animals in realist novels did not veer far from the kind of representations we see in these political and scientific texts, although at times they pushed back against claims that humans can definitively know and represent animal subjectivity.

Many Victorian animal characters are pets, reflecting the intensification of pet-keeping as an institution throughout the period. Most famous, perhaps, are the many pets – most often dogs – throughout the novels of Charles Dickens. Although they often help to characterize their human companions, Dickens represents animal subjectivity as part of his realist aesthetic. In *Oliver Twist* (1838), for example, Bill Sikes's ferocious dog Bull's-Eye has "faults of temper in common with his owner" and represents the immorality of the criminal gang.[7] When Oliver asks the Dodger if he is a thief, Dodger replies, "I am [. . .] so we all are, down to the dog, and he's the downiest one of the lot."[8] And Dickens does not shy away from entering into the dog's point of view. While in a fight with Sikes, for example, Dickens describes Bull's-Eye as "appearing to entertain some unaccountable objection to having his throat cut," and when Sikes attempts to murder him at the end of the novel, "[t]he animal looked up into his master's face while these preparations were making, – and, whether his instinct apprehended something of their purpose, or the robber's sidelong look at him was sterner than ordinary, – skulked a little farther in the rear than usual, and cowered as he came more slowly along."[9] Yet it is not just pet dogs whose interiority – however minor or passing – is represented in *Oliver Twist*, as we see with Gamfield's donkey: "The donkey was in a state of profound abstraction, – wondering, probably, whether he was destined to be regaled with a cabbage-stalk or two, when he had disposed of the two sacks of soot with which the little cart was laden; so, without noticing the word of command, he jogged onwards," and with the famous early descriptions of Chesney Wold in chapter 7 of *Bleak House* (1852), where Dickens wanders through the thoughts of horses, dogs, rabbits, turkeys, and a goose to emphasize the dreariness of Lady Deadlock's abode.[10]

Even given these novels' interest in animal subjectivity and characterization, pets such as Bull's-Eye and Grip the raven in *Barnaby Rudge* (1841) often destabilize assumptions that humans can know the inner lives of animals, and thus critique the liberal politics of animal welfare discourse that assumes such knowledge. For these animals are often represented with a striking amount of distance or alterity, suggesting that humans can only make assumptions or guesses about animal interiority. Consider Barnaby's pet raven Grip, who when we first meet him, is called "a dreadful fellow" and "knowing imp" by Gabriel Varden, yet proceeds to say, "'Halloa, halloa, halloa! What's the matter here! Keep up your spirits. Never say die. Bow wow wow. I'm a devil, I'm a devil, I'm a devil. Hurrah!" and then begins to whistle.[11] Characters are consistently unsure how to read Grip, whether as a loyal pet to Barnaby, an evil omen, or part of the novel's mystery plot. This alterity demonstrates an uneasiness about incorporating animals into the realist novel. Animals are incorporated and represented as individualized subjects with thoughts, feelings, and desires, yet there is often ambivalence about whether we can ever know what such animals are thinking, as seen above with Dickens's hesitancy in describing Bull's-Eye's actions: "appearing to," "whether his instinct apprehended [...] or the robber's sidelong look," and "wondering, probably." In other words, Victorian novels seem to acknowledge the difficulties in accessing animal interiority through human constructions.

This uneasiness about representation and the limits of human knowledge – of realism itself – mirrors anxieties about the instability of identity and its reliance on relationships with animals. As a constructed space delineating bourgeois values, what does it say about the human that certain animals are brought into the domestic sphere so closely alongside us? As Kreilkamp has argued, animals throughout Dickens's novels often represent "anxieties of dehumanization and fears of animalization," seen throughout representations of animals who disappear from the narrative, never to return.[12] "To be a dog," Kreilkamp argues, "is to occupy a shadowy realm of incomplete identity, identity that may not possess permanence or leave permanent traces."[13] Keridiana Chez goes so far as to argue that throughout Victorian literature dogs complete humanity and function as "emotional prostheses [...] to enhance [...] affective capacities."[14] Emotional relationships with and care for animals thus mark us as distinctly human. Yet animals within Victorian literature can also push back against the restraints of domesticity and the family, offering alternative visions of human identity and belonging. Philip Howell and Monica Flegel, for example, suggest pet animals can resist attempts at domestication and "stretch" hegemonic understandings of "family and domesticity in ways that acknowledge alternate sexualities, power structures, and ways of understanding time."[15] Count Fosco in Wilkie Collins's *The Woman in White* (1859), for example, can be read as queer through his relationship with pet mice, as Flegel argues, to parody "English masculinity and the English family" and "reveal the centrality of dominance to the patriarchal home."[16] Thus for good or ill, animals were explicitly tied to understandings of the Western human and British bourgeoise identity.

While the realist novel and its attendant genres (such as industrial fiction and the sensation novel) incorporate individualized animals as characters, animal autobiographies intensified the individuation of animals – most often pet or working animals – with an explicit political purpose. Anna Sewell's *Black Beauty* (1877), for example, is a piece of protest fiction about the treatment of working horses, most especially the bearing rein, a fashionable headpiece among the upper class that when forced upon horses made them hold up their heads unnaturally high.[17] Excerpts from *Black Beauty* circulated widely in support of abolishing this cruel contraption, and Sewell hoped for her novel to have tangible effects on the lives of animals.[18] She tries to accomplish this by showing animals with good character who accept a human-animal hierarchy.

Beauty's mother explains to him early on that "the better I behaved, the better I should be treated, and that it was wisest always to do my best to please my master; [. . .] I hope you will fall into good hands." She warns him that "a horse never knows who may buy him, or who may drive him; it is all a chance for us, but still I say, do your best, wherever it is, and keep up your good name."[19] Although Beauty protests against the treatment he receives at the hands of individual humans, he never critiques the structure that exploits him. Early in the text when Beauty is owned by an upper-class man, he notes he was not "discontented" but did miss his liberty. "I was quite happy in my new place," he says,

> and if there was one thing I missed, it must not be thought I was discontented; all who had to do with me were good, and I had a light airy stable and the best of food. What more could I want? Why, liberty! [. . .] I must stand up in a stable night and day except when I am wanted, and then I must be just as steady and quiet as any old horse who has worked twenty

years. Straps here and straps there, a bit in my mouth, and blinkers over my eyes. Now, I am not complaining for I know it must be so.[20]

Beauty's language at first seems somewhat radical. He emphasizes his lack of agency over his own body and movements, and a desire for liberty that harkens back to the abolition movement. He is, quite literally, strapped into his position as a proletariat. Yet Sewell neglects to offer any further critique. Beauty's statement "I am not complaining for I know it must be so" suggests that the social structure in which animals circulated as commodities forced to work for humans is natural, and not so bad as long as the humans who participate in this structure have good character. Both Beauty and his more rebellious friend Ginger emphasize that they are willing to work for humans. Ginger tells Beauty, "I was willing to work, and ready to work hard too; but to be tormented for nothing but their fancies angered me," while Beauty tells readers that "[w]e horses do not mind hard work if we are treated reasonably."[21]

Black Beauty thus cultivates individual human character while showing that animals have not just their own individualized histories – a biography – but comparable forms of liberal character. Although forcing humans to look at their behavior toward animals, this animal subjectivity reifies animals in positions of exploitation. Beauty is part of a larger discourse that regulated animal conduct, wherein animals were imagined as complicit in a human-animal hierarchy, even desiring to work for the ends of humans. Such texts suggest that the liberal social reform discourse that was supposed to change the lives of animals ends up reinforcing and reifying their oppression.[22]

Animals beyond Character

As we can see, it was not only pet animals who were used to cultivate a sympathetic and middle-class reader who treats animals well. Other domestic animals such as sheep were incorporated into the Victorian novel as it shifted toward a more diffuse representation of animal "characters," from interiority to their physical lives. For example, Thomas Hardy's *Far from the Madding Crowd* (1874) represents the lives of sheep to highlight Gabriel Oak's good character and to argue for the better treatment of animals raised for their products. In an early moment of financial ruin, when the young unnamed dog chases Oak's flock of sheep off a cliff, Hardy emphasizes Oak's feelings of pity for the dead animals: "Oak was an intensely humane man: [. . .] A shadow in his life had always been that his flock ended in mutton – that a day came and found every shepherd an arrant traitor to his defenceless sheep."[23] Not only demonstrating Oak's own good character, the scene explicitly references the consumption and commodification of animals, encouraging the reader to ethically reflect on the treatment of animals other than pets and horses.

Throughout the novel, Hardy, who was deeply invested in animal welfare, asks for political change for animals by positing them as thinking, feeling subjects for whom we should have sympathy, yet without an emphasis on liberal animal character. The 1860s and 1870s saw many debates over how to treat animals who were raised for consumption and as capital, especially in relationship to public health. Not only were there concerns over the slaughter and transport of animals, animal disease, and the humane sheering of sheep, but veterinary science also became more authoritative during this time. *Far from the Madding Crowd* is deeply engaged with these concerns. Throughout the novel Hardy represents detailed moments of physical care for animals, from warming and nursing lambs and gorgeous representations of shearing carefully and lovingly to leading the animals to a fair to be sold.[24] Significantly, Hardy represents the inner struggles of sheep even as they are sheared with care:

> Here the shearers knelt, the sun slanting in upon their bleached shirts, tanned arms, and the polished shears they flourished, causing these to bristle with a thousand rays, strong enough to blind a weak-eyed man. Beneath them a captive sheep lay panting, increasing the rapidity of its pants as misgiving merged in terror, till it quivered like the hot landscape outside.[25]

And later, as they are driven to the sheep fair to be sold by kind shepherds:

> Men were shouting, dogs were barking, with the greatest animation, but the thronging travelers in so long a journey had grown nearly indifferent to such terrors, though they still bleated piteously at the unwontedness of their experiences[.][26]

Hardy marks a shift in the incorporation of animals in the realist novel, as the care he takes to represent them emerges within both the plot and the novel's style. There is a focus on animal welfare and contemporary debates over legislation, yet this emphasis emerges through an alternate form of representation, one Kreilkamp has called a "less anthropocentric literary form."[27]

The expansion of the realist novel to include more kinds of animals and representations of animals beyond liberal character intensifies in Hardy's next novel, *The Return of the Native* (1878). Here, animals are more diffuse but no less important, as Hardy shows a near-obsession with animal perspectives. I have argued elsewhere that in this novel Hardy incorporates a multiplicity of animal perspectives – many of which are often fleeting – to help readers see differently and recognize the ethical and political claims animals have on humans.[28] Hardy's novels thus not only destabilize an anthropocentric representation and novel-form, but also imagine animal experience from an ethical lens, cultivating a more democratic, multi-species politics. While on the surface animals seem merged into the environment, Hardy often emphasizes their point of view. Detailing Diggory Venn's walk through the heath, for example, Hardy points out an avian perspective: "Though these shaggy hills were apparently so solitary, several keen round eyes were always ready [. . .] to converge upon a passer-by."[29] Later, the heath-croppers, small, semi-wild ponies, approach Venn and Damon Wildeve as they gamble: "their heads being all towards the players, at whom they gazed intently."[30] In another moment, the narrator pauses to show the life of a small pool, seen only by looking closely:

> The pool outside the bank by Eustacia's dwelling, which seemed as dead and desolate as ever to an observer who moved and made noises in his observation, would gradually disclose a state of great animation when silently watched awhile. A timid animal world had come to life for the season. Little tadpoles and efts began to bubble up through the water, and to race along beneath it; toads made noises like very young ducks, and advanced to the margin in twos and threes; overhead, bumble-bees flew hither and thither in the thickening light, their drone coming and going like the sound of a gong.[31]

Hardy shows readers how to pay attention to, and consider the lives of, a wide variety of animal life often seen as part of the background.[32] Thus, the expansion of the realist novel to include more animals encapsulates a more democratic, ecological, and ethical impulse used to level representation, although of course this leveling can never be total, and comes only as a result of a human mediator.

Animals and Racialization

Olive Schreiner's *The Story of an African Farm* (1883) also represents farm animals, but without the explicit goal of cultivating sympathy for ostriches, who were raised for their feathers by Dutch and British colonists throughout South Africa. Instead, ostriches destabilize biological notions of gender and offer a white feminist argument for a change in gender expectations

toward women. Ostriches are aligned with the feminist character Lyndall
early on in the novel when they attack the Irish colonist Bonaparte
Blenkins, taking an almost immediate dislike to him, as Lyndall does.
When Bonaparte is searching through Otto's things after he has died, for
example, Hans the ostrich taps Bonaparte on the head, unseen, and
frightens him so badly he runs out of the house, thinking he was touched
by a ghost. Lyndall says to Waldo: "Why do you think I was driving that
bird? That was Hans, the bird that hates Bonaparte. I let him out this
afternoon; I thought he would chase him and perhaps kill him."[33] Later,
after Lyndall returns from finishing school, she looks to animal life as an
example of how men and women can live more equally. Instead of
distancing herself from the animal world, she notes there is something
admirable there, which humans should replicate:

> "Let us wait at this camp and watch the birds," she said, as an ostrich hen
> came bounding towards them, with velvety wings outstretched, while far
> away over the bushes the head of the cock was visible as he sat brooding on
> the eggs. [...] "I like these birds," she said; "they share each other's work,
> and are companions. Do you take an interest in the position of women,
> Waldo?"[34]

Importantly, this alignment between the novel's white feminism and the
ostriches, animals used to bolster the British economy and its colonization
efforts, highlights how relationships with animals worked as a form of
racialization. For Lyndall's admiration of animals from a distance, and
their relationship to her feminism, emphasizes her whiteness, whereas the
Khoisan characters in the novel are often working with animals, out of
necessity rather than desire, and their Blackness becomes tied to animals
more directly and thus offsets the whiteness of the main characters.[35]
Indeed, the "African farm" that serves as the setting for the novel represents a space of control of both animals and Africans, a place of displacement and occupation of Indigenous land enacted in part through animal
husbandry. Not only are Schreiner's Khoisan characters emptied of interiority – indeed, they are all unnamed – but they are mostly only ever seen
working with the sheep or ostriches, or in the house for Tant Sannie. From
the small boys in the kraal forced to listen to Otto's lecture on the end of
the world to the herder who steals sheep and to the man Em watches milk
"unwilling" cows, the Khoisan characters are represented in conjunction
with animal husbandry.[36] The white characters, however, own and profit
from animals – Tant Sannie mentions that her future husband Piet Vander
Walkt owns 12,000 sheep, for example, and Em offers to give Lyndall
some of her own sheep – or admire them from a distance, as Lyndall does.

Thus throughout novels such as *The Story of an African Farm*, relationships with animals assemble racial categories. Whiteness emerges as an ability to profit from animals, control, trade, and enclose them in a transactional relationship that reflects the economic circumstances and oppressive nature of colonial domination. It is a structure that regulates animals and how others are placed in relationship to them. Blackness, on the other hand, emerges through a working relationship with animals – herding them, milking them, or even stealing them as a mode of resistance – and thus is aligned with the animals who occupy Indigenous land.[37] Ostriches, who were once resources for African communities such as the Khoisan, are now resources for British colonists.[38] The Khoisan characters and animals are aligned throughout the novel, but they are often placed in a hierarchical relationship below the animals. Animal characters such as Doss, Waldo's dog, and even Hans the ostrich are given a subjectivity, interiority, and agency that is denied to the Khoisan characters. The humanization of animals can thus work at the expense of colonized subjects and their own humanity.

Animals in Victorian literature therefore racialize in important and significant ways, whether through literary devices such as metaphor or simile, or through representations of relationships with animals. While critics often focus on racialization within literature set in the colonies or other imperial locations, we can locate this earlier in the Victorian novel, as most of the relationships with animals we have seen in Victorian literature demarcate whiteness. If animals within Victorian literature produced a sympathetic middle-class reader, this was a *white* reader whose whiteness came into being in part through a particular, often benevolent, relationship with animals. So, while the incorporation of animals into the Victorian novel signifies a new form of literary and political representation for animals, and a recognition that they may think and feel in ways similar to humans, it also signals an intensification of the way representations of animals can humanize, dehumanize, and racialize humans. In Victorian literature this takes a new intensity with the abolition of slavery, the expansion of the British empire, and the "scientific" solidification of racial categories.

In what is perhaps the best-known example, Charlotte Brontë's *Jane Eyre* (1847), the Creole woman Bertha is often racialized through references to animals. When Jane enters the third story to nurse Mason after he is attacked by Bertha, she hears "a snarling, snatching sound, almost like a dog quarrelling," a "snarling, canine noise," and describes Bertha as "the wild beast" and "a carrion-seeking bird of prey."[39] Mason tells the doctor that Bertha "bit me [. . .] She worried me like a tigress."[40] Similarly, after Mason and Briggs disrupt Jane and Rochester's wedding and Rochester takes them to Bertha, Jane observes that

> [i]n the deep shade, at the farther end of the room, a figure ran backwards and forwards. What it was whether beast or human being, one could not, at first sight, tell: it groveled, seemingly on all fours; it snatched and growled like some strange wild animal: but it was covered with clothing, and a quantity of dark, grizzled hair, wild as a man.[41]

Here Bertha is not a human being to meet or shake hands with; rather, Rochester "shows" her as if he is displaying a dangerous zoo animal. As not-quite-human, Bertha is locked in the attic as an animal from the empire might be kept in a zoo cage, put on display to highlight racial and moral differences from the demure domestic British animals with whom most were familiar.

These animalized representations of Bertha enunciate Jane's whiteness, Britishness, and humanness; Rochester tells the crowd before opening the door to the attic: "You shall see what sort of a being I was cheated into espousing, and judge whether or not I had a right to break the compact, and seek sympathy with something at least human."[42] Later Rochester compares Jane to birds: "It seemed as if a linnet had hopped to my foot and proposed to bear me on its tiny wing," he says when reminiscing about how they met, emphasizing that "[y]ou open your eyes like an eager bird."[43] When Jane returns to Rochester at the end of the novel, he calls her his "skylark."[44] Bertha's imprisonment and comparison to savage animals is thus juxtaposed with Jane's avian-like freedom; she can take "flight" at any moment, as she does after the disrupted wedding, unlike Bertha, whose freedom has been taken away. Both are compared to animals, but Bertha's comparisons serve to mark her as less-than-human, whereas the animals Jane is associated with, somewhat paradoxically, emphasize her humanity.[45]

Animalization thus works vis-à-vis the *specific kinds* of animals used in comparison to human characters. In other words, animalization cuts both ways, demarcating both whiteness and non-whiteness; it thus becomes crucial to attend to which animals are used and how they are represented next to certain characters. Comparisons to animals racialize both Jane and Bertha while emphasizing particular qualities associated with Britishness and Creoleness. Bertha – a Creole woman often racialized as Black – must be dominated by someone like Rochester and cannot assimilate into white British society, whereas Jane – the white, female, liberal individual – has a freedom and liberty accorded only to white British citizens. Similarly, Rochester is a "caged eagle" in his blindness, his "thick and uncut locks" reminding Jane of "eagles' feathers," also representing whiteness as freedom.[46] She says of his blindness, "The water stood in my eyes to hear this avowal of his dependence; just as if a royal eagle, chained to a perch, should be forced to entreat a sparrow to become its purveyor."[47] While comparisons to animals, or any kind of animalization, is often read as a way to mark someone as not-white, animals and animalization also assemble a white, Western humanity.

This interconnection between animals, animalization, and racialization emerges most fully within the literature of empire in the latter half of the period, from adventure novels and hunting narratives to travel narratives and colonial memoirs. In H. Rider Haggard's adventure novel *King Solomon's Mines* (1885), whiteness and Blackness are produced through animals in ways similar to Schreiner's novel. However, Haggard emphasizes a genocidal violence toward animals that mirrors a similar disregard for Black life, a hunger for animal capital reflective of a larger drive for the resources and wealth of places such as Africa and India. There is an excessiveness in the colonist's relationship to animals showcased in chapter 5, "An Elephant Hunt," where Captain Good, Allan Quatermain, and Sir Henry Curtis stumble across a large group of elephants – "a paradise of game" – and Quatermain notes that "it went against my conscience to let such a herd as that escape without having a pull at them."[48] The slaughter of animals becomes a moral issue, just not in the way we would imagine, as displays of extravagant violence teach readers that white British masculinity emerges through animal death.[49]

Yet if this hunting scene demonstrates white British masculinity and the profits gained by colonial exploration, Black characters such as Khiva, Good's servant, gain humanity through a willing sacrifice in relation to animals, as Khiva is killed trying to defend Good from an angry elephant, torn in two and stomped upon. Representing both a Black disposability and a courageousness exceeding the white characters, this gruesome death is reflective of the mass slaughter of the elephants and later of the Kukuanas. Yet through this moment of death Khiva is humanized, for as Umbopa claims, "he is dead, but he died like a man."[50] And at the end of the novel, animal and African death and objectification are memorialized in a grotesque collection of objects in Sir Curtis's house. He writes to Quatermain: "The tusks of the great bull that killed poor Khiva have now been put up in the hall here, over the pair of buffalo horns you gave me, and look magnificent; and the axe with which I chopped off Twala's head is stuck up over my writing table."[51] The novel's ending ties together the relationship between animal products and African death, a Blackness and animality that must be contained, wiped out, and yet memorialized and put on display. Whiteness thus emerges through the simultaneous control of Africans and animals, whereas Blackness is solidified as an objectification and commodification reminiscent of British slavery.[52]

These racialized relationships with animals were supplemented and reinforced through nonfictional accounts of imperial travel. In contrast to the excessive death on display in adventure novels and hunting narratives, travel narratives such as Mary Kingsley's *Travels in West Africa* (1897) show a humanization of animal life that exceeds representations of Black humans. One of the most striking instances of this occurs when Kingsley and her group stumble across a family of crocodiles. Although they are generally seen as violent animals, Kingsley represents them as a peaceful family enjoying a nap:

> These interesting animals are also having their siestas, lying sprawling in all directions on the sand, with their mouths wide open. One immense old lady has a family of lively young crocodiles running over her, evidently playing like a lot of kittens. [...] [W]e feel hopelessly in the wrong in intruding into these family scenes uninvited, and so apologetically pole ourselves along rapidly, not even singing.[53]

This playful humanization, respect for animal life, and acknowledgment that Kingsley and her group are outsiders is contrasted merely a few paragraphs later when she arrives in a Fon village and encounters "a brown mass of naked humanity," where "[t]hings did not look restful, nor these Fans [Fons] personally pleasant."[54] Whereas Kingsley refuses to disrupt the crocodile family, respecting their "siesta," she purposefully breaks etiquette when coming upon the Fon community: "I got up from my seat in the bottom of the canoe, and leisurely strolled ashore, saying to the line of angry faces 'M'boloani' in an unconcerned way, although I well knew it was etiquette for them to salute first."[55] Reading animality, humanity, and race as an assemblage helps emphasize how deeply relationships with animals were tied to the production of race and the human.

Travels in West Africa contains a similar desire for the taking of animal life that we see in *King Solomon's Mines*, just one that is not so violent on behalf of the British. Through humane discourse, a white, civilized humanity emerges in contrast to Blackness. Writing of all the birds, for example, Kingsley notes, "I expect an ornithologist would enjoy himself here, but I cannot – and will not – collect birds. I hate to have them killed anyhow, and particularly in the barbarous way in which these natives kill them."[56] This racialized relationship to animals, wherein whiteness functions as humaneness, not only looks back to representations of birds such as we saw above in *Jane Eyre*, but is further exemplified by RSPCA discourse and its attempts throughout the latter half of the period at starting branches in colonies such as Egypt, India, and Jamaica. This production of whiteness through animal welfare is best represented in an 1875 letter to the editor of *Animal World*, the journal of the RSPCA: "Wherever the English flag is hoisted, there likewise should a Royal Society for the Prevention of Cruelty be in full operation."[57] Englishness serves as code for whiteness, emphasizing that white people can best exemplify proper relationships with animals throughout the globe.

Richard Marsh's sensation novel *The Beetle* (1897) also represents a racialized and animalized anxiety about British relationships with people from the colonies as a fear of reverse colonization. In this novel, the liberal politician Paul Lessingham is stalked by a magical creature from his youth, a being who has the ability to switch genders and species, most especially the ability to shape-shift into a beetle. Representing not only the alternative epistemologies of Egyptian mythology, the Beetle also represents fears that Britain risks revenge for its colonizing efforts. This intertwined animalization and racialization also looks back to novels like *Jane Eyre*, demonstrating the long history and permanence of using animals as a means of racialization. Not only is the Beetle explicitly referred to as an "Arab," but he frequently comments on the whiteness of the British characters. He says to Robert Holt, a houseless man he has mesmerized: "What a white skin you have, – how white! What would I not give for a skin as white as that," and also comments on the whiteness of Lessingham's skin.[58] This stands in stark contrast to the grotesque descriptions of the Arab character's transformation into an insect as he approaches Holt:

> On a sudden I felt something on my boot, and, with a sense of shrinking, horror, nausea, rendering me momentarily more helpless, I realized that the creature was beginning to ascend my legs, to climb my body. Even then what it was I could not tell, – it mounted me, apparently, with as much ease as if it were some gigantic spider, – a spider of the nightmares; a monstrous conception of some dreadful vision. It pressed lightly against my clothing with what might, for all the world, have been spider's legs. There was an amazing host of them, – I felt the pressure of each separate one. They embraced me softly, stickily, as if the creature glued and unglued them, each time it moved.[59]

The multiple forms of dehumanization, animalization, and monstrosity represented by the Arab character, who remains nameless throughout the novel, is more intense than the dehumanization and animalization of *Jane Eyre*'s Bertha, but we can discern a clear thread between the two. Both the Beetle and Bertha are dehumanized and racialized through becoming animal, while the whiteness of the British characters comes from controlling animals, or being aligned with a more easily humanized animal. The animalization we see in *The Beetle* represents a more total othering of Black and Brown humans alongside a fear that such animalization can invade Britain's shores and pollute its whiteness. Animals and humans are merged in ways that signal an intensified anxiety about the limits of white human identity and about the implications of the imperial project at home.

***

As we have seen, representations of animals in Victorian literature are wide-ranging and diverse, often serving multiple political goals and intersecting with themes such as domesticity, identity, animal welfare, gender, empire, and race. They appear as minor characters and subjects with an interiority meant to encourage political protection and emphasize their human characteristics alongside the humanity of white British subjects. At the same time, animals deemphasize the humanity of nonwhite subjects from the British colonies while offering opportunities for their resistance. Throughout Victorian literature there is a consistent anxiety about what it meant to be a racialized human, an anxiety informed by what it meant to be animal. There is a tension between animalization and seeing animals as subjects, animals as something to be dominated and used as resources, and animals to be pampered and protected through law and legislation. What becomes clear is that the kinds of human-animal relationships we see throughout Victorian literature show us how deeply the Victorian era animated versions of "the animal" and "the human" that remain with us today.

Notes

1 *Animal World* was first published in 1869, and the version for children, *Band of Mercy*, started in 1879. For in-depth discussions of the RSPCA and Victorian animal welfare, see Anna Feuerstein, *The Political Lives of Victorian Animals: Liberal Creatures in Literature and Culture* (Cambridge: Cambridge University Press, 2019); Hilda Kean, *Animal Rights: Political and*

Social Change in Britain since 1800 (London: Reaktion, 1998); and Arthur Moss, *Valiant Crusade. The History of the R.S.P.C.A.* (London: Cassell, 1961).

2 The Vegetarian Society was formed in Manchester in 1847 and was originally a temperance society invested in health and well-being, not necessarily the treatment of animals.

3 Feuerstein, *Political Lives of Victorian Animals*.

4 For example, see R. M. Ballantyne's adventure novel *The Settler and the Savage* (London: James Nisbet, 1877), Annie Martin's memoir *Home Life on an Ostrich Farm* (London: George Philip & Son, 1890), and the how-to guide by Arthur Douglass, *Ostrich Farming in South Africa* (London: Cassell, Petter, Galpin, 1881).

5 Ivan Kreilkamp, *Minor Creatures: Persons, Animals, and the Victorian Novel* (Chicago: University of Chicago Press, 2018), 17.

6 John Styles, *The Animal Creation: Its Claims on Our Humanity Stated and Enforced* (London: Thomas Ward, 1839); William Drummond, *The Rights of Animals and Man's Obligation to Treat Them with Humanity* (London: John Mardon, 1838); Charles Darwin, *The Expression of the Emotions in Man and Animal* (London: Penguin, 2009); George Romanes, *Animal Intelligence* (New York: D. Appleton, 1906).

7 Charles Dickens, *Oliver Twist* (London: Penguin, 2008), 117.

8 Ibid., 148.

9 Ibid., 117, 406.

10 Ibid., 18–19; Charles Dickens, *Bleak House* (London: Penguin, 2003), 105.

11 Charles Dickens, *Barnaby Rudge* (Oxford: Oxford University Press, 2013), 61.

12 Kreilkamp, *Minor Creatures*, 76.

13 Ibid., 83.

14 Keridiana Chez, *Victorian Dogs, Victorian Men: Affect and Animals in Nineteenth-Century Literature and Culture* (Columbus: Ohio State University Press, 2017), 2.

15 Philip Howell, *At Home and Astray: The Domestic Dog in Victorian Britain* (Charlottesville: University of Virginia Press, 2015), 44; Monica Flegel, *Pets and Domesticity in Victorian Literature and Culture: Animality, Queer Relations, and the Victorian Family* (New York: Routledge, 2015), 6.

16 Flegel, *Pets and Domesticity*, 125, 128.

17 Anna Sewell, *Black Beauty* (London: Penguin, 2008).

18 See Moira Ferguson, "Breaking in Englishness: Black Beauty and the Politics of Gender, Race and Class," *Women: A Cultural Review* 5.1 (1994), 34–52.

19 Ibid., 15.

20 Ibid., 26.

21 Ibid., 37, 213.

22 *Black Beauty* is often erroneously referred to as children's fiction, perhaps in part because so much children's fiction from the period included animals and their perspectives, with the next most famous being *Alice in Wonderland*. For a discussion of animals in Victorian children's literature, see Tess Cosslett,

Talking Animals in British Children's Fiction, 1786–1914 (Aldershot: Ashgate, 2006).

23 Thomas Hardy, *Far from the Madding Crowd* (London: Penguin, 2003), 33.

24 Ibid., 11, 98, 127–9, 294–5.

25 Ibid., 127.

26 Ibid., 295.

27 Kreilkamp, *Minor Creatures*, 116.

28 Anna Feuerstein, "Seeing Animals on Egdon Heath: The Democratic Impulse of Thomas Hardy's *The Return of the Native*," *19: Interdisciplinary Studies in the Long Nineteenth Century* 26 (2018).

29 Thomas Hardy, *The Return of the Native* (London: Penguin, 1999), 88.

30 Ibid., 228.

31 Ibid., 189.

32 Animals and their perspectives also appear often throughout Hardy's poetry. For a full-length study of Hardy and animals, see Anna West, *Thomas Hardy and Animals* (Cambridge: Cambridge University Press, 2017).

33 Olive Schreiner, *The Story of an African Farm* (Peterborough: Broadview Press, 2003), 107.

34 Ibid., 183–4.

35 Ryan Fong explains that "'Khoisan' was originally developed as a category by settler ethnologists to refer to the various peoples that have lived in southern Africa for over 20,000 years. Khoisan is a combined moniker for the Khoekhoe and San, who are themselves made up of diverse communities." *The Story of an African Farm* includes people from Khoekhoe, San, and Xhosa communities. Ryan Fong, "The Stories Outside the Farm: Indigeneity, Orality, and Unsettling the Victorian," *Victorian Studies* 62.3 (2020), 421–32, 423, 429.

36 Ibid., 50, 91, 94–5, 175.

37 This kind of working relationship with animals also shows a deep connection with enslaved people who were often forced to work with animals.

38 This connection between animals as resources and the occupation of Indigenous land can be seen in other kinds of literature, such as Samuel Butler's collection of letters *A First Year in a Canterbury Settlement* (1872).

39 Charlotte. Brontë, *Jane Eyre* (London: Penguin, 2006), 241, 243.

40 Ibid., 245.

41 Ibid., 338.

42 Ibid., 337.

43 Ibid., 360, 358.

44 Ibid., 506.

45 Birds were humanized throughout the Victorian era, in a drive to educate children in being kind to animals, and later in the period, to bolster support for legislation limiting the shooting and capturing of certain birds. See Feuerstein, *Political Lives of Victorian Animals*, chapter 2.

46 Ibid., 498, 503.

47 Ibid., 507.

48 H. Rider Haggard, *King Solomon's Mines* (Oxford: Oxford University Press, 2006), 39.

49 For further discussion of animals in the empire, see Ann Colley, *Wild Animal Skins in Victorian Britain: Zoos, Collections, Portraits, and Maps* (Aldershot: Ashgate, 2014); John Miller, *Empire and the Animal Body: Violence, Identity and Ecology in Victorian Adventure Fiction* (London: Anthem, 2012); and Shefali Rajamannar, *Reading the Animal in the Literature of the British Raj* (New York: Palgrave, 2012).

50 Haggard, *King Solomon's Mines*, 43.

51 Ibid., 199.

52 This alignment with British slavery is made clearer when we remember that enslaved people were traded and sold alongside animal products such as ivory and hides, and that cowrie shells were the main form of currency used for such transactions.

53 Mary Kingsley, *Travels in West Africa* (London: Phoenix Press, 2000), 98.

54 Ibid., 99.

55 Ibid.

56 Ibid., 94.

57 E. Jesse, "Cruelties at Port Elizabeth," *Animal World* 6.65 (February 1875), 30.

58 Richard Marsh, *The Beetle* (Peterborough: Broadview Press, 2004), 55, 64.

59 Ibid., 51.

CHAPTER 6

Modernist
Invention and Otherness

Paul Sheehan

Through much of the postwar era, modernism acquired a reputation for promoting certain reactionary tendencies. Its fiercest opponents claimed that it was elitist, imperious, obscurantist, declinist, Eurocentric, and aloof. But if certain modernist writers were dismissive or disdainful of women, minorities, and/or middle-class taxpayers, their attitudes to nonhuman animals were not often addressed. Even with this oversight, though, a disregard for creaturely life was retrospectively imputed to be a pernicious side-effect of modernist poetics. This was so pronounced that acolytes of postmodernism, who liked to distance themselves from modernist values and techniques, could establish their own concern with animal life by highlighting the blind spots or predispositions of their forebears. Textually and epistemically, this argument went, animals were reduced to formal designs, abstractions, and symbolic markers by literary-modernist practices. Steve Baker, in *The Postmodern Animal* (2000), concluded that the "animal is the very first thing to be ruled out of modernism's bounds."[1] Although Baker was writing primarily about the visual arts, his plaint has been ascribed to other modalities of modernism.

If the situation has largely changed, over the past twenty years – although similar criticisms are still to be heard in some quarters[2] – that can be put down to two factors. In the first place, the field of modernist studies is no longer so orthodox or canon-focused, nor are its borders policed so rigidly. To the contrary, it is more expansive, flexible, and accessible than it has ever been – or, in institutional terms, more global, multimodal, and pedagogically affirmed than hitherto. Such concepts as "pulp modernism," "jazz modernism," "middle-brow modernism," "cold (fashion-oriented) modernism," "regional modernism," and "mid-century modernism" would have been anathema to even the most liberal modernist scholar of the last century, yet now are the subjects of book-length studies. To the list just cited could be added the following: "primordial modernism," "beastly modernism," and "zoological modernism," all denoting an attentiveness to multispecies diversity and to the textual embodiments of that diversity. *Pace* Baker, then, animals of all varieties can be located within the bounds of modernism, and they are legion.

The second major change is the transformation and advancement of animal studies. As a field of inquiry, its initial emphasis was on animal ethics – the rights, protection, and liberation of animals. These objectives were pursued via rational debate, which drew (paradoxically) on emotional-empathic connections to the nonhuman world. But animal studies only really spread across the humanities once it had taken a more poetic turn, in the sense of looking beyond the arguments made for animal welfare and accepting the realities of animal agency and ontology. Jacques Derrida acknowledges this shift in his seminal 2002 book, *The Animal That Therefore I Am*, when he avers that no theorist, philosopher, judge, or even citizen has ever attempted both to *see* the animal and *to be seen* by it. That particular maneuver, in Derrida's view, is unique to "those signatories who are first and foremost poets or prophets"; indeed, "thinking concerning the animal [. . .] derives from poetry."[3] A reorientation such as this attunes human subjectivity not just to animal life but also to the body, to the emanations of language, and to that which is marginal, forgotten, inscrutable, and/or repressed.[4] In this broader understanding, animal theory intersects with the concerns of environmental and ecocritical studies, with the prognoses of the Anthropocene, and with the troubling insights of posthumanist critique.

Critical modernist studies has also been affected by the widening reach of animal studies. Charles Darwin, of course, played a role in the literary-modernist field since its inception, although more as a shadowy presence than an active agency.[5] Darwinian naturalism may have served to fortify certain nineteenth-century beliefs in social progress, laissez-faire capitalism, and human betterment, but there is also an anti-progressivist version of Darwinism, more amenable to modernism, which punctures these shibboleths. Thus, Philip Armstrong, in *What Animals Mean in the Fiction of Modernity* (2008), defines modernist human-animal relations in terms of "therio-primitivism," a mindset that sees animality as desirable and even redemptive – not humanity's enemy, as it was for many Victorian writers and thinkers, "but its possible, perhaps its only, salvation."[6] Carrie Rohman, by contrast, is more ambivalent. In *Stalking the Subject: Modernism and the Animal* (2008), she figures modernist literature as first reluctantly Darwinian (Eliot, Conrad, early Lawrence), in that traces of human animality are identified, then repressed, but ultimately receptive to Darwin's evolutionary radicalism (mid- and late Lawrence, Barnes).

The prominence that Rohman gives to D. H. Lawrence is indicative; as she notes, "Lawrence is perhaps the British modernist most engaged with the species problem throughout his work."[7] Central to this "problem" are swans and snakes, Lawrencian archetypes that denote the range of his zoopoetic imaginary. In the so-called Leda poems, for example, swans appear as pure sound, as beating wings that "whistle," "hiss," and generate "drum-winds" (which complement their "singing").[8] Lawrence also weds them to the unsettled processes described by the new physics, observing the swan's motility "within vast chaos, within the electron" ("Swan"). In the poem "Snake," the speaker's reflections resemble the unfixed, unruly behavior of the swan – alternating between fascination and fear, respect and malice, and torn between upbringing ("He [the snake] must be killed") and instinct ("I liked him"). The tension is elaborated after the speaker throws a "clumsy log" at the water pitcher, although the snake has departed: "I despised myself and the voices of my accursed human education."

If literature is a form of knowing, the literary-modernist animal makes that knowing sensible and legible – and also unavoidable. At the same time, this apparent impasse is mediated by another, equally entrenched modernist propensity. In the penultimate verse, the snake is given an anthropomorphic semblance – "Like a king in exile, uncrowned in the underworld" – before the speaker declares it to be "one of the lords / Of life."[9] Lawrence's conferral of a mythic aspect neutralizes the biblical condemnation of the snake, as the evil creature that precipitates mankind's expulsion from paradise. In overwriting the Edenic myth, Lawrence reasserts the snake's otherness, while consolidating the forms of inventiveness that have come to define modernist animal aesthetics. Additionally, for Rohman, this human-reptile encounter provides relief from the overbearing superiority of traditional species hierarchies.[10]

Is there an alternative to the subject-centered orientation of modernism? For Caroline Hovanec, a more heterodox pathway is through animal subjectivity, a concept that she explores in *Animal Subjects: Literature, Zoology, and British Modernism* (2018). Darwin, says Hovanec, proposes an "intercorporeality" of species as they coevolve, identifying continuities between human and nonhuman animals that (implicitly) extend the notion of the intersubjective.[11] Given that many modernist authors were exposed to the public culture of science of the time, they would have absorbed Darwinian conceptions of animal life along with other scientific precepts, and at least been aware of the decentering implications of natural selection enough to sharpen their own radical critiques of human primacy.

Moreover, if Jonathan Greenberg's proposition is correct, that "Darwin makes possible modernism itself,"[12] then the intricacies of human-animal relations have been nested in modernist poetics from the start.

But even as modernism promulgates certain antihumanist axioms, it nonetheless exhibits a residual anthropocentrism (the stubborn persistence of the subject). Cathryn Setz attempts to minimize this residue in *Primordial Modernism: Animals, Ideas, transition (1927–1938)* (2019). Setz's method is to use modernist print culture to plot the imbrication of animals, language, and meaning. Her case study is *transition*, one of the most outré and influential of modernist magazines, wherein she finds "an enormity of symbolic creatures" slithering across its pages. For these are not domesticated or farmyard animals, but those life-forms that are most alien to us: amoeba, fish, lizard, and bird; "primordial" creatures that are, in Setz's words, "freighted symbols rather than textually fortified agents."[13] This fantastic zoology is singularly modernist, as we will see, in that it heralds a movement away from more realist, propitious depictions of animal life.

If there is a precedent for the recent surge of modernist animal studies, it is Margot Norris's *Beasts of the Modern Imagination* (1985). Norris outlines a "biocentric" tradition, a line of thought congruent with the multispecies life-world that houses all living creatures. She examines those writers and thinkers "who create *as* the animal [. . .] with their animality speaking." The tradition begins with Darwin, continues through Nietzsche (who "transform[ed] his work into bestial acts and gestures"), and culminates in a trio of modernists: Franz Kafka, Max Ernst, and Lawrence.[14] Norris presents this as a paradox: modernist figures celebrate "unmediated experience," which can only be individuated, but they do so in writing (or painting) that must draw on art's shared conceptual resources. This problematic is endemic to literary-modernist practice. In what follows, I suggest that the otherness of creatures whose ontologies can be imputed, but never properly apprehended, becomes legible when modernism asserts itself against the mandates of verisimilitude. The modernist animal, as a result, is stretched between the fabulous and the mundane, the singular or extraordinary and the commonplace. I show how these two apparently distinct currents are also inescapably, even necessarily entangled, and that this reveals the intricate workings of the modernist animal.

Fantastic Beasts: Hybridity in Melville, Yeats, and Barnes

In the early 1870s, Friedrich Nietzsche begins publishing the essays that are eventually collated as the *Untimely Meditations*. For Nietzsche, to be "untimely" (*Unzeitgemässe*) means "acting counter to our time and thereby acting on our time and, let us hope, for the benefit of a time to come."[15] The history of modernism contains many instances of its own untimeliness, working against and on the present, sowing seeds for future readerships. Perhaps the signal instance of untimely modernism is Herman Melville's whale epic, *Moby-Dick* (1851), published some twenty years before Nietzsche's declamation. However, the novel did not gain serious critical recognition (or commercial support) until the 1920s, when modernism provided a lens through which it could finally be read and understood. Central to this belated acceptance is Melville's relentless testing of boundaries – of what a novel could be, of how a (marine) animal should behave, and of whether or not the latter's elusive, unfathomable qualities can be textually embodied.

Modernist contravention also coincides with what has been termed the "age of extremes,"[16] a period marked by the upheavals of total war, unprecedented urban and industrial expansion, and the slow, agonizing death throes of Empire. Attuned to this unrest, much modernist work was an *art* of extremes, striving to overcome the interdictions of language and representation, of temporal congruity and regularity, and the dehumanizing realities of metropolitan life. This kind of radical overcoming can also be seen in Melville's White Whale, which breaches the text through its sheer size and bulk. As a "Sperm Whale of uncommon magnitude and malignity," this particular leviathan is given an almost supernatural countenance, sustained by the "unearthly conceit that Moby Dick was ubiquitous; that he had actually been encountered in opposite latitudes at one and the same instant of time." More than ubiquitous, Moby Dick is seen as immortal, "for immortality is but ubiquity in time."[17] One of the most fabulous creatures in the modernist bestiary, Moby Dick's sublimity and majesty – and its ineluctable menace – give it an aura of dread, a quasi-mythical bearing that attests to its destructive capability.

As a species, whales are strange hybrids of anthropoid (mammals, like us) and extraterrestrial (their monstrous proportions). Roger Payne, for example, puts the emphasis on the former: "I think it more appropriate that whales are our apotheosis than our nemesis"[18] – a view underwritten by his exposure to whale song ("humans and whales share a startlingly similar musical aesthetic" [703]). Yet the poet Heathcote Williams, although equally sympathetic, nonetheless sees whales as "Alien beings" that can literally swallow up a dozen or more human bodies, "with headroom" to spare.[19] As the extreme embodiment of its species, Moby Dick's prodigious size issues a bold challenge to humanistic ways of thinking and understanding. In Susan Stewart's words, "[t]he giant, from Leviathan to the sideshow freak, is a mixed category; a violator of boundary and rule; an overabundance of the natural and hence an affront to cultural systems."[20] As well as species-confusion, then, Moby Dick's mixed nature makes it resistant to conventional or consistent hermeneutical norms.

To give a dog a name is to elevate it into an individual, a principle that could be extended beyond domesticated animals. The name "Moby Dick" precedes Ahab, but even as it individuates the whale, it marks it out to be hunted and killed – for sport, effectively, its corporeal value temporarily suspended. In being marked, Moby Dick charges the narrative with shape and purpose (the much-anticipated hunt). But the novel also contains seventeen chapters on whale anatomy and/or behavior, reflections that Jonathan Lethem reads as "freaky poetical crypto-zoological musings."[21] Indeed, Moby Dick's singularity renders it not just a quasi-cryptid, like the rest of its species, but a metaphysical force that almost defies meaning. A parallel could then be drawn between Ahab's monomaniacal pursuit of the whale and Ishmael's exhaustive attempts to capture its meaning, ostensibly contained in its mysterious whiteness. Both lead to an impasse: the whale escapes not only Ahab's ropes, harpoons, and lances, but also every form of semblance and identity that Ishmael tries to impose on it. Moby Dick's semantic elusiveness suggests, then, a template for modernist animality, in which the calibrations of the real – the would-be knowability (and measurability) of the whale by means of its immense magnitude – cannot accommodate its creaturely otherness.

In the three-day chase that closes off the novel, Melville's cetological modernism asserts itself, via a sensorium of animal reflexes. The first sighting of Moby Dick, at daybreak, is preceded by the "peculiar odor" that emanates from "the living sperm whale," which guides the mariners to their prey. On the third day, it is an aural alert – a "low rumbling sound [. . .] a subterranean hum" – that heralds the whale's final reappearance and the ultimate fate of Ahab and the *Pequod*. In between and alongside of these sensory cues, Melville presents a phenomenology of the hunt. Day two is defined by the whale's speed, which, in turn, impels its pursuers and sends "their wild craft [. . .] plunging towards its flying mark." In the controlled chaos that follows, the ship's crew instinctively recomposes itself: "They were one man, not thirty. [. . .] [A]ll varieties were welded into oneness. [. . .] The mast-heads [. . .] were outspreadingly tufted with arms and legs." Yet this spontaneous fusion of man and man – and, more strikingly, of man and mast – is overtaken by the spectacle of the whale, as it both absorbs and sheds the ocean, "piling up a mountain of dazzling foam [...] the torn, enraged waves he shakes off, seem his mane."[22] The odors, sounds, and images of Melville's leviathan delineate it as the creature that seeds (or at least anticipates) the modernist fascination with fabled, chimerical beasts, as often as not taking the form of fantastic hybrids.

W. B. Yeats takes up the mantle, seventy or more years later. In its late Romanticist phase, Yeats's poetry is famously attuned to the natural world and the range of creaturely existences – birds and beasts, for the most part – that abide in it. But as he becomes more enticed by modernist tenets, Yeats's treatment of animals changes accordingly. This can be seen in the signature animal of his oeuvre, the swan – a vital presence in at least four major poems, and a significant figure in several minor ones. The centerpiece of this mini-canon, "Leda and the Swan" (1924), goes further than Melville's myth-enshrouded whale by revising and condensing an actual myth. The rape of Leda, Queen of Sparta, by Zeus, in the guise of a swan, has prompted a good deal of painterly and poetic renderings. In Yeats's version, there is nothing divine about Zeus/the swan in his attack, which begins the poem with a violent irruption:

> A sudden blow: the great wings beating still
> Above the staggering girl, her thighs caressed
> By the dark webs, her nape caught in his bill.[23]

The "great wings," "dark webs," "his bill" – the swan's anatomy is presented realistically, creating a short-circuit between the Olympian king and his graceful, but mundane, animal form. In fact, it is only the speaker's musing that reaches beyond the physical immediacy of the act to consider the repercussions, both impersonal (the Trojan War) and intimate (the "knowledge" that Leda may have acquired). As Elizabeth Cullingford suggests, "hybridization" is the poem's underlying principle, because there is "no simple opposition between the carnal and the spiritual."[24] Yeats further complicates the physicality of the assault by referring to "the brute blood of the air," as if the swan's violent agency were suddenly transferred to the ether.

We learn certain things about the myth-based swan in "Leda," but very little about Yeats's *other* posthuman creature, the monstrous entity that spreads its darkness over "The Second Coming" (1919). More prosaic animals fleetingly appear in this poem, both innocent (the falcon) and ominous (desert birds, reduced to shadows), to quicken the sense of crisis and set the scene for the final, prophetic declamation: "And what rough beast, its hour come round at last, / Slouches towards Bethlehem to be born?"[25] The implied answer – a demon, a diabolical force, the Antichrist – might seem to suggest an occult entity from a gothic or decadent fantasy. But given that this creature has a "shape with lion body and the head of a man," the rough beast is also a kind of cryptid, able to be named and described but not proven to exist (cryptids, too, are often hybrid creatures, amalgams of known and unknown, veridical and fantastical). Yeats's demonic hybrid projects the ancient world into the future, a symbolic upheaval made more scarifying by its vivid, corporeal countenance.

As an apocalyptic carrier of darkness, the rough beast epitomizes the "polemically anti-mimetic" basis of the Yeatsian aesthetic, which yields "an art of extravagant imagination."[26] Yet there is another, more innocuous figure that also illuminates these precepts, even as it usurps the nature-poet of yore. In the Byzantium poems, the poet-speaker articulates a desire to become an aesthetic animal, a mechanical bird spun out of pure gold. Despite this wish, "Sailing to Byzantium" (1926) begins in nature, with the "birds in the trees / [. . .] at their song" (239), providing background ambience for the carefree posturing of the young. The "sensual music" that resonates through the mortal cycle of *birth-life-death* is a reproof to the sexagenarian speaker, whose soul must be taught how to sing. And so, he sails to the holy city of Byzantium, where he asks the sages to "be the singing-masters of my soul," to take him out of nature and into the "artifice of eternity." The allusions to song – a synecdoche for art and creative vitality – culminate in the poet's desire to be transformed into

> such a form as Grecian goldsmiths make
> Of hammered gold and gold enamelling
> To keep a drowsy Emperor awake,
> Or set upon a golden bough to sing.[27]

Like Payne and his avowal about the "oceanic exhalations" of whale song, which hint at a shared musical aesthetic between mammals, Yeats reminds us that birdsong is the meeting-point of nature (the creatural) and art (musical vocalization). Yet he tips the balance in favor of artifice, to suggest that art is, or can be, eternal rather than ephemeral. Thus, even if the creaturely aspect is merely nominal or associative, an extrapolation of the organic, it nevertheless reasserts Yeats's attitude to the natural world. It is as if to say: all animals are subject to decay and death, but it is nonhuman animals that keep the imagination alive, hence they are the true bearers and emissaries of art.

In "Byzantium" (1930), the sequel to "Sailing," *image* replaces *song*, as a sensual thread connecting the poem's five stanzas. Walking through the city as night descends, the speaker witnesses a series of unearthly sights: ghosts, or shades (a play on *Hades*); the eternal, golden bird, crowing "like the cocks of Hades"; and self-renewing fire, with its Hadean overtones. "In glory of changeless metal,"[28] the bird disdains its terrestrial counterparts, singing under the starlit, moonlit dome of eternity its song of imperishable abidance. As with Yeats's other mythic animals, it recalls Moby Dick's doubled, undefinable nature (mammal/monster), in the poet's construal of beastly hybridity: animal/god (the violent swan), animal/demon (the rough beast), and now animal/art-object (the singing bird). Like the white whale, these creatures move restlessly between the literal and the symbolic, their material substance taking on different valences and different semantic inflections. But given the modernist investment in art, abstraction, reflexivity, and linguistic verve, must all of its animals be determined by symbolic inference, in one form or another?

Derrida's acknowledgment of the poetic turn in animal philosophy is exemplified by one of his famous neologisms, pointedly questioning the privilege accorded speech over writing. The term he coins, *animot* – "a sort of monstrous hybrid"[29] – is a singular noun that sounds identical to *animaux*, the plural form of *animal*. Derrida thus contends that *an* animal should never be conflated with *the* animal: each creature's specificity ought not to be dissolved into an overall category that denies or eschews species diversity. At the same time, the coinage also asserts another kind of materiality, in the substantive properties of language that brace the word (or *mot*) "animal." Language has the capacity to divest from its referents, thanks to the resources of symbol, metaphor, metonym, analogy, trope, and so on – the language of the poets. But modernist uses of language add something more. In drawing attention to themselves, these uses have the potential to move beyond divestment and overwrite the operations of literal language, to find an alternative pathway back to the referent. Recognition of the *material substance* of language can thus restore (or at least preserve) the *material traces* of animal singularity.

In the multi-generic writings of Djuna Barnes, the signifying functions of language and their modes of displacement are impugned. This can be seen in the very format of *Creatures in an Alphabet*, a work composed throughout the 1970s and published posthumously in 1982, long after historical or first-wave modernism had abated. Despite its "untimely" appearance, the book is at once a modernist bestiary, taxonomy, encyclopedia, and inventory, even as it puts the adequacy of all these cataloguing systems in question. And so, *Creatures*, a hybrid of written text (twenty-seven quatrains) and illustration, runs from A to Y (not Z); the entry for

A is not an animal but, "Alas!"; for X, "The X has crossed himself away" – all of it, in the assertion of the first quatrain, "as the Lord planned it."[30] But if the Lord planned it this way, then the textual menagerie that results is founded on, in Zhao Ng's words, a "logic of self-sabotage," a misshapen world populated with miscreated animal figures. Or as Ng writes, it houses a "common carnival of unfinished creatures: the ontologically incomplete animal [. . .] shape-shifts into a series of transient hybrids."[31] The alphabet that postulates a kind of textual order is, in fact, undone by the hybrid creatures that (provisionally) furnish it, which do not obey the unvarying principles of codification.

Before Barnes's unruly "creatures," in the earliest phase of her writings, there were her untamed "beasts."[32] They feature prominently in her first novel, *Ryder* (1928), a Joycean experiment in stylistic (and scatological) abundance. Barnes's protagonist, Wendell Ryder, is a kind of nature man who communes with beasts of the field and spreads his own seed far and wide. In "The Occupations of Wendell," a chapter written in iambic pentameter, he laments that "animal and man be set apart" and spurns the interdictions of language/speech. As the speaker tells us:

> So while his beasts about him browse and graze,
> He set a plan a-crawling up the maze
> Of his mind's wit, a wizardry to seek
> That every beaste in kindë might speak.

Animal speech, Wendell believes, will make humans less carnivorous ("For man be fright to pick the rack of bone / That to him spoken has" [83]) and more inclined to see these beasts as equals. Later in the novel, Wendell recounts the fable of the "Beast Thingumbob," a composite creature with wings, horns, paws, and a tail, who mates with the unnamed "beast woman," a creature of the underworld who will bear him ten sons (153);[33] the sexual profligacy, in Wendell's telling, is personal. The fable is also a prelude to the mysterious human-animal mergings in *Nightwood* (1936), announced by that novel's implied narrator, Doctor Matthew O'Connor: "Sometimes one meets a woman who is a beast turning human."[34] The nature of this "turning" is not always clear-cut, though, given that *Nightwood* has "more animal characters than people," from lions, cows, and fish to "an extraordinary number of birds."[35] The latter might include the central female personage, Robin Vote, who has a bird's name, is steeped in their song, and has a propensity for flight in her nighttime wanderings about the city. Robin's avian characteristics, however, are only one part of her beastly identity.

"The Irish may be as common as whale-shit [...] on the bottom of the ocean": the slur is cast by O'Connor, an unlicensed (Irish American) physician, who believes that the Irish are moving *down* the evolutionary scale, becoming more atavistic and animalistic. But similes do not define *Nightwood*'s conflux of species. When O'Connor is called on to revive the elegant yet disheveled Robin, who has fainted in a nearby hotel room, he detects a whiff of damp plant matter, "overcast with the odour of oil and amber, which is an inner malady of the sea."[36] That this evocation of whale effluvium, or ambergris – the "whale-shit" mentioned earlier – should be seen as a "malady" suggests that Robin has succumbed to oceanic torpor. One mammalian species is superseded by another, in the novel's discomfiting final scene, where Robin goes down on all fours and barks like a dog. Through bird, whale, and dog, Robin bears out Jane Marcus's claim that "*Nightwood* is about merging, dissolution, and above, all hybridization."[37] The novel mixes metaphors, genres, high and low discourses and technical languages, ignoring species distinctions and anthropological seemliness. Formal hybridity, then, is congruent with the "beast turning human" schema that shapes Barnes's fascination with interspecies relations.

Domestic Creatures: Canine/Feline Modernism in Woolf, Eliot, and Joyce

From the sublime to the domestic, or from gods and monsters to dogs and cats, creaturely modernism is marked by a propensity to imagine, not just the far-flung but also the near-to-hand, in ways that are emblematic of the wider field. Which is to say, within modernist animal studies there are fantastic hybrids that betoken an art of extremes, as we have just seen, but also more common, unremarkable creatures that denote an art of the mundane or everyday. This bilateral distinction can be understood through a key constituent of modernist poetics. The "radiant moment" – the epiphany, the moment of being, the ebullient impression – elicits a ray of awareness that can light up the everyday. If the latter requires illumination, though, that is because it is often treated as invisible, or at least concealed, standing out in plain sight yet somehow veiled or just beyond reach. However, the everyday can also be, as Ben Highmore notes, "a form of attention that attempts to animate the heterogeneity of social life, the name for an activity of finding meaning in an impossible diversity"[38] – a question of *honing*, then, rather than of illuminating. The animals most commonly associated with everyday (private) life, the companion species of dogs and cats, can actuate or vivify this disclosure of meaning. Through their proximity and active presences, such animals have the potential to enliven domestic routines and agitate the settled orthodoxies of *Anthropos*.

"The most controversial animal in *Nightwood* is clearly the dog,"[39] writes Bonnie Kime Scott, the novel's final, inscrutable scene of implicit human-canine kinship underpinning this assertion. A similar claim could be made for the writings of Virginia Woolf, suggesting that dogs might be the most consequential animals in modernism. As Karalyn Kendall-Morwick notes, "canine agency asserts itself much more forcefully in modernism" than it does in any earlier literary-cultural formation.[40] Woolf's oeuvre is inconsistent, however, in her treatments of species-being. In *Mrs Dalloway* (1925), for example, dogs (and birds) recur throughout the novel, although not necessarily in zoological form. On the surface of the narrative, the Dalloways are a family of dog-lovers: Clarissa, the society hostess, makes generous and affectionate overtures toward her "great shaggy dog." Even more devoted are her daughter and husband, both practically defined by their caninophilia. Elizabeth has no interest in gloves or shoes, the trappings of her class; to Clarissa, she "really cared for her dog most of all." And Richard, despite his career as a Conservative politician, is still merely "a sportsman, a man who cared only for dogs." Beyond such tokens of sympathy, Woolf's inventiveness shows itself in those indices of animality distributed through the text.

Both Clarissa and her shadow protagonist, the war veteran Septimus Warren Smith, are likened to birds in various ways, whether it be their physiognomies or their movements (Septimus "hops" where Clarissa "crouch[es]," both with avian poise). Alongside these straightforward, metaphorical usages, however, is evidence of Septimus's mental infirmity. So, he hears the voices of birds "before waking," as if dreaming them into existence – even though he has already been privy to a sparrow singing "freshly and piercingly in Greek words," while wide awake. Similarly, Septimus's relationship with his wartime officer, Evans, is compared to "two dogs playing on a hearth-rug," one snarling and snapping at the other.[41] But the canine analogy is preceded by a *Nightwood*-like experience that fills Septimus with horror:

> [A] Skye terrier snuffed his trousers and he started in an agony of fear. It was turning into a man! He could not watch it happen! It was horrible, terrible to see a dog become a man! At once the dog trotted away.

Septimus falls into a kind of posthumanist stupor, feeling cursed with the ability to "see through bodies, see into the future, when dogs will become men." The horror is compounded because, he believes, human beings are neither kind, nor loyal, nor charitable: "They hunt in packs. Their packs scour the desert and vanish screaming into the wilderness. They desert the fallen" – an image of species atavism, of *Canis familiaris* regressing back into *Canis lupus*, or wolf. (Richard Dalloway, mirroring Septimus, cares for Clarissa's dog with its damaged paw, "all the time talking to the dog as if it were a human being.") Like the birds and their voices, dogs also have an auricular presence in *Mrs Dalloway*: both Clarissa and Septimus respond to "dogs barking and barking far away";[42] and in the background of the dinner party that concludes the novel is the (real or imagined) howling of Elizabeth Dalloway's fox terrier, locked away so as not to disturb the guests. Dogs and birds are, then, pushed to the background, where they can be summoned back into the text in more or less oblique or associative ways, reduced to being zoomorphic inferences or aural signifiers. But if Woolf's formidable inventiveness here comes at the cost of any canine agency, she does bring the two together convincingly in a later, and for a long time overlooked, quasi-novel.

In fact, Woolf's *Flush: A Biography* (1933) presents itself as a biographical work, purporting to tell the life story of Elizabeth Barrett Browning's cocker spaniel. But the canine-centric perspective is made possible only through free indirect discourse, restricted point of view, anthropological defamiliarization, and other novelistic devices. By using these creative instruments, Woolf relays to us directly the sensorial reflexes of Flush, the dog, thereby certifying the "pretense of unmediated access to the canine mind."[43] However, although Flush's world is bounded by his olfactory and tactile responses, they are still couched in language, having been translated for us by the narrator. Questions concerning language are also raised in other ways by Flush's owner, Elizabeth Barrett (not yet wed), when she contemplates the nature of their relationship:

> The fact was that they could not communicate with words [. . .] Yet did it not lead also to a peculiar intimacy? [. . .] After all, she may have thought, do words say everything? Can words say anything? Do not words destroy the symbol that lies beyond the reach of words? Once at least Miss Barrett seems to have found it so.

As do all poets, Elizabeth has faith in language to do certain things – "communicate" and "express," for example. But here, human-canine interaction gives her pause to question that faith and to wonder if words, the basis of her craft, might not rescind or annul rather than create.

Doubts about poetry are raised throughout the text by Woolf's narrator, reminding us that poetry is an "untrustworthy medium" and that poetic diction is riven with "inaccuracies," and that even the poet's imagination "could not divine what Wilson's [the maid's] wet umbrella meant to Flush."[44] For all of Woolf's anthropomorphic conjuration – the "pretense" mentioned above – canine *quidditas* is still treated as something radically untranslatable, even for a poet as gifted as Elizabeth Barrett. Where, then, does that leave Derrida's "poets and prophets," the only ones who know what it is to be seen by nonhuman eyes? Does Flush's life story undermine this claim? For Derrida, it is not *poetry* so much as *poetic thinking* that is at stake ("For thinking concerning the animal, if there is such a thing, derives from poetry").[45] With that in mind, Elizabeth's recognition that words cannot "say everything" exemplifies this way of thinking, which acknowledges poetry's competencies *and* its limitations: "The greatest poets in the world have smelt nothing but roses on the one hand, and dung on the other. The infinite gradations that lie between them are unrecorded. Yet it was in the world of smell that Flush mostly lived." This is less a reproach than an indicator of Elizabeth's awareness that poetry cannot accomplish the impossible, that it cannot cross the species barrier. And yet the question of poetry does not stop there. "Flush was not a poet but a red cocker spaniel," the narrator reminds us. But Flush is in some ways much *more* than a poet, his canine sensorium opening onto a terra incognita too radically singular and alien for poetic-linguistic apprehension.

There is a point in chapter 2 where Flush has a moment of zoomorphic uncertainty, wondering when *he* might blacken "a white page with a straight stick," as his poetry-writing mistress does, and become human like her. But the "strange stirrings" pass and Flush accepts his dogginess – until, that is, he becomes more sensitized to art and to life indoors, which is when "he came to prefer the silence of the cat to the robustness of the dog."[46] Feline "silence" could be read as a distinctively modernist pursuit, as a way of approaching those aspects of the unsayable that are intrinsic to the real. For T. S. Eliot, silence is consonant with his poetic practice and its evasive, allusive, and impersonal tendencies; or rather, that practice strives for the condition adverted to in one of Eliot's earliest poems, which scrutinizes the moment when

> The seas of experience
> That were so broad and deep
> So immediate and steep,
> Are suddenly still.[47]

The silence or sudden stillness of cats is most acute when juxtaposed with the rowdiness of dogs: "They often bark, more seldom bite."[48] The line is from *Old Possum's Book of Cats* (1939), the volume in which Eliot strays furthest from his modernist roots into the whimsical realm of light verse. But *Old Possum's* does share one important thing with its author's earlier, more momentous work: a toning-down, even disavowal, of cats as domestic creatures.

The work in which Eliot both exhibits and enshrouds his feline aesthetic is "The Love Song of J. Alfred Prufrock" (1915). The third stanza establishes a relationship of reciprocity between cat and "fog":

> The yellow fog that rubs its back upon the window-panes,
> The yellow smoke that rubs its muzzle on the window-panes,
> Licked its tongue into the corners of the evening,
> Lingered upon the pools that stand in drains.[49]

For most critics, the "yellow fog"/"yellow smoke" is a metaphorical foil for an actual cat that rubs its back or muzzle, licks its tongue, and lingers around drain effluence. But the absence of the word "cat" in the stanza makes the meaning reversible, so that it is the yellow fog that rubs, licks, and lingers, in characteristically cat-like ways. This reading evokes the ur-imagism formulated by T. E. Hulme, of which Eliot was an unstinting admirer. Hulme's poetry invites a process of optical misrecognition, in which, say, a farmer's "ruddy" face at dusk could be mistaken for a reddish, rising moon – and vice versa.[50] In Eliot's poem, the feline is shown to be detachable from an actual cat, and versatile enough to incarnate a weather formation.

Elsewhere in Eliot's poetry, cats are exoticized and sensualized – which is to say, de-domesticated. "Whispers of Immortality" (1919) surveys the death-obsessed doctrines of Webster and Donne, before introducing Grishkin, a modern woman with a "Russian eye" (sight) and a "friendly bust" that exudes the promise of "pneumatic bliss" (touch). The poem then shifts again, to the Amazonian jungle:

> The couched Brazilian jaguar
> Compels the scampering marmoset
> With subtle effluence of cat;
> Grishkin has a maisonnette.[51]

The jungle cat is initially given a separate existence, until brought into alignment with Grishkin via the near-homonymic "marmoset"/"maisonn-ette" rhyme. Grishkin is feline, then, not in the manner of the stealthy,

preening yellow fog, but in her erotic, kittenish allure and "subtle effluence" (odor). Indeed, even the jaguar's "feline smell" is no match for
Grishkin's, as she seduces or preys on visitors to her drawing room. Eliot
is exploiting here the centuries-old prostitutes-as-cats association, and the
dangers and lures of unfettered sexual desire.

But Eliot's feline aesthetic extends beyond the carnal-sensual to the
religious-biblical: the tiger as punitive, devouring deity in "Gerontion,"
and the "three white leopards" that consume the speaker in "Ash-
Wednesday" (1930). More implicitly, Eliot addresses Christian persecution in the sixth chorus from *The Rock* (1934), rhetorically asking if lions
"no longer need keepers" to restrain them, in an impious and corrupt
world.[52] All these beasts of prey are fearsome and appetitive, threatening
and unnerving. And yet, for Eliot, even jungle cats are preferable to dogs,
whether it be the "friend to men" in *The Waste Land* with a propensity for
digging up corpses or the "frequently undignified [. . .] easy-going lout[s]"
of *Old Possum's*.[53] Canine modernism thus has little purchase in Eliot's
writing, beyond voicing his distaste for dogs as dirty, contemptible
creatures.

For James Joyce, canine and feline poetics also serve very different
purposes, as evidenced in *Ulysses* (1922). Although not often read in this
way until recently, the novel is a compendious book of animals, a textual
menagerie that includes horses, bulls, panthers, gulls, rats, foxes, owls, and
goats.[54] But it is dogs that demonstrate the novel's transformative aesthetic. The protean forms that they will take begin in the third episode
("Proteus"), when Stephen Dedalus is confronted with a high-spirited dog,
Tatters, on the beach at Sandymount Strand. As Tatters frolics on the
sand, Stephen likens him to a "bounding hare" with a "bearish fawning"
and a "wolf's tongue," then watches him loping off at a "calf's gallop" to
paw the sand like "a panther [. . .] vulturing the dead." Tatters's owner
scolds him ("you mongrel"), anticipating the arrival of Garryowen, the red
setter wolf-dog under the care of the Citizen, in "Cyclops." The narrator
refers multiple times to Garryowen as a "bloody mongrel," a slur that
signals his hybrid, canine-anthropoid abilities, brought to light when he is
"rechristened" Owen Garry and recites a Celtic Irish poem. The fantastic
implications of this feat are tempered in the following episode, "Nausicaa,"
when Gerty MacDowell thinks of Garryowen as the "lovely dog [. . .] that
almost talked, it was so human."

Garryowen makes a final, fleeting appearance in "Circe," when he
follows Leopold Bloom into Bella Cohen's brothel. Or rather, a stray
retriever follows him in, which Bloom thinks he ought to acknowledge

("Better speak to him first [. . .] Good fellow! Garryowen!")[55] and which is then described as a "wolfdog" – as if Bloom's address causes the dog spontaneously to change breed. Nor does it stop there. Garryowen (if it is indeed him) reappears later as a bulldog, then a beagle, and finally a dachshund. "Circe" recodes events and occurrences from earlier in Bloom's day, so his wariness of the Citizen resurfaces here as an abiding uncertainty about his dog's genus. Thus, Joyce's canine modernism may initially promise a realist poetics, initiated by a bathetic incursion into Stephen's stream of consciousness as he wanders along the beach. But it becomes clear soon enough that dogs are "fungible beasts, ever-transforming into other figures," whether via Stephen's interspecies metaphorics or Bloom's troubled imaginings.[56]

Like Eliot, Joyce preferred cats to dogs. Rather than resort to jungle cats or other exotic predators, though, Joyce construes a feline modernism that is both realist and expressive. It centers on Bloom's interactions with his cat, Pussens, in the domestic space. "They understand what we say better than we understand them," reflects Bloom. "Wonder what I look like to her." In adopting the stance unique to Derrida's "poets and prophets," by ruminating on what it is to *be seen* by this animal, he defines himself as a cat person. But so too is Molly, albeit only briefly ("I wonder do they see anything that we cant," she muses), and also, more implicitly, Milly, their daughter. Bloom draws up a list of "similar differences" between Pussens and Milly, conjoining the latter with the former's "neckarching," "mousewatching," "earwashing," and "hearth-dreaming" propensities.[57] For Bloom, these zoomorphic quirks provide consolation, allowing him to commune with his absent daughter through a kind of feline meta-language. Just as the Dalloways are a family of dog lovers, the Blooms are all cat people, their domestic pet mediating certain familial bonds.

Notes

1 Steve Baker, *The Postmodern Animal* (London: Reaktion, 2000), 20.
2 See, for example, Mario Ortiz Robles, *Literature and Animal Studies* (London: Routledge, 2016), 6; and Carrie Rohman, *Stalking the Subject: Modernism and the Animal* (New York: Columbia University Press, 2009), 17.
3 Jacques Derrida, *The Animal That Therefore I Am*, trans. David Wills, ed. Marie-Luise Mallet (New York: Fordham University Press, 2008), 14, 7.
4 See Kári Driscoll and Eva Hoffmann, "Introduction: What Is Zoopoetics?," in Driscoll and Hoffmann (eds.), *What Is Zoopoetics?: Texts, Bodies, Entanglement* (Cham: Palgrave Macmillan, 2018), 3.

5 See Jonathan Greenberg, "Introduction: Darwin and Literary Studies," *Twentieth-Century Literature* 55.4 (Winter 2009), 423–44, 423.

6 Philip Armstrong, *What Animals Mean in the Fiction of Modernity* (London: Routledge, 2008), 143.

7 Rohman, *Stalking*, 100. See also Jeff Wallace's chapter "Animals" in *D. H. Lawrence, Science and the Posthuman* (Basingstoke: Palgrave Macmillan, 2005); and Rachel Murray's chapter on Lawrence's insects, "Formication," in *The Modernist Exoskeleton: Insects, War, Literary Form* (Edinburgh: Edinburgh University Press, 2020).

8 See "Won't It Be Strange," "Leda," and "Give Us Gods," in D. H. Lawrence, *The Complete Poems*, ed. Vivian de Sola Pinto and F. Warren Roberts (Harmondsworth: Penguin, 1977), 438, 436, 436.

9 Ibid., 350, 351.

10 Rohman, *Stalking*, 92.

11 Caroline Hovanec, *Animal Subjects: Literature, Zoology, and British Modernism* (Cambridge: Cambridge University Press, 2018), 5–6.

12 Greenberg, "Introduction," 432.

13 Cathryn Setz, *Primordial Modernism: Animals, Ideas, transition (1927–1938)* (Edinburgh: Edinburgh University Press, 2019), 7, 8.

14 Margot Norris, *Beasts of the Modern Imagination: Darwin, Nietzsche, Kafka, Ernst, & Lawrence* (Baltimore, MD: Johns Hopkins University Press, 1985), 1.

15 Friedrich Nietzsche, *Untimely Mediations*, trans. R. J. Hollingdale, ed. Daniel Breakzeale (Cambridge: Cambridge University Press, 1997), 60.

16 See Eric Hobsbawm, *Age of Extremes: The Short Twentieth Century, 1914–91* (London: Abacus, 1995).

17 Herman Melville, *Moby-Dick*, 3rd ed, ed. Hershel Parker (New York: W. W. Norton, 2018), 144, 146, 147.

18 Roger Payne, "Melville's Disentangling of Whales," in Melville, *Moby-Dick*, 703.

19 Heathcote Williams, *Whale Nation* (New York: Harmony, 1988), 18, 22.

20 Susan Stewart, *On Longing: Narratives of the Miniature, the Gigantic, the Souvenir, the Collection* (Durham, NC: Duke University Press, 1993), 73.

21 Jonathan Lethem, *"Moby-Dick,"* in Melville, *Moby-Dick*, 701.

22 Melville, *Moby-Dick*, 391, 305, 398, 398, 399.

23 W. B. Yeats, *The Poems*, ed. Daniel Albright (London: Everyman, 1992), 260.

24 Elizabeth Butler Cullingford, *Gender and History in Yeats's Love Poetry* (Syracuse, NY: Syracuse University Press, 1996), 149. Cullingford also suggests that the poem (a sonnet) is a hybrid in its very form, combining a "Shakespearean" octave of two quatrains with a Petrarchan sestet (ibid.).

25 Yeats, *The Poems*, 235.

26 Nicholas Grene, *Yeats's Poetic Codes* (New York: Oxford University Press, 2008), 129.

27 Yeats, *The Poems*, 239, 240.

28 Ibid., 298.

29 Derrida, *Animal*, 41.

30 Djuna Barnes, *Creatures in an Alphabet* (New York: Dial Press, 1982), 1.

31 Zhao Ng, "After *Physiologus*: Post-Medieval Subjectivity and the Modernist Bestiaries of Guillaume Apollinaire and Djuna Barnes," *symploke* 29.1–2 (2021), 401–29, 422.

32 For Peter Adkins, "Beasts are of clear centrality to Barnes's oeuvre." He shows how they differ from the more prosaic "animals," and how beastliness and species discourse more broadly are fundamental to Barnes's modernist aesthetic. See *The Modernist Anthropocene: Nonhuman Life and Planetary Change in James Joyce, Virginia Woolf and Djuna Barnes* (Edinburgh: Edinburgh University Press, 2022), 90–1.

33 Djuna Barnes, *Ryder* (New York: St. Martin's Press, 1956), 77, 81, 83, 153.

34 Djuna Barnes, *Nightwood* (London: Faber and Faber, 2001), 33.

35 Jane Marcus, "Laughing at Leviticus: *Nightwood* as Woman's Circus Epic," *Cultural Critique* 13 (Autumn 1989), 143–90, 187.

36 Barnes, *Nightwood*, 28, 31.

37 Marcus, "Laughing," 146.

38 Ben Highmore, *Everyday Life and Cultural Theory: An Introduction* (London: Routledge, 2002), 175.

39 Bonnie Kime Scott, *Refiguring Modernism: Postmodern Feminist Readings of Woolf, West, and Barnes* (Bloomington: Indiana University Press, 1995), 117.

40 Karalyn Kendall-Morwick, *Canis Modernis: Human/Dog Coevolution in Modernist Literature* (University Park: Pennsylvania State University Press), 168.

41 Virginia Woolf, *Mrs Dalloway* (London: Penguin, 1992), 65, 12, 207, 26, 94.

42 Ibid., 74, 74, 98, 82, 153.

43 Kendall-Morwick, *Canis*, 61–2.

44 Virginia Woolf, *Flush: A Biography* (London: Hogarth Press, 1963), 38, 14, 37.

45 Derrida, *Animal*, 7.

46 Woolf, *Flush*, 122, 39, 39, 45.

47 T. S. Eliot, "Silence" (June 1910), in *Inventions of the March Hare: Poems 1909–1917*, ed. Christopher Ricks (New York: Harcourt Brace & Company, 1996), 18.

48 T. S. Eliot, *Old Possum's Book of Practical Cats* (London: Faber and Faber, 2001), 44.

49 T. S. Eliot, *Collected Poems 1909–1962* (London: Faber and Faber, 1974), 3.

50 See T. E. Hulme, "Autumn," in *The Collected Writings of T. E. Hulme*, ed. Karen Csengeri (Oxford: Clarendon Press, 1994), 3.

51 Eliot, *Collected Poems*, 45.

52 Ibid., 164.

53 Eliot, *Old Possum's*, 45.

54 See, for example, the two journal special issues, "Joyce, Animals and the Nonhuman," ed. Katherine Ebury, *Humanities* 6.3 (September 2017); and

"Joyce and the Nonhuman," ed. Katherine Ebury and Michelle Witen, *James Joyce Quarterly* 58.1–2 (Fall 2020–Winter 2021).

55 James Joyce, *Ulysses* (London: Penguin, 1992), 58, 458, 580.

56 Sam Slote, "Garryowen and the Bloody Mangy Mongrel of Irish Modernity," *James Joyce Quarterly* 46.3–4 (Spring–Summer 2009), 545–57, 547.

57 Joyce, *Ulysses*, 65–6, 907, 813.

CHAPTER 7

Contemporary
Animal Form and Zoontology

Robert McKay

For, certainly, works of art are not really organisms with biological functions. Pictures do not really pulse and breathe; sonatas do not eat and sleep and repair themselves like living creatures, nor do novels perpetuate their kind when they are left unread in a library.[1]

Perpetuating Their Kind in a Library

If we are to respond to the literary portrayal of animal life in the contemporary period, we must reject some very conventional ideas about the matter of species, and in turn about what is happening when we encounter animals in literature. This chapter adopts a principally literary-theoretical approach, and proceeds by discussing some key contemporary critical and theoretical approaches to making sense of animal life, in the context of which I explore literary writing. Then, to instantiate the argument, I turn specifically to George Orwell's *Animal Farm* (1945), widely regarded as a foundational work for the appreciation of literary animals in the contemporary period. There are two main reasons for this status. For one, as I show, discussion of *Animal Farm* plays a key role in contemporary debates about the scope of literature, and literary interpretation, to "represent" animals, in the vexed senses of speaking about and speaking for them. Second, strategies for reading *Animal Farm* are instructive across the period to the present because – from its pivotal position, published at the end of World War II – it so powerfully reenergizes several trajectories of literary animal writing, which are impossible to properly understand outside the novel's influence. These include, most importantly, the long tradition of animal satire, which explodes into new life in response to Orwell's imagining of human political follies in animal form: from Sławomir Mrożek's *The Elephant* (1957) and Stevie Smith's *Some Are More Human Than Others* (1958) to Romain Gary's *White Dog* (1970) and Brigid Brophy's *The Adventures of God in his Search for the Black Girl*

(1973) to Will Self's *Great Apes* (1998) and NoViolet Bulawayo's *Glory* (2022). *Animal Farm* also resets the agenda for the tradition of the talking animal tale, which finds remarkable iterations in William Kotzwinkle's *Doctor Rat* (1976), Timothy Findley's *Not Wanted on the Voyage* (1984), and Scott Bradfield's ironic late capitalist reworking of Orwell, *Animal Planet* (1995). In more narrowly thematic terms, *Animal Farm* is the standard-bearer for critical agricultural fictions that track radical changes in the reality of animal farming across the period: from James Agee's "A Mother's Tale" (1952) through Alice Walker's "Brothers and Sisters" (1975) and "Am I Blue" (1986) to Ruth Ozeki's *My Year of Meat* (1998) and Michel Faber's *Under the Skin* (2000). What is important about all these texts – and what marks them as heirs of Orwell's work – is their determination to connect humans' and nonhuman animals' experiences, understanding them as existentially intertwined, and putting literary writing to work in ways that firmly refuse distinctions between them.

My purpose, then, is specifically to problematize two widely held notions that lie behind many interpretations of literary animal writing. The first is the idea that so-called animal beings, and by extension (though perhaps less surprisingly) so-called human beings, have a simple or essential existence: a consistent, persistent, and generalizable "animal form" – a species morphology and correlative set of species behaviors – by which we can reasonably recognize, describe, and know them.[2] This kind of idea is at work, for instance, if when asked "what is a chicken like?" and "where do chickens live?" we confidently reply: "feathery with a beak," and "in a farmyard," as though no chicken has ever lost their feathers or beak or, for instance, inhabited the kitchen and the kitchen terrace of an apartment of an unnamed city.[3] The point here is not that the immediate response is wrong and my qualification right; rather, that what we generally consider "right" as a way of recognizing animals is authorized by a particular way of knowing them – thinking about them in terms of species types – which treats normative aspects of their bodies and experiences as the reality of those animals, discounting the remarkable variety of individual animals' experience.[4] By complicating our knowledge about animal life, the shift in interpretation I argue for here asks that we stop reading cultural texts in terms of such normative quasi-zoological knowledge about what an animal being is. This, furthermore, is knowledge to which we implicitly refer when we simply and confidently distinguish *actual* embodied animal life from the *textual* form in which we encounter it. And so, the second, even more challenging, notion I hope to undermine is the very distinction between the preexisting, essential, and *embodied* (or we could say) "natural" animal and the *formed*, variable, and (we could say) "cultural" animal re-presented in literary texts. These two discreditable notions – that animals can be known by way of a consistent and essential embodied form and that that form preexists its representation in literature – are, I think, remarkably persistent across literary and other cultural understandings of animal life, but they are simply no longer useful.

One way of framing this thesis is to say that I am offering an essay in understanding *literary zoontologies*. This term signifies the literary presentation of animal existence, or of social relations amongst animals and humans, as an intertwined story of the reality of more-than-human life and literary meaning, in the form of a work with its own multiple priorities. I also find it helpful to say, when talking about this strange and chimerical kind of beast – a story of animal lives that demands not to be dissected into actual and imaginary, embodied and aesthetic, parts – that such a text has *animal form*. The potential confusion caused by my use of this term, given its use in the preceding paragraph, is quite deliberate: my aim, here and throughout, is to make it difficult to distinguish between that sense of "animal form," meaning the embodied shapes and behaviors of this or that animal species as they are normatively conceived, and the irreducibly hybrid *animal form* that I find, for example, in *Animal Farm*.

To read in terms of literary zoontologies is to heed a challenge posed by the philosopher Matthew Calarco: that critical thought must move "beyond the anthropological difference," which is to say beyond the human-animal distinction.[5] One means of doing this that is particularly difficult in the field of literary interpretation – and therefore especially important – is to "disarticulate the problem of a properly postmodern pluralism from the concept of the human," as Cary Wolfe puts it.[6] Wolfe wants us to reject the idea that if *human* life and meaning are plural, for instance, in the fact that they are multicultural, then this distinguishes them from a "natural" animal life that is not so conceived. Indeed, while literary criticism is well versed in acknowledging pluralisms of meaning at the level of interpretation, separating that pluralism from the figure of human demands, I suggest, that we not draw easy distinctions between the form and the matter of cultural texts – between text and world, word and body, interpretation and text. For such line-drawing is at work when multiple understandings of animal life are understood as *really* the preserve of plural *human* understandings about, cultural responses to, and textual representations of animals.[7] This is another widely held realistic notion that the concept of animal form explored here aims to debunk. As such, this concept is intended to contribute to the transdisciplinary endeavor of animal studies in redirecting "the humanities" away from their all-encompassing affirmative goal to "understand what it means to be human." The valuable aim of animal studies is instead to explore what it means, for the more-than-human world, that structures of knowledge keep reproducing the phantasm of the human by way of the intellectual and material ownership of animals and animality.[8]

And so, to the extent that I am able in my writing to perpetuate the kinds of animal form that live in the examples I discuss, I respond to Suzanne Langer's perfectly realistic suggestion that literary works are not "really" animals with a resounding: *get real.* To do so, I first offer a fuller theoretical rationale for the ideas I have just set out about contemporary animal form, and then turn to Orwell's novel as an exemplary case.

Cultural Zoontologies

Let me begin with the notion of *cultural zoontology*, a concept I loosely define as a shared or shareable account of the reality of animal life: a general set into which literary zoontology can be aligned. The term "cultural zoontology" is intended to connect ideas from two areas of intellectual inquiry: theoretical animal studies (and posthumanism) and the anthropology of ontologies. In the arena of animal studies and post-humanism, a linked set of ideas has developed under the rubric of "the question of the animal," posed in such terms originally by Jacques Derrida and first elaborated under the sign "zoontology" by the theorist Cary Wolfe.[9] The principal and influential innovation of zoontology in this mode is to account for the historically variable discursive construction of the human/animal divide. This approach connects inquiry focused on theorizing and understanding the complexity and value of animal existence to other analyses that address the discursive manipulation of animal ontologies for the purpose of political management of human life (especially in social arenas like Indigeneity, gender, sexuality, race, and ability).[10] Often, in zoontological studies that retain an ethical focus on nonhumans, as happens in Wolfe's work, this view is linked to increased philosophical, ethical, and political attention to differences between animals (usually taken at a species level), which reveals the evident stupidity of generalizing about "the animal."[11] Finally, these attitudes are connected to innovations in scientific understanding of the capabilities of different animals, which simultaneously underscore the need to attend to the diversity of animal ontologies (again, at a species level) and successively undermine the ontological gamesmanship that posits this or that capacity (language, culture, tool-use, grieving, altruism, etc.) as the preserve of the human.

The legacy of this work is an exponential increase in the complexity and richness with which the reality of animal life is understood. However, even in its most sophisticated elaborations, a tendency persists toward neglecting some of these advances while elaborating others. Here, for instance, is Wolfe, reaching a key moral conclusion from this kind of zoontological thought:

> Is there not a qualitative difference between the chimpanzee used in biomedical research, the flea on her skin, and the cage she lives in – and a difference that matters more (one might even say, in Derridean tones, "infinitely" more) to the chimpanzee than to the flea or the cage? I think there is.[12]

We can and should read this rhetorical Q&A as an exercise in literary zoontology: it is an imaginatively formed story about the reality of animal life embedded within the larger intellectual priorities of Wolfe's book. "The chimpanzee" is speculatively narrated with some specificity here (marked with a gender and a captive-institutional locale and her skin invested with feeling) and on the basis, presumably, of decades of research on chimpanzee cognition. Nevertheless, there remains a vague – and because of this rhetorically powerful – generalizing sentiment aimed at the level of species. This stems from Wolfe's broad allusion to "biomedical research" and the slippage, implicit in the use of the definite article, between a unique individual and the individual as species type. This is part and parcel of an essentializing and schematizing point being made about chimpanzees, fleas, and cages, which presents the matter of "mattering" – of having different existential investments in having preferences – as if it exists somewhere *in* these beings, by virtue of their species being, which Wolfe refers to as their "form of life." What this point glosses over is precisely the very *creative* zoontological work that narrating the meaning of animal life in this way – fixing it at the level of species by way of this kind of speculative, generalizing and comparative schema – itself performs.

And here is where the "anthropology of ontologies" comes in. This is how the theoretical anthropologist Eduardo Kohn has described work by Eduardo Viveiros de Castro, Phillipe Descola, Bruno Latour, and others that has – in various ways – analyzed the practices and concepts by which different societies variously imagine the reality of existence.[13] (A broad focus on existence of any sort rather than animal life per se means that "ontology" rather than "zoontology" is the term of choice here.) Perhaps the most significant innovation here, developed at length by Kohn in his own work, is Viveiros de Castro's account of what he calls "multinaturalism." In short, his point is that, rather than there being a "multiplicity of representations of the same world," as in a multi*cultural* understanding of a supposedly singular nature, in multi*naturalism* "all beings see ('represent') the world the same way – what changes is the world that they see."[14] This idea is based on analyzing instances of the perspectival ontologies of Amerindian peoples, in which (according to Viveiros de Castro) all beings, from their own subjective position, "see themselves anatomically and culturally as humans." In turn "snakes and jaguars see humans as tapirs or white-lipped peccaries [...] because they, like us, eat tapirs and peccaries, people's food. It could only be this way, since, being people in their own sphere, non-humans see things *as* 'people' do."[15] Kohn describes this argument as "metaphysical," because it offers "systematic attention to [and] the development of [...] forms of thought that change our ideas about the nature of reality."[16] One important thing that is happening here, which connects the shift from a multi*cultural* to multi*natural* approach in the anthropology of ontologies to zoontological work in theoretical animal studies, is precisely the separation of pluralism from a concept of the human.

David Herman, whose book *Narratology beyond the Human* (2018) is ground-breaking in exploring the implications of anthropological metaphysics for literary studies, develops it into his notion of "cultural ontologies." Herman glosses this term as: "a framework for understanding that circulates more or less widely in a given (sub)culture and that specifies, in the form of common knowledge, (1) what sorts of beings populate the world and (2) how those beings' qualities and abilities relate to the qualities and abilities ascribed to humans."[17] A key point Herman is making – different (sub)cultures understand the lives of other beings and things only *relative* to their ideas about humans – is perhaps the key feature of this approach for my argument. It clarifies that rather than being a "description" of actual animals, any cultural ontology is a complex and differential parceling-out of attributes of being. Herman goes on to indicate a key role that literary texts might play here. Against a background condition that such ontologies "are partly worked out in and through a culture's or subculture's storytelling practices," he argues that literary, filmic, and other narrative practices can "both unmask and help consolidate the species hierarchies that humans have used to legitimate their self-serving attitude toward – and destructive treatment of – other animals as well as the larger biosphere."[18] This project can proceed, for example, when experimental literary form works to "defamiliarize – and thereby disrupt – established narratives about other-than-human worlds and human–animal relationships." Or (and here the positive influence of the anthropology of ontologies is felt) we can encounter stories that "explore the boundaries of the category of person and extend it across species, thereby denying *Homo sapiens* preeminence or centrality across other creatural kinds."[19] From the perspective of the reader of contemporary literature, Herman's account has the signal benefit of emptying out conventional ideas about animal life of most of their authority (treating them as "just" a cultural ontology, rather than fact); in the literary and other cultural texts around us we will thus find both reactionary instances and progressive recalibrations of such ontologies.

But I want to add something here, recalling how the relations posited by Wolfe *between* the interests of a speculative generalized flea, chimpanzee, and cage were crucial to his particular literary zoontology. For the relational ascription Herman mentions in his gloss on cultural ontology surely itself extends far beyond the dyad of human-other being. It is not just that cultural ontologies involve understandings of other beings relative to the human (and vice versa); they surely also involve understanding the plurality of different beings (e.g., chimpanzee, flea, and cage), and indeed different scales of being (such as individual and species) in relation to each other. And, crucially for my argument, they also understand what we might call different *zones* of being in relation to one other; by this I mean, for instance, the idea, within a realist cultural ontology, that hypothetical things are not existent or that representations are not real. An ontology of the human is therefore established partly by way of asserting different animals' different kinds of difference from the human, in terms of such zones. A simple example, here, would be the oft-repeated zoontological notion that animals (unlike humans) cannot properly act or perform.[20] To return to my example from Wolfe, I would argue that there the analytical mode of theoretical or philosophical discourse shifts into a hypothetical or speculative one, which fantasizes the existence of the abstract beings that it simultaneously presents as real ("the chimpanzee," "the flea," and "the cage"); it does this in the very act of establishing a comparative moral claim about them. The claim also arranges these supposed beings in the context of a presumption that qualitative differences are the basis for the kinds of preferences that self-evidently matter to humans, and which ethics therefore respects. A moral claim is thus seemingly based on existing distinctions between four kinds of beings (chimp, flea, cage, human), but it in fact *produces* those distinctions and species forms in a speculative drama of abstract comparison. This is literary zoontology at work.

My interest in how stories of animal existence play out *across* the real/represented boundary clarifies the part played by the literary text in relation to cultural zoontology. For, if cultural zoontologies *also* necessarily involve the relative parceling-out of zones of being (along spectrums such as speculative to existing, abstract to concrete, species to individual, and, crucially, imaginary to real), then we can no longer happily distinguish between cultural zoontologies (i.e., culturally shared systems of ideas and stories *about* animal life) and kinds of life "per se." It is equally questionable to retain a distinction between shared stories about supposed "actual" animal beings, and the modes of relation with them that such cultural zoontologies understand, and those stories that appear as "imaginatively" posited or made possible in the form of literary texts. For to do so would be to presume one cultural ontology (realism, which carefully distinguishes the imaginary or represented from the real) as having authority over others; yet this is something that the very notion of plural cultural ontologies undermines. As a result, the "*Homo sapiens*" and the other "creatural kinds" whose relative value Herman finds experimental literature reconfiguring are themselves no more and no less than particular species forms taking shape in cultural zoontological configurations. This shifts the sand under some of our firmest assumptions about the literary experience, such as that writers and readers of texts are by definition human or that the language used in them is human. Once we discover ourselves in the wild realm of cultural zoontology, the kinds of distinctions and the distinctions between kinds that once seemed solid melt into air. The radicalism of the concept is that it does not just "separate pluralism from the concept of the human," as Wolfe puts it; *it separates the human from the concept of the human.* And, indeed, it separates any animal or other living being from a reality its species concept supposedly designates. Here, then, we arrive at a substitution of the realistic notion of species with that of cultural zoontology: no more, and no less, than a shared or shareable story of animal life.

Meaningless and Meaningful Animals

What does thinking about animals in terms of this or that cultural zoontology *allow us to know* about more-than-human life? If we only have literary and other cultural zoontologies, rather than actual animal realities, at our disposal as we interpret the existence of animals in texts, then the demand, now, is to read such stories of animal being for what they say about how so-called animals did, might, should, or will live, and how so-called humans did, might, should, or will live with them.[21] A step in this direction is to consider nonhuman animal life *as itself meaningful*. We can do this by working against the following logic of interpretation: "animal body or lifeform X is the bearer of (human) cultural meaning Y"; and so, when reading cultural texts in which animals appear: "we should read X as meaning Y – animal representation X *means* human significance Y." This set of ideas – which certainly allows for cultural texts to contain multitudes of meaning about animals – nevertheless implies *animal* meaninglessness. But the concept of cultural zoontology illuminates the limitations of this approach.

The linguistic or cultural turn in humanities inquiry (since about 1970) has influenced animal studies with the idea that, as opposed to being straightforwardly knowable as fact, animal life is an endlessly complex bearer of cultural meaning. This appears to be generous in the attribution of meaning to animal life, in that it profusely multiplies the possible meanings of animal existence. But it is profoundly parsimonious to the extent that *human cultural* variation is treated as the meaningful signification of (themselves implicitly meaning-less) animal bodies. This notion is perfectly exemplified (to return to the influence of theoretical anthropology on my account of zoontologies) by the work of Clifford Geertz, in a major work of the cultural turn, *The Interpretation of Cultures* (1973). "Believing that man is an animal suspended in webs of significance he himself has spun," Geertz writes (in the gendered idiom of his day), "I take culture to be those webs."[22] It is a striking metaphor that does a wonderful job of normalizing the spider in general as a web-maker (plenty of spiders don't make webs, incidentally) so as to inject its stereotypical proteinaceous creative energy into the engine of human cultural meaning-making. The zoontological understanding this produces, clearly enough, is that human culture is meaning-full while spiders' web-making is meaning-less.

The pro-animal literary theorist Josephine Donovan offers a trenchant critique of how such notions undergird what she terms the "formalist aesthetics of modernity." Such aesthetics, she argues, insist on the radical separation of human cultural *form* from nonhuman "reality." Such a view, for Donovan, "overrides and suppresses the living subjecthood of [animals] relegating [them] to the status of inert matter to be manipulated and shaped according to aesthetic constructs."[23] Indeed, cultural inquiry with an ethical interest in animals has a long history of being critical of animal metaphors – and beyond this the larger repertoire of animal symbolism – to the extent that such metaphors' assumed prioritizing of whatever animals are made to signify celebrates human interests and denigrates animal being.[24] Ironically, though, it has been a feature of theories of metaphor since at least I. A. Richards's *Philosophy of Rhetoric* (1936), that rather than *distinguishing* vehicle from tenor, metaphors actually produce a "meaning [. . .] which is not attainable without their interaction."[25] The suggestion that both aspects of an animal metaphor are meaningful offers a helpful way of thinking zoontologically with literary writing; it helps us develop critical responses to anthropocentric ways, such as Geertz's, of harnessing animal meaning and putting it to work, meta-phorically or not, but crucially without invoking a view from nowhere about what animals *really* are, or want.

Geertz himself surprisingly intuits the possibility of responding to animals otherwise, as *meaning-full*, in excess of his own account of how they participate in human meaning-making. His richly literary interpreta-tion of cockfighting in Bali, for example, famously explains how this cultural practice should be read as a form of "deep play," of "saying something of something" (i.e., as a kind of cultural text with an expressive form). Cockfighting in Bali has a meaning that can be interpreted, and this meaning emerges in the allowance it gives participants in that culture to work through, or to play out, sensibilities that would otherwise be too difficult for them to externalize – principally, in Geertz's interpretation, status anxiety. "An image, fiction, a model, a metaphor, the cockfight is a means of expression; its function is neither to assuage social passions nor to heighten them [. . .] but, in a medium of feathers, blood, crowds, and money, to display them."[26] Yet, even here, the meaning of a cockfight as *human* cultural play whose "significant form" is a particular configuration of cockfighting practices, and whose material medium is chicken feathers and blood, is not offered as simple truth. Rather, it is the invocation of a *particular* interpretive response. Geertz acknowledges that to connect "the collision of roosters with the divisiveness of status," as he does in his interpretation of the cockfight, "is to invite a transfer of perceptions from the former to the latter, a transfer which is at once a description and a judgment."[27] But he then offers an astonishing admission. "Logically, the transfer could, of course, as well go the other way; but, like most of the rest of us, the Balinese are a great deal more interested in understanding men than they are in understanding cocks."[28] It is quite possible to interpret this scene otherwise, finding the entire human melodrama around the cockfight to be expressing an elaborate story of the life (and death) experience of the chickens at its center.

Here, in a particularly acute way, we encounter the wonderful zoonto-logical indeterminacy of animal metaphors in a more-than-human world. For Geertz helps us to realize that it is only by way of a prejudiced, limited, and anthropocentric practice of interpretation – in the interests of, as he puts it, "most" of "us" – that animals mean something for humans and not the other way round. Practicing interpretation in such a way, as Geertz's offhand but mind-blowing aside reveals, is the peculiar product and not the general proof of a particular cultural zoontology. But "we" need not share those priorities; there are, of course, "others of us." One of those, in fact, is George Orwell, who offers his own literary zoontology by way of the animal form of *Animal Farm*.

The Animal Form of *Animal Farm*

Reading Orwell's novel as a site of contestation about how literary repre-sentations might take animals seriously is perhaps literary animal studies' own inversion of the interpretive cliché that *Animal Farm* is what Sean Meighoo has called a "humanimallegory" – a text in which animals are put to use in symbolic ways to tell a story about human life.[29] In the case of *Animal Farm*, the basic outline of that reading is, of course, that a tale of a liberatory revolution by the animal inhabitants of a farm in rural England, and its degeneration into a disenchanted dictatorial aftermath, really conveys the story of communist revolution ceding to totalitarianism in its Stalinist guise. Susan McHugh, by contrast, has importantly explored how *Animal Farm* (not unlike Geertz's cockfight) might be read otherwise so as to stress what I have called the meaningfulness of literary animals. She does this by giving her account of "a progressive reading of *Animal Farm* as a novel about animals."[30] Such a reading, she argues, emerges across fragmentary interpretations of Orwell's work by several critics, including D. B. Asker, Jeffrey Moussaief Masson, Helen Tiffin, and Raymond Williams. The key context guiding it is Orwell's preface to the Ukrainian edition of *Animal Farm*, in which he describes the creative genesis of the novel in the moment he witnesses a "little boy" controlling a "huge cart-horse" with a whip. Orwell responds, rather as if he has experienced a visionary *coup de foudre*, in a stunning moment of zoonto-logical speculation:

> It struck me that if only such animals became aware of their strength we should have no power over them, and that men exploit animals in much the same way as the rich exploit the proletariat.[31]

For Tiffin, this moment epitomizes a different "impetus and trajectory" for *Animal Farm*'s meaning than the convention learned in childhood to read "through the 'animal' characters" – by which, for example, Mary Mapes Dodge's 1874 fable "*The Little Red Hen* is really about human social co-operation." In this zoontological approach, "the presence of the animal in narrative [is] denied."[32] For Tiffin et al., by contrast, the context of the *Animal Farm*'s genesis insists on that presence.

But McHugh, rather than claiming that *Animal Farm* is *really* about animals and so is *not* an allegory, instead stresses that all interpretations of the book (including animal-centered ones) are themselves necessarily the products of histories of literary critical strategy, and such strategy can always be directed. For McHugh, "more than any final agreement about its one, true meaning, the precise struggle through which literary history has arrived at what now seems so patently obvious indicates what remains at stake for reading animals in and around disciplinary structures."[33] She suggests that *Animal Farm*'s place as a canonical text in English-speaking (especially secondary-level) education in the second half of the twentieth century is rooted in the fact that it especially rewards the orthodox practice of reading in the postwar era known as the "New Criticism." Crucially, however, for McHugh, the general interpretive work of animal studies is, by contrast, to "focus on how people make animal selves and others (dis)appear."[34]

Indeed, I prefer to describe Orwell's account of the boy and cart-horse as a speculative literary zoontology, rather than as being in any simple way about the "presence" of animals, to stress that what is happening in it remains a process of interpretation and narrative imagining of animal life. A key effect of the narrative form of the moment, as Orwell recounts it, is that it allows him to move smoothly through a slippery metonymic argument by presenting parallel impressions as "striking" him simulta-neously out of this one vision.[35] A careful configuration of human and animal subjects and collectives, and of ethical and political values about them, is thus made to seem entirely straightforward as Orwell extrapolates from the behaviors and implied attitudes of individual characters (a boy and a cart-horse) to various and distinct collectives (first "such animals" and "we," and then "animals" and "men," and then "rich" and "proletariat"). This moment, I am suggesting, is an assiduously formed literary characterization of life that imagines, configures, and presents animals' interests as meaningful in particular relational ways by virtue of particular rhetorical methods (and that is where its radicalism lies). Offering such a literary zoontological account of this moment's animal form, I suggest, is quite different from taking it as proof that Orwell's writing might be "'really' about animals," which is how McHugh explains it has been used by the pro-animal critics she discusses.[36]

On the one hand, then, we must be careful to sidestep the futile hope that we can find the "presence" of animals in literary texts, by looking "through" nonanthropocentric logics of animal life – as if doing so would not simply enact a further zoontological proliferation. But conversely, we also must not agree to confine our analysis of literary texts to a uniquely human realm of cultural reproduction, leaving animals themselves in ontological abeyance – a conventional approach by which cultural attitudes about animals might be diverse, but remain straightforwardly understood to be the property of "humans" to be passed on to other humans through representations of them.[37] For this determinate parsing of zones of being in terms of the discourse of species remains itself a cultural zoontology; it performatively enacts the human by claiming for the human the absolute right to account for animal life in texts. Finding common ground instead with McHugh's attentiveness to the species-politics implied by literary criticism's fundamental gestures, my alternative is this: we need to develop readings that aim to explicate *how* literary works and their receptions enact, reproduce, and proliferate specific literary zoontologies, specific stories of animal life. For *these* are the true living denizens of any text's animal form, whose meaningful life it is our duty to respond to in our readings.

And so, to offer just one example of how we might do this, let me take inspiration from the potentially meaningful chickens that scratch their way through this essay, and turn now to the disobedient civil collective of hens who live on *Animal Farm*. For perhaps the best way to understand literary zoontology is to attend carefully, as Geertz suggested we might, to the indeterminate co-presence of different meaningful elements in specifically figurative language – not because figuration is a special case, but because tropes such as metaphor can be taken to enact in miniature the larger process of discursive world-creation that goes on in any literary text.[38]

In chapter 7 of *Animal Farm*, the farm's hens are presented with a sudden and shocking demand to surrender their eggs because Napoleon, a pig who is the animals' dictatorial leader, has entered a contract with a neighbor to trade eggs for grain in response to an apparent crop failure. In turn, "led by three young Black Minorca pullets, the hens made a determined effort to thwart Napoleon's wishes. Their method was to fly up to the rafters and there lay their eggs, which smashed to pieces on the floor."[39] In response to various measures to repress this political action, and after nine die, reportedly of coccidiosis, the hens eventually capitulate.[40] Later in the same chapter, at an abrupt show trial where a number of pigs are summarily executed at Napoleon's behest by "his nine huge dogs," the three hens offer a seemingly forced confession that they were incited to rebel by the politically exiled revolutionary leader Snowball, who appeared to them in a dream. "They, too, are slaughtered."[41]

These moments can be read, in conventionally allegorical terms, as figuring events in Soviet history in the text's characteristically condensed and vivid way: the forced collectivization and dekulakization that followed the dreadful famine of 1930–3 (i.e., the expropriation of possessions as part of an intended destruction of the entrepreneurial peasant class) and Joseph Stalin's purges of his political enemies in the years afterward, conducted in the shadow of his paranoid fear of the political influence of Leon Trotsky. In this reading, the Black Minorca pullets and other hens allegorize the recalcitrant rural peasantry, while the pigs Napoleon and Snowball portray Stalin and Trotsky, and the dogs represent Stalin's henchmen in the People's Commissariat for Internal Affairs (NKDV).[42] On the other hand, we could read against allegorical convention, finding in the hens' disobedience (and the sovereignty over their own bodies it implies) a fantastic and crystalline example of the "history of animal resistance" documented by the historian of animal labor Jason Hribal.[43] We could even insist that the animals remain animals, as even McHugh does when she recognizes that of course many dogs have been themselves made into violent agents of the state; in which case, the failure to address the coercion of canine labor in that role is a "gaping hole in the plot" of animal liberation in *Animal Farm*: these "dogs remain dogs, serving not as extensions of anyone's ego."[44]

However, the problem with insisting too firmly on either of these interpretations is that they both equally obscure the particular kind of zoontological story that is at work in *Animal Farm* precisely *because* of the double-voiced nature of its figurative fictional language. Put simply, this is a story that can be told because, like the complexity of metaphorical meaning itself, the world is full of surprising and unexpected equivalences, similarities, and solidarities across and athwart different experiences of life, irrespective of species. McHugh gestures toward this, I think, when arguing that in *Animal Farm* "the story [of the dogs] builds in limits to both metaphorical and anthropomorphic projection."[45] Indeed, if we do find Stalinist henchmen to be the "attack dogs" allegorized in these attacks by dogs, we should thereby recognize the more-than-human indeterminacy of metaphor and remember that the derivation of the term "henchman" lies in the Old English word "hengest" meaning male horse or gelding, and so a henchman is a horseman, someone to accompany a monarch or other nobleman on horseback.[46] Moreover, whether or not there is any firm evidence to show that Orwell knew about the precise context, Napoleon's commandeering a litter of puppies and instrumentalizing them as agents of the state certainly bespeaks the contemporaneous work to develop a Russian military dog breed from the 1920s onward.[47] In this case, then, we find that the zoontological indeterminacy of animal allegory – the core of *Animal Farm*'s animal form – allows it to characterize state repression in a violent form of life lived by henchmen and attack dogs alike.

To redouble the point, let me highlight one final facet of such animal form by returning to those egg-destroying Black Minorca pullets, because the indeterminacy of their figural meaning also allows them to instantiate a remarkable zoontology of Soviet collectivization. Ironically enough, the point is suggested in a more literal fashion by Trotsky himself in 1936:

> Collectivization appeared to the peasant primarily in the form of an expropriation of all his belongings. They collectivized not only horses, cows, sheep, pigs, *but even new-born chickens*. They "dekulakized," as one foreign observer wrote, "down to the felt shoes, which they dragged from the feet of little children." As a result there was an epidemic selling of cattle for a song by the peasants, or a slaughter of cattle for meat and hides.[48]

What this startling context allows us to see is that the hens' destruction of their eggs is not simply a symbolic trope in which the behavior of farm animals allegorizes civil disobedience in a human political realm; rather, it is a complex and ambivalent metonymic portrayal of acts of violence in which farmed animals themselves were quite central. And yet the point of such eye-opening consonances across different lived experiences in these particular historical phenomena is not – to reiterate – that *Animal Farm* really is a story of nonhuman animal life. For reading it in that way would mean looking past the haunting experiential connections drawn by Trotsky in this moment between newborn chicks and shoeless children, and erroneously generalizing across the quite different lived experiences of collectivized chickens and slaughtered cows (not to mention the peasant-owned sheep whose wool made possible the existence of those felt shoes). Yet these are the animal lives that indeed come into existence within the text's meaningful literary zoontology of a more-than-human Soviet history.

The animal form of *Animal Farm*, then, poses challenging questions for literary animal studies. How might we interpret the zoontologies – the shared and shareable stories of animal life – that literary texts bring into being, and how, by retelling them, might we perpetuate and proliferate them in our analyses? Can we read in ways that do not eradicate, but instead recreate and give form to the lives that such stories narrate? To approach literary texts as a set of zoontologies, as I have suggested we should, is to understand contemporary storytelling by investing little interpretive faith in ideas about species and species difference or in hard-and-fast distinctions between zones of being. In particular, it is to resist the way that such ideas imply that the lives and experiences of humans and animals should not be collocated together. Such an approach allows us instead to see how the animal form of contemporary literature configures *together* what are normally and normatively understood as essentially different "kinds" of living and being: human and animal, species and individual, speculative and actual, aesthetic and real. As such, it is one way that literary reading might (as it should) take us beyond the human-animal divide.

Notes

1 Suzanne Langer, *Problems of Art: Ten Philosophical Lectures* (New York: Scribner's, 1957), 45.
2 I write "so-called" only here but intend it to condition every other usage of a term designating a species.
3 Clarice Lispector, "The Hen," trans. Elizabeth Bishop, *Kenyon Review* 26 (1964), 507–9, 509.
4 See further Tom Tyler, *Game: Animals, Video Games, and Humanity* (Minneapolis: University of Minnesota Press, 2022), 137.
5 Matthew Calarco, *Beyond the Anthropological Difference* (Cambridge: Cambridge University Press, 2018), 42–6.
6 Cary Wolfe (ed.), *Zoontologies: The Question of the Animal* (Minneapolis: University of Minnesota Press, 2003), xiii.
7 See further Jamie Lorimer, "Multinatural Geographies for the Anthropocene," *Progress in Human Geography* 36 (2012), 593–612.
8 See further Cary Wolfe, "Human Advocacy and the Humanities: The Very Idea," in Michael Lundblad and Marianne DeKoven (eds.), *Species Matters: Humane Advocacy and Cultural Theory* (New York: Columbia University Press, 2011), 27–48.
9 See Wolfe, *Zoontologies*.
10 For an introduction to this "biopolitical" work, see Dinesh Joseph Wadiwel, "Biopolitics," in Lori Gruen (ed.), *Critical Terms for Animal Studies* (Chicago: University of Chicago Press, 2018), 79–98.

11 See Jacques Derrida, "The Animal That Therefore I Am," *Critical Inquiry* 28 (2002), 369–418.

12 Cary Wolfe, *Before the Law: Humans and Other Animals in a Biopolitical Frame* (Chicago: University of Chicago Press, 2011), 83.

13 Eduardo Kohn, "Anthropology of Ontologies," *Annual Review of Anthropology* 44 (2015), 311–27.

14 Eduardo Viveiros de Castro, "Cosmological Deixis and Amerindian Perspectivism," *Journal of the Royal Anthropological Institute* 4 (1998), 469–88, 477.

15 Ibid., 477–8.

16 Kohn, "Anthropology," 312.

17 David Herman, *Narratology beyond the Human* (Oxford: Oxford University Press, 2018), 335.

18 David Herman, "Experimental Writing as Autoethnography: Thalia Field's Decentered Stories of Personhood," *Transpositiones* 1 (2022), 15–32, 25, 15.

19 Ibid., 16.

20 This idea is debunked by Una Chaudhuri in *Animal Acts: Performing Species Today* (Ann Arbor: University of Michigan Press, 2014), 7.

21 See also Herman, *Narratology*, 5.

22 Clifford Geertz, *The Interpretation of Cultures* (London: Fontana, 1993), 5.

23 Josephine Donovan, *The Aesthetics of Care* (London: Bloomsbury, 2016), 45.

24 Ibid., 45–50, which draw on Carol Adams's idea of the absent referent; see also John Simons, *Animal Rights and the Politics of Literary Representation* (London: Palgrave 2002), 85–115.

25 I. A. Richards, *The Philosophy of Rhetoric* (London: Oxford University Press, 1936), 100. For further complications of animal metaphor, see Mario Ortiz-Robles, *Literature and Animal Studies* (London: Routledge, 2016), 16–18.

26 Geertz, *Interpretation*, 444.

27 Ibid., 447–8.

28 Ibid., 448.

29 Sean Meighoo, "The Function of HumAnimAllegory," *Humanities* 6.2 (2017), doi:10.3390/h6010002.

30 Susan McHugh, "*Animal Farm*'s Lessons for Literary Animal Studies," *Humanimalia* 1.1 (2009), 25–39, 24–5.

31 George Orwell, "Preface to the Ukrainian Edition of *Animal Farm*" (1947), www.orwellfoundation.com/the-orwell-foundation/orwell/books-by-orwell/animal-farm/preface-to-the-ukrainian-edition-of-animal-farm-by-george-orwell/.

32 Helen Tiffin, "Pigs, People and Pigoons," in Philip Armstrong and Laurence Simmons (eds.), *Knowing Animals* (Leiden: Brill, 2007), 254, 252.

33 McHugh, "*Animal Farm*'s Lessons," 28.

34 Ibid.

35 Orwell, "Preface."

36 McHugh, "*Animal Farm*'s Lessons," 28.

37 See, for instance, Simons, *Animal Rights*, 86.

38 See Ortiz-Robles, *Literature*, 1–25.

39 George Orwell, *Animal Farm* (Harmondsworth: Penguin, 1951), 66–7.

40 This little moment, encapsulating how the more-than-human political agencies that shape farmed chickens' lives and deaths also include the political management of disease, attests to a whole complicated world of biopolitical control of animal life. Avian influenza is a compelling contemporary galline case in point, on which, see Natalie Porter, *Viral Economies: Bird Flu Experiments in Vietnam* (Chicago: University of Chicago Press, 2019).

41 Orwell, *Animal*, 73.

42 Donald Rayfield, *Stalin and His Hangmen: An Authoritative Portrait of a Tyrant and Those Who Served Him* (London: Viking, 2004).

43 See *Fear of the Animal Planet: the Hidden History of Animal Resistance* (Petrolia: Counterpunch, 2010).

44 McHugh, "*Animal Farm's* Lessons," 29.

45 Ibid., 182.

46 *Oxford English Dictionary*, "henchman."

47 See Xenia Cherkaev and Elina Tipikina, "Interspecies Affection and Military Aims: Was There a Totalitarian Dog?," *Environmental Humanities* 10.1 (2018), 20–39.

48 Leon Trotsky, *Revolution Betrayed*, trans. Max Eastman (Newburyport: Dover, 2012), 30 (my emphasis). For corroboration, see C. J. Storella and A. K. Sokolov (eds.), *The Voice of the People: Letters from the Soviet Village, 1918–1932* (New Haven, CT: Yale University Press, 2013), 355; and J. Arch Getty and Oleg V. Naumov, *The Road to Terror: Stalin and the Self-Destruction of the Bolsheviks, 1932–1939* (New Haven, CT: Yale University Press, 2010), 30.

PART II

Contexts and Controversies

CHAPTER 8

Religion
Reformation Christianity and Biblical Rhetoric
Karen L. Edwards

Early modern Protestants who were engaged in religious controversy regularly called each other by the names of animals. Dogs and curs, swine, beasts, locusts, vipers, vermin, foxes, wolves – all of these names, and others, were wielded against opponents in the polemical writing that poured from England's printing presses in the century after Reformation. This essay is concerned with how the standard practice of employing animal names against opponents affected their controversial exchanges. The practice, at least in formal political debate, is no longer acceptable. We need to ask why it was acceptable in the early modern period. How did the practice arise? What rhetorical benefits were gained, or assumed to be gained, from calling an opponent by the name of an animal? In the century during which the practice flourished, the function and even the choice of rhetorical animals shifted as political conditions changed. In this essay I will analyze representative controversial pieces from the early Reformation, the Elizabethan era, and the early Stuart period to consider the nature and function of their animal epithets, before turning in conclusion to two larger questions raised by the analysis: What political and religious consequences arose from the practice of using animal names for religious-political opponents? And what does it tell us about the era's attitude toward actual animals?

It is impossible to say where and how human beings began to use animal metaphors for themselves and other human beings; such metaphors are present in the earliest literature extant. John Berger suggests that human animals learned to think by comparing themselves to nonhuman animals, asking what they had in common and what distinguished them from each other.[1] It is, however, relatively easy to locate a specific and authoritative source for the use of animal metaphors in the sixteenth and seventeenth centuries. The Bible, translated into English by early reformers, swiftly became England's central cultural text and remained so for hundreds of years.[2] Those whom the Bible portrays as the enemies of God and of God's people are compared to predatory or degraded carnivores, venomous reptiles, and noxious insects. In the Old Testament, those who attack the faithful are represented as fierce animals.[3] In the New Testament, Christians animalize false prophets, hypocrites, and enemies who persecute them for their faith.[4]

Such biblical name-calling was taken as a model and a justification by religious controversialists as the Reformation unfolded in England. Until the end of the sixteenth century, most of their animal epithets were copied from the Bible, a practice having many rhetorical advantages. Most importantly, writers could rely on their readers to know the entire passage or context from which an animal epithet was taken. The Bible provided a sort of cultural code for the population: readers' thorough familiarity with it meant that a single word was enough to evoke a web of biblical associations. Thus when clergy of the English Church call puritans "vipers," they know that readers will immediately call to mind Matthew 3.7, in which Jesus condemns hypocritical Pharisees as a "generation of vipers." Moreover, vipers populate the desolate landscape prophesied by Isaiah, if God's people disobey him.[5] There may also be in "vipers" a subdued allusion to the serpent that tempts Eve in Genesis 3, although the serpent's precise species was a vexed issue for early modern biblical commentators.[6]

The Bible not only provided a supply of animals for rhetorical use. Repeating the names of scriptural animals also clothed the words of a controversialist in biblical authority. These animals played an important role in the rhetorical power struggles of the Reformation's first decades, as writers pitted their biblical animals against those of other writers.[7] In response to the claims of established churchmen that dissenters were hypocritical vipers, dissenters hurled back the charge that the clergy were wolves in sheep's clothing, a charge based on Jesus' warning: "Beware of false prophets which come to you in sheepes clothing, but inwardly they are ravening wolves" (Matthew 7.15).[8] The adjective "ravening," which occurs in early modern Bibles from Tyndale's New Testament to the King James Version, derives from the verb "raven," meaning to eat greedily and voraciously.[9] The verb could also mean to plunder or maraud, or to carry off as prey, implications that darken "ravening" even further with notions of greed and theft.[10] Moreover, to Jesus' words, reformers could add Paul's warning to the Christians at Ephesus: "Take heed therefore unto your selves, & to all the flocke, over the which the holy Ghost hath made you overseers, to feed the Church of God, which he hath purchased with his own blood. For I know this, that after my departing shall grievous wolves enter in among you, not sparing the flocke" (Acts 20.28–9). Paul's words are rich in oppositions – between feeding the flock and devouring it, between gentle innocence and cruel ferocity – allowing reformers to characterize themselves (the flock) even as they denounce their enemies (the wolves).

The meaning conferred on animals by the Bible was amplified even further by two influential books from late antiquity. Both attempted to fuse the representations of animals in the Bible with their representations in classical literature and ancient pagan lore. The first of these works, *Physiologus*, was composed in Greek between the second and fourth centuries AD. The title means "the natural philosopher"; the book is composed of what this anonymous author teaches about animals (and a few trees and stones). The viper entry, after quoting Jesus' condemnation of the Pharisees, states that at copulation the female viper bites off the head of the male, and when her offspring are born, they avenge their father by bursting through the mother's entrails and killing her.[11] This piece of lore, which has no basis in scripture (or zoology), lies behind the viper insult aimed by established clergy at those who were demanding further reform of the Church. The implication is that ungrateful, seditious reformers are intent on tearing through the bowels of their mother church and destroying her. There is no entry for the wolf in *Physiologus*, but the creature has a striking entry in the second work, a work that influenced the rhetorical deployment of early modern animals perhaps more than any other.

The Etymologies of Isidore, Bishop of Seville, has been called "an encyclopedia [. . .] [a] compendium of much of the essential learning of the ancient Greco-Roman and early Christian worlds."[12] Written in Latin in the early seventh century, the book is based on the assumption that a word's origins reveal its true meaning. Isidore devotes book 12 (out of twenty) to animals. In his entry on the viper he remarks: it is "so named because it is 'born through force' (*vi parere*) [violence + to bring forth]."[13] Accordingly, in his retelling of the story of the murderous female and her matricidal offspring, Isidore gives particular emphasis to the vicious gnawing of the young vipers as they burst out of their mother's body. The violence he attributes to them is present in the medieval bestiary tradition, which developed from *The Etymologies*, or at least from the assumptions that govern it. Thus in the twelfth-century bestiary translated by T. H. White, the viper is said to be so named "because it brings forth in violence."[14] When sixteenth-century conformists called dissenters a brood of vipers, they imply that those who would claim to reform the Church are raging, ungovernable, and utterly destructive, a danger to the civilized nation itself.

Of the wolf, Isidore declares that the name *lupus* came into Latin through its Greek name (*lykos*), which signifies that it slaughters everything it sees in an enraged frenzy. Or perhaps, Isidore admits, the name is a corruption of *leopos*, which combines *leo* (lion) and *pes* (paws), because the lion's paws are so strong that whatever it steps on, it kills. The point, he continues, is that the wolf "is a violent beast, eager for gore."[15] When sixteenth-century reformers called bishops of the English Church "wolves," they are thus accusing them of profoundly perverting their Christian calling. Instead of feeding the sheep as a shepherd, bishops devour the sheep in their bloodthirsty greed. The implication here is that in their resistance to reforming the Church, bishops are motivated not by love of their flock but by an unchristian love of wealth and worldly power, which they are ready to defend by violently persecuting anyone who threatens their position.

Metaphorical wolves and vipers confront each other in two well-known pamphlets from the earliest years of the English Reformation. In 1529, as Henry VIII contemplated assuming supremacy over the English Church and its vast properties, a fiercely satirical, anticlerical, unlicensed pamphlet appeared. Written by the reformer Simon Fish, *A Supplicacyon for the Beggers* was boldly addressed to the king and begins with a stark warning: England's genuine beggars, the "nedy, impotent, blinde, lame, and sike, that live onely by almesse," are dying of hunger because "counterfeit holy, and ydell beggers and vacabundes" – by which Fish means bishops, priests, monks, and friars – soak up the kingdom's money, which they demand in return for praying to release souls from Purgatory.[16] Yet there is no biblical authority for Purgatory, Fish declares; Purgatory is a fiction designed solely to raise money. This means, he continues, that the clergy are "not the herdes [i.e., shepherds], but the ravenous wolves going in herdes [shepherds'] clothing devouring the flocke."[17] Monks, mendicants, and priests are hypocrites, Fish charges, who murder the souls of their parishioners for material gain. Their crimes are thus both spiritual and economic, an accusation Fish renders with dramatic efficiency by invoking two further biblical animals. The Greeks would never have taken Troy, Fish asserts, "if they had had at home such an idell sort of cormorauntes to finde," nor would the Turk (i.e., Suleiman I) have conquered so much of Christendom "if he had yn his empire suche a sort of locusts to devoure his substaunce."[18] Cormorants are among the unclean birds forbidden as food at Deuteronomy 14.17. Regarded as insatiable devourers of fish, they represent the symbolic opposite of Jesus and his disciples, salvific fishers of men. Locusts are notable for devouring the green shoots of the earth (as at Nahum 3.15); more sinister still, scorpion-like locusts emerge from the smoke of the Bottomless Pit at Revelation 9.2 to torment the godly. While cormorants were a familiar (if misunderstood) sight in early modern England, wolves had become extinct long before the Reformation, and locusts had never ravaged the English countryside. But Fish is not interested in what we would today think of as a naturalistic understanding of such creatures. Rather, he is drawing on deeply entrenched lore about wolves, cormorants, and locusts to make concrete his argument that the clergy of the Church in England are a "ravenous cruell and insatiabill generacion."[19]

Fish's sixteen-page pamphlet provoked anger among Church authorities, and Thomas More was ordered to answer it. The rhetorical problem he faced was complicated. To deny that clergy are locusts, cormorants, or wolves would mean repeating Fish's terms – and also sounding foolishly literal. More ignores Fish's animal epithets and instead guides readers into seeing Fish as a kind of serpent – or, rather, *the* serpent. Narrated by the pitiful souls suffering in Purgatory, *The Supplycacyon of Soulys* presents Fish as one who leads his readers into ignoring the terrible plight of the departed. Fish is not directly called a serpent or a viper; readers are allowed to draw that conclusion themselves, as the souls in Purgatory warn readers about "hys venymous wrytynge."[20] The book is so "contrived" that "by the secrete inwarde wurkynge of the devyll that holpe [helped] to devyse yt / a simple reder might by delyte in the redyng be dedely [deadly] corrupted and venemed."[21] More's readers would not miss the implication of these words. Fish is a tempter, for subtlety is the chief characteristic of the serpent of Genesis, "more subtill than any beast of the fielde, which the Lord God had made" (3.1).

As the unsettled political and religious situation that marked the early Reformation gave way to the apparent stability of Elizabeth's reign, the controversy between dissenters and conformists changed in character. For all her Protestant credentials, Elizabeth I would not, it had become clear, accept the reforms that puritans had been advocating for decades. The animals that appear in controversial tracts during her reign reflect the hardening of the political-religious situation – intransigence on the part of established clergy, frustration on the part of puritans. The wolf still appears in puritan tracts, the viper, in conformist tracts. But with increasing regularity, as angry puritans call attention to the poor quality of the clergy of the English Church, "beasts" and "dumb dogs" begin to appear in their writing, the latter sometimes signaled simply by the repeated use of "dumb" or by allusions to dogs and curs. Behind this terminology lies the prophet's condemnation of Israel's failed leaders at Isaiah 56.10–11:

> 10 His watchmen *are* blinde: they *are* all ignorant, they *are* all dumbe dogs, they cannot barke; sleeping, lying downe, loving to slumber.

> 11 Yea they *are* greedy dogges *which* can never have ynough and they *are* shepheards *that* cannot understand: they all looke to their owne way, every one for his gaine, from his quarter.

Although dogs were valued as hunters and companions in early modern Europe, they were regarded as shameless, filthy, and unreliable in the Ancient Middle East. A watchdog that does not bark cannot protect the flock, leaving the sheep vulnerable to the wolf's ferocity. The fact that the dumbness of these dogs may result from their "loving to slumber" frequently leads nonconformists to employ the phrase "idoll shepheards" in combination with "dumb dogs." "Idoll" neatly captures the danger represented by unfit ministers: their idleness allows idolatry (i.e., papistical superstition) to flourish unchecked in the people. Not to preach is thus tantamount to soul murder.

The epithet "beasts" reflects another aspect of what puritans regard as the inadequacy of conformist ministers: their worldly and material preoccupations. The term implies that, like beasts, such ministers cater only to the needs of their bodies, caring nothing for their souls or the souls of their congregation. "Beast," moreover, hints at the kinship of such worldly clerics to the Beast of the Apocalypse: "And I stood upon the sand of the sea: and saw a beast rise up out of the sea, having seven heads, and ten hornes, and upon his hornes ten crownes, and upon his heads, the name of blasphemie" (Revelation 13.1). The Beast is generally regarded as a manifestation of Antichrist, interpreted by many Protestants as the papacy. Through their use of "beast," that is, puritan controversialists reinforce their argument that conformists are moving ever closer to Catholicism.

Church authorities, who are confident of Elizabeth's support and consequently wield political power with growing confidence, charge puritans with sedition as well as hypocrisy. They lead the people astray, declare the prelates; they are the "false prophets" about whom Paul warns early Christians: "Beloved, beleeve not every spirit, but trie [test] the spirits, whether they are of God: because many false prophets are gone out into the world" (1 John 4.1). Conformists represent false prophets not only as venomous serpents but also as animals given to predatory violence. Indeed, lists of such noxious animals become a feature of conformist polemics, as if metaphoric multiplicity conveys the threat of what the bishops see as an ever-increasing number of nonconformists.

The new rhetorical situation is demonstrated with particular clarity in one of the most notorious exchanges of the Elizabethan period, that between an unidentified puritan and a bishop of the Church of England. When a series of pamphlets appeared between 1588 and 1589 written by one Martin Marprelate, church authorities were outraged by the audacious nature of the writing, which failed to adhere to what had hitherto been the conventions of controversial exchange. The author's name is clearly a pseudonym: "Martin" alludes to Martin Luther; "Marprelate" is composed of *mar* + *prelate*, a clear indication of the writer's antagonism toward bishops. The six Marprelate pamphlets were printed without license; even worse, in the eyes of the Church, were their satirical, disrespectful tone and their detailed accounts of the peccadillos and misdeeds of individual clerics. Chief among the objects of Martin's ridicule is the uneducated state of the clergy. Their veniality, ignorance, and lack of learning make them wholly unfit to feed the flock, he argues, an attitude he conveys even on the title page of the first tract, known as the *Epistle*. The book has been "compiled," announces the title page, "for the behoof and overthrow of the Parsons, Fyckers, and Currats, that have learnt their catechisms, and are past grace."[22] Leaving aside the insulting wordplay involved in "Fyckers," "behoof" suggests an animal's foot or possibly the Devil's cloven hooves, and the term "Currats" combines *cur* + *rats*.[23] As the tracts' modern editor observes, "past grace" means both that Church of England clergy "have fulfilled the requirements of a degree" but also that they are "'beyond' grace or redemption."[24]

Martin gleefully names and exposes the inadequacies and shortcomings of several clerics. A favorite target of his satire is John Aylmer, Bishop of London. "Who made the porter of his gate a dumb minister?" asks Martin and answers his own question: "Dumb John of London."[25] By "the porter of his gate" Martin refers to Aylmer's appointment of "an unlearned and (literally) purblind porter to serve a congregation in Paddington" because, maintained Aylmer, the parish was too poor to pay for a better minister.[26] Martin provides a full list of Aylmer's other "carnal" activities, as, for instance, his failure to honor the Sabbath: "Who goeth to bowls upon the Sabbath?" Martin asks. The answer is, again, "Dumb dunstical John of good London hath done all this."[27] Later, Martin sheds his satirical tone and pleads with those in power: "may it please you to let the gospel have a free course, and restore unto their former liberty in preaching all the preachers that you have put to silence."[28] There is an implied contract here between dumb (conformist) preachers and silenced (puritan) preachers. In an attack on another of his favorite targets, Martin says of Bishop Thomas Cooper that he is "like a monstrous hypocrite, for he is a very duns, not able to defend an argument, but till he come to the pinch, he will cog [cheat] and face it out, for his face is made of seasoned wainscot, and will lie as fast as a dog can trot."[29] The concluding simile – one of several irreverent sayings involving dogs in the *Epistle* – reinforces the tract's insistence on Church of England ministers as dumb dogs.[30] The frequent pairing of "dumb" and "duns" indicates that the dumbness of conformist clergy is not a literal dumbness. Rather, being dumb means preaching sermons that provide no spiritual nourishment, or reading a Bible passage to the congregation without offering a commentary on it, a practice that puritans call "bare" reading. "Dumb," in short, means vacuous speaking. Hence Martin refers to the Archbishop of Canterbury as "my Lord of Cant."[31]

In the face of the *Epistle*'s revelation of the clergy's worldliness, greed, and ignorance, Martin professes himself astonished that the Archbishop can assure the Queen that the Church of England is flourishing. "Is it any marvel," Martin demands,

> that we have so many swine, dumb dogs, nonresidents with their journey-men the hedge priests, so many lewd livers, as thieves, murderers, adul-terers, drunkards, cormorants, rascals, so many ignorant and atheistical dolts, so many covetous popish bishops in our ministry and so many and so monstrous corruptions in our church, and yet likely to have no redress?[32]

Martin thus summarizes what the rest of his tract has demonstrated. The animal names here ("swine," "dumb dogs," "cormorants") have the weight of Martin's evidence behind them. What is most notable about this list may be the fact that swine, dumb dogs, and cormorants are on a rhetorical level with drunkards, dolts, and nonresidents, as if the figurative status of the animals has been lost.

The listing or accumulation of epithets is not a technique used regularly by puritan controversialists. However, perhaps suggested by the passage above, the technique is employed to considerable effect by Bishop Richard Bancroft in his (first) answer to Martin, a sermon delivered at Paul's Cross in February 1589. The gist of Bancroft's argument is that those who criticize the "unreformed" English Church are heretics, sectaries, schis-matics, and hypocrites. They are, in short, the false prophets about whom Paul warns at 1 John 4.1. Their sole aim, Bancroft charges, is to create dissatisfaction with the established order in the Church so that they themselves can take control of it and its wealth. To accomplish their purpose, they present themselves as "humble and lowlie in outward shew," interested only in spiritual matters, but in fact they are "verie contentious and unquiet, doting about questions and strife of words: wherof cometh envy, strife, railings, and evill furnishings."[33] Under the pretense of instructing their flock in the reading of scripture, they undermine accepted interpretations of the Bible, or as Bancroft puts it: "They murder the Scriptures to serve their owne purpose."[34] Even worse, in Bancroft's opinion, is their arrogant contempt for the established clergy. Their condemnation of those whom they ought to respect – and to whose understanding of scripture they ought to defer – encourages the people to interpret the Bible for themselves, which leads to contention in the church and in the nation.

Bancroft represents these false prophets as fearsome animals, exotic beings, and loathsome diseases. Puritans can be compared, he announces,

> to the mermaids bicause they hide their errours under their counterfeit and faire speeches: to *Helena*, of Greece, for that they move as great contention in the church as she did troubles betwixt the Grecians and the Troians: to the diseases called the leprosie and the cankar, in that their corruption taketh deepe roote and spreadeth so farre: to a serpent that is lapped up together, bicause they have many windings and contradictions: to the fish named a Cuttle, for that they infect men with their blacke and slanderous calumniations: to snakes or adders, the poison of aspes being under their lips: to the viper, bicause they regarded not to wound & destroie their mother the church: to tigers and lions, for that they are verie cruell and fierce: and to diverse other such things as ought to make them odious to all that love the truth.[35]

The passage's cumulative effect relies not only on the number of its similes but also on the variety of sources from which they come. Most of these sources are secular. The treacherously deceitful mermaid, matricidal viper, and ferocious tiger are creatures about which everyone has heard but which no one (in England) has seen. The story of Helen is inherited from classical literature. Although the cuttlefish is a familiar species to Europeans, the function of its "ink," not well understood at the time, is declared here to infect and contaminate. The serpent and its windings may be derived from direct observation, as may "the cankar," the name for any devouring sore. Of Bancroft's remaining similes, leprosy and lions have a presence in the Bible, but knowledge about them is available through other routes. Only asps (lumped here with snakes and adders) are provided with a recognizably biblical context: "the poyson of Aspes is under their lippes" (Romans 3.13).

Bancroft briefly returns to the winding serpent later in his sermon: "though (as the serpent before mentioned) they [i.e., puritans] have many implications and turnings, yet they have always means and waies to shift for themselves."[36] But he does not develop the simile or any of the others in his initial list. He merely sketches in the resemblance between animals and puritans. At other points in the sermon, that resemblance is suggested by the attribution of a nonspecific animality to his opponents. It is a technique he may have learned from Thomas More, who refers to venom without calling Fish and his cohorts vipers. Bancroft, too, refers to puritans' venom,[37] but he most strikingly implies animality with his use of "pray," that is, "prey." Puritans argue that ministers should take a vow of poverty, he claims, "to the intent that they [themselves] might obtain the pray."[38] Their argument, he means, is greedily self-interested; they wish to obtain the Church's wealth for themselves. Addressing them directly, Bancroft urges them to cease criticizing "the present governement of the Church" unless you are "willing and readie to deliver out of your hands such spoiles and praies thereof, as you have alreadie."[39] At the conclusion of his sermon, Bancroft warns readers once again of the hypocrisy of those who "exclaime against the pride of B[isho]p[s]": such exclaimers, "the better to creep into your harts," are merely "pretend[ing] great humilitie."[40] "Creep" is a verb consistently associated in the early modern period with insects and reptiles and small, verminous mammals. The unspecified nature of the animals arguably makes Bancroft's portrait more sinister by allowing readers' imaginations to flourish.

While both Bancroft and Martin attach demeaning animal names or animal behavior to their opponents, they derive their rhetorical animals from different sources and put them to different uses. Martin's use of "dumb dogs" and "beasts" is intimately related to his central argument, that clergy of the Church of England are unqualified to be the spiritual shepherds of the flock. His animal names draw their meaning from relevant passages in the Bible, demonstrating that the problem he perceives is one that the Bible itself recognizes. Bancroft's animal names draw their meaning from the surrounding culture, both secular and religious. He does not directly answer Martin's arguments. Rather, his comparison of puritans to animals aims to demolish the character and motives of those who criticize the government of the Church, to paint them as dangerous enemies of the established order. Against Martin's biting satire, wittily irreverent tone, and biblical allusiveness, Bancroft opposes cultural commonplaces that evoke superstition, fear, misogyny, and disgust.

Almost forty years of polemical quiescence followed the Marprelate scandal, but in the early years of Charles I's reign, religious hostilities broke out again. In 1629, the radical Scottish reformer Alexander Leighton published *An Appeal to the Parliament; or, Sions Plea against the Prelacie*, a lengthy and virulent attack on Arminian bishops.[41] Furious church authorities likened it to the Marprelate Tracts. In at least one respect, however, *Sions Plea* (as the book came to be known) is closer to Bancroft's sermon: the animal epithets that fill the tract are drawn from an extraordinary range of sources. Leighton is particularly fond of comparing the bishops to raptors and other profane birds. Bishops' harassment of nonconformists, he declares in his preface, is like the *"terrible noyse"* that bitterns make *"in their hollowe canes."*[42] Naturalists describe the bird's call as a "strange, even unearthly" "boom" that was "long steeped in mystery and inspired fear."[43] In the King James Bible, the bittern is among the creatures that will haunt the ruined landscape of Israel's enemies, as foretold by Isaiah (34.11).[44] But Leighton's chief source for his episcopal bitterns is an emblem book by Henry Peacham, *Minerva Britanna* (1612). In an emblem entitled *"In timidos et iactantes"* (Among the faint-hearted and the boastful), the bittern with its booming call is described as an apt symbol for two kinds of "base" people: the coward, who "will with words affright" but will not stay to face "true Valor," and "the proude vaine-glorious wight," who makes "a goodly show / Of wit, or wealth, when it is nothing so."[45] Leighton's point is that bishops do not have the courage or acuity to respond to nonconformist arguments; instead, they use their high position to bully and intimidate – and punish – all who disagree with them.

Leighton draws again on familiar but sinister birds as he asks how there can be any comfort to the people, or honor to Parliament, or blessings from God "To have the *Doves* thus beaten and the *Ravens* & *Pye-Maggotts* to prey upon the State."[46] Leighton means that the bishops, because of their own papist proclivities, allow Catholics (ravens and magpies) to worship openly, in defiance of the law, while they enforce harsh measures against puritans (doves). He returns to rapacious birds later in *Sions Plea*, demanding that Parliament end the rich remuneration offered to bishops. It is the desire for wealth rather than a true spiritual calling that attracts them to the prelacy: "take away the *Carion*," he proclaims, "and the *Kites* will be gone."[47] Kites have little biblical resonance; in the King James Version, they are mentioned only in lists of prohibited food (as at Deuteronomy 14.13). Their exploits as petty thieves and scavengers of rubbish, however, were thoroughly familiar to residents of early modern cities.[48] Ravens appear several times in the Bible, once as nurturers of the prophet Elijah (1 Kings 17.2–16). But by pairing them with magpies (which do not appear in the Bible) and assigning the verb "prey" to both of them, Leighton emphasizes the common belief that the two species are ominous. Ravens were known to peck out the eyes and strip the flesh from corpses hanging from gibbets; magpies were thought to bring bad luck, which might be warded off by uttering charms.

Leighton does not confine himself to foul fowls in his portrait of the bishops as rapacious devourers. To make his point that the great number of established clergy consumes the wealth of the nation, he likens them to insects (and sharks, to which I will return). Simon Fish calls them locusts; Leighton calls them by the names of more familiar insects, notable for their reproductive success and their destructiveness. Bishops and the minor clergy "devour the Kings wealth," Leighton declares; "what a numberless number of *Mothes*, drones, and *Caterpillers*, they keepe in their Cathedrall and Collegiate Churches, we are not able to expresse. Some have summed them up to the number of 22000. Or there about, what a huge deal of meanes will so many *Sharks* devoure."[49] He repeats the image several pages later, calling established clergy "the *mothes hornetts & Caterpillars* of the state."[50] The capacity of moths and caterpillars to destroy earthly treasures is briefly mentioned in the Bible; drones and hornets do not appear at all. What matters in Leighton's metaphors is the theme of widespread devastation, a theme that culminates in "sharks." The name was relatively new, introduced when "a marveillous strange fish" was displayed in a London fish market in 1569, advertised on an illustrated broadsheet, and given the name "shark."[51] The rhetorical metamorphosis effected by Leighton is deft: the mouthparts of insects have been writ large in the new fish's jagged, tearing teeth.

With "sharks," Leighton introduces a new range of animal metaphors into *Sions Plea*, metaphors that merge the animal with the monster. It is true that monstrous apocalyptic animals such as the Beast, the locusts from the Bottomless Pit, and the Dragon have a presence in Leighton's book. But they are standard fare in puritan polemical tracts. Leighton reaches for monsters that are new to religious controversy. He compares bishops to "the Arabian monster Caccus, which sets all on fire with its breath, and yet lives like a salamander in the flame"; "Harpies, that is monstruous byrdes with maiden visages, but ravenous tallants, leaving an ill smell upon all that they touch"; and (several times) a "Hydraes head."[52] These monstrous creatures are drawn from classical literature, as if Leighton's fury and frustration have outstripped the rhetorical resources that the Bible can offer. Gone is the careful argumentative approach of his Tudor predecessors, intent on persuading readers of the righteousness of their case for reform. What replaces that approach is a spewing out of metaphors drawn from the furthest and darkest reaches of the imagination. Bancroft's metaphors aim to demonstrate the traitorous sedition of nonconformists; Leighton's metaphors aim to represent a horrifying new political and religious reality in which Church courts (operating without oversight from Parliament) are used by tyrannical and nominally Protestant bishops to persecute true Protestants.

Responses to *Sions Plea* were immediate and plentiful. But the most dramatic response was the one imprinted on Leighton's body. Found guilty of sedition in the Court of Star Chamber in 1634, he was fined and imprisoned in the Fleet, pilloried, and whipped; one of his ears was cut off; his nose was slit; and his cheek was branded with the letters SS (standing for Sower of Sedition). In a poem probably written while he was in prison, Leighton reflects on his mutilated body:

> Begoard in bloud of cruell p[relates] scourge
> Dismemberd nose, eares, stigmatized, to urge
> Me to despaire of earths and heavens grace.
> That to the sunne I nere might showe my face.
> A dismal, savage spectacle I rise
> An act unparalleled to eternize. [...]
> I both condemned and execrated stand
> As the doung and offskouring of the land.
> A marke for men and angells to behold
> A gazing stocke become to younge and olde.[53]

I have become a spectacle horrifying to all who see me, Leighton mourns, and he understands his mutilation as a physical transformation into the monster that he is called by his enemies.

Historians agree that the causes of England's civil war were multiple, including political, economic, social, and religious factors, although there is little agreement about which of those causes is primary. But the role of rhetorical conflict and the increasing violence of its metaphors in the outbreak of war also deserves consideration. In the early decades of the Reformation, the practice of giving animal names to opponents belonged to what might be called a decorum of insult, in that it was controlled by biblical precedent. But with the growing division between conformists and nonconformists, the resources of early modern culture were rifled for the most frightening and grotesque animals with which to liken the enemy, and the bounds of convention – and of physical restraint – were broken.

The potential for violence that perhaps always lurks in the willingness to call human beings by the names of fierce animals was unleashed. Repeated name-calling seems to have blunted the perception of metaphoricity in early modern controversial writing, as indicated by the slippage between metaphoric and embodied animals in Martin's list: "swine, dumb dogs, nonresidents [. . .] adulterers, drunkards, cormorants, rascals." Becoming convinced that another human is an animal engenders and is engendered by disgust and fear, emotions that undermine the possibility of negotiation. On the contrary, disgust and fear encourage violence: that which is disgusting must be got rid of, and that which causes fear must be attacked before it attacks.

Let us ask, finally, what a willingness to deploy animal names as rhetorical pawns reveals about early modern attitudes toward animals. It is noticeable that the animals chosen for polemical purposes were, with a few exceptions, animals that either were or could be rendered unfamiliar. Wolves, tigers, vipers, and asps; harpies, hydras, and mermaids; locusts; probably sharks and lions – all of these were known almost exclusively by reputation or through literary representations.[54] Even those creatures that would have been familiar in daily life – caterpillars, moths, hornets, drones, bitterns, ravens, magpies, cormorants, cuttlefish, dogs – appear strange and sinister in the pages of controversial tracts. Insects are represented as swarming horribly in vast numbers; black-feathered birds, as portending disaster; dogs, as refusing to bark. What was known about them through everyday experience was not allowed to impinge on the exaggerated, fearsome, villainous roles they were assigned in polemical writing. What matters for purposes of early modern religious controversy was not the biological reality of the animals – although writers would not have thought about it in such terms – but the reactions stirred up by their names.

The ability to keep separate the characteristics of actual and rhetorical animals did not long outlast England's civil war. By the end of the seventeenth century, it was no longer acceptable in formal dispute to call opponents by the names of animals.[55] There are no doubt many and profound reasons for the change, but the most obvious is the triumph of the established political and religious order at the Restoration in 1660. Hope for reform of the Church of England once so passionately advocated by nonconformists was at an end, and vigorous religious controversy no longer claimed a central place in the nation's cultural life. Indeed, dissenters who argued too passionately for religious reform were accused of dangerous delusion, or "enthusiasm." But it is also possible to point to another development that affected the rhetorical deployment of animals. The emergence of the new natural philosophy between the sixteenth and seventeenth centuries advanced at different speeds in various branches of inquiry. Cosmography was one of the earliest to be affected by new ways of thinking about the natural world; zoology was one of the last.[56] Nonetheless, the distance between what observant naturalists were discovering about animals and what had been handed down about such animals from ancient sources and popular superstition was growing noticeably wider by the late sixteenth century. In the post-Restoration period, the distance between them became too great to bridge. The animals that once filled the pages of controversial literature had finally to be recognized as fictions and banished from political and religious writing that wished to be taken seriously as a quest for truth.

Notes

1 John Berger, *About Looking* (London: Writers and Readers, 1980), 4–5.
2 For a concise history of English translations of the Bible in this period, see Gerald Hammond, *The Making of the English Bible* (Manchester: Carcanet, 1982).
3 As, for instance, at 1 Sam. 17. 34–36; Psalm 22.13, 57.4, 58.6, 91.13.
4 As, for instance, at Matt. 7.15 (discussed below).
5 See Isa. 30.6 and 59.5.
6 On the species of serpent that tempted Eve, see Thomas Browne, *Pseudodoxia Epidemica* (1646), 2 vols., ed. Robin Robbins (Oxford: Clarendon, 1981), vol. 1, 539.
7 At the outset of the Reformation in England, controversy centered on whether the structure of the newly Protestant English Church was to be hierarchical and episcopal (a structure supported by Henry VIII and his Protestant successors) or presbyterian and quasi-democratic, with self-governing congregations. Because bishops played an integral role in the governing of the state – politics and religion being inextricable in the early modern period – criticism of the Church's episcopal structure could be, and was, interpreted as sedition. There was in fact a range of opinions about how the English Church should be governed, but for my purpose here it is fair to speak generally of nonconformists and conformists. Nonconformists go by many names, some of which I will use in this essay: the godly, the flock, presbyterians, puritans, hot Protestants, dissenters, and sectaries, among others. The same terminological variety does not exist for those whom I am calling conformists, that is, those who support the episcopal Church of England and its established clergy (whom opponents often simply call bishops or prelates). A caveat: "conformist" does not necessarily imply an active choice; undoubtedly many who conformed never considered *not* conforming.

8 I quote from the King James version in this essay. Although it was not published until 1611, its language, like that of other early modern English Bibles, is strongly indebted to William Tyndale's early sixteenth-century translation.

9 *OED*, "raven," v., 2a.

10 *OED*, "raven," v., 1a, 1b.

11 *Physiologus: A Medieval Book of Nature Lore*, trans. Michael J. Curley (Chicago: University of Chicago Press, 2009), 16.

12 Stephen A. Barney, W. J. Lewis, J. A. Beach, and Oliver Berghof, "Introduction," in Stephen A. Barney et al. (eds.), *The Etymologies of Isidore of Seville* (Cambridge: Cambridge University Press, 2006), 3.

13 Isidore, *The Etymologies of Isidore of Seville*, ed. Barney et al., 255.

14 T. H. White (ed. and trans.), *The Book of Beasts* (London: Jonathan Cape, 1954), 170.

15 Isidore, *The Etymologies*, 25.

16 Simon Fish, *A Supplicacyon for the Beggers* ([Antwerp?] 1529), fol. 1^v.

17 Ibid., fol. 1^v.

18 Ibid., fol. 3^r.

19 Ibid., fol. 2^v.

20 Thomas More, *The Supplycacyon of Soulys* (London, 1529), fol. ii^r.

21 Ibid., fol. ii^v.

22 *The Martin Marprelate Tracts: A Modernized and Annotated Edition*, ed. Joseph L. Black (Cambridge: Cambridge University Press, 2008), 5. Martin has never been certainly identified; see Black's Introduction at pp. xxxiv–xlvi for possible candidates.

23 For a discussion of "Fyckers," see *Martin Marprelate*, 211, n. 4.

24 *Martin Marprelate*, 211, n. 5.

25 Ibid., 21.

26 Ibid., 211, n. 96.

27 Ibid., 21.

28 Ibid., 27.

29 Ibid., 31.

30 See, for instance, a story about William Turner, Dean of Wells, whose dog snatched a bishop's four-cornered cap, mistaking it for a cheese cake, a story that satirizes ecclesiastical vestments (*Martin Marprelate*, 38).

31 *Martin Marprelate*, 30.

32 Ibid.

33 Richard Bancroft, *A Sermon Preached at Paules Crosse the 9. of Februarie . . . 1588* (London, 1589), 5.

34 Ibid., 11.

35 Ibid., 6, 68, 84.

36 Ibid., 65.

37 See, for instance, Bancroft, *A Sermon*, 30, 92.

38 Ibid., 28.

39 Ibid., 29.

40 Ibid., 93.

41 Arminian clergy emphasized ritual and formality in worship, including such material aids to worship as incense and candles, "innovations" that noncon-formists regarded as heralding a return to Roman Catholicism.

42 Alexander Leighton, *An Appeal to the Parliament; or, Sions Plea against the Prelacie* (Amsterdam, 1629), sig. A2ᵛ.

43 M. Cocker and D. Tipling, *Birds and People* (London: Jonathan Cape, 2013), 134. *Botaurus*, the bittern's generic name, "means 'to roar like a bull'" (134).

44 In modern translations, the horned owl or the ruffed buzzard, more appro-priate for a desert landscape, replaces the bittern, a wetland bird (Cocker and Tipling, *Birds and People*, 134).

45 H. Peacham, *Minerva Brittana* (London, 1612), 63.

46 Leighton, *Sions Plea*, 35.

47 Ibid., 334, 336.

48 See K. Thomas, *Man and the Natural World: A History of the Modern Sensibility* (New York: Pantheon, 1983), 274.

49 Leighton, *Sions Plea*, 121.

50 Ibid., 155.

51 C.R., *The True Discription of this Marveilous Straunge Fishe* (London, 1569).

52 Leighton, *Sions Plea*, 148, 255, 256, 263, 264.

53 F. Condick, "The Self-Revelation of a Puritan: Dr. Alexander Leighton in the Sixteen-Twenties," *Bulletin of the Institute of Historical Research* 55 (1982), 202.

54 Some English naturalists suspected that the adder was a viper. See Browne, *Pseudodoxia Epidemica*, vol. 1, 220, and E. Topsell, *The History of Four-Footed Beasts and Serpents and Insects* (London, 1658), 801. The lions in the Tower would have been seen by some Londoners and visitors to the capital, but the impact of the sight would no doubt have been outweighed by popular and ubiquitous representations of the kingly lion.

55 It could still be used in satire, however.

56 The word "zoology" itself did not come into existence until the third quarter of the seventeenth century (*OED*).

CHAPTER 9

Anthropomorphism
Violence and Law
Monica Flegel

Debates about the usefulness of anthropomorphism in terms of representing the animal other are common in animal studies, with the word "usually applied as a term of reproach, both intellectual and moral."[1] A primary problem with anthropomorphic texts for those of us invested in animal rights is that their focus on animal characters who speak and act like humans often "means that the differences between animal and human consciousness are not much explored."[2] This is certainly true for the two texts I will be discussing in this chapter: Alfred Elwes's *Adventures of a Bear, and a Great Bear Too!* (1853) and *The Adventures of a Dog, and a Good Dog Too!* (1854). While all three of the novels in the fictional Caneville universe, which also includes *The Adventures of a Cat, and a Fine Cat Too!* (1857), focus on the importance of good conduct, these first two novels feature characters on opposite sides of the law-and-order divide, with a bear engaged in criminal activity that leads to his downfall, and a dog who becomes an exemplary police chief beloved and admired by all. In this chapter, I want to explore Elwes's choice of a fictional, anthropomorphized world of animals to teach child readers about the importance of law and order.

Both texts intervene in nineteenth-century panics about the perceived rise of violent crime, particularly as it was connected to fears of social unrest and anxieties about lower-class morality. But the stories also delineate the complicated work that animal protagonists are called to perform in terms of representing a battle between "instinct" and "discipline." Both Bruin and Job are presented as individual personality "types," thus doing the work of aligning one's position under the law with one's character, but both are also assigned traits that are linked to species and instincts, raising the specter of social categories of criminality. I examine what the violence in these stories can tell us about the use of anthropomorphism to disavow structural explanations for oppression. By punishing nonhuman animals for being nonhuman animals, the anthropomorphism contained in these novels actually works against their ideology and ends up revealing the contradictions within character-based law-and-order discourse.

The Role of "Character" in Nineteenth-Century Legal Discourse

"The law" as a grand narrative in Western culture is strongly linked to Enlightenment ideals of humanity and civilization. To have law, and to follow law, is what distinguishes humans from nonhuman animals, with "the law of the jungle" standing in as the violent opposite of ordered, rational systems of justice. In short, "law is not simply a corpus of practical rules, but a part of ongoing 'discourse about good and bad states of society.'"[3] Animals are still, of course, caught up in human law as it plays a key role in "maintaining man's dominion over the animal kingdom."[4] While there have been instances of animal defendants whose actions came under the scrutiny of law,[5] generally animals are *objects* under the law, and their entry into law is in relation to human concerns: the policing of human violence and cruelty under animal protection laws, or the policing of human property, the primary category covering most domestic animals. As Lesli Bisgould asserts, "people do not treat animals badly because animals are property, animals are classified as property so that people can treat them badly. We can choose to classify them differently and to act accordingly."[6] Law as a social construct largely governs and defines human behaviors and societies, mostly to nonhuman animals' detriment.

This chapter focuses on the role of animals in representing early nineteenth-century law, which, as Martin Wiener highlights in *Reconstructing the Criminal* (1990), was situated in a period of moral panic around criminality. The vast changes to English society resulting from industrialization meant that "[v]irtually all the developments of the age were working to multiply the effective force of human desires and will. As a consequence, the question of control came to the fore."[7] This desire for greater social control, largely from the middle and upper classes and aimed at the lower ones, was driven by the perception of an "ever-rising amount of criminality of all kinds,"[8] though "Modern historians have found contemporaries' excited accounts of this supposed 'crime wave' to be highly misleading."[9] Rather than an accurate depiction of criminality, then, the early nineteenth-century discourse on the crime problem can be linked to "rising anxieties about impulses and will out of control; crime was a central metaphor of disorder and loss of control in all spheres of life."[10]

Crime was seen not as the result, primarily, of poverty or unequal power relations and access to resources, commentators asserted, but instead as arising from moral flaws. The solution to criminality, therefore, was through "character": "Underlying early Victorian reform of criminal policy was the supposition that the most urgent need, and possibility, of the age was to make people self-governing and that the way to do this was to hold them, sternly and unblinkingly, responsible for the consequences of their actions."[11] To make a man lawful, that is, one needed to make him "rational and responsible."[12] We can see this in early English laws protecting animals; Harriet Ritvo notes that "it was widely believed that habitual brutality to animals on the part of members of the lower classes resulted from their general inability or disinclination to 'subjugate the passions.'"[13] The policing of animal cruelty, that is, was often about fears of the undisciplined, irrational, and violent man and the effect he would have on society beyond his cruelty to animals. Crime was primarily, then, about a lack of discipline, reason, and self-control.

Elwes's two novels operate very much within this framework, as he makes clear from his juxtaposition of Master Bruin and honest Job that environment is not, at heart, the cause of criminality. Of the two, Master Bruin has a better start in life, as "our bear [...] had a mamma and papa, and some brothers and sisters [and] he lived in a cavern surrounded by trees and bushes."[14] By contrast, Job is born into extreme poverty:

> I do not remember either my father or my mother. An old doggess, who was the only creature I can recal to mind when I was a pup, took care of me. At least, she said she did. But from what I recollect I had to take most care of myself. [...] But how I came to be under the care of herself, and how it happened [...] that I should be forced to be so poor and dirty, I cannot tell.[15]

If environment was the primary cause of crime, then Bruin should have been the more lawful of the two, given his birth into a complete and stable, if somewhat feckless, family. The stories therefore reject structural explanations for criminality because none of Bruin's siblings turn out as badly as he, and because Job's escape from his life of poverty is presented solely as the result of his own individual choices.

The story of Master Bruin is that of someone unable to master his passions and of the attempts by the law to control or reform him. Bruin is set apart from his parents and siblings by his aggressivity, as he "was often out of temper, or rather, was always *in* temper, only that temper was a very bad one."[16] The lesson he offers for young readers is the extent to which possessing a good character is essential to health, happiness, and success in life: "unfortunately for his own happiness, he laid the blame of his mishap on any one or any thing, rather than the right being or circumstance."[17]

His story can therefore be read as a critique of a particularly grouchy and inflexible disposition, with Bruin's downfall serving as a warning to the child reader about the consequences of being ill-tempered.

By contrast, "honest Job" is distinguished from those around him by an inborn "spirit of goodness" that guides him out of poverty and through the many ordeals of his life.[18] He forms an early distaste for the dog-eat-dog world in which he is born and raised, reflecting, "This sort of life, wherein one was compelled either to fight for every bit one could get to eat or go without food altogether, became at last so tiresome to me that I set about for some other means of providing for my wants."[19] What he desires most is respectability; he reflects, "my only wishes were the desire to do some good for myself and others, and earn my meat."[20] For Job, "earning" is inherently linked to "goodness," falling very much in line with Victorian narratives of self-help. He is not afraid of engaging in violence, whether to threaten bullies or in "fights we had in protecting the property of our master."[21] But his violence is always kept in check, and always in service of the larger social order.

However, if both novels reject poverty and social inequity as the primary causes of criminality, they do not deny the role played by upbringing; when it comes to parental discipline, Elwes's novels suggest that violence is both necessary and curative of a bad disposition. He lays partial blame for Bruin's character at the feet of his parents, opining, "Now I privately think, that if a good oaken stick had been applied to his shoulders, or any other sensitive part of his body [. . .] the exercise would have had a very beneficial effect on his disposition."[22] Elwes's text clarifies, very early on, that law and order must be established within the home, and that properly wielded violence prevents a child from becoming an unruly member of society. We see this too in Job's origins, in which he is beaten by the "old doggess" after falling in the river:

> after I had escaped so great a danger, I flew to her paws, in the hope of getting a tender lick; but as soon as she recovered breath, she caught hold of one of my ears with her teeth, and bit it till I howled with pain [. . .] I remember at the time thinking it was not very kind of her, but I have since reflected that perhaps she only did it to brighten me up and prevent me taking cold.[23]

Both Bruin's and Job's upbringing are used to suggest that character is not solely an inborn quality, but also one that can be inculcated in a child through violent discipline. If the parent lays down the law, then the child will grow up to respect the law. The right kind of violence is therefore

salutary to the development of character and will result – as in Job's case –
in using violence in proper ways as an adult.

The novels continually focus on the *influence* that upbringing and
environment can have, for good or ill, but in the end, it is their individual
characters and the choices they make at crucial points in their journeys that
determine where both Bruin and Job end up in the social hierarchy. For
example, at low points in their stories both are exposed to criminal
elements, but it is only Master Bruin who is fatally harmed by such
contact. After experiencing a fall in fortunes due to his own failings, Bruin

> directed his steps to those parts of the town where poverty and vice were
> accustomed to assemble, strong in their numbers and their misery. Among
> them he now strove to bury his griefs and acquire consolation; but, alas, it was
> at the cost of every hope of virtue which might yet lurk in his nature!
> Characters like Bruin's, that are ever more apt to imitate the evil than the
> good which is around them, can only acquire some fresh stain from every
> contact with the wicked; and thus our bear sunk lower and lower in the scale
> of beasts, till many even of his new associates at last shrunk from him.[24]

Elwes's description here suggests that even proper parental discipline might
not have been enough to save Bruin from his criminal nature; any contact
with "the wicked" is dangerous for Bruin, with criminality depicted as a
contagion to which he is particularly vulnerable. In fact, Bruin outdoes
even those criminals with whom he comes into contact, given that they "at
last shrunk from him." Throughout the story, we see various characters
provoked to violence by the bear's actions: a boar who castigates him for
his ingratitude after sharing food with him, a pack of dogs that he
deliberately provokes, and violence caused by his presence at a fair "either
as an instigator or a principal."[25] Master Bruin is born bad, further harmed
by a lack of parental discipline, and either is made worse by, or makes
worse, any company he chooses to keep.

Job, by comparison, uses each encounter of suffering, danger, or violence as an opportunity to make the right choices and ascend to greater
roles of power and authority. Like Bruin, Job possesses great strength and
the ability to use it for ill, but he chooses always to align his power with
lawfulness. As he proclaims, "such work as a dog *can* do should be sought
after and done, for nothing can be more shocking than to see an animal's
powers, either of body or mind, wasted away in idleness."[26] His strength
must be geared toward the maintenance and preservation of the social
order, because above all, Job believes in earning his keep, a quality that is
central to everything good he represents: "These paws, large and strong as
they are, were never intended for idleness; this back, broad as it is, was

meant for some other purpose than to show off a fine coat; this brain, which can reflect and admire and resolve, had not such capabilities given to it in order that they might be wasted in a life of ease."[27] He describes the perfect combination of upbringing and personality that make him the ideal worker: "I was very poor – one good reason for his employing me, as I would be contented with little; I was strong, and should therefore be able to get through the work; I was willing, and bore a reputation for honesty."[28] These qualities, combined with his strong sense of "duty" and numerous acts of courage, lead to Job occupying powerful law and order positions: first, as the caretaker of a lord and lady's estate "to save them from the depredations of thieves," then finally as "chief of the Caneville police."[29] Furthermore, throughout his many troubles and his successes, Job is markedly modest and grateful, as, unlike Bruin, he expects nothing from the world and offers to give everything in return. Gratitude, a strong work ethic, and a belief that his strength must be used in the service of protecting others and preserving order are all qualities native to Job's character that align him with propriety, lawfulness, and, ultimately, social success and happiness.

The depiction of the contrasting personalities and experiences of Bruin and Job thus firmly operate within the narrative of criminality as a problem of character. Importantly, in the novels' focus on personality, there is little about either Bruin or Job that has to do with animality (beyond, arguably, their physicality and violence, which I will discuss in the next section). Each could be characters within the kinds of moral tales told by Hannah More: flat, allegorical types offering clear models for the child reader as to how one should comport oneself in order to stay on the right side of the law. But when Bruin and Job *are* marked by their species and their animality, this idea of character becomes far more complicated, undermining (if only unintentionally) the texts' devotion to morality as the cure for criminality.

Nature in Conflict with the Law: The Specter of Instinctualism

Given the focus on upbringing and personal character as essential to lawfulness, the choice of animal protagonists to represent the conflict between law and order would seem to be a strange one. However, "animality" as a metaphor haunted early nineteenth-century concepts of law, both supporting and complicating notions of criminality as a character flaw. If the lawful citizen is, arguably, the most humane, at least according to Enlightenment principles of subjectivity, then the corollary of this is that the criminal person is, problematically, still yet a "natural" one. That is, aligning criminality with unregulated passions meant positioning law-lessness as something "deeply rooted in human nature, in the 'natural man' (and woman) who lay underneath the thin crust of civilization."[30] This "natural man" is closer to the animal world, aligned with "savagery" in opposition to the civilized, lawful subject who, according to John Stuart Mill, exhibits self-control and "mastery over his 'animal nature' that impelled him, to his ultimate harm, towards immediate, usually sensual gratification."[31] The "instincts and impulses, identified with 'barbarism' or 'savagery'" had to be managed and controlled, and therefore "much legal reform of the first three-quarters of the nineteenth century aimed to encourage and enforce the growth of a more self-restrained character type in the general public, one that deferred immediate gratification and looked toward the distinct consequences of actions."[32] To be humane, to be a person of character, to be *lawful*, is to fight back against the animal within, and to reject passion for reason, instinct for regulation.

In early nineteenth-century legal discourse, the violent, passionate crim-inal is problematically natural, but he is also almost always still othered. Hubert Malfey identifies the following links "to be found between the issues of criminality and animality in the Victorian Age": "the criminal was considered to be outside the law in the same way as the animal was outside the realm of *anthropos*. Apart from pets that may have had the guarantee of a privileged place inside the bourgeois standards of home, 'instinctual' animals shared with criminals a certain form of separate status from the world of men."[33] Part of how this separate status is constructed is through reference to metaphors not just of animality but also of class. As J. Carter Wood explains, "'Civilisation' was a word with great currency in the nineteenth century, reflecting a particular set of attitudes towards behav-iour that became most strongly associated with middle-class cultural tastes,"[34] especially those shaped by the Evangelical revival. This framing led to a construction of the lawful subject as, ideally, enacting middle-class values, and "much legal reform during the first three-quarters of the nineteenth century aimed to encourage and enforce the growth of a more self-restrained character type in the general public."[35] Controlling the criminal required policing and educating the lower classes, and inculcating within them middle-class notions of character, so as to combat the "natural man" coming too near the surface.

But to identify such "brutality" at the heart of English culture risked making it seem indelible to Englishness, and that problem was often managed through the construction of criminals as foreign, ethnically "other," and a race apart. In part, this othering is achieved through depicting the criminal world as almost another country, with the "perception that crime constituted a world of its own, one that invertedly mirrored the respectable world as a nightmare mirrors the day world."[36] The dwellers in that criminal world were often conceived, then, as members of a different "tribe," as foreigners within England (importantly, such characterizations of the criminal world often linked criminality with travelers, Irish immigrants, and other ethnic groups who made up some portion of the lower and working classes). Thus, the construction of criminality in the early part of the nineteenth century operated on overlapping categories of otherness, all linked by the "specter of instinctualism" and a focus on "the critical distinction between savagery and civilization."[37] The focus on species in these texts therefore both makes the "animal within" metaphor literal and also reveals the extent to which narratives of class, race, and ethnicity were used to identify the "natural criminal."

As discussed, Bruin's and Job's positioning in relation to the law is continually underlined as resulting from their individual characters; nevertheless, the fact of them being a bear and dog is also tied to their respective ends. Bruin's family might not be criminals, but Elwes opines to his audience: "You are, perhaps, aware that bears, being of rather an indolent disposition, are not accustomed to hoard up a store of provision for their wants in winter, but prefer – in their own country, at least – sleeping through the short dreary days and long bitter nights."[38] Here, the flaw in Bruin and his family, that of being "indolent," is a characteristic that is not individual solely to him, but, Elwes makes clear, shared by all "brown" bears as a species. Furthermore, the attention to Bruin's ursine presence as that of an outsider to the city folks begs for him to be read through the lens of race/ethnicity. Elwes describes how Bruin first appears on his arrival to Caneville, positioning him both as rube and as savage other. He notes the strangeness of Bruin in the eyes of the "the more civilized animals, particularly in regard to his "untrimmed hair and beard, his ragged coat, his queer gait."[39] Only a "learned pig" who had "travelled much and was acquainted with the peculiarity of bears" is level-headed enough to make use of Bruin's size and behavior, making him part of his performing act as a "foreigner."[40] Throughout the novel, Bruin's inability to fit into the proper class structure of Caneville, or to abide by its many laws and customs, is assigned at least in part to his otherness, as much as to his character.

Though the novel invokes species and, by association, race and ethnicity, as an explanation for some forms of criminality, Elwes is clearly

uncomfortable with this, preferring the narrative of character and individ-
uality as responsible for one's position in relation to the law. After
explaining that the species is "rather indolent" and that "there are few
more disagreeable beings in creation than ill-nurtured bears," he cautions
his reader against stereotyping:

> here we may observe, that they are such characters as Bruin who bring
> disrepute on the whole tribe; for we are too apt to form our opinions of a
> nation by the few individuals we may happen to fall in with, although,
> probably, no conclusions can be falser. Let us, therefore, be careful ere we
> form our judgements, and let us not believe that all Bruin's kindred and
> compatriots were sulky and ill-tempered because he himself was such a
> disagreeable lump of a bear.[41]

Instead, Elwes highlights how "sullen, cross-grained and ill-tempered
beasts" might be the result of them being "ill-licked" and "ill-nurtured
bears."[42] Similarly, Elwes opens Job's story with an introduction that
cautions the reader to recognize that "the dispositions of dogs are as various
as their forms – although education, connections, the society they keep,
have all their influence." Nevertheless, he cannot leave behind the role
played by species either, as he states, "to the credit of their name be it said,
a dog never sullies his mouth with an untruth. His emotions of pleasure
are genuine, never forced. His grief is not the semblance of woe, but comes
from the heart. His devotion is unmixed with other feelings. It is single,
unselfish, profound."[43] Job is good because his character is good, but his
character is good at least in part because he is a dog.

   Elwes's reliance on and disavowal of species and kind as an explanation
for criminality reveals the contradictions in instinctualism as the source of
criminal behavior. In Elwes's two novels, this need to fight against one's
own instincts is seen in the animalistic violence within the texts, much of
which is linked to food and eating. Characters in the text are continually
depicted as food-driven, but the texts also call on them to resist the need to
feed, to predate, and to survive. In Bruin's case, the novel depicts the
family of bears awaking from their hibernation:

> The smell of the fresh air [. . .] caused him a tremendous appetite, which
> was every moment becoming greater; and then it entered his bearish brain
> that where there was a smell there must be something to occasion it.
> Whereupon, following that great nose of his – and he could not have had
> a better guide – he scuffled out of the cavern and down the path [. . .] With
> his great paws he soon demolished the entrance to his mamma's larder, and
> lost no time in pulling out some of the dainties it contained which, without
> more ado, he set about devouring.[44]

Reading Bruin as an anthropomorphized naughty child, his raiding of his mother's larder is clearly an unworthy act, and an opportunity to teach the child reader about restraint. But in this moment, Bruin and his family are most definitely also *bears*, engaging in ursine behavior, with Bruin's actions described as highly instinctual, following as he does his "bearish brain" and his "great nose."

But the novel vacillates, in this scene, between normal and forgivable behavior for a bear, and the use of Bruin's actions as somehow applicable to humans engaged in wrongdoing. Bruin's brothers

> were by this time also wide awake, and had quite as good appetites as Bruin himself; and though on ordinary occasions they stood in great awe of that most ill-tempered brute, it must be admitted that this was an extra-ordinary occasion, and they acted accordingly. Just fancy being months without anything to eat, and having appetites fierce enough to devour one another![45]

The brothers' voracious feeding on the hoard leads to violence, as Bruin strikes them both, resulting in his expulsion from the home. Clearly, the actions of all three are characterized by a lack of restraint, but this violence – even to the point of engaging in cannibalism – is portrayed as understandable or even sympathetic, given their long sleep and their great hunger: Elwes even instructs his readers as to how bears in winter sleep "through the short dreary days and long bitter nights, and thus avoid the necessity of taking food for some weeks, although they grow very thin during their lengthened slumbers."[46] This focus on the desperate hunger of the bears presents their fierce behavior as perfectly natural, yet the novel also puts boundaries around the aggression their privation invokes, appealing to their animality in one moment, and then erasing it in an anthropomorphized scene of familial conflict the next. The novel's rendering of Bruin's expulsion captures this juxtaposition perfectly, describing how his father tells him "that if he ever expected to get through the world with credit to his name, and even comfort to his person, he must be honest, good-tempered, and forbearing," to which Bruin just "growled out some unintelligible words."[47] Bruin is oddly pathetic in this moment, and in many others, seemingly trapped between his nature as a bear, captured in his "unintelligible" growling, and a culture that makes demands of him that he is unable to meet.

The trials that Job endures make clear just what is necessary for an animal to be a *person* of law and order. *The Adventures of a Dog*, like *The Adventures of a Bear*, has numerous scenes of conflict over food during

times of great hunger, but in Job's case, starvation is presented as preferable
to lawlessness. Left adrift after attempting to save others in a flood, Job
almost kills and eats a fellow stowaway, before the bird discerns his intent
and flies away. Job reflects, "I am sorry to say my only thought at first was
the having lost my dinner: but as I watched him [. . .] until he diminished
to a misty speck, and then disappeared, my better feelings came back to me
and said, 'let Job rather die, than do what he would live to feel ashamed
of.'"[48] Like the biblical Job, he despairs but ultimately keeps his faith in
the ideals of honor and respectability. And, through this parallel, we see
the purpose of employing animal characters in these stories: we humans,
the texts suggests, are like animals in relation to a higher power, and we
struggle with inborn drives that point us toward violence. We are meant to
understand these characters' animal desires to hunt and eat, but still to see
the battle against these instincts as necessary. Hunger is not about need in
these novels; instead, hunger is about what one has earned:

> I had no right to eat the food of idleness where so many dogs, more
> deserving than I, were often in want of a bone, but whose modesty
> prevented them making known their necessities. [. . .] [T]hey must permit
> me to do something which might be useful to the city in return, for I should
> devour the fare provided for me with a great deal more appetite, if I could
> say to myself when I felt hungry, "Job, brother Job, eat your dinner, for you
> have *earned* it."[49]

The fact that Job is physically capable of satisfying his perfectly natural
hunger is not presented in the novel as justification for predation; instead,
it is offered as an inborn temptation in Job that he must battle
and overcome.

Though the purpose of animal characters fighting against their animality
highlights the struggle to be lawful, it also makes the law itself seem
unnatural, even unreasonable. Job's first employment as a keeper of law
is in patrolling the grounds at Sir John Bull's estates, protecting the lord of
the manor's prized birds from feline and fox poachers. Job describes his
charges as "a delicate kind of bird; much esteemed by himself and his
family, and which was induced to flock there by regular feeding and the
quiet of the situation."[50] This arrangement requires the policing of predatory appetites, as others "just as fond of the birds as [Sir John] himself
[. . .] were accustomed to pay nightly visits to the forbidden ground, and
carry off many of the plumpest fowl. The wood was known to shelter
many a wandering fox, who, although dwelling so near the city, could not
be prevailed on to abandon their roguish habits and live in a civilised
manner."[51] The phrasing – "although dwelling so near the city" – implies

that these foxes should have been transformed by the urban landscape, leaving behind their animality and their appetites with it. It is not just country foxes who must be guarded against, however, as "stray curs" and "the cat population, who have a general affection for most birds, and held these preserved ones in particular esteem"[52] also threaten the flock. Sir John Bull's birds, that is, offer temptation to every predatory species in the vicinity who regularly feast on birds. As such, the policing of these kept birds offers a strange view of law and order: rather than highlighting how important it is to fight against natural instincts, this scene in the novel instead begs the question of just why Job is engaged in the seemingly useless work of policing natural and necessary species behavior. Here, it is the ownership and policing of nature that seems absurd, particularly as the passing on of the estate after the death of the owner leads to the new owner simply "killing off the birds."[53] The wastefulness and violence of this act is presented as nothing less than the owner exercising his rights under the law.

The choice of animal protagonists, then, works both within and against the idea of character as essential to lawfulness. Certainly, using animal protagonists actualizes the metaphor of the "animal within," the supposed baser self that must be governed by education, law, and order. If Job can suppress his need to survive with narratives of self-help and self-abnegation, then so too should the child audience. As well, using species to stand in for metaphors of class and species works within the stereotypes of problematic "natural man" current at the time, however much Elwes might want to caution against generalizations; his stories still rely on narratives of inborn goodness that are linked, at least in part, to species and kind. But setting these stories in an anthropomorphized animal world also subtly highlights the violence of the law, particularly in terms of how concepts like private property and ownership violate basic needs for sustenance and survival.

These contradictions caused by using animal characters to tell us about human laws are useful, I argue, because they reveal the ideological fissures at the heart of early nineteenth-century legal discourses. And, most painfully, the scenes of Bruin imprisoned for his criminal acts highlight the incredible cruelty of carceral discourses. Captured by the police after many transgressions, Bruin is thrown into "a wretched place of confinement," where he is left "tearing round and round and round the confined space of the cell." The image recalls animals trapped in enclosures, and his pain and suffering are presented as profoundly instinctual and natural: "He howled till the dirt sticking about the vaulted ceiling, and the earth choking up the airhole, dropped piecemeal to the ground, and every insect that had ears covered them up the best way it could to prevent its becoming simultaneously deafened by the horrid sound."[54] This moment highlights what Teresa Mangum has identified as animals writing back within anthropomorphic genres:

> In each of these forms of art and literature, the human genre tames the animal with an anthropomorphic whip. The humanness of these genres and modes consume, sympathize with, and strain against animalness. Yet animal alterity also bites back, ripping at the human flesh of genres, exposing the amorality of the animal, and inviting curiosity, fear, shame, and compassion of a writer, painter, reader, or viewer willing to bare the throat of her own imprisoning, anthropocentric expectations.[55]

Bruin is an animal trapped in an anthropomorphized world, unable to coexist within the legal confines of a society and culture that is inherently alien to him. In this moment, Elwes captures his pain and frustration, revealing how cruel and inhumane this punishment is and, ultimately, how unnatural. But if the animal character "bites back" in this moment against anthropocentrism, so too does this representation encourage us to see the pain of discourses that dehumanize those outside the bounds of limiting and often arbitrary legal discourses.

Notes

1 Lorraine Daston and Gregg Mitman, "The How and Why of Thinking with Animals," in Daston and Mitman (eds.), *Thinking with Animals: New Perspectives on Anthropomorphism* (New York: Columbia University Press, 2005), 2.
2 Tess Cosslett, *Talking Animals in British Children's Fiction, 1786–1914* (Aldershot: Ashgate, 2006), 70.
3 Martin Wiener, *Reconstructing the Criminal: Culture, Law, and Policy in England, 1830–1914* (Cambridge: Cambridge University Press, 1990), 4.
4 Piyel Haldar, "Law and Animalities," *Law and Humanities* 3.1 (2009), 71–85, 71.
5 Edward Payson Evans, *The Criminal Prosecution and Capital Punishment of Animals* (London: William Heinemann, 1906).
6 Lesli Bisgould, *Animals and the Law* (Toronto: Irwin Law, 2011), 8.
7 Wiener, *Reconstructing the Criminal*, 11.
8 Ibid., 15.
9 Ibid., 14.
10 Ibid., 11.
11 Ibid., 11–12.
12 Ibid., 11.

13 Harriet Ritvo, *The Animal Estate: The English and Other Creatures in the Victorian Age* (Cambridge, MA: Harvard University Press, 1987), 149.

14 Alfred Elwes, *The Adventures of a Bear, and a Great Bear Too!* (London: Addey and Co., 1853), 2.

15 Alfred Elwes, *The Adventures of a Dog, and a Good Dog Too!* (London: Addey and Co., 1854), 17.

16 Elwes, *Adventures of a Bear*, 2.

17 Ibid., 18.

18 Elwes, *Adventures of a Dog*, 15.

19 Ibid., 21–2.

20 Ibid., 41.

21 Ibid., 13, 48.

22 Elwes, *Adventures of a Bear*, 3.

23 Elwes, *Adventures of a Dog*, 19.

24 Elwes, *The Adventures of a Bear*, 53.

25 Ibid., 14–15, 17–18, 56.

26 Elwes, *The Adventures of a Dog*, 89.

27 Ibid., 89

28 Ibid., 23.

29 Ibid., 41, 92.

30 Wiener, *Reconstructing the Criminal*, 25.

31 Ibid., 39.

32 Ibid., 26, 56.

33 Hubert Malfray, "Freak Shows on the Page: Defining 'Criminanimality' in Newgate Fiction (1830–1847)," *Cahiers victoriens & édouardiens* 85 (Spring 2017).

34 J. Carter Wood, "A Useful Savagery: The Invention of Violence in Nineteenth-Century England," *Journal of Victorian Culture*, 9.1 (2004), 22–42, 27.

35 Wiener, *Reconstructing the Criminal*, 56.

36 Ibid., 20.

37 Ibid., 26, 34.

38 Elwes, *Adventures of a Bear*, 5–6.

39 Ibid., 22.

40 Ibid., 25, 26. 29.

41 Ibid., 5, 18.

42 Ibid., 5.

43 Elwes, *Adventures of a Dog*, iv.

44 Elwes, *Adventures of a Bear*, 7

45 Ibid., 7.

46 Ibid., 6.

47 Ibid., 9.

48 Elwes, *Adventures of a Dog*, 77.

49 Ibid., 90.

50 Ibid., 43.

51 Ibid., 43–4.
52 Ibid., 44.
53 Ibid., 51.
54 Elwes, *Adventures of a Bear*, 72, 73.
55 Teresa Mangum, "Narrative Dominion or the Animals Write Back? Animal Genres in Literature and the Arts," in Kathleen Kete (ed.), *A Cultural History of Animals in the Age of Empire* (New York: Berg, 2007), 153–73, 157.

CHAPTER 10

Habitat
Worlds of Wildlife

Tobias Menely

The Earth is the shared home of all known living beings, yet our world can also be said to contain many worlds. Each species has evolved to occupy a specific habitat, an environment conducive to its unique mode of life. A habitat, put simply, is where a species lives, an envelope of habitability, the geophysical conditions and distribution of resources that support its survival and reproduction. While biologists generally emphasize the availability of food, habitat may be understood to include the entire milieu in which animals live as active subjects: hunting, foraging, or grazing, but also bathing, grooming, exploring, playing, communicating, mating, and raising young. Any species occupies a habitat and also transforms it, through niche construction, such as nest- or dam-building, and insofar as their presence (as predator or prey, pollinator or distributor of seeds) shapes the habitat of other organisms. An ecosystem is the collectively constituted totality of relations among organisms each occupying its habitat.

In the early twentieth century, the Estonian-German biologist Jakob von Uexküll pioneered the concept of *Umwelt* – literally, a "surrounding world" – to refer to the perceptual field of an organism, the subjective experience of living in habitat. For the physicist, Uexküll writes, "there is only one real world"; for the biologist, by contrast, "there are as many worlds as there are subjects."[1] The *Umwelt* concept draws attention to the way animals navigate their habitat as subjects: perceiving and interpreting, remembering and anticipating, making choices. No animal apprehends all of the potential information in the world around it. Rather, animals notice aspects of the environment available to their perceptual apparatuses and relevant to their mode of life. An animal is a subject relating to its world according to its specific needs. "Every subject," Uexküll writes, "spins out, like the spider's threads, its relations to certain qualities of things and weaves them into a solid web, which carries its existence."[2] The same object within an environment may have profoundly different meanings for the animals that relate to it. Uexküll gives the example of "the stem of a blooming meadow flower," which for a young girl is an "ornament," for an ant is a "path" to reach the leaves of the flower, for cicada larva is a "spigot," and for a cow is a "clump of food."[3] There is no single, objective flower or meadow. The significance of the flower or the meadow differs depending on its function in the relation between an animal and its world.

Habitat remains a relatively underexplored topic in the field of animal studies. It has been taken up primarily through the *Umwelt* concept, particularly as it influenced biosemiotics and Continental theory (including the work of Martin Heidegger, Jacques Lacan, Maurice Merleau-Ponty, and Giorgio Agamben).[4] Scholars working in animal studies have attended less to wildlife inhabiting ecosystems than to domesticated animals (such as pets, work animals, meat animals) inhabiting anthropogenic environments (homes, farms, confined feeding operations). We have focused more on representations of animal subjectivity, on the question of human/animal difference, and on forms of sociopolitical recognition within human communities than on the dynamic ecological relations animals establish with other beings in a web of life. To take up habitat as a key concept for animal studies requires us to ask how animals occupy and navigate worlds often independently of human actors and points of view – if also, in the Anthropocene, worlds everywhere shaped by human activity.

Literary texts that accomplish the imaginative feat of depicting the worlds inhabited by wildlife are rare, which is perhaps evidence that literature inclines toward anthropocentrism, focalizing around human points of view, treating the human *Umwelt* as the norm. Even more than everyday speech, literature – in its modes of address, semantic density, and second-order reflexivity – would seem to fatally detach humans from an awareness of the worlds we share with other animals. Yet literature also has the power to incorporate animal voices, adopt animal points of view, and imaginatively transport readers into animal worlds. In recent years, scholars working in literary animal studies have identified a range of texts, from across historical periods and cultures, that succeed in decentering the human, and they have begun to rethink critical concepts to account for such texts. David Herman, for example, develops a narratology concerned with works in which "non-human animals are focal participants in storyworld events."[5] Like most narratology, however, an emerging "narratology beyond the human" has primarily emphasized characterization, point of view, and plot. Not only in literary animal studies but in literary studies more generally, *setting* – the representation of a shaping place, milieu, territory, environment, ecosystem, or *Umwelt* – remains an undertheorized concept.

In this chapter, I survey a range of literary texts that center on wildlife and feature habitat as a setting: John Clare's poetry (mostly published between 1820 and 1835); J. A. Baker's work of literary natural history, *The Peregrine* (1967); Barbara Gowdy's novel, *The White Bone* (1998); and Ted Chiang's short story, "The Great Silence" (2016). I have chosen these texts because, despite their generic and historical variety, they similarly manage something unusual: to represent wild creatures perceiving *Umwelt*, navigating territory, negotiating worlds. They are not only about animals as acting subjects, with minds and intentions; they are also about habitat, the specific life-world of a species, the web of relations it inhabits.

In each of these texts, animal worlds are threatened by human encroachment. These works, written over the past two centuries, give expression to the geohistorical event we are learning to call the "sixth mass extinction," the primary driver of which is a calamitous loss of habitat. Globally, populations of wild vertebrate species have declined by more than half since 1970. Wild mammals now make up less than 3 percent of total mammalian biomass on Earth; the rest is humans, our pets, and our food animals. Anthropogenic climate change contributes to this extinction event by rapidly transforming the envelope of habitability to which species are adapted. Climate change pushes species to move, to adapt, and to evolve, but, given the fragmentation of habitat and the speed of warming, such changes are often impossible. Some animals require large territories; many are highly specialized, with respect to food or climate. This is not to say that "anthromes" (anthropogenic biomes, or human-built environments) such as cities and farmland cannot serve as habitat. Some of the most interesting recent work in multispecies ethnography has focused on those wild animals that successfully negotiate human environments, including rhesus macaques living in New Delhi and crows living in Brisbane.[6] These species – undomesticated but suited to survive in human-made environments – tend to be similar to us: intelligent and adaptable generalists. Yet there are many species that survive and flourish only within a distinct habitat, an ecological web in which they have evolved and to which they are adapted. This chapter explores the imaginative work of evoking such wildlife worlds.

Clare's Dwelling Places

The son of a farm laborer, John Clare made his name as the self-described "Northamptonshire Peasant Poet" with four volumes of verse, published between 1820 and 1835. Although Clare fell into obscurity in the century after his death, in recent decades he has been reclaimed as a central figure of Romanticism, a poet with an ecological vision quite distinct from that of famous contemporaries such as William Wordsworth. James McKusick

calls Clare the "first 'deep' ecological writer in the English literary tradition," referring to deep ecology, a philosophy that rejects human
supremacy.[7] Clare is known for his meticulous descriptions, in poetry
and prose, of local flora and fauna, particularly birds, and for his outraged
documentation of the enclosure of rural land. These two forms of attention were closely connected. Clare's sensitivity to animal life-worlds was
inseparable from his experience of the disappearance of a social life-world
organized around what John Barrell calls the pre-enclosure "open-field
sense of space."[8] Clare thought hard about inhabitation, for humans and
animals alike, because he recognized what it meant to lose a home and a
way of life. Indeed, Clare sold his first volume of poetry in a desperate
attempt to pay the rent on his family's house.

Clare is often referred to as the finest naturalist among English poets.
He identified around 150 wild bird species and 135 plant species in his
poems.[9] Clare was influenced by Enlightenment natural history, particularly as popularized by works such as Gilbert White's *Natural History of
Selborne* (1789), the record of a lifetime of observations in a single parish
concerned with what White called "the life and conversation of animals."[10]
Clare, who owned a copy of *Selborne*, hoped to publish a "Natural History
of Helpston," modeled on *Selborne*, although his detailed prose natural
history writings remained unpublished until the twentieth century.

In the eighteenth century, the word "habitat," from the Latin *habitāre*,
had come to be used to refer to the locality inhabited by a plant or animal.
Carl Linneaus, the great Swedish naturalist, used the term in his *Systema
naturae* (1735) to designate the region where a given species dwells.
Habitat – along with appearance, diet, and habits – was an identifier used
to taxonomically distinguish one species from another. Clare never uses the
word "habitat," which remained a specialized scientific term until the mid-
nineteenth century, but he uses a range of synonyms. "Dwelling place" is a
favorite; "haunt," "home," "spot," and "nook" also appear frequently.
Clare, moreover, attends to the relation between territory and the character
of a species. He considers not only the "actual locality" inhabited by a
given species, its regional distribution, but also the "kind of locality" it
inhabits, anticipating a modern scientific understanding of habitat.[11]

In his poem "Shadows of Taste," Clare attributes to animals a faculty
akin to aesthetic judgment, a distinct experiential orientation to the
specific milieu they inhabit:

> Taste is their joyous heritage and they
> All choose for joy in a peculiar way
> Birds own it in the various spots they chuse

Some live content in low grass gemmed with dews
The yellowhammer like a tasteful guest
Neath picturesque green molehills makes a nest.
[. . .]
Birds bolder winded on bushes love to be
While some choose cradles on the highest tree.[12]

Expanding on the taxonomic tradition, Clare identifies specific organisms with the "various spots" they inhabit, a niche within a broader ecology. He also attends to the subjective experience of such inhabitation, as an expression of volition (choice) and a unique perceptual relation (taste) to one's surroundings. Barrell's observation about Clare's landscape aesthetics, that he aims not to "*describe* each place" but to "suggest what it is like to be in each place,"[13] can be applied equally to Clare's representation of the manner in which animals experience the "spots" they inhabit, the satisfactions they find in the worlds they occupy. Among animals, there are as many ways of perceiving the world – indeed, there are, as Joseph Albernaz argues, as many "worlds," overlapping but distinctly apprehended – as there are definitions of taste among humans: "Minds spring as various as the leaves of trees" (53–4).[14] Removing an organism from its native habitat, as might a scientific collector, leads to an impoverished and inadequate conception of its identity: "take these several beings from their homes / Each beauteous thing a withered thought becomes" (147–8).

In his lyrics of creaturely life, Clare rarely loses sight of his own embodied human perspective and presence. To observe animals in their native habitat, the poet must stoop and wade, clamber and climb through furze-covered heath and tangled brambles. He must sit quietly for hours. In "The Nightingales Nest," for example, the speaker warns his companion to close a gate softly so as not to frighten the sought-after bird. He looks for her nest, "creeping on hands and knees through matted thorns."[15] For hours he sits still and listens to her song (repeating a common error, since only male nightingales sing), "But if I touched a bush or scarcely stirred / All in a moment stopt" (28–9). Finally, he observes her sitting silently on an oak bough, "Mute in her fears our presence doth retard / Her joys" (65–6). Clare's consistent attention to the conditions of observation, the way his presence itself alters animal behavior, distinguishes his poems from scientific natural history. Lyric poetry foregrounds the perspective of the speaker. By recognizing that we perceive and move through the world in particular ways, occupying an *Umwelt* even as we shape the *Umwelten* of others, we become sensitized to the distinct life-worlds of the animals we observe. Whether they enter the "wilderness of listening leaves" (32) as nest-robbers, hunters, shepherds, or even quiet observers, humans comprise a significant presence in the experience of other animals, who are keenly sensitized to human intrusion. When the nightingale detects the human interloper and silences her song, Clare's reader is made to recognize the human from a nonhuman stand-point – to ask, perhaps, how other animals perceive our troublesome species as a distinct category of being within their environment.

In 1809, enclosure began to transform Clare's native village of Helpstone. Enclosure was a legal process, often formalized by an act of Parliament, of appropriating common land and turning it over to a single owner who could maximize its profitability. Enclosure brought about a profound transforma-tion of the countryside. Common fields were fenced; marshes were drained; forests were felled; springs were channeled into irrigation ditches; hills were leveled; roads were straightened. Wastes, where locals might graze livestock and forage for food or fuel, were brought into cultivation. Land came to be regarded primarily as a source of profit. In his poetry, Clare conveys the lived experience of enclosure using analogies with animal experience. In the first poem, "Helpstone," of Clare's first volume, *Poems Descriptive of Rural Life and Scenery* (1820), the narrator compares himself to the "little birds in winters frost and snow / [. . .] / Searching for food."[16] The seasonal subsis-tence struggles of the birds stand for the narrator's experience of loss. The birds are resilient; they "still chirp and hope" (31). But as they fly higher, just as the narrator's worldly experience increased, they realize that winter's grasp is inescapable. While the poet compares his human situation to that of the birds struggling to survive winter, he avoids naturalizing the forces trans-forming his rural community. Seasonal dearth is distinguished from "Accursed wealth" (127): "Thou art the cause that levels every tree & woods bow down to clear a way for thee" (133–4). Capitalist accumulation is the cause; enclosure is the tool; and the consequence is a profound diminish-ment of what Clare calls "nature's freedom" (96), the independent lives, human and animal alike, supported by the woods, hedges, brambles, streams, and swamps.

Several of Clare's most elegiac poems, such as "The Mores" and "The Lament of Swordy Well," specifically document the loss of animal habitat brought about by enclosure. In "Swordy Well," written in the early 1820s though unpublished until 1920, the poet adopts the first-person point of view of the marshland, and describes the consequences of agricultural improvement:

> The bees flye round in feeble rings
> And find no blossom bye
> Then thrum their almost weary wings

Upon the moss and die
Rabbits that find my hills turned oer
Foresake my poor abode.[17]

The "hasty plough" cuts down the "clover bottle," leaving the butterflies homeless (89–96). The narrator complains, "I've scarce a nook to call me own / For things that creep or flye" (113–14). What causes this destruction of animal abodes is not an innate human tendency to seize and repurpose natural habitat but rather "the price of grain" and the political system that prioritizes property and profit (145). Enclosure diminishes the prospects – and, indeed, the "freedom" – not only of an independent peasantry but also of the various creatures that rely on the "commons wild & gay."[18]

The Peregrine's Freedom

A century after Clare's death, J. A. Baker published an extraordinary work of literary nonfiction, *The Peregrine*, recounting his observations of falcons around the Essex marshes between October 1962 and April 1963. That bitterly cold winter was the culmination of a decade in which Baker, severely arthritic and myopic, traversing the ground on bicycle and by foot, dedicated himself to observing raptors whose aeronautical freedom and keen vision acutely contrasted with his earthbound condition. Reading *The Peregrine* can be a disorienting experience. There is no narrative arc, no satisfying human story. The temporal organization is diurnal and seasonal. Each daily entry begins and ends out-of-doors. Baker's prose is concrete but also ecstatic and angry. Language, the privileged medium of human consciousness, will never exactly convey a nonhuman point of view, but in his chiseled prose Baker captures something of the peregrine's perspective, its lack of interest in what is superfluous to its needs, the violent attention with which it regards those with which it shares its world: its prey.

The concentrated attention required to observe falcons in flight reorients Baker's perception, in line with the falcon's *Umwelt*. He watches peregrines with the intensity with which peregrines hunt small birds. As he writes of his growing infatuation with the raptors: "the eye becomes insatiable for hawks. It clicks toward them with ecstatic fury, just as the hawk's eye swings and dilates to the luring food-shapes of gulls and pigeons."[19] Baker imagines the raptor's view of the territory as it sweeps across the sky. "The peregrine," he writes, "lives in a pouring-away world of no attachment, a world of wakes and tilting, of sinking planes of land

and water. [...] The peregrine sees and remembers patterns we do not know exist: the neat squares of orchard and woodland, the endlessly varying quadrilateral shapes of fields."[20] The land that for Baker is full of obstacles extends for the raptor outward toward a distant horizon, flowing water-like below as the bird glides through the air. Immersed in this rushing world, the hawk is keenly attentive to prey, of course, in a sky "drifted with gulls and plover and curlew," but also to the "gravelly streams" in which it likes to "bathe every day" to rid itself of feather lice.[21]

Baker longs to be subsumed by the nonhuman point of view, to transcend his lumbering human locomotion and scattered human consciousness. In this passage, the discovery of the corpse of a woodpigeon, butchered by a tiercel (male falcon), enables a new intensity of direct identification:

> I found myself crouching over the kill, like a mantling hawk. My eyes turned quickly about, alert for the walking heads of men. Unconsciously I was imitating the movements of a hawk, as in some primitive ritual; the hunter becoming the thing he hunts. I looked into the wood. In a lair of shadow the peregrine was crouching, watching me, gripping the neck of a dead branch. We live, in these days in the open, the same ecstatic fearful life. We shun men. We hate their suddenly uplifted arms, the insanity of their flailing gestures, their erratic scissoring gait, their aimless stumbling ways, the tombstone whiteness of their faces.[22]

Baker's identification with the peregrine does not provide the basis for an ecological politics, a recognition of common right or a shared sovereignty, as identification with animals does for Clare. Rather, it measures a mortified disassociation with the human, a misanthropic alienation, a desire for a way of life unavailable to us. As Baker writes, "I have always longed to be a part of the outward life, to be out there at the edge of things, to let the human taint wash away in emptiness and silence [...] to return to town a stranger."[23] For some readers, this human self-loathing will be discomforting. But it is worth trying to understand that Baker's disidentification with his own species expresses his sense that what we lack, in our human lives, is an experience of being fully absorbed in a habitat. "We have no element," he writes.[24] For Baker, fully occupying habitat – the experience of being immersed in a highly specific world, to which one is perceptually attuned – amounts to a form of liberty unavailable to us who, insulated by our infrastructures and technologies, can occupy any environment. "You cannot know what freedom means," he writes, "till you have seen a peregrine loosed into the warm spring air sky to roam at will through all the far provinces of light."[25] Strikingly, for both Clare and Baker, freedom is not understood as an absence of constraint, the ability to be anywhere or do anything. Freedom, rather, is what habitat enables, a mode of autonomous life that comes from being supported within a territory.

The Peregrine is haunted by the forces transforming the countryside, above all the intensification of industrial-scale farming and the use of toxic pesticides. The patchwork of small farms were being replaced by giant monocultural fields. Hedgerows, offering habitat for the small birds on which peregrines prey, were being ripped out. The pesticide DDT was used beginning in the mid-1950s, around the time Baker began his observations, and the population of raptors plummeted. In 1962, Rachel Carson published *Silent Spring*, exposing the catastrophic effects of DDT on bird life. Baker vividly evokes these conditions, although he does not dwell on them. "Few peregrines are left," he writes, "there will be fewer, they may not survive. Many die on their backs, clutching insanely at the sky in their last convulsions, withered and burnt away by the filthy, insidious pollen of farm chemicals."[26] Baker believed that peregrines in England were doomed. As Robert Macfarlane notes, however, Baker's elegiac tone may have been premature. The population of peregrines has increased since the publication of *The Peregrine*, mainly due to the banning of DDT.[27] While many raptors are still killed, illegally, by game-keepers preserving the upland moors for pheasant-hunting, in recent decades peregrines in the United Kingdom and elsewhere have adapted to a new type of habitat: cities. Large human-built structures provide ideal nesting sites and vantage points. Cities also provide prey: doves, pigeons, and small mammals. Perhaps Baker's very awareness of the extent to which the peregrines were embedded within a specific habitat blinded him to the possibility that they could adapt to a changing world.

The Elephant Domain

In recent decades, a number of novels have explored the politics of conservation, habitat loss, and the complex ways human and animal lives enmesh in disputed territory, including R. K. Narayan's *A Tiger for Malgudi* (1983), Amitav Ghosh's *The Hungry Tide* (2004), T. C. Boyle's *When the Killing's Done* (2011), and Barbara Kingsolver's *Flight Behavior* (2012). These novels are, however, focalized around human perspectives and perceptions. Animal habitat also features prominently in classic adventure stories, often read to and by children, such as Jack London's *White Fang* (1906), Henry Williamson's *Tarka the Otter* (1927), Robert O'Brien's *Mrs. Frisby and the Rats of NIMH* (1971), and Richard Adams's *Watership Down*

(1972). These stories, with animal characters speaking and behaving like humans, grow out of the tradition of beast fables, in which anthropomorphized animals teach moral lessons. In each of these adventure novels, though, aspects of the distinct species-being of the central animal characters are expressed in their relation to habitat: in the repeated subsistence crises in *White Fang*; in the otter hunts and traps navigated by Tarka; when Mrs. Frisby, a field mouse, seeks to relocate her den to avoid the spring plowing; and in the destruction of the rabbit warrens and the threat of predators faced by the rabbits in *Watership Down*. In these adventure stories, the unique life-worlds of wild animals are explored less through characterization (since in each story the animal characters are granted human-like minds) than in setting, in the representation of habitat.

Barbara Gowdy's *The White Bone* is an extraordinarily inventive novel focalized around nonhuman animals, African bush elephants, living in their wild, though increasingly encroached on, habitat. Unlike the adventure stories just discussed, *The White Bone* is written for an adult audience. It features graphic depictions of animal sexuality and harrowing depictions of poachers massacring elephants. Rather than offering a rousing moral, its tone is tragic.

Gowdy negotiates a fine line in her representation of elephant subjectivity. In some ways, her elephants act like real elephants: forming matriarchal herds, jockeying for dominance, perceiving the world primarily through scent, and mourning their dead. Yet, more fantastically, her characters also speak, sing hymns, create rock art, and comprehend the causal forces in their worlds in ways that are both religious and scientific. In granting language and reason to elephants, Gowdy, we might conclude, anthropomorphizes them. Yet anthropomorphism is a troubled concept because it presupposes that a wide range of subjective capacities are innately and uniquely human.[28] Consider, for example, religion. Elephants are known for their elaborate practices of mourning, which Gowdy represents as a form of collective ritual. And, as Donovan Shaefer asks, should we not consider the complex modes of sociability, repetitive behavior, and heightened affective responses to death that we see in animals the basis for what we call religion?[29] Yet Gowdy pushes further, into the realm of fantasy, when she grants her characters an ornate belief system, with a benevolent deity ("the She"), a creation story, and an embodiment of cosmic evil: human beings.

In representing elephant minds in a human language, English, Gowdy's omniscient narrator certainly anthropomorphizes (and Anglicizes) her nonhuman characters. Yet Gowdy repurposes English in order to show that elephant language, in its associative logic, gives expression to elephant

Umwelt, a singular way of knowing and inhabiting a dynamic environment. The novel is prefaced with a detailed glossary. A cricket is a "creaker"; a snake is a "flow-stick"; humans are "hindleggers"; helicopters are "roar flies"; fences are "webs."[30] These words attest to the unique manner in which elephants perceive their world. Gowdy's elephants, like actual elephants, also communicate in ways alien to human experience, trumpeting, groaning, growling, and utilizing infrasonic underground rumbles to send messages across long distances. They negotiate complex relations, affects, and hierarchies within the herd and with other species, as when Date Bed finds herself conferring with flies who in their zooming and buzzing appear to help her locate water.

Foregrounding the importance of habitat, the first page of *The White Bone* features a map of "The Domain," with rivers, salt licks, notable trees used for orientation and feed, and impassable fence lines. Route-finding is key to survival, which means closely attending to subtle details such as "bird calls, the shape of the horizon, the exact placement of bushes, rocks, the texture and incline of the ground, the light."[31] Elephant territory is defined primarily by the distribution of water (rivers, swamps, mud wallows) and graze. The novel is set during the "worst drought in the matriarch's memory," forcing long periods of migration in search of water.[32] Elephant territory is marked, as well, by the presence of other animals, with whom the elephants have an uneasy relation, and by human objects, such as fences, villages, and the mysterious hubcap Date Bed discovers. Geography is remembered with a precision and intensity unmatched by human memory. It is also interpreted. Elephants, such as the "Link Bull" Tall Time, study the country's portentous signs and omens, each "pointing to something else," which, though often ambiguous, evince deep causal connections within the web of life.[33]

As in the other texts surveyed here, in *The White Bone* the human presence is disastrous. The novel's tragic mood expresses not the difficulty of life for mortal beings but a loss of meaning in a world of indiscriminate slaughter. Repeated massacres traumatize the survivors and fray the social relations within the herd that comprise a form of collective intelligence. For the elephants, humans are enigmatic and terrifying. Unlike with other animals, communication with "hindleggers" is impossible. The trauma of massacres, human encroachment, and the unrelenting drought create, among the elephants, a need for solace. The plot of the novel follows the search for a rumored "Safe Place." The "white bone" is a mystical object that would direct the elephants to this "refuge" – perhaps a wildlife park – where there is "permanent green browse" and where humans peacefully observe the creatures congregating there.[34] For the elephants, the Safe Place is a source of "hope," though the novel implies that it may be only a wishful fantasy, sustaining them as they navigate a degraded and dangerous landscape.[35]

Gowdy's "fantastical anthropomorphism," as Onno Oerlemans argues, may inspire incredulity in the reader, positioning us to ask what we can and cannot know about the minds of other highly intelligent animals, compelling us to reckon with the "imaginative leaps" that enable us to know other minds of any sort.[36] It is particularly notable, then, that Gowdy's elephant characters themselves often wonder about the minds of others, asking what it is like to be a warthog, or cheetah, or eagle. *The White Bone*, though, is not just a fantasy novel. There is a naturalism, and a powerful imaginative sympathy, in its depiction of the trauma and social breakdown caused by habitat loss and poaching, and of the difficult choices that elephants make, individually and collectively, as they negotiate a frayed world.[37] Not unlike Clare's elegiac poetry, *The White Bone* is a study of dispossession and displacement, of what it means for wild creatures to negotiate the loss of habitat.

Vanishing Worlds

While the narrator of *The White Bone* is omniscient (and, implicitly, human), Ted Chiang's short story "The Great Silence" is narrated by a parrot directly addressing the human reader. The narrator inhabits the Río Abajo forest in Arecibo, a region on the north coast of Puerto Rico known for the observatory that, until recently, housed a radio telescope. For the parrot, this scientific instrument exposes a contradiction in human nature: our fascination with the possible existence of extraterrestrial life contrasts with our disregard for our intelligent terrestrial kin. The parrot introduces the Fermi Paradox, one of the great problems of twentieth-century cosmology. In our vast and ancient universe, life must have arisen on many planets, and yet "there is no sign of life anywhere except on Earth."[38] The parrot considers possible solutions to this paradox. Perhaps intelligent life chooses to hide its presence. "Speaking as a member of a species that has been driven nearly to extinction by humans," the narrator observes, "I can attest that this is a wise strategy."[39] Another explanation is that intelligent life tends toward self-extinction. From the perspective of the narrator, the human capacity for ecocide, the anthropogenic destruction of the biospheric foundations of planetary life, supports such a solution: "Hundreds of years ago, my kind was so plentiful that the Río Abajo forest resounded with our voices. Now we're almost gone. Soon this rainforest may be as silent as the rest of the universe."[40]

The parrot sympathizes with our curiosity about extraterrestrial life but cannot understand our apathetic relation to the extraordinary living beings with whom we share the Earth. As the narrator observes,

> We Puerto Rican Parrots have our own myths. They're simpler than human mythology, but I think humans would take pleasure from them. Alas, our myths are being lost as my species dies out. I doubt the humans will have deciphered our language before we're gone. So the extinction of my species doesn't just mean the loss of a group of birds. It's also the disappearance of our language, our rituals, our traditions. It's the silencing of our voice.[41]

Like Gowdy, Chiang attributes to the parrots a unique species lifeworld expressed in culture, a mythic worldview. Both writers use this fantastical conceit to evoke the loss of a distinct animal *Umwelt*. In similar though more naturalistic terms, Eileen Crist observes that declining wildlife populations and species extinctions amount to a loss of diversity not only of life forms but also of ways of life, of inhabiting, perceiving, and interpreting:

> The world that gopher tortoises create – or beavers, bison, fungi, mosses, hub trees, coral reefs, sea otters, elephants, and sharks for that matter – invites us to pause and view it. In viewing their world, we might understand it as the imprint of a "worldview" – call it the gopher tortoise worldview – on the landscape.[42]

What is necessary to sustain such diverse "worldviews," Crist insists, is the preservation of habitat, above all in the form of wilderness, "lands and waters sizeable enough to support wide-ranging species, especially big carnivores and herbivores who need largely people-free, expansive spaces to live, disperse, and migrate."[43] A wilderness is more than a source of scenic beauty or a temporary refuge from the demands of modern life. Wilderness is a place of inhabitation, a world harboring multiple worlds, territory where animals, many of which cannot survive in anthropogenic environments, live with a degree of autonomy, where ecological processes unfold not entirely determined by human will.

It is easy to despair when confronted with habitat loss and species extinction, the extinguishing of the unique *Umwelten* of our nonhuman kin. The writers discussed in this chapter all experienced such despair, along with a painful human self-awareness brought on by the imaginative act of viewing our species from the perspective of wild animals. Yet it is also important to recognize that the work of protecting habitat is ongoing, in efforts to conserve the wild habitat that remains and to restore damaged ecosystems. In the United Kingdom, one of the most nature-depleted nations in the world, such efforts, in recent years, have taken form in initiatives to rewild regions denuded of biodiversity. Clare's "Swordy Well" has been resurrected as a nature preserve, Swaddywell Pit. After being used as a rubbish dump for much of the twentieth century, it was set aside as a preserve in 2003 – in part, due to its association with a Romantic poet – and now provides habitat for great crested newts and a variety of other plants, insects, birds, and mammals.

Notes

1 Jakob von Uexküll, *Theoretical Biology* (New York: Harcourt, Brace & Co., 1926), 70.
2 Jakob von Uexküll, *A Foray into the Worlds of Animals and Humans*, trans. Joseph D. O'Neil (Minneapolis: University of Minnesota Press, 2010), 53.
3 Uexküll, *Foray*, 143.
4 On Uexküll's broad influence, see Carlo Brentari, *Jakob von Uexküll: The Discovery of the Umwelt between Biosemiotics and Theoretical Biology* (Dordrecht: Springer, 2015). On Uexküll's influence on animal studies, see Giorgio Agamben, *The Open: Man and Animal* (Stanford, CA: Stanford University Press, 2004), chapters 10 and 11; Inga Pollmann, "Invisible Worlds, Visible: Uexküll's *Umwelt*, Film, and Film Theory," *Critical Inquiry* 39.4 (Summer 2013), 777–816; and David Herman, *Narratology beyond the Human: Storytelling and Animal Life* (Oxford: Oxford University Press, 2018), chapter 4.
5 Herman, *Narratology beyond the Human*, 119–20.
6 See Radhika Govindrajan, *Animal Intimacies: Interspecies Relatedness in India's Central Himalayas* (Chicago: University of Chicago Press, 2018), chapter 4; and Thom Van Dooren, *The Wake of Crows: Living and Dying in Shared Worlds* (New York: Columbia University Press, 2019), chapter 1.
7 James McKusick, *Green Writing: Romanticism and Ecology* (New York: St. Martin's Press, 2000), 78.
8 See John Barrell, *The Idea of Landscape and the Sense of Place 1730–1840* (Cambridge: Cambridge University Press, 1972), 103.
9 See *John Clare's Birds*, ed. Eric Robinson and Richard Fitter (Oxford: Oxford University Press, 1982), xii and xix.
10 Gilbert White, *The Natural History of Selborne*, ed. Anne Secord (Oxford: Oxford University Press, 2016), 120.
11 Joseph A. Veech, *Habitat Ecology and Analysis* (Oxford: Oxford University Press, 2021), 24.
12 John Clare, "Shadows of Taste," in *Major Works* (Oxford: Oxford University Press, 2004), 170–4, lines 5–16; cited hereafter in text by line number.
13 Barrell, *Landscape*, 166.
14 Joe Albernaz, "John Clare's World," *European Romantic Review* 27.2 (2016), 189–205.
15 John Clare, "The Nightingales Nest," in *Major Works* (Oxford: Oxford University Press, 2004), line 13; cited hereafter in text by line number.

16 John Clare, "Helpstone," in *Major Works* (Oxford: Oxford University Press, 2004), 1–5, lines 22–4; cited hereafter in text by line number.

17 John Clare, "[The Lament of Swordy Well]," in *Major Works* (Oxford: Oxford University Press, 2004), 147–52, lines 81–6; cited hereafter in text by line number.

18 John Clare, "The Mores," in *Major Works* (Oxford: Oxford University Press, 2004), 167–9, lines 8 and 39.

19 J. A. Baker, *The Peregrine*, 1967 (New York: New York Review of Books, 2005), 12.

20 Ibid., 35.

21 Ibid., 86, 22.

22 Ibid., 95

23 Ibid., 10.

24 Ibid., 171

25 Ibid., 178.

26 Ibid., 14–15.

27 Robert Macfarlane, "Violent Spring: The Nature Book That Predicted the Future," *The Guardian*, April 15, 2017.

28 See Eileen Crist, *Images of Animals: Anthropomorphism and Animal Mind* (Philadelphia: Temple University Press, 1999).

29 Donovan O. Shaefer, *Religious Affects: Animality, Evolution, and Power* (Durham, NC: Duke University Press, 2015).

30 Barbara Gowdy, *The White Bone* (New York: Metropolitan Books, 1998).

31 Ibid., 227.

32 Ibid., 20.

33 Ibid., 135.

34 Ibid., 44.

35 Ibid., 158.

36 Onno Oerlemans, "A Defense of Anthropomorphism: Comparing Coetzee and Gowdy," *Mosaic* 40.1 (March 2007), 181–96.

37 See Charles Siebert, "An Elephant Crackup?," *New York Times Magazine*, October 8, 2006.

38 Ted Chiang, "The Great Silence," in *The Best American Short Stories 2016* (Boston: Mariner Books, 2016), 69–72, 69.

39 Ibid., 69.

40 Ibid., 70.

41 Ibid., 72.

42 Eileen Crist, *Abundant Earth: Toward an Ecological Civilization* (Chicago: University of Chicago Press, 2019), 218.

43 Ibid., 116.

CHAPTER 11

Captivity
Zoos as Scenes of Nonencounter

Antoine Traisnel

As far as I can recall, the initial shiver of inspiration was somehow prompted by a newspaper story about an ape in the Jardin des Plantes, who, after months of coaxing by a scientist, produced the first drawing ever charcoaled by an animal: the sketch showed the bars of the poor creature's cage.[1]

Zoogoing

Lydia Millet's 2009 short story "Zoogoing" begins with boredom. On a business trip to Arizona, a young real-estate developer known as "T." visits the Scottsdale zoo "to fill an empty afternoon" (35).[2] T.'s interest is moderately piqued by the caged animals, who seem equally indifferent to him, until an incident interrupts the stillness of the afternoon: he witnesses two young boys throwing litter at a black bear so their father can snap a decent shot of the sleepy animal. Seized with a feeling between rage and excitement, T. jumps to the bear's rescue, threatening to punch the father in the face if he does not leave the bear alone. As the family flees the scene, T. realizes that he has found his calling: "He was elated. This was who he was, he thought; he was a person who would defend, who would swear and threaten and feel the heat and the cliff-edge of opinion."[3] A person who would defend ... *what*? By stripping the verb of a direct object, Millet hints that the bear is superfluous to T.'s grand epiphany. The sentence reenacts grammatically the "quiet mass disappearance" of the sixth extinction, which passed unnoticed "outside fringe elements and elite groups, professors and hippies."[4] The verb's unsettling intransitivity compounds the irony of T.'s vacuous pledge to defend something that is already being defended – and, in a sense, that is already gone. After the incident, T. stands "in rapture," basking in the altruistic glory of his newfound vocation; meanwhile the bear tosses "his head as though trapped in a nightmare" and goes back to sleep.[5]

Because it was never about the bears. T.'s solipsistic awakening hyper-
bolizes the paradox of zoogoing as described by John Berger: "Public zoos
came into existence at the beginning of the period which was to see the
disappearance of animals from daily life," Berger observes. "The zoo to
which people go to meet animals, to observe them, to see them, is, in fact,
a monument to the impossibility of such encounters."[6] What Millet's
protagonist had hoped to find at the zoo, tellingly, was not living animals
but "the wildness it contained. [. . .] He wanted to meet it."[7] From the
outset, animals are reduced to an abstraction. For T., captive animals
embody the solitude of the modern condition. Not the trivial loneliness
endemic in individualist Western societies but the radical aloneness of
being the last of one's species – a unique, irreplaceable life-form barreling
toward extinction, "a whole volume in the library of being" about to go
out of print forever.[8] As much as he laments the loss of their "particular
way of existence,"[9] T. cannot help but regard endlings as canaries in the
coal mine of the Sixth Extinction, "pioneers [. . .] sent ahead to see what
the new world was like" and prepare him for the day "it would be men that
were last."[10] When he decides to climb into the enclosures of endangered
specimens under the cover of night, it is not to raise awareness about their
vulnerability or the poor conditions of their custody, but simply to be
"alone with" them.[11] Stepping into their exhibits does nothing to bridge
the distance that separates him from them, and the story ends just as it
begins, with boredom. Ironically, this is the only thing T. seems capable of
sharing with vanishing animals. Once he surrenders to boredom, he
manages to fall asleep next to his encaged companions, like the black bear
in the opening scene. Only then is he truly "alone with" animals.

Built around this aberrant syntagma, "alone with," the story dramatizes
Berger's insight that animals have been "rendered absolutely marginal"
with the advent of capitalist culture in the Global North. "The public
purpose of zoos is to offer visitors the opportunity of looking at animals,"
Berger observes. "Yet nowhere in a zoo can a stranger encounter the look
of an animal. At the most, the animal's gaze flickers and passes on. They
look sideways. They look blindly beyond. They scan mechanically."[12] Zoo
animals, Berger argues, have been utterly "immunised to encounter."[13]
But should we assume that all zoogoers "miss" animals in the same way
T. misses the bear he vows to protect? T. is a traveling salesman who
approaches endlings the way Silicon Valley CEOs approach NFTs.
Through the lens of his myopic idealism – his quixotic promise "to
defend," his fetishization of "wildness," his narcissistic misanthropy –
animals cannot but appear "out of focus," as Berger laments.[14] Yet even

if we accept Berger's premise that zoos inoculate against species encounter, can we not imagine different forms of nonencounter? Different manners of looking at zoo animals, and thus different ways of *not seeing* them?

In this chapter, I consider three literary *scenes of nonencounter* with captive animals in Rainer Maria Rilke's poem "The Panther" (1902/3), Julio Cortázar's fantastic tale "Axolotl" (1957), and Marie NDiaye's experimental novella *La naufragée* (*The Castaway*, 1999). These three texts stage a missed encounter with an animal at the Jardin des Plantes' zoological garden in Paris. It is in this zoo that Nabokov claims to have found his muse for *Lolita* in an ape cajoled into producing "the first drawing ever charcoaled by an animal" but who could sketch only the bars of its cage.[15] Given Nabokov's admiration for Kafka, it is likely that his ape is the descendant of Red Peter, the simian protagonist of the 1917 short story "A Report to an Academy."[16] Captured in West Africa and shipped to Europe by Carl Hagenbeck's company of animal traders, Red Peter must learn to speak German to avoid ending his days locked up in a zoological garden. When pressed to give a report about his previous life as an ape, he informs his captors that he cannot comply, as though acquiring human speech caused him to forget everything about his past apehood. Stepping into language does not emancipate Red Peter from animal muteness. For him, ironically, speech is just an expedient, a more spacious enclosure in which humans find themselves unwittingly trapped. In the scenes examined below, captive animals appear similarly unapproachable but, unlike Kafka's and Nabokov's apes, they are not explicitly prompted to express themselves on behalf of their species, nor are they observed with a view to lay bare the secret of animal life. Although species do not meet in Rilke, Cortázar, and NDiaye, the singular ways in which they miss one another suggest that *nonencounter* is eminently contingent. Respectively written in German, Spanish, and French, these texts spanning the twentieth century have little in common except that each posits that captivity radically alters the experience of looking at and interacting with animal(ized) others. The nonencounters they stage are not simply the negation of encounter since animals are obviously *there*, before the zoogoer. Nonencounter, instead, is a paradoxical measure of interspecies cohabitation when coexistence appears impossible.[17] If Berger is right that zoos epitomize the systemic disappearance of animals in Western modernity insofar as they disallow human-animal encounters, then focusing on the distinct forms assumed by nonencounter might help us to articulate the shifting epistemological and political stakes of looking at captive animals. It also allows us to sketch the lineaments of an ethics of viewing and reading that is predicated not on direct contact, visibility, and sympathy, but rather on entanglement, reflectivity, and detachment.[18]

Nonencounters at the Jardin des Plantes

As the world's second oldest zoological garden and the first one open to the general public, the Jardin des Plantes has been a frequent source of inspiration for writers since it opened its doors in 1794. Romantics such as William Wordsworth and Ralph Waldo Emerson report being deeply impressed by the Jardin des Plantes, to the extent that the latter claims that it is in the menagerie arranged in accordance with French naturalist Georges Cuvier's classificatory system that he first glimpsed nature's harmonious composition;[19] it is in one of its enclosures that the very first criminal of modern detective fiction was locked up at the end of Poe's "Murders in the Rue Morgue" (1841); and its quaint layout has served as a backdrop for countless novels and poems, from Victor Hugo, Honoré de Balzac, and Emile Zola in the nineteenth century to W. G. Sebald, Yasmina Reza, and Christine Montalbetti more recently. Such appeal is not surprising since the menagerie was explicitly designed to attract artists from the outset. Established in the wake of the French Revolution on the recommendation of the botanist and novelist Bernardin de Saint Pierre, the zoo was meant to benefit "the nation rather than a select few."[20] It would provide scientists and artists an opportunity to try their hand at the "living monuments of nature," explained Bernardin de Saint Pierre, when all they had at their disposal before were the fossils and skeletons on display at the Natural History Museum.[21] Despite concerns about captivity's tendency to "weaken the character of animals," its founders were confident that imported specimens would eventually acclimatize to the French soil by being surrounded by plants indigenous to their places of origin.[22] Financial and spatial constraints, however, consistently challenged this attunement to the animals' environmental needs.[23] When Irish poet Louis MacNeice visited the menagerie in 1938, he described it as a vermin-infested "glory in decline" whose poor approximations of natural habitats paled in comparison with the modern Zoo de Vincennes, which had adopted the "Hagenbeck principle – bars or wire being replaced by ditches between the animals and the visitors."[24]

Because its baroque layout makes it particularly unsusceptible to reform, the menagerie at the Jardin des Plantes betrays more than other zoos that the "benefits of containing animals for education and entertainment" are often overstated, as Derek Ryan observes.[25] Ryan turns to Jacques

Derrida's *The Beast and the Sovereign* (2009) to understand how the emergence of public zoos at the end of the eighteenth century perpetuated and even accelerated the exploitation of animals while ostensibly marking the dawn of a more enlightened and humane period in their treatment. Derrida ventures that the Jardin des Plantes, despite its revolutionary ambitions, did not really topple the structure of scientific knowledge, which remained predicated on the sovereign power to see without being seen. Relocating animals from the royal menagerie to the Jardin des Plantes, Derrida argues, was little more than a "transfer of power."[26] And yet, even as he laments that the fundamental architecture of power-knowledge was maintained under the guise of radical change, the philosopher sheepishly admits that he "nevertheless remain[s] enamored of the Jardin des Plantes."[27] What are we to make of this passing confession? It is tempting to contrast this fondness for the old Paris zoo with the malaise Derrida experiences after being "seen naked under the gaze of a cat" in his bathroom.[28] It is unlikely that the well-known scene that opens *The Animal That Therefore I Am* (2008) – in which the philosopher describes a cat entering his space, coming "into this place *where it can encounter me, see me*"[29] – could have taken place at a public zoo, where "people go to meet animals, observe them."[30] It is surprisingly in the privacy of one's home that the eyes of an animal can unexpectedly be met (even as the animal's gaze remains absolutely "bottomless").[31] But in a zoo, such chance encounters seem impossible precisely because zoos, "even when they are instituted for the purpose of knowledge or for the protection of animals, [...] are also places of spectacle, theaters."[32] Both the private home and the public zoo are designed to shield from animal encounters, albeit in different ways. The zoo appears as the mirror image of the home: the latter is the site of a *possible impossibility* (the animal appears where you least expect it, yet it remains "wholly other" despite its "intolerable proximity");[33] the former stages an *impossible possibility* (animals are not where you most expect to find them; they are overexposed yet unseen as seeing beings).

The scenes of nonencounter at the Jardin des Plantes recounted by Rilke, Cortázar, and NDiaye register a similar sense of estrangement, only one magnified by the authors' difficulty to feel entirely "at home" in the French capital.[34] While one essay cannot do justice to the complexity of these texts or to the expansive secondary literature devoted to them, my ambition here is simply to consider how such different authors have responded to the same historical phenomenon. When they evoke captive animals, they focus less on what has been lost (wildness, the possibility of encounter) than on the material, cultural, and epistemological conditions under which humans approach animals *as lost*. Rilke primarily ponders over the epistemological implications of this epochal nonencounter: his poem describes the panther's gaze as wholly barred from the outer world, but it also suggests that the human eye is just as limited by comparing the zoo enclosure to another apparatus of capture, the camera, which promises increased access to its object but radically desynchronizes the observer from the observed and makes their coexistence unthinkable. Cortázar's short story inscribes nonencounter in the colonial context that made faraway creatures available for European amusement and edification. Paradoxically, the hypervisibility to which axolotls are subjected in their aquarium only increases the viewer's sense of alienation from the animals. In their utter inscrutability, the axolotls nonetheless present "another way of seeing"; they are "witnesses of something."[35] That vague "something" is the repressed history of colonial capture out of which European zoos were born and to which the narrator becomes alert at the price of losing his humanity – of becoming the axolotl he scrutinizes. NDiaye's *La naufragée* connects this colonial history of zoological capture to the forcible dislocation and subjugation of enslaved Africans to reflect on the dangers of aesthetic sublimation and art's responsibility toward an "event" of such magnitude. The title's castaway, who is half-woman, half-fish, remains unintelligible when she speaks, but as soon as she sings, her voice is deemed invaluable – a "natural" reserve mineable by artists who approach her song as a source of inspiration, not a medium of expression. NDiaye's magical-realist tale suggests that the dialectic of Enlightenment consists not in resisting the song of Sirens but rather, as Adorno and Horkheimer had recognized, in absorbing it for the benefit and enjoyment of a select few.[36] Exoticized and animalized bodies are deemed immiscible with human modernity even as they are consumed for its material and aesthetic advancement.

Entangled Visions

Of all the animals that caught Rilke's eye during his visits to the Jardin des Plantes, the panther is by far the most charismatic. In English alone, one can easily find more than thirty translations of "The Panther." Below is Stephen Mitchell's translation:

> The Panther
> *In the Jardin des Plantes, Paris*

His vision, from the constantly passing bars,
has grown so weary that it cannot hold
anything else. It seems to him there are
a thousand bars; and behind the bars, no world.

As he paces in cramped circles, over and over,
the movement of his powerful soft strides
is like a ritual dance around a center
in which a mighty will stands paralyzed.

Only at times, the curtain of the pupils
lifts, quietly –. An image enters in,
rushes down through the tensed, arrested muscles,
plunges into the heart and is gone.[37]

On the face of it, the poem describes a panther rendered impotent by captivity, its mighty will "stupefied" (*betaübt*) by solitary confinement, its gaze so exhausted that it can no longer "hold" anything beyond the bars of its cage. From the outset, however, the poem drifts into abstractions, presenting the reader, not with eyes but a visionless gaze (*Blick*), not with the organs of sight but their inoperative function. Rilke shifts from the indicative to the subjunctive to account for the animal's diminished condition, speculating that the cage does not simply restrict its movements but obliterates the/its world ("behind the bars, no world"). This evocation of the animal's world put under erasure reads as a preemptive response to Heidegger's infamous thesis, formulated some twenty-five years later, that the animal is essentially "poor-in-world." Where Heidegger dogmatically assumes *Benommenheit* (stupor, captivation) to be "the essence of animality,"[38] Rilke presents the panther's mental state of captivation as an effect of its physical captivity. This explains why the Estonian ethologist Jakob von Uexküll found in "The Panther" a perfect illustration for his concept of *Umwelt*, the subjective lifeworld that "surrounds" every organism. Rilke's poem, explains Geoffrey Winthrop Young, "is an *ex negativo* depiction of Uexküll's Umwelt: a snapshot of a defunct Umwelt destroyed by the removal of the animal from the habitat that contained all the perceptual markers it had been 'fitted into.'"[39]

The poem describes the destructive powers of captivity while hinting that captivity is also productive in the sense that it gives access, albeit negatively, to the animal's subjective phenomenal world. The deprivations captivity inflicts on the panther make knowable what *was* or *might have been* meaningful to it. To heed the animal's unresponsive gaze is thus to acknowledge that it inhabits an altogether different world, or at least that its way of inhabiting the world is incommensurable with ours. Yet even as it appears unencounterable, a new image of the panther flickers through the bars of the cage. The poem invites the reader to *imagine* the panther by combining "snapshots of a defunct Umwelt" just as a movie creates an impression of movement by stringing together a sequence of still images.[40] The bars perform the dual function of keeping the animal out of reach and making it legible, effectively reanimating it before the eyes of the reader/viewer. "Constantly passing," the bars evoke the lines of the poem, whose first and last word is *sein*, which makes it seem trapped in a virtually endless cycle of recurrence, not unlike its subject pacing "in cramped circles, over and over."[41] But the bars also conjure up the "frame lines," this unused space on a film strip between two contiguous images. Cinematic vision is predicated on the disappearance of these vertical dividers, which become invisible to the human eye only when the film runs at the appropriate speed. The poem, however, refuses to give a seamless impression of the panther. Instead, it makes its object quiver by foregrounding the bars, to the extent that it is the captive subject (and not the bars) that *appears to disappear* before the reader/viewer's eyes. The panther is simultaneously there and not there, detained but unholdable, exposed yet unseeable.

Because it is not just the panther's gaze that is blurred by capture. In a recent reading of the poem, Kári Driscoll observes that we are led to assume that the pronoun *sein* with which the poem opens refers to the panther, "but it can with equal justification be taken to refer metatextually to the reader." Driscoll cleverly plays on the etymological affinity between bars (*Stäbe*) and the letters of the alphabet (*Buchstaben*), which imperceptibly pass "before the reader's eyes as we scan the lines of the poem."[42] It is this undecidable equivocation over whose gaze no longer can see the world beyond the bars (or can no longer see the bars through which the world manifests itself) that justifies Driscoll's "zoopoetic" reading of "The Panther."[43] Thematically, "the poem forecloses any contact between the panther and the outside world," but "formally it establishes an empathic connection between the reader/observer and the animal."[44] Insofar as it enables the reader to "imagine ourselves in the panther's place," Driscoll argues, it can be read as the "record of an engagement" with an animal.[45] I find Driscoll's interpretation compelling, but it might be more accurate to view the poem as the record of an *entanglement*, rather than engagement. Rey Chow defines entanglements as "the linkages and enmeshments that keep things apart; the voidings and uncoverings that hold things together."[46] Her formulation emulates the chiasmic topology of entanglement staged by the poem: to see the panther is to see a nonseeing being; to imagine a seeing panther demands acknowledging the untranscendable limits of one's own sight. The poem therefore invites its readers not to "empathize" with the panther, as Driscoll suggests, so much as to contemplate themselves in the diffracted image of a captive animal.

Fantastic Reflections

"The Panther" hints that the spatial restrictions imposed by captivity also affect the subject's experience of time. Condemned to repeat the same meaningless "dance" around an ever-narrower center, the panther appears trapped in an interminable present. The poem alludes to a time *prior to* the suspended temporality of captivation – the gaze "no longer holds" anything (*nichts mehr hält*) – but it is more interested in the effects of captivity than in its prehistory. Had Rilke consulted the Jardin's catalog of acquisitions, he might have been able to trace his panther's place of origin.[47] Was it the African leopard named Wasiri, a "gift" of the French explorer M. Versepuy? Or this panther sent from Gabon in 1896 by Pietro Savorgnan di Brazzà, the governor-general of the French Congo?[48] While we cannot ascertain which panther Rilke beheld at the Jardin des Plantes, we know that of the specimens present at the time, none was born in captivity. All had been recently captured in Africa or Asia. It is to this unaccounted history of colonial appropriation that "Axolotl" bears witness. The narrator of Cortázar's story reports developing a sudden obsession for axolotls after stopping one morning by the Jardin des Plantes to visit his "friends" the lions and panthers.[49] Disappointed by what he finds in their enclosures ("The lions were sad and ugly, and my panther was asleep"), he falls back on the "dark, humid building" of the aquarium and unexpectedly "hit[s] it off" with axolotls.[50] Although axolotls are being observed through the glass of an aquarium, not the bars of a cage, and although unlike panthers axolotls cannot shut their eyes to the world since they "have no lids," they appear infinitely more distant than Rilke's dejected feline.[51]

At first, the narrator tries to familiarize himself with axolotls by consulting a dictionary, in which he gleans facts about their place of origin, name, physiology, and culinary uses. But this specialized knowledge seems inadequate to the task of apprehending his subject. Empirical observation likewise appears limited, as the axolotls' description betrays the narrator's anthropomorphic proclivities: "On both sides of the head *where the ears should have been*, there grew three tiny sprigs, red as coral, a vegetal outgrowth, the gills, I suppose."[52] The use of the conditional hints at the normative bias that informs the narrator's description, who surveys axolotls with the assumption that their anatomy *should be* comparable with his own. As it becomes clear that this expectation will not be satisfied, the text lingers on all that separates humans from axolotls, both physiologically (they are amphibians living in a perpetual larval state) and morphologically (only their hands are humanlike, but this similarity is quickly dismissed as irrelevant). The "vegetal outgrowth" of their gills, their mineral translucence, and eerie stillness even suggest that they are "not *animals.*"[53] Most otherworldly are their eyes, "two orifices [. . .] lacking any life but looking, letting themselves be penetrated by my look, which seemed to [. . .] lose itself in a diaphanous interior mystery."[54]

"And nevertheless they were close."[55] Despite his inability to establish contact with axolotls, the narrator cannot shake the feeling that they are somehow related: "I knew that we were linked, that something infinitely lost and distant kept pulling us together."[56] To account for this indeterminate "something" that makes his narrator gravitate toward axolotls, Cortázar does not resort to the lexicon of kinship, affinity, or proximity. Their bond utterly defies comprehension ("I knew that no understanding was possible").[57] It is a matter of *re*cognition beyond any positive cognition, beyond logic or even analogy: "The absolute lack of similarity between axolotls and human beings proved to me that my recognition [*reconocimiento*] was valid, that I was not propping myself up with easy analogies."[58] The narrator confesses feeling haunted by axolotls even in their absence, "as though I were being affected from a distance."[59] Evocative of Einstein's description of quantum entanglement as "spooky action at a distance," this formulation suggests that the tale's spooky turn – the narrator's sudden realization that he has become "prisoner in the body of an axolotl" – does not signal a rejection of realism so much as an attempt to model an alternative relation to and representation of reality. The fantastic, for Cortázar, is a means to explore what Aristotelian laws dismiss as irrational.[60]

It is not wrong, therefore, to read "Axolotl" as an investigation of species difference when we remember that Aristotle defines the human as the only rational animal, or more precisely the animal endowed with language (*zōon logon echon*).[61] Axolotls are indeed perceived as impenetrable beings purely driven by their instincts. But Cortázar suggests that what separates humans from axolotls is less a function of biology than technology by repeatedly drawing attention to the transparent partition of the aquarium. The glass does not keep its promise of unbarred access to the animal. In fact, it acts as a mirror more than a window. The narrator appears unable to do more than project his own image on the captive animals until he suddenly and inexplicably finds himself on the other side of the looking glass. When he finally sees the world through the eyes of an axolotl, ironically, the glass loses its reflective faculty and what he beholds is (still) his former human self: "I saw my face against the glass, I saw it on the outside of the tank."[62] This statement is logically sound but phenomenologically impossible: in principle, one can never see one's own eyes, except in a reflection or an image. The story's tour de force is to assign the same grammatical position to two different subjects. In the space of three words in the English translation, the first-person pronoun skips from the observing axolotl to the observed human ("*I* saw *my* face"). The Spanish original is even more economical: "*vi mi cara contra el vidrio.*" Without any transition (*sin transición*), the narration is surreptitiously handed over to the captive animal. By exploding narratological conventions, the tale introduces the unthinkable notion that thinking is not a human prerogative: "He was outside the aquarium, his thinking was a *thinking outside the tank.*"[63]

The human/animal distinction is no longer articulated along the thinking/unthinking dichotomy, as in the Aristotelian typology of living beings, but it is organized topologically, in terms of outside versus inside. From this vantage, the narrator's initial suspicion that the axolotls' stillness issues from some anarchistic "will to abolish space and time"[64] gets reframed as a quintessentially human thought, a quintessential example of "thinking outside the tank." Once an axolotl, the narrator knows better: "It's that we don't enjoy moving a lot, and the tank is so cramped [...] The time feels like it's less if we stay quietly."[65] The tale's ultimate "recognition" is that axolotls are "suffering, [...] lying in wait for something, a remote dominion destroyed."[66] Their present condition – their sentence without parole, their utter dependence on the guardians' benevolence, their inability to hide from inquisitive visitors – is the product of an untold history of colonial subjugation. The allusions to their "Aztec faces"[67] make axolotls cryptic emblems of decimated pre-Columbian civilizations. Capture is recognized as the precondition of their captivity, but the violence of capture remains unspeakable. It is conceivable only through the irrealistic lens of the fantastic tale (*cuento*). Hence the axolotl narrator concludes with the dubious hope that the man he once was one day will write about axolotls, knowing full well that the man will believe that he's just "making up a story [*creyendo imaginar un cuento*]."[68]

Letting Go

Cortázar greatly admired Poe, so it is not surprising to find in "Axolotl" echoes of "The Murders in the Rue Morgue." Both stories deal with the unsettling possibility that a humanlike consciousness might be trapped – or in Poeian fashion, "buried alive"[69] – inside an animal body. Poe's "tale of ratiocination" ultimately rejects this possibility by enlisting the services of a detective, who reassures the good people of Paris that no reasonable creature would have committed the gruesome murders of the L'Espanaye women. A series of inductions leads Dupin to pin the killings on an orangutan, who from a distance might pass as human but on close inspection is *nothing but an animal*.[70] The police are at a loss because they stubbornly assume that the deed must have been committed by a rational actor with a motive. Only when Dupin suspends this rationalist assumption does the perpetrator manifest itself, albeit negatively, in the figure of an ape whose acts appear entirely unmotivated and whose voice is "devoid of all distinct or intelligible syllabification."[71] Just as the detective pictures the ape as a purely instinctive creature deprived of *logos*, Cortázar's narrator views axolotls as "slaves of their bodies, condemned infinitely to the silence of the abyss."[72] But there is a crucial difference: the former ends up detained at the Jardin des Plantes *because* he is assumed to lack *logos*, whereas the latter come across as without reason (*alogon*) or stupefied *because* they are held captive (hence the idioms of enslavement and punishment). By turning the causality upside down, "Axolotl" reminds us that, after all, a detective story is but a fantastic tale contained within a rationalist frame.

Perhaps Marie NDiaye also had Poe's story in mind when she wrote *La naufragée*. This short book was published as part of Flohic Press's "Secret Museums" series, in which a French-speaking author is invited to write a text inspired by the work of an artist of their choosing (NDiaye's muse is the English painter J. M. W. Turner). A playful take on Hans Christian Andersen's 1837 fairy tale *The Little Mermaid*, *La naufragée* recounts the tribulations of a hybrid creature, part-woman, part-fish, who finds herself marooned in nineteenth-century Paris after being accidentally caught by fishing nets trailing in the open seas. She asks the locals for help but soon realizes that "outside of the water, I'm nothing but a fish."[73] No one can understand her any more than they understand "the stupefied fish [*les poissons hébétés*] that approach the glass wall of their aquarium with their big mute talking mouths opening and closing mutely, stupidly [*muettement, bêtement*]."[74] Indifferent at first, the Parisians quickly become fearful and cruel, and soon an angry mob gathers on the Quai de la Seine threatening to cut off her tail. Fearing for her life, the woman-fish (who dislikes the designation *sirène*) suddenly begins singing a song she did not remember knowing and for a brief moment the crowd is petrified by the inhuman beauty of her voice.[75] Although she is injured and famished, she manages to escape and drag herself to the Halles de Paris, where she is captured and sent to the Jardin des Plantes. There she is found languishing at the bottom a dingy tank by an unnamed painter whose atmospheric landscapes are evocative of Turner's marine landscapes. At this point, the narrative abandons the woman-fish's perspective to relate the rest of her story in the third person. This surreptitious removal of narrative agency enacts at the level of discourse the protagonist's dispossession of a speaking voice in the diegesis. From then on, it becomes clear that her singing voice is her only means to interact with her captors. Mesmerized by the creature's song, the painter appeals to the zoo's humaneness and arranges to acquire her. Once she is "undeniably his thing," he puts her in a trunk, takes her to England, and locks her up in his London apartment.[76] He promises that he will release her if she sings for him (although he does not understand her when she speaks, he has no trouble figuring out what she wants from him). She complies, but he keeps deferring her manumission until he has infused "all her voice" into his paintings.[77]

The text of La naufragée is printed on the right page of the book, with a Turner painting reproduced on the left page. Twice, NDiaye writes opposite details from Turner's 1840 painting The Slave Ship, initially titled Slavers Throwing overboard the Dead and Dying – Typhon Coming On. From a distance, the painting looks rather abstract: three vertical lines figuring the masts of a ship disappear in a tempest signified by a swirling blur of bright reds, yellows, and whites. A closer look, however, reveals a horrific scene taking place in the ship's wake: manacled limbs pierce the surface of a turbulent sea, their dark flesh attacked by hungry fish and seagulls. The painting is believed to refer to the Zong massacre, where more than 130 enslaved Africans were thrown overboard when the ship began running out of drinking water so the owners could file an insurance claim for "lost cargo." Turner's intention was doubtless to denounce the atrocities of the slave trade, but whether his painting succeeds in doing so has been the subject of many debates.[78] The painter's trademark refusal to subordinate color to form can be read as an erasure of the enslaved bodies, reduced in the painting to indistinct silhouettes drowning in a sea of light. Just as Turner has been accused of aestheticizing the violence of the Middle Passage for his artistic gain, NDiaye's fictional painter is introduced as a self-serving artist hoping to transubstantiate the suffering of his model into a self-referential, subjectless, even worldless artwork.

To exploit the woman-fish's mournful song requires acknowledging her pain while denying her humanity altogether. When he looks at her, the painter sees only a "thoughtless and lucid beast" capable of looking back but unable, he convinces himself, to see him the way he sees her (*il eut la conviction, plutôt, qu'elle le voyait d'une manière inimaginable pour lui, à sa façon de bête lucide et sans pensée*).[79] One of her desperate attempts to escape fills him with pity, and for a moment he cannot tell if he sees her cry or if he is the one crying. But this confusing sympathy is quickly repressed when he reasons that he "could not let her go. His work needed something, and this something might be her."[80] He is similarly troubled to feel somewhat aroused when he inspects his model's naked body, but his attraction gives way to repulsion as soon as his gaze moves from her human breasts down to her fish tail. The twin sexualization and bestialization of the woman-fish evokes the treatment of Saartjie Baartman, a Khoi woman exhibited as the "Hottentot Venus" by an animal trainer in London and Paris at the beginning of the nineteenth century. Baartman was sometimes suspended in a cage as an audience of curious visitors was invited to examine and even prod her naked body.[81] She also fascinated the scientific community, to the point that she "spent three days at the Jardin des Plantes [where] she posed nude for the images that appeared in the first volume of [...] *Histoire naturelle des mammifères*."[82] After her death in 1815, Georges Cuvier acquired and dissected her corpse. His autopsy report repeatedly compares her anatomy to the body parts of various apes and reveals an obsession with her genitalia, which the naturalist preserved in a jar (along with her brain) and put on display in the Musée National d'Histoire Naturelle, adjoining the Jardin des Plantes and founded one year prior to the menagerie.

Although she laments that her "part of humanity" is not being recognized, the woman-fish never expresses the desire to be incorporated in the human community that rejects her, in striking contrast to the protagonist of Andersen's fairy tale.[83] All she asks throughout the story is to be returned to the sea. What the painter wishes, on the other hand, is to transcend his own human limitations: "he tried to paint exactly what he was hearing, and precisely what he did not know in the siren's song, all the unknown that constituted it, its absolute and candid inhumanity."[84] His main fear is that if he lets her go, there is no guarantee that she will return to him given that she is "not trained to come back."[85] And yet, paradoxically, it is this very evanescence that he is so desperate to capture. What most transfixes him is her song's perceived ability to forgo objects and subjects alike: "The siren's song ignored images and the evocation of places, beings, or things, so he removed all these things. He kept the pervasive light, sovereign on the canvas, knowing full well that this light was a threat to him: that one day he would not survive the voice."[86] Shortly after smuggling her into London, the painter is found dead alone in his apartment. The narrative concludes where Poe's story began, with a locked-room mystery. Only here it is the master's body that is found lifeless, where in Poe it was innocent bystanders, and no detective is hired to chase the animalized fugitive and put her behind bars at the Jardin des Plantes (where Cuvier taught his courses in comparative anatomy).[87] The painter's friends are puzzled to find an empty tub, but they quickly forget about it "because it was without importance."[88] The woman-fish has vanished beyond the bounds of the narrative.

How are we to interpret this final disappearing act? The epigraph for "Murders in the Rue Morgue" might give us a clue: "What song the Sirens sang," it suggests, is "not beyond all conjecture."[89] And indeed, Dupin succeeds in tracking a voice deemed senseless down to its nonhuman emitter, finding an orangutan at its source. He manages to do this without ever hearing that voice precisely by using conjectures. Poe's epigraph introduces the detective as a modern incarnation of Ulysses, who alone managed to hear the sirens' song by tying himself to the mast of his ship. Ulysses will dare to listen only after ensuring himself against the possibility of succumbing, or perhaps simply responding, to their call. By letting her heroine disappear without a word of explanation, NDiaye intimates instead that we must be willing to let them go if we want a chance of hearing them. Detachment is the improbable condition for approaching the other *as other*. Does this dramatic refusal to tie up loose ends and inform its reader about the fate of its heroine mean that fiction is just another instrument of capture? There is no attempt at transcribing the woman-fish's song into words, as though rendering her singing voice on the page will make her susceptible to capture, and the novella complicit with the extractive process it denounces in the painter's work. Unless perhaps the novella is her song, and the protagonist vanished not outside the fiction but within it. The novella's inconclusive ending performs the very subjectlessness that the painter sought to fix on his canvas.

***

Animal nonencounters can be read as critical engagements with the *what* of literature, that is, with the responsibility literature entertains toward its objects when these objects are captive animals. For Rilke, Cortázar, and NDiaye, depicting captive animal subjects is an occasion to reflect on the epistemological, political, and ethical stakes of their own writing practice.

Each author ponders the affordances and the limits of capture as a representational mode and invites the viewer/reader to recognize how deeply they are implicated in the spectacle they consume. In each case, capture is more than a one-time event that led to the animal's display at the Jardin des Plantes; it has become a representational grammar whose operations are all the more naturalized because they are underacknowledged. But the poem, the short story, and the experimental novella do more than reflect critically on their own enmeshment in the logics of capture. They also push this regime of representation beyond its intended effects of preserving and presenting the animal *as it is* to show instead that it always conjures an undefinable, unexpected "something" that has the power to undo the work of capture.

Notes

1 Vladimir Nabokov, *The Annotated Lolita*, ed. Alfred Appel (New York: Vintage, 1991), 311.
2 Lydia Millet, "Zoogoing," in Mark Martin (ed.), *I'm with the Bears: Short Stories from a Damaged Planet* (New York: Verso, 2011), 35–54. The story is excerpted from Millet's 2009 novel *How the Dead Dream*.
3 Ibid., 38.
4 Ibid., 44.
5 Ibid., 38–9.
6 John Berger, "Why Look at Animals?," in *On Looking* (New York: Pantheon, 1980), 21.
7 Millet, "Zoogoing," 39.
8 Ibid., 53.
9 Ibid.
10 Ibid., 39, 54.
11 Ibid., 49.
12 Berger, "Why Look," 24, 28.
13 Ibid., 28.
14 Ibid., 24.
15 Nabokov, *Annotated Lolita*, 311.
16 Franz Kafka, "A Report to an Academy," in Gabriel Josipovici (ed.), *Collected Stories* (New York: Knopf, 1993).
17 The strange phenomenology of what I call nonencounter, wherein humans and animals appear to belong in distinct planes of existence, is epitomized by but by no means unique to the zoogoer's experience. One finds a similar model of interaction extended to all interspecies relations in Donna Haraway's *When Species Meet*, for instance. Species do not coexist, Haraway contends; in fact, they "do not precede the meeting" *as species*, but they shape one another in a contingent and asymmetrical "dance of encounters." See Donna

Haraway, *When Species Meet* (Minneapolis: University of Minnesota Press, 2008), 4. This reconceptualization of encounter (from an action that species do to an "ontological choreography" that makes species what they are) has profound epistemological and ethical consequences (ibid., 19). By challenging the assumption that species is a preestablished biological category, Haraway asks what it means for "us humans" to know ourselves as a species and conjures up the formation of new and "unpredictable kinds of 'we'" (ibid., 5). "It would be a mistake," she argues, "to assume much about species in advance of encounter" (ibid., 18).

18 On the epistemo-historical conditions under which animals came to be known as unseeable and unencounterable, see Antoine Traisnel, *Capture: American Pursuits and the Making of a New Animal Condition* (Minneapolis: University of Minnesota Press, 2020). For a model of reading "out of focus" when we behold literary animals, see Thangam Ravindranathan's invitation to suspend realist habits favoring considerations "of vulnerability, suffering, empathy, justice, interspecies relation and difference" for fear of "unwittingly supply[ing] animals' missing limbs, presence, perspective, blood, breath" and thus *missing how animals are missing*. Thangam Ravindranathan, *Behold an Animal: Four Exorbitant Readings* (Chicago: Northwestern University Press, 2020), 6, 9.

19 William Wordsworth, "Letter to the Earl of Lonsdale," in *The Letters of William and Dorothy Wordsworth*, vol. 3 (Oxford: Oxford University Press, 1970), 42; Ralph Waldo Emerson, *The Journals and Miscellaneous Notebooks of Ralph Waldo Emerson*, ed. William Gilman et al., 16 vols. (Cambridge, MA: Harvard University Press, 1960–82), 4: 197.

20 Eric Baratay and Elizabeth Hardouin-Fugier, *Zoo: A History of Zoological Gardens in the West* (London: Reaktion, 2002), 73.

21 Henri Bernardin de Saint-Pierre, *Mémoire sur la nécessité de joindre une ménagerie au Jardin National des Plantes de Paris* (Paris: Didot le Jeune, 2020), 14 (my translation).

22 Ibid., 34 (my translation).

23 Maria P. Gindhart, "Liberty, Utility, Proximity: Animals and Animaliers at the Jardin des Plantes Menagerie in Paris," Age of Revolutions, July 26, 2021, https://ageofrevolutions.com/2021/07/26/liberty-utility-proximity-animals-and-animaliers-at-the-jardin-des-plantes-menagerie-in-paris/.

24 Louis MacNeice, *Zoo* (London: Faber and Faber, 1996), 242, 230.

25 Derek Ryan, *Animal Theory: A Critical Introduction* (Edinburgh: Edinburgh University Press, 2015), 4.

26 Jacques Derrida, *The Beast and the Sovereign*, vol. 1, trans. Geoffrey Bennington (Chicago: University of Chicago Press, 2009), 282.

27 Ibid., 275.

28 Jacques Derrida, *The Animal That Therefore I Am*, trans. David Wills (New York: Fordham University Press, 2008), 11.

29 Ibid., 9, my emphasis.

30 Berger, "Why Look," 21.

31 Derrida, *Animal*, 12.

32 Derrida, *Beast*, 283.

33 Derrida, *Animal*, 12.

34 Rilke complained about his limited linguistic abilities to Auguste Rodin, who encouraged his Austrian protégé to look for inspiration at the Jardin des Plantes; Cortázar regarded axolotls as fellow South American expatriates; NDiaye is a well-established French author, but her writings often reflect her experience of alienation as a biracial subject living in a country that refuses to confront its colonial history.

35 Julio Cortázar, "Axolotl," in *Blow-Up: And Other Stories*, trans. Paul Blackburn (New York: Pantheon Books, 1985), 7.

36 The sirens, in Adorno and Horkheimer's reading, represent the temptation of relapsing into the animalized prehistory against which enlightened "humanity" fashions its identity. Odysseus recognizes this danger but insists on hearing their song, which he alone is in a position of "using as the material of progress." Theodor Adorno and Max Horkheimer, *Dialectic of Enlightenment: Philosophical Fragments*, trans. Edmund Jephcott (Stanford, CA: Stanford University Press, 2002), 25.

37 Rainer Maria Rilke, *The Selected Poetry of Rainer Maria Rilke*, ed. and trans. Stephen Mitchell (New York: Vintage, 1982), 24–5.

38 Martin Heidegger, *The Fundamental Concepts of Metaphysics: World, Finitude, Solitude*, trans. William McNeill and Nicholas Walker (Bloomington: Indiana University Press, 1995), 248.

39 Geoffrey Winthrop-Young, "Afterword," in Jakob von Uexküll, *A Foray into the Worlds of Animals and Humans, with a Theory of Meaning*, trans. Joseph D. O'Neil (Minneapolis: University of Minnesota Press, 2010), 232.

40 This is perhaps why the jaded gaze of the first stanza returns in the third as a photographic apparatus, with the "curtain of the pupil" acting as a shutter mechanically processing an image that leaves the viewer's heart unmoved. On this analogy, see Kenneth S. Calhoon, "The Eye of the Panther: Rilke and the Machine of Cinema," *Comparative Literature* 52.2 (2000), 143–56.

41 The claustrophobic impression conveyed by the epanalepsis is somewhat deceiving, because the poem begins and ends with the same cluster of letters but not the same word. The first "*sein*" is the possessive pronoun "his," the second the verb "to be" in the infinitive. Does the poem surreptitiously introduce difference under the appearance of repetition? Or does it do exactly the opposite, smuggle (literal) sameness by way of (semantic) difference?

42 Kári Driscoll, "Second Glance at the Panther, or: What Does It Mean to Read Zoopoetically?," *Frame* 31.1 (2008), 40.

43 Ibid., 33. Reading zoopoetically means being attuned to animals in literature as material-semiotic figures rather than indexes of real specimens or abstract symbols.

44 Ibid., 40.

45 Ibid., 33.

46 Rey Chow, *Entanglements, or Transmedial Thinking about Capture* (Durham, NC: Duke University Press, 2012), 12. Interestingly for us, Chow focuses on

entanglements to reflect on the epistemological and political implications of technologies of capture.

47 *Registre d'entrée des mammifères et oiseaux, 30 octobre 1895–4 mai 1914* (https://bibliotheques.mnhn.fr/medias/detailstatic.aspx?INSTANCE=EXPLOITATIO N&RSC_BASE=IFD&RSC_DOCID=MNHN_MEN_19).

48 There is no "exit date" (*date de sortie*, a euphemism for death) for this specimen, which likely did not survive until Rilke's visit in late 1902 given zoo animals' short life expectancy at the time. To compensate for outrageous mortality rates, the Jardin required very high volumes of importations to restock its menagerie (Baratay and Hardouin-Fugier, *Zoo*, 123–4).

49 Cortázar, "Axolotl," 4.

50 Ibid.

51 Ibid., 7.

52 Ibid., 5 (emphasis mine).

53 Ibid., 5–6.

54 Ibid., 5.

55 Ibid., 6.

56 Ibid., 4.

57 Ibid., 8.

58 Ibid., 6.

59 Ibid., 7.

60 Ibid., 8. Jean Capello reads Cortázar's fantastic fiction as representative of a new genre she calls "new physics realism" (Jean Capello, "Science as Story: Julio Cortazar and Schrodinger's Cat," *Revista de Estudios Hispanicos* 31.1 [1997], 41). Capello builds on an interview in which Cortázar calls "fantastic" these phenomena "at the margin of Aristotelian laws" that "our logical brain does not grasp [*capta*]" but that our bodies nonetheless register and which obey perfectly valid laws of physics (qtd. by Capello, 41, my translation).

61 Aristotle, *Nicomachean Ethics*, trans. C. D. C. Reeve (Indianapolis, IN: Hackett, 2014), 10.

62 Cortázar, "Axolotl," 8.

63 Ibid., 8 (emphasis mine).

64 Ibid., 5.

65 Ibid., 6.

66 Ibid., 8.

67 Ibid., 6.

68 Ibid., 9.

69 Ibid., 7.

70 On this, see Akira Mizuta Lippit, "Afterthoughts on the Animal World," *MLN*, 109.5 (1994), 786–830.

71 Edgar Allan Poe, "Murders in the Rue Morgue," in *Poetry and Tales* (New York: Library of America, 1984), 423.

72 Cortázar, "Axolotl," 7.

73 Marie NDiaye, *La naufragée – J. M. W. Turner* (Paris: Le Flohic, 1999), 17. All the translations of NDiaye's text are my own.

74 Ibid.
75 Ibid., 29.
76 Ibid., 71.
77 Ibid., 69.
78 On the ethical implications of Turner's representation of the Zong episode, see Ian Baucom, *Specters of the Atlantic: Finance Capital, Slavery, and the Philosophy of History* (Durham, NC: Duke University Press, 2005).
79 NDiaye, *La naufragée*, 65–7.
80 Ibid., 75.
81 The audience was especially fascinated by Baartman's steatopygia, or protruding buttocks, a condition common among women of the Khoi tribes.
82 Sadiah Qureshi, "Displaying Sara Baartman, the 'Hottentot Venus,'" *History of Science* 42 (2004), 241.
83 NDiaye, *La naufragée*, 35.
84 Ibid., 77.
85 Ibid., 73.
86 Ibid., 79.
87 Poe's narrator remains dubious about Dupin's demonstration until the detective invokes Cuvier's "minute anatomical" description of the orangutan, after which he understands "the full horrors of the murder at once" (Poe, "Murders," 424).
88 NDiaye, *La naufragée*, 81.
89 Poe, "Murders," 397.

CHAPTER 12

Indigeneity
Posthumanist Fantasy and Weird Reality

Melanie Benson Taylor

Reader, I'm making this up, but face it:
The strange world is below us, above us, and beyond.
— Janet McAdams, "The Children's Map of Antarctica," in *Feral* (2007)

It would be perhaps prosaic, but not hyperbolic, to assert the uniquely world-altering capacities of the recent epistemological and ontological reorientations animated by animal studies and its cognate fields of inquiry. This is mostly a good thing: in a moment of global ecological emergency, one of the most constructive measures we can take as an academic community is to explode and expand the *Anthropos* monolith within the Anthropocene, to more capaciously reimagine human subjects as – following Timothy Morton and others – "subscendent" elements of a radically correlationist whole, dependent on realizing our shared kinship and care in order to forge functional solidarity. But this course correction has also at times resulted in well-meaning but pernicious overcorrection: in earnest efforts to disrupt the largely white, racialized space of Anthropocene conversations, Indigenous epistemological alternatives in particular have emerged as exceptional antidotes to ecological despair with privileged access to nonhuman, natural, and interspecies lifeworlds. While many Indigenous approaches do offer pertinent, beneficent measures, their broadscale characterization and application has the effect of depositing fresh essentialisms in the wake of the old, and battles over intellectual privacy and appropriation trouble the larger, coalitional urgency. As a result, the very incommensurability that these new approaches seek to demolish – those nourished by the imperial practices we aim to counter[1] – are rejuvenated in perdurable ways.

This shift has come in many theoretical guises, which we call variously the ontological turn, object-oriented ontology, new materialism, posthumanism, and interspecies kinship, building on foundational thinking elaborated by Michel Foucault, Gilles Deleuze and Félix Guattari, Bruno Latour, Elizabeth Povinelli, Graham Harman, Timothy Morton, Donna

Haraway, Sylvia Wynter, Anna Tsing, and others' efforts to level the hierarchical distinctions between human, nonhuman, and "natural" inhabitants of the biosphere. These turns have produced a range of relational concepts about leveled and imbricated "landscapes,"[2] "making kin" and "Chthulucene,"[3] "ethical mutualism,"[4] "entangled spaces,"[5] and an "implosive whole" or "symbiotic real."[6] Many of these formulations build explicitly on Indigenous cultural knowledge, sometimes without formally crediting those sources, as Sarah Hunt, Zoe Todd, and others have contended. Some Indigenous thinkers themselves have entered traditional phenomenologies and material practices fruitfully into mainstream scientific discourse, such as the Indigenous Climate Change Studies movement facilitated by Potawatomi scientist Kyle Whyte.[7] Despite their significant differences, these approaches are united by a common ethical drive toward human humility rather than hubris in a world critically leveled by catastrophe. Yet repeatedly they are stymied by assumptions of cultural disparities that apportion blame and salvation differently according to the differential logics and politics of settler-colonial repair.

We already know (at least most of us) that capitalism and racism are inextricable and that together they have ravaged our world with stark inequity;[8] we are desperate now for solutions. To borrow the title (I wish I came up with) of a recent essay cowritten by a group of *Social Text* editors: "We Already Know How Fucked Up the World Is." As those writers put it, addressing a range of perversities in state and political regimes: "We already know what is happening – being told over and over as though that will make a difference only prompts anger."[9] Rather than participate further in the endlessly reiterative meme machine of liberal critique, those invested in Indigenous epistemological tutoring and revolt – what we're now calling "Indigenous resurgence"[10] – are intent on mobilizing. And, as Arundhati Roy puts it, "the first step towards reimagining a world gone terribly wrong would be to stop the annihilation of those who have a different imagination."[11] In scholarly circles, even the hard sciences have turned seriously to non-Western and especially Indigenous "traditional" practices of "radical sustainability," "grounded normativity," and a functional embrace of ontological connectedness and "interspecies kinship" as lifelines to an ecological future. These theoretical principles have gained credence in social movements such as the Dakota pipeline protests at Standing Rock and the Idle No More drive in Canada, and with a broader, growing recognition that Native communities are uniquely equipped to address not just global climate catastrophe but its larger racial capitalist etiologies. Aboriginal nations in Australia, New Zealand, and

Canada have managed to launch highly effective alliances with political and federal entities to develop sustainable ecological programs and recognition of nonhuman life-forms as sovereign elements of their societies and economies. In a range of cli-fi works and other speculative narratives about the hypothetical survival of humankind, Indians are frequently the lifelines. Take, for example, Bong Joon-hoo's apocalyptic climate thriller *Snowpiercer*, in which the Earth's two sole survivors are an Inuit girl and an African American boy, symbolic vestiges destined to "spread the human race."[12] Similarly, in *The Mermaids, or Aiden in Wonderland* (2018), a recent short film by the influential anthropologist Elizabeth Povinelli, we encounter a near future where "the world is being poisoned and Europeans are unable to step outside, while *Indigenous people are able to*."[13] In other words, Indigenous epistemologies and politics are having a moment.

The impulse to disambiguate the elect from the suppressed in these reckonings is both rational and redemptive; but the functional applications of identity-bound logics stumble on the impractical or the impolitic. The question remains, especially in the United States, of how – and whether – to share and scale up local, tribal, often protected and emplaced methods to materially alter the destructive trajectories of colonial-capitalist horror writ large. More fundamentally, how do we unmake the world that made us, without also obliterating ourselves? As Saidiya Hartman puts it, "[t]he hope is that return could [. . .] make a victory out of defeat, and engender a new order. And the disappointment is that there is no going back [. . .] Loss remakes you."[14] Lisa Lowe similarly stakes a capacious claim for the "intimacies" that emerge when we read comparatively across asymmetrical cultural, discursive, and political frameworks, a method of elision that produces a fundamentally "different kind of thinking, a space of productive attention to the scene of loss."[15] While the larger critical tide moves boldly through these stark vicissitudes of loss and sacrifice, Indigenous critical thought continues to herald its singular capacities for reclamation, and at the same time to police its appropriation, at once demanding and rejecting inclusion in serious academic and scientific conversations. These are essential conceits, without which sovereignty claims founder, but it remains problematic that Indigenous resurgence aims to have it both ways: we cannot stake a proprietary claim to the salvation of radical connectedness and altered ecological futures without including the artifacts of colonial-capitalism in the web, without including ourselves and our pageants of partition in the matrix of all that anthropogenic modernity has issued.

A flotilla of paradoxes demonstrate that fix: a constant toggle between kinship and essentialism, coalition and prohibition, alliance and annexation. We have scholars claiming, on the one hand, that the now largely endorsed concept of slow violence against the poor and marginalized does not apply to Indigenous communities, where "water, land, and ecosystems under the[ir] care [...] have been kept more in-tact [*sic*],"[16] and, on the other hand, the urgent declaration that "structural colonial violence has created ideal conditions for [things like our current pandemic] to have devastating impacts on Indigenous, Black, and Latino communities."[17] As a rejoinder, many Indigenous critics – like the First Nations political theorist Glen Coulthard – have called for the removal of "all of the colonial, racist, and patriarchal legal and political obstacles" that have punished Indigenous communities. "For Indigenous nations to live," Coulthard argues, "capitalism must die."[18] This "will not be easy," he admits. And yet the twinned mystifications of Indigenous alterity and anticapitalist futurity are the ineradicable fossil fuels for the posthumanist escape fantasy.

A politics of action based on exceptional epistemologies and myths of alterity cannot succeed precisely because all of it – our imaginations, identities, Indigeneity itself – are epiphenomena of a world that cannot be selectively reduced, a world that includes capitalism and nature and humans alike in a subscendent association – no part bigger or smaller or more innately powerful than another, but tangled indissolubly in a structural platform where fictions of difference – not just between humans and nonhumans, but among humans themselves – emerge from the very systems we seek to explode. Morton reminds us that we miss the point entirely when we use terms like "survival" or "sustainability," which are surface-level adjustments that do nothing to address the brokenness and the violence produced by the structures themselves, the volatile apartheids and brutal violence that result from our unwillingness to reckon with our elemental entanglement. Until we can manage a sober rejection of the very terms that contravene any possibility of solidarity to begin with, then this is *merely a poetics, not a politics, of progress.*

As Tiffany Lethabo King puts it, the work of confronting racial capitalism's apocalyptic afterlives "really has to fuck us up in our core and make us relentless about seeking out and making alternatives possible."[19] In that spirit, I want to propose a concept that might capture a range of catalyzing new writing that vastly exceeds, even explicitly rejects, the more rigid, sectarian, essentialist impulses of the theoretical debates: "Weird Indigeneity," inspired partly by Timothy Morton's notion of weirdness as he elaborates it in *Dark Ecology* (2016) and elsewhere. The "weird" has long functioned in literary criticism as a descriptor for

Lovecraftian horror narratives that frequently foreground strange, destabilizing, deformative embodiments and the unsettling unknown; a more recent wave of so-called New Weird speculative fiction carries this tradition forward in provocative ways. For Morton, "weird" is a way of conceptualizing human embeddedness in a vast biosphere of nonhuman others that both contains and erases us, an uncanny awareness that is dark and enlivening all at once. Drawing on the Norse origins for weird meaning "twisted" or "in a loop," Morton suggests that to exist "means to be a loop, a twisted loop, like a Möbius strip [...] a non-orientable surface [where] every attempt to locate the twist on some precise region of the loop is impossible: there is no part of the surface that is not already twisted." For Morton, this is "the same as saying that reality does not come with a dotted line and a picture of scissors saying 'Cut Here,' to separate [...] its components like a good butcher (Phaedrus). Butchering reality becomes impossible."[20] This kind of thinking is essential for ecological awareness, because it allows us to see moments when "two levels that appear utterly separate – [such as geology and humanity] – flip into one another."[21] This weirdness may seem at first glance just another twist in the ontological turn, but its difference is its expansiveness, one fundamentally incompatible with the identity-rooted logics that allow us to include and exclude selectively, and which prevent us from seeing our true positionality in the biosphere and our responsibilities to it and to one another. There is inherently more humility, as we have to admit that there are elements of our shared existence that we can't know, which extends fundamentally to ourselves, caught in the loop. Here, we're all suspended in an uncanny state of partial awareness, permeated by a metaphysics of simultaneous presence and absence, here and not-here, past and futurity, a "nowness" in which we're caught. We can be imagined no longer as discrete, as contained or interpellated in any authoritative way, but as dynamic beings in kinetic co-constitution with animals, nonhumans, objects, viruses – a landscape of being where all things are "actors," and "[r]eality, in the end, is a kind of drama."[22]

The components of all this are not really new but are the result of Morton's painstaking reinterpretations of, among others, Immanuel Kant, Martin Heidegger, Michel Foucault, Jacques Lacan, Karl Marx, Friedrich Nietzsche, Deleuze and Guattari, Michael Hardt and Antonio Negri; he wants to embed this weird familiarity as always already haunting continental philosophy. This is because endowing only certain non-Western cultural perspectives with exclusive access and authority, no matter how outwardly redeeming or ethical, is another wrong turn on the same road map. As David Graeber puts it, we engage in mystifications as an "ethical imperative" to exercise "respect for [Indigenous] otherness"; but this narrowness impedes real solidarity by denying "one of the most important things all humans really do have in common: the fact that we all have to come to grips, to one degree or another, with what we cannot know."[23] Integral to the concept of weirdness is the understanding that we can never fully understand it in isolated snatches but only collectively, implosively, and spectrally.

Thus, the final feature of this "weird" Indigeneity I'd like to propose is that it need not – in fact, it cannot – be "Indigenous" in the ways and terms we have come to define it. Once again, solidifying any cultural group – particularly a pan-tribal, motley, global aggregate such as that bundled awkwardly in the modern signifier of "Indigenous" – only enables the pernicious politics of settler colonial and capitalist logics that depend on facile divisions. Scholars have remarked on the obstinacy of the "overly reductive binary of 'settler' and 'native'" that "has contributed to a simplified opposition that assumes the self-evidence of 'indigeneity' and the singular category of 'settler,' rather than querying the analytic coherence of these categories, of how the distinctions themselves are bound up with the colonial definition and management of difference, in the interest of perpetuating a semblance of coherence for colonial declarations of sovereignty."[24] In other words, maintaining the heteroglot fiction of "Indigeneity" is, ironically, compulsory ground for leveraging tribal sovereignties that incorporate ecological preservation efforts. The route out of this bind can't simply be to revise political terms or power differentials, but to more elementally reassess the ontological rigidity that allows for such stubborn bugs in the posthumanist agenda. In his work with Sudanese Indigenous tribes including the Nuer people, Graeber concludes similarly that, in the ethical insistence on "drawing borders," "one can't simply follow 'native categories' because you need to have those borders to know who the relevant 'natives' are" – a problem that necessitates the determination both of those borders as well as of "who, inside those borders, gets to define what should be considered [for example] 'Nuer ideas.' Chances are there's next to nothing that every single individual you have just defined as 'Nuer' will agree on." The simplification compounds, as does the attendant hostility, when "one decides one cannot stand in judgment over the views of someone residing in a different cultural universe" and develops "a special supercategory – such as 'modern' or 'Western' – in which to include those views one feels one should be allowed to disagree with or condemn."[25]

To be sure, either because of or despite the politicized performance of ecological shamanism, Indigenous thinkers and artists are often very much attuned to the architecture of these weird logics, and they lead us substantially toward its haunting revelations. But the most fully weird and (to my mind) most energizing Indigenous writing resists the ideological off-ramps of embedded resurgence and exceptionalism, exercising instead uncompromising inclusivity – not repudiating Indigeneity but refashioning it as open, permeable, epiphanic. As Morton suggests, this "indigeneity to the symbiotic real" lingers as latent knowledge within humans generally; it is recoverable. By contrast, "the thing we keep telling ourselves with our words and our social space and our philosophy and our Stockholm syndrome feelings, that we are outside of [the geological and natural and the consumer] world [. . .] is killing us and all life on this planet."[26] So, ultimately, the only way to engineer a truly correlationist world and a constructive politics based on Indigenous wisdom is to utterly repudiate Indigenous identity as we have previously framed and politicized it. Weird Indigeneity may offer one such template for functional solidarity. It's another paradox in the end, but perhaps the most animating one we have stumbled on yet.

There are any number of Weird Indigenous artists who could introduce us to this universe, but I will briefly introduce two contemporary poets, voices refreshingly distinct from the mold of much Indigenous literature and, additionally, from one another. First, Tommy Pico, a Kumeyaay poet, podcaster, and screenwriter from the Viejas reservation near San Diego, California. In his brilliant tetralogy of poems, we follow a queer, urban Indian speaker named Teebs, a self-described "weirdo NDN faggot."[27] In his 2017 *Nature Poem*, composed loosely in the epic form, Teebs muses on the many reasons why he won't write a nature poem: "bc it's fodder for the noble savage / narrative"; and then (and yet), he cleverly reclaims both nature and poetry altogether. "You can't be an NDN person in today's world // and write a nature poem. I swore to myself I would never write a nature / poem. Let's be clear, I hate nature – hate its *guts* // I say to my audience. There is something smaller I say to myself: // *I don't hate nature at all.*"[28] Teebs is no Quentin Compson, who famously "do[es]n't hate the South";[29] but like Quentin's, Teebs's self-perception is structured explicitly by a kind of ambient, acculturated, primary negation. To produce a self we must not be something else, and especially not the thing that most determines and delimits us; the consequence of this dissociation is a mash-up of abjection and craving. Nature's guts are Teebs's guts, of course, and while he doesn't hate it he also can't love it as it currently exists, because neither entity is real or separate or articulable except in the toxic containers we peddle and pretend to inhabit. "Nature" and "poem" are separated by a line break here so we can visually digest their cautious estrangement, a silent divorce of their caustic intimacy. Teebs's aversion starts to feel more like injunction: "You *can't* be an NDN person in today's world" is followed by a full stanza break, which lets the declaration linger briefly on its own as a statement. But its refusal is also additive "[y]ou can't be an NDN in today's world AND *write a nature poem*" – the nihilism of both projects is aligned, with a subtle shift toward the imperative and generative: "*write* a nature poem" – a response to the awareness of co-creation. But who is he actually instructing here? He is not just addressing his audience but telling us that he is telling his audience, and talking to himself at the same time. The drama of this shared reality is dizzyingly multiple, fractal, and ultimately sensual. Audience and self, NDN and nature – partial and indissoluble conceits; too much the same, they express both a queer ecology and a homophobia of the self's transgressive desires: "I get so disappointed by stupid NDNs writing their dumb nature poems like grow up faggots," he says; "I look this thought full in the face and want to throw myself into traffic."[30]

Erasure and presencing thus battle erotically throughout the poem. Teebs self-consciously performs his own suicidal theatrics of resistance to the elements of nature he craves. "Admit it," he writes near the end, on a page by itself: "This is the poem you wanted all along."[31] His window onto the symbiotic real is at once a snuff poem, an erotic assault, and a queer fantasy. As Morton would encourage, these vistas onto the weird webs of ecological embeddedness can be intent not on reduction or restriction but on the expression of enjoyment and desire, which is fundamentally the organizing principle of economics and the pathway to true solidarity.[32] Teebs doesn't shy away from showing us his voracious attraction to all the things that compose his version of a nature poem, which includes gummy bears and hashtags and advertising slogans as well as hills with backs and magnetic, enigmatic starscapes. He is attracted viscerally to all of it, but also repelled by the self-symmetry, expressed again as a kind of self-effacing homophobia: "I literally hate all men bc literally men are animals," he declares.[33] The emphasis here is on the colloquialism "literally," a reminder of language's sweeping Stockholming effects (he does at one point call English "some Stockholm shit"), but in its reiterative appearance we realize the negation of the negation is true. The queer body, the natural world, the NDN, and the world of objects and fetishes writ large are all keening to overflow their artificial levies, and it both terrifies and titillates him.

Pico relies on the play of language to flirt with both its hostile boundaries and its ungovernable eruptions. The result is a toggle between seduction and prohibition, expressed at times in parodic play: "Sky mother falls thru / a hole, lands on a turtle. // Hole is my favorite band" (67). His intention is to undercut Indigenous folklore with pop culture, linguistic echoes that render each hole equally sacred (or not), but what lingers are the cavities themselves: gaps and hungers that cannot be uttered in the "Stockholm shit" that is English, nor by the Indigenous narratives that are differently coercive and incomplete, tuned diametrically for false disambiguation. The poem thus takes us on an escapade of ontological anarchy, where nature is at once a needling interlocutor and a bad date: "Nature asks aren't I curious abt the landscapes of exoplanets – which, I / thought we all understood planets are metaphors / like the Vikings, or Delaware [. . .] It's hard for me to imagine curiosity as anything more than a pretext for colonialism," he concludes, "so nah, Nature I don't want to know the colonial legacy of the future."[34] Whatever is literal here is also metaphor, the residue of processes of exploration, extraction, interpretation – a Viking, a Delaware, a planet, Teebs himself, all bundled in disconnected pockets of a universe imprinted by colonial curiosity and desire.

That curiosity lingers in the persistent interrogations of identity and the weirdness of Indigeneity throughout the poem:

> WHAT'S YR NATIONALITY!?!? This guys shouts at me during drag queen karaoke at this gay bar two stops down the line.
>
> In order to talk about a hurricane, you first have to talk about a preexisting disturbance over the ocean, so you have to talk about mean ocean temperature, so you have to talk about human industry and sun rays, so you have to talk about helium, so did you know helium was named for the sun god Helios and was defined by a gap in the solar spectrum so literally not itself but what surrounded it, so of course we have to talk about the solar system, the Milky Way, the networks of universe and the Big Bang.
>
> How far back do you have to go to answer any question about race?[35]

Breathlessly, Teebs makes clear that hurricanes and racism are part of the same ecology of contingency, no one element explicable on its own terms, and further, never the thing itself but a "gap" discernible only by the architecture of its surroundings. Race, too, lives in this archaic web, a modern invention and an invisible gap bound and conscripted within a world of concatenation. In an imploded universe that we cannot see for what it is, we feel only the embodiment and contingency that imprisons us as artifacts of past and history.

For Pico, poetry is an opportunity to pause, to perform a forensics of present and presence, to play with the collision of bodies, impulses, curiosities, and demarcations that both enliven and undo us: "in order to get inside," he tells us, "a poem has to break you." There is a little bit of Kafka's axe for the frozen sea metaphor here, but for Pico, the poem that shatters you is the lyric of the body finding its compass in a world of reiterative removes. Poetry's unique capacity to distill and collapse, to perform the weird flips that exceed analogy, make it an apt instrument for rupturing our delusions of wholeness, partiality, essentialism, community, nationality, race.[36] But it also reveals our detention within those interpellating structures. To not-hate nature's – and your own – guts, you first need to spill them, to understand that their immersion in any one body or culture or lyric is desperately artificial, that part of our current crisis is our prism of parallel narcissisms and parodies. This is why the colonial curiosity about Teebs's race is shouted at him in full caps during "drag queen karaoke," a hyperbolic moment of performativity and hyper-duplication, the decibels tuned to unbearable pitch. Kumeyaay is simultaneously who he is and not who he is; consumerism and spectacle are leveraged precisely to stage this "chasing of self," and the theater and digital platforms are all fragments of whatever real we have access to. In the collection's opening lines, Teebs is worried that "[t]he stars are dying," but "I feel fine, in the sense that I feel very thin – I been doin Tracy Anderson DVD workouts on YouTube, keeping my arms fit and strong. She says *reach, like you are being pulled apart //* I can't not spill."[37] Like the recessional of drag queen karaoke, here Teebs chases himself – and hurricanes and stars – via a diluted pathway: a live workout to a DVD on a YouTube clip – Tracy Anderson in dialogue with her audience, as Teebs is with his, yet estranged and reaching. It's *You*Tube for a reason, a mirror show to our hyper-constructed selves as we engage in delusions of connection that only pull us further apart – the centrifugal evisceration of the techno-consumer-capitalist society that ensnares and then refuses to nourish us.

But, as Morton reminds us and Pico underscores, the goal is not to rebuild, at least not with the tools we are used to: one cannot "heal one's intrinsic brokenness," Morton avers, because this inherent permeability "is a possibility condition for your existence."[38] Morton would probably diagnose Teebs as an ambivalent ambassador to this symbiotic real, simultaneously attuned to the specific hungers and desires of his partial self and eager to abandon or disclaim them, his embodiment an embarrassment: "I am not my body. Get me out of here," he begs, and later, in direct address: "Body: *don't get too attached to me.*"[39] The poem ends largely as it begins, with a "very thin" Teebs gently registering a "rotting" Earth while "petting kitties" on a porch with "lavender in the air." "The air is clear, and all across Instagram – peeps are posting pics of the sunset."[40] This is the kind of nature he can write about, the only kind he or we know, no less real for its technological mediation, but impoverishing in its partiality. The poem acknowledges the truth of this condition, the hauntedness and the gauntness, and while Teebs yearns for the fullness of real solidarity he recognizes the layered limits of his alienating and alienated identities: "I will always be alone," he predicts.[41]

Perhaps he is right. There are so many conceptual and political obstacles to realizing the plenitude of Weird Indigeneity's liberations; Pico experiments with their possibilities and limits, reaches across distances that pull and allows himself to be drawn apart, includes within the looping frame of human experience the motley elements that compose us, that make us want to claim and reject our bodies all at once and by turns. There is some combination of exhilaration and evacuation in the poem, and throughout Pico's work generally, because he refuses steadfastly to submit to any easy, interim, stock-Indigenous panaceas for the wounds and the isolations of anthropocentric modernity.

There are myriad other examples of Weird Indigeneity, drawn from Indigenous literature alone, that I could include here. Poetry by Natalie Diaz and Sherman Bitsui that plays wildly with form and bodies and nonhuman agents; speculative fiction by Stephen Graham Jones, where the deviant and the unreal function as a portal to uncloaked relations and revelations;[42] even the ostensibly not-weird but actually sometimes-deeply-weird Louise Erdrich, musing on our arrest in the violent, mundane in between zones of being and not-being, on the threshold of Schrödinger's dilemma of unknowing. We can be neither alive nor dead in these works, Indian or otherwise, but some frustrated being warped in a fabric of contingency drawn increasingly to explosively weird imaginings and openings. None of these Indians has solutions for our current state of anthropocentric crisis; they refuse to be ecological warriors or shamans or anticapitalist, decolonizing crusaders, but are simply explorers – with tentativeness, with traumatic stress responses, with reluctance and curiosity.

In the remaining space, I'll end with just one more brilliantly weird Indian: Alabama Creek poet Janet McAdams. In her poetry collections *The Island of Lost Luggage* (2000), *Feral* (2007), and *Seven Boxes for the Country After* (2016), as well as her lyrical novel *Red Weather* (2012), she returns insistently to the twisted landscapes of history, haunting, excavation, and the porous boundaries between humans, animals, and the elements that variously inspire, invent, sustain, and undo us. For McAdams, the racialized Indigenous body is a sentient but ultimately imperfect vehicle – her words are "inexact" and "messy"[43] – for carrying one's identity into the twenty-first century, for mapping its vast coordinates of loss and alienation. Instead, she deterritorializes both her Indigeneity and her Southernness, setting her poetry in disparate geographies and cultures that are rarely discernible or specific. The effect is distinctly and deliberately disorienting, as she interrupts the lore of tribal tradition and identity as privileged access points to histories that are indiscriminately leveling. In other words, she is intent to canvas the Indigenous body in its weird symbiotic orientations: "Our deepest metaphors are the furniture, language, oxygen of that other world, the 'unacknowledged' world," she asserts. "It is a life's work to understand them. It is the lifework of a poet to write them down."[44]

Feral is her collection most explicitly concerned with recovering bodies unfettered from the coordinations of so-called civilization, but also from nation, region, tribe, and earth altogether, and then charting their disaffected reentries. In *Feral*'s final poem, "Earth My Body Is Trying to Remember," McAdams's speaker addresses "Earth" and "my body" simultaneously – enjambed in a continuous space of loss:

> We were born but born too young to remember.
> The land they took us from, the mothers' milk dried up,
> every womb a dried-up
> crackle of flesh. Earth my body
> is trying to remember.
> Child-That-Was, don't try to remember, but lean back
> into this place outside history.

McAdams deflates any mythologies about contemporary Indigenous subjects' blood memories of intimacy with land, here a metonymy for a barren inheritance. In the elision of "Earth" and "my body," both entities are ruined by history and struggling to remember one another and themselves all at once. Paradoxically, to first evoke and then shatter that slippage becomes an unexpectedly decolonizing gesture of sorts, a radical inhabitation of a place "outside history," which is at once impossible and inevitable – the only place we can be with cognition, there but not-there. In the poem's final lines, the Indigenous body's fatal land-anchored value is again underlined: "They chipped away at us, / hammered us out like gold." More and less than bodies, Indigenous subjects "were cell and stone and field, the sky: / Stars pulled down from their wandering."[45] This is not the end at all, but a haunting tautology. Just as in Pico's poem, the stars are dying anyway, "like always."

This futility haunts not just McAdams's poetry but so much contemporary Southern and Indigenous literature, two weird institutions that get weirder together. In the final prose poem of McAdams's most recent collection, *Seven Boxes for the Country After* (2016), she offers a vision of a stripped-down future at a mythical waypoint: "We undress behind a screen in a small room in the space between countries. They search our pockets, tossing it all in a box marked THINGS, half full with false teeth, a tangled wig, a book losing the old skin of its binding. They search our folds, our stories [. . .] They take: our shoes, our pockets, the hole from the lobe of your left ear [. . .] They take until we are tender as babies, until we have nothing left to declare."[46]

Nothing left to declare. Bodies grown thin, thrown into traffic, riddled with holes, bodies without organs, or at least without teeth and hair – decaying specimens of human hubris. In a response to escalating, multi-scale global emergency, Donna Haraway calls for "stories (and theories) that are just big enough to gather up the complexities and keep the edges open and greedy for surprising new and old connections."[47] Poets like Pico and McAdams offer just such openings, returns to rawness and rebirth, "more than meat" again and always. How far back do we need to go to indigenize ourselves? they ask. Where is this country outside and after history? In the speculative worlds of weirdness, we find grace and novelty, beauty and absurdity and greed for something other than – but inclusive of the "THINGS" that tether and create us – who we are and what we own functioning together. To have "nothing left to declare" is to be without a passport, one that so deeply imprints and supplements the body; there is mourning in the loss but also, perhaps, weird, greedy hope for new beginnings, stories, alliances, and skins.

Notes

1 As Timothy Morton puts it, scholars' legitimate fears of appropriating non-Western cultural knowledge "miss the target because they rely on an idea of the incommensurability of cultures," which is itself "a symptom of the very imperialism from which one is trying to rescue thinking by departing from strong correlationist orthodoxy. How ironic is that?" See *Humankind: Solidarity with Non-Human People* (London: Verso, 2017), 12.
2 Anna Lowenhaupt Tsing, Heather Anne Swanson, Elaine Gan, and Nils Bubandt (eds.), *Arts of Living on a Damaged Planet: Ghosts of the Anthropocene; Monsters of the Anthropocene* (Minneapolis: University of Minnesota Press, 2017).

3 Donna J. Haraway, *Staying with the Trouble: Making Kin in the Chthulucene* (Durham, NC: Duke University Press, 2016).

4 Deborah Bird Rose, "Slowly: Writing into the Anthropocene," *TEXT*, Special Issue Website Series 20: Writing Creates Ecology and Ecology Creates Writing, ed. Martin Harrison, Deborah Bird Rose, Lorraine Shannon, and Kim Satchell, October 2013, www.textjournal.com.au/speciss/issue20/Rose .pdf, accessed August 2, 2022.

5 David Farrier, *Anthropocene Poetics: Deep Time, Sacrifice Zones, and Extinction* (Minneapolis: University of Minnesota Press, 2019), especially chapter 2.

6 Morton, *Humankind*.

7 Kyle Whyte, "Indigenous Climate Change Studies: Indigenizing Futures, Decolonizing the Anthropocene," *English Language Notes* 55.1–2 (2017), 153–62.

8 Across disciplines, we have developed more granular accounts of climate change as elaborated viciously by and through the global flows of capital that laid waste to human and natural ecologies simultaneously. See pivotal works such as Kris Manjapra, "Plantation Dispossessions," in Sven Beckert and Christine Desan (eds.), *American Capitalism: New Histories* (New York: Columbia University Press, 2018), 361–88; Sylvia Wynter, "Unsettling the Coloniality of Being/Power/Truth/Freedom: Towards the Human, after Man, Its Overrepresentation – An Argument," *CR: The New Centennial Review* 3.3 (Fall 2003), 257–337; and Katherine Yusoff, *A Billion Black Anthropocenes or None* (Minneapolis: University Minnesota Press, 2018).

9 After Globalism Writing Group, "We Already Know How Fucked Up the World Is," *Social Text* 36.1 (2018), 113–16, 113–14.

10 For elaborations of Indigenous resurgent principles and practices, see especially Leanne Betasamosake Simpson, *As We Have Always Done: Indigenous Freedom through Radical Resistance* (Minneapolis: University of Minnesota Press, 2017); Glen Sean Coulthard, *Red Skin, White Masks: Rejecting the Colonial Politics of Recognition* (Minneapolis: University of Minnesota Press, 2014); and Jaskiran Dhillon's edited volume, *Indigenous Resurgence: Decolonialization and Movements for Environmental Justice* (Brooklyn, NY: Berghahn Books, 2022).

11 Quoted in Dhillon, "Indigenous Resurgence, Decolonization, and Movements for Environmental Justice," in Dhillon (ed.), *Indigenous Resurgence*, 7.

12 Quoted in Rebekah Sheldon, *The Child to Come: Life after the Human Catastrophe* (Minneapolis: University of Minnesota Press, 2016), vii.

13 Karrabing Film Collective, "The Mermaids, or Aiden in Wonderland," IFFR, https://iffr.com/en/2020/films/the-mermaids-or-aiden-in-wonderland. The film has been lauded as "a powerful intervention in contemporary debates about the future present of climate change, extractive capitalism, and industrial toxicity from the point of view of Indigenous worlds."

14 Saidiya V. Hartman, *Lose Your Mother: A Journey along the Atlantic Slave Route* (New York: Farrar, Straus and Giroux, 2007), 100.

15 Lisa Lowe, *The Intimacies of Four Continents* (Durham, NC: Duke University Press, 2015), 41.

16 Dhillon, "Indigenous," 1.

17 Ibid., 2–3.

18 Coulthard, *Red Skin*, 172–3.

19 Interview with Dr. Tiffany Lethabo King, *feral feminisms: Complicities, Connections, and Struggles: Critical Transnational Feminist Analysis of Settler Colonialism*, no. 4 (Summer 2015), https://feralfeminisms.com/lethabo-king/.

20 Timothy Morton, "Weird Embodiment," in Lynette Hunter, Elisabeth Krimmer, and Peter Lichtenfels (eds.), *Sentient Performativities of Embodiment: Thinking alongside the Human* (Lanham, MD: Lexington Books, 2016), 19–34, 20.

21 Morton, *Dark Ecology* (New York: Columbia University Press, 2016), 7.

22 Morton, "Weird Embodiment," 29.

23 David Graeber, "Radical Alterity Is Just Another Way of Saying 'Reality': A Reply to Eduardo Viveiros de Castro," *HAU Journal of Ethnographic Theory* 5.2 (2015), 1–41, 22.

24 Manu Vimalassery, Juliana Hu Pegues, and Alyosha Goldstein, "Introduction: On Colonial Unknowing," *Theory & Event* 19.4 (2016), muse.jhu.edu/article/633283.

25 Graeber, "Radical," 33.

26 Morton, *Humankind*, 118.

27 Tommy Pico, *Nature Poem* (Portland, OR: Tin House Books, 2017), 2. "NDN" is a shortened form of "Indian."

28 Ibid., 67.

29 In the closing moments of Faulkner's *Absalom, Absalom!*, Shreve asks Quentin "Why do you hate the South?" and Quentin responds, "I don't! I don't hate it! I don't hate it!" Critics have read this moment as an epiphany of the Southerner's fatal romance with the region's dark histories and conditioning.

30 Pico, *Nature*, 72–3.

31 Ibid., 73.

32 Morton, *Humankind*, 119–20.

33 Pico, *Nature*, 2.

34 Ibid., 40.

35 Ibid., 9.

36 As David Farrier has argued, poetry as a genre is distinctively suited to the "rhetorical manifestations of the Anthropocene [. . .] Poetry can compress vast acreages of meaning into a small compass or perform the bold linkages that it would take reams of academic argument to plot; it can widen the aperture of our gaze or deposit us on the brink of transformation" (*Anthropocene Poetics*, 4–5).

37 Pico, *Nature*, 1.

38 Morton, *Humankind*, 134.

39 Pico, *Nature*, 38–9.

40 Ibid., 74.

41 Ibid., 53.
42 "I think the more we center the deviations, the less stable the perception of 'reality' becomes, and then more and more stuff either is possible, or it seems possible," Blackfeet horror author Stephen Graham Jones said. "I want to walk through a wardrobe, into another world." Erika T. Wurth, "Not Your Grandmother's Native American Fiction," All Arts, www.allarts.org/2021/03/speculative-native-american-fiction-erika-t-wurth/.
43 McAdams, "From *Betty Creek: Writing the Indigenous Deep South*," in Geary Hobson, Janet McAdams, and Kathryn Walkiewicz (eds.), *The People Who Stayed: Southeastern Indian Writing after Removal* (Norman: University of Oklahoma Press, 2010), 251–6, 256.
44 McAdams, "From *Betty Creek*," 256.
45 Janet McAdams, "Earth My Body Is Trying to Remember," in *Feral* (Norfolk: Salt Publishing, 2007), 76.
46 Janet McAdams, *Seven Boxes for the Country After* (Kent, OH: Kent State University Press, 2016), Kindle edition.
47 Haraway, *Staying*, 160.

CHAPTER 13

Biocentrism
Sexuality, Coloniality, and Constructing the Human
Nathan Snaza

Let me say right away that I will take "sexuality" less as a discrete set of acts, pleasures, and identities than as a specifically biopolitical field, not a description of a purportedly "natural" cluster of phenomena but a means of modulating the social production of entities, including those entities we have come to call "humans" and other "animals." This is a Foucauldian framing of sexuality,[1] but one I want to prod toward an orientation attuned to how "sexuality" – as "patterned discursive incitements and stimulations that facilitated the penetration of social and self-disciplinary regimes into the most intimate domains of modern life" – is, first and foremost, a colonial and racial field.[2] This framing will ultimately push me to claim that the same thing is true of "the human" and "the animal": far more than conceptual catachreses or "animots," these terms are part of the patriarchal and colonial grammars of the modern, homogenized world of Man in the post-1492 moment of European imperialism.[3]

One way to say this is to claim that "the human" and "the animal" are inseparable, as categories of thought, not only from each other but from the operations of de/humanizing assemblages, or what Alexander Weheliye calls "assemblages of the human, not-quite-human, and nonhuman."[4] In a resonant formulation, Judith Butler notes that "these excluded sites come to bound the 'human' as its constitutive outside, and to haunt those boundaries as the persistent possibility of their disruption and rearticulation."[5] For Butler this insight – that the production of the human necessarily entails the production of its nonhuman constitutive outsides – enables a theory of gender as performative, where iterative praxis immanently materializes the sexed and gendered scripts that govern how subjects emerge and endure in social fields (fields that I see, although Butler doesn't frame it this way, as always more-than-human). Sylvia Wynter, whose work is one point of departure for Weheliye's theory of racializing assemblages, speaks in an interview with Katherine McKittrick about how her project of decolonizing the human – a project that guides this chapter – might be understood as a decolonial generalization of Butler's argument. She writes, "Butler's illuminating redefinition of gender as praxis rather than a noun, therefore, set off bells ringing everywhere! Why not, then, the performative enactment of *all our roles*, of all our *role allocations* as, in our contemporary Western/Westernized case, in terms of, inter alia, gender, race, class/underclass, and, across them all, sexual orientation?"[6] Sexual orientation, or simply sexuality, works here as a biopolitical modulation of subjects as they come into being and endure as praxis, and it has come to mark the hegemonic form of the human – what Wynter calls Man – that is presumptive in the overwhelming majority of contemporary thought, from global capitalism to international law to critical theory. At stake in this chapter, then, is showing how that idea of the human – which must "have" a sexuality and a race to be legible in a colonialist world oriented around Man – and "the animal" as one of its constitutive outsides (which is also an inside) are also bound up with particular ideas about what "literature" is and does.

These are enormous questions, but I want to broach them modestly by simply juxtaposing two different uses of the adjective "biocentric," uses that despite their polarization on some axes both find "literature," "the human," "the animal," and "sexuality" inextricably bound up with each other and with the proper name of Charles Darwin, and more broadly with the evolutionary episteme his name connotes. The first section will look at the way literary critic Margot Norris charts a "biocentric" tradition that includes Darwin and Friedrich Nietzsche and modernist artists such as Franz Kafka, Max Ernst, and D. H. Lawrence. For these biocentric thinkers, the human *is* an animal, and their aesthetic, creative praxes foreground the animality of the human and the biological or instinctual nature of art. More than two decades later, a similar biocentric lineage, modulated now by a reading of Gilles Deleuze, shapes the accounts of animality and (bio)politics offered by Elizabeth Grosz and Brian Massumi. In all of these thinkers, the question of how animals and literature relate isn't primarily one of representation (how animals are depicted in literary texts), but one of how "literature" itself names practices that can be called, non-anthropomorphically and without risking the "abuse" of metaphor we call "catachresis," "animal."

The second section takes up Sylvia Wynter's use of "biocentric" to describe a specifically *colonial* and racializing concept of the human(imal), one whose genealogy and effects can be sensed only when one foregrounds the entanglements of "biological" science with (Western) imperialism and racisms. Wynter's account, which in one of its lines works by taking up an idea of Frantz Fanon – "sociogeny" – and reconfiguring it through a careful reading of cybernetics, foregrounds not just how literature is an expression of (hum)animality, but how literature is part of the biocultural emergence and endurance of *all genres* of human praxis. As she puts it, "it is we who are the function" of literature.[7] Wynter's is a "hybrid bios/mythos" conception of the human, one that is positioned specifically against a "biocentric" understanding of what a human *is*.

Holding these two uses of the same concept in tension, the third section articulates a cluster of questions that might guide our future interests in how "animals" and "literature" relate. These include questions about how "sexuality" and discourses of species are inseparable from each other and from discourses of racialization/coloniality. I turn here to Zakiyyah Iman Jackson's *Becoming Human* (2020) as exemplary of the kinds of literary reading that Wynter's project allows, even as she pushes us toward a reckoning with how this "sociogenic principle" (potentially) operates beyond a narrowly "human" field.[8] This necessarily entails some further questions about how we understand literary practices in relation to the work of sciences that simultaneously shores up and reconfigures dominant notions of what "the human" is. By thinking through the racial biopolitics of sexuality as the surround of what we call "literature," I hope to tap into other genres of the human, as Wynter calls them, that simultaneously entail otherwise worlds: more-than-human(ist) socialities that are structured by storytelling, no longer understood as merely "human" phenomena, but not quite "animal" either: an anima-literature where stories animate and are animated by more-than-human socialities, what Jayna Brown calls "genres of existence" that deviate from Man and generate otherwise worlds.[9]

Biocentrism One

Margot Norris's 1985 *Beasts of the Modern Imagination* offers a careful, complex articulation of what she calls a "biocentric tradition," founded by Charles Darwin, and including "writers whose works constitute animal gestures or acts of fatality."[10] She situates this tradition (which "is no tradition at all")[11] in relation to what she calls "an anthropocentric universe" structured by a presumptive rupture between "the human" and "the animal," a rupture adhering around, most importantly, *language*.[12] In the anthropocentric (or simply "humanist") cosmology, only humans "have" language, which means that, since literature is language pushed to its utmost intensity, literature is not just uniquely human but a lodestar of human potentiality.[13] Thus conceived, if a writer – who is always and necessarily a "human" – writes like or as "the animal," it is at worst a dangerous anthropomorphism and at least a catachrestic tropological swerve. After Darwin, though, Norris is interested in writers "who create *as* the animal – not *like* the animal, in imitation of the animal."[14]

Animality here is what Norris calls a "plenum": the very source of creativity that biocentric artists tap into and express.[15] This is a source of both the novelty of their modern(ist) creations and their cultural misunderstanding: "Biocentric art therefore eschewed realism in favor of new, experimental modes that are easily confused with the visionary, the allegorical, or the satirical, if we consider only their representations and disregard the destructive rhetorical strategies aimed at representation." Biocentric art is antirepresentational, not nonrepresentational, such as when Kafka's "narration cancels itself in the act of telling: his argument retracts itself after every point."[16] While Norris worries about the ways that anthropocentrism pointedly misreads such works by "taming" (in the Nietzschean sense) biocentric art and insisting on its legibility within humanist rhetorical frames like "allegory" and "satire," she still wants to track the tradition by following rhetoric. Put schematically, art always links the rhetorical and the representational; anthropocentric art shores up representation through rhetorical practice, while biocentric art lobs rhetorical bombs against representation's operations. For the creators in Norris's post-Darwinian (non)tradition – Nietzsche, Kafka, Ernst, and Lawrence – rhetoric is (or can be) an animal practice that militates against human(ist) representation. Animality here is not the what of (literary) art, but the *how*. It's legible not in the characters and plots of the texts so much as in the specific enunciative moves that bring trembling worlds into being through creative destruction.

This implies a Nietzschean commitment to violence, where "animal violence is restored to its amoral Dionysian innocence."[17] There is, here again, a kind of reversal, a transvaluation, of the humanist cosmology in which "violence has been traditionally attributed to the beast."[18] Norris is interested in violence as it blurs into creation. This is the precise point at which sexuality enters the frame: Nietzsche "equates [. . .] artistic productivity with sexual prowess."[19] In a quasi-Freudian move (one elaborated by Lawrence in his book *Fantasia of the Unconscious* [1922]), art is here a kind of sublimated libido or what she calls, in her reading of Kafka's "pornology," "the libidinalization of thought."[20] The upshot is that biocentric art is not just "animal" but "sexual" since those terms aren't able to be held apart from each other for long. "The animal" that is the human for Norris is irreducibly sexual or libidinal and those terms are used nearly synony-mously with "natural."

This parsing of nature and culture snaps most clearly into focus when Norris has to address the ways that this framework risks what is to her a mistaken appropriation by racist social politics including those of the Third Reich (whose members were avid, if partial and idiosyncratic, readers of Nietzsche). One of the key moments here is worth quoting at more length:

> But the tasks of distinguishing biocentrism from its cultural parodies, and of distinguishing myriad false doubles created by the insertion of the lack and the "other" into the libidinal realms, are not easily mastered. Biocentrism, with its affirmation of the animal and, by possible extension, physical prowess, genetic constitution, and racial destiny, has therefore undergone intellectual repression along with fascist ideology in the after-math to World War II.[21]

Starting with the obvious, stating the difficulty of this "distinguishing" – a task that compels most of *Beasts of the Modern Imagination*'s arguments – is a way of authorizing the correctness, counterintuitively, of what she calls the "innocence" of animal violence. It is only, Norris claims, when anthropocentric cultural practices *parody* this innocent animal violence that it tips into the kinds of racist and masculinist violence we have learned to see as constitutive of the Third Reich.[22] She presumes here some concept of animality, or bios, outside of what any particular culture represents that to mean. Put more simply, Norris is implying that the masculinist and racist projects that attach themselves to Darwin's name – including eugenics – are in effect *bad readings* of this tradition, readings that refuse the ontogenic capacities of the bios in favor of a generalized form of what Donna Haraway has called "simian orientalism" where the work of purportedly (social) "scientific" knowledge is little more than a symptom of a racialist and patriarchal program masking itself via natural-ization.[23] But, she thinks, it might be otherwise if we were more open to thinking about art – including literature – not as a sign of human exceptionalism but as one version of nature's plenum operationalized as animal expressiveness.

If Norris's elaboration of a biocentric tradition runs into the ways that tradition has been yoked to racist and heteropatriarchal understandings of evolutionary politics – understandings that aren't fully alien to the mod-ernist texts she engages – we might see an attempt to induce a swerve away, toward more progressive futures in the work of Elizabeth Grosz and Brian Massumi, work that doesn't mark itself as "biocentric" but draws its

potentiality from a similar set of texts and an affiliated axiomatic commitment to human animality, or the irreducibly "natural" facticity of humans.
For Grosz, who reads Darwin, Nietzsche, and Henri Bergson through
Deleuze in order to think about the "untimely" future of progressive
politics, the primary thrust is locating political action not in the rational
operations of planning that authorize actions but in an aleatory excess that
she articulates as evolutionary or "natural." She writes:

> The human is fundamentally an elaborate and relatively adaptable animal,
> an animal whose future is not within its own control, though cultural
> systems cannot function without a certain level of (voluntary) social partic-
> ipation. This participation, though, exerts less control over human social
> arrangements than the self-organizing structures of human "products":
> language, the economy, law, justice, and so on. These are not the emer-
> gence of "higher" qualities but the elaboration and expansion of certain
> animal impulses.[24]

Rather unlike the eugenicist framing that would read evolutionary drift
through a presumptive telos in the human – or, to anticipate Wynter's
genealogy of modern humanism, Man – which allows for hierarchized
attributions of differential humanity, Grosz here sees evolution as a useful
frame for politics precisely because of the more- or other-than-conscious
propulsion of a natural becoming that works through the human but is not
(agentially) located within it. "Animal" names that excess, and for her it
leads to politics not as the asymptotic approach of a critical Ideal but as
something "endless'" and "unattainable."[25]

I want to amplify a tension in Grosz's work. On the one hand, this
commitment to "nature" leads her to hypostasize binary sex difference, a
difference she sees as pre- or more-than-human, and one that "is the very
motor of life's self-variation, life's most ingenious invention for its own
variability, regeneration, self-surpassing, and elaboration."[26] Needless to
say, this has some troubling implications for Grosz's relationship to
contemporary theories of trans, intersex, and nonbinary life.[27] On the
other, one of her crucial interventions – and one clearly aligned with the
biocentric artists Norris analyzes – is to see, after Darwin, language as *itself*
a field of evolution: "the development of language is not just *like* evolution,
it is evolution."[28] The tension adheres in how language's evolution –
which strikes me as no less elaborate and literally wonderful than the
evolution of multicellular organisms – cannot be dependent on the binary
sexual difference and sexual selection that her work sometimes seems to
privilege. That is, I would propose we might see the focus on language as
an animal capacity – where "some of the rudiments or preconditions of

language [. . .] are there in animals"[29] – as allowing a foregrounding of
nonsexual reproduction, replication, and evolution, one that doesn't run
headlong into the binary essentialisms of second wave feminism and
its afterlives.

This may be partly why in *What Animals Teach Us about Politics*,
Massumi specifically doesn't follow sexual difference in his attention to
animal politics. The concept that figures most prominently in his account
is "play": "In play, the human enters a zone of indiscernibility with the
animal."[30] Following the work of Gregory Bateson, Massumi sees play as a
matter of the *conditional*, a kind of subjunctive modal swerve from
denotative, indicative seriousness that is specifically not "human." This
grammatical account unsurprisingly also foregrounds the animality of
language: "it is actually in language that the human reaches its highest
degree of animality";[31] or language is where the human expresses the
"highest animal power."[32] The specifics of Massumi's account – which
rereads "instinct" through Bergson, Gilbert Simondon, and Deleuze away
from determination toward the very source of improvisational worldmaking – lead to the necessity of attaining a specific conception of the human
for politics precisely because the human isn't thinkable apart from a
concept of the animal: "to evoke the posthuman is to evoke the postani-
mal."[33] Rejecting the posthuman, and reaffirming the animality of the
human, is part of an affirmation that the human is always "more-than-
human," always activating a kind of virtual potentiality of the political that
he anchors in a conception of animal instinct as improvisational
tendency.[34] As with Grosz, we see how thinking language *as* animal
capacity leads to a notion of the human not as telos, and not as Man,
but as the name for an always unfolding evolutionary tendency that we
might call "animality."

Biocentrism Two

To understand the role of "biocentrism" in the thought of Sylvia Wynter,
one has to first back up to see the ways that her project reconceives of the
human not as a noun – say, a "species" – but as a verb, as a praxis. The
human is a performance of being that takes its specific form(s) in cultural,
economic, political contexts. Her massive career-spanning genealogy of
modernity – whose beginning can be indexically marked as 1492 when
Spain expelled Jewish people and Christopher Columbus launched his
voyage[35] – is attentive to how a specific form of the human (a white,
masculinist, imperialist one) "overrepresents itself as if it were the human

itself."[36] This development happens for her in two distinct moments, or across two thresholds: a passage from divine causality into a "natural causality" linked to renaissance humanism's secular heresy, which she associates with "Man1," and a subsequent revision based in "the natural sciences" that produces "Man2" in the nineteenth century.[37] She notes that in this Man2 moment – where we see the emergence of "our present Darwinian'" understanding of Man[38] – what is at stake is the circulation of a specifically "biocentric descriptive statement" of the human that is constitutively colonial/racist. The global ubiquity of racism and the idea of race is possible only because of how specific scientific concepts – developed within imperialist or colonialist contexts – have proposed a purportedly natural, neutral, or universal understanding of the world.[39] Racism here is not a psychological phenomenon affecting persons (legible in their biases or prejudices), but rather an inextricable part of the grammar of not just political theory but the entire project of articulating "universal" or objective knowledge of "the" world in which specific post-Enlightenment subjects (endowed with self-determinative autonomy) move.[40]

Descriptive statements – particular narratives, stories, or scripts about what it means "to *be*, and therefore what it is *like to be*, human" – matter for Wynter because of the way she takes up Frantz Fanon's concept of sociogeny from *Black Skin, White Masks* (1952) and reconceives of this through cybernetics.[41] Specifically, she's interested in how, for (at least) human beings, descriptive statements are not "culture" that appears after the fact of a purportedly "natural" evolutionary emergence of humans, but a *constitutive part* of evolutionary becoming at both the individual (pheno-typical) and social levels. Descriptive statements are part of the autopoetic system functioning of the beings-in-and-as-praxis that we are. The milieu in which any human becomes and endures includes ideas of what it is to be human, and the geopolitics of coloniality adheres in large measure in how Man becomes *the* measure of all things. For Wynter, the human, as praxis, as genre, as performance, is always articulated in relation to circulating descriptive statements that are materially co-compositional with a particular human's affective apparatus: it's about how it feels to be human, what it "is like" to be human, and what it feels like to encounter others in their more- and less-than-humanness according to Man's overrepresentation.

Within Man2, the crucial thing is that various genres of humanness are marked in their colonial hierarchy specifically in terms of evolutionary selection, where non-Man genres of the human are "dysselected," disqua-lified, marked for elimination.[42] In an essay written in the immediate aftermath of the Rodney King beating and news that the LA Police

Department marked certain encounters as "N.H.I." (no humans involved), Wynter writes that within this present moment:

> The human can be [. . .] conceived *as if it were* a mode of being which exists in relation of pure *continuity* with that of organic life. Whilst it is only within these terms, that the N.H.I. acronym and its classificatory logic is to be understood as part of the *genetic status-organizing principle* of which the phenomenon we have come to know as "race," is the expression.[43]

Race and racism are not nature, not culture, but rather part of a specific, historically contingent if world historical concept of the human – Man – that achieves a kind of global hegemony through enormous, centuries-long violence, one part of which has to be understood as the circulation – through "literature," through law, through all educational and cultural institutions marked by modernity – of stories about what it is to be human. For Wynter, who is here seemingly now opposed to Norris, seeing the human in biocentric terms is the clearest expression of a racializing, colonialist worldview rather than a minor claim that would disrupt humanist thought.

Wynter is clearly rejecting the kind of biocentric understanding of the human that Norris proposes, instead insisting on some kind of human distinction from the natural. She often calls this difference *story*: "*storytellers who now storytellingly invent themselves as purely biological.*"[44] This might look, from a certain angle, like a reassertion of traditional human exceptionalism, or even the kind of anthropocentrism that Norris sees as in need of biocentric disruption. Such a reading might underline moments when Wynter makes claims that such hybridity is related to "the mode of consciousness unique to humans."[45] But Wynter's entire concept of sociogenesis – which unlike Fanon's "sociogeny" is not circumscribed within humanist psychoanalytic frames – works, on the other hand, to resist any kind of human exceptionalism that would resonate with Man's humanism. At stake is the way that something outside "the human" affects it, works through it, animates it. She does this by foregrounding, like Grosz and Massumi, the ways that language itself evolves, and the always and necessarily unfinished, nonteleological unfurling of genres of humaning. In the interview with McKittrick, she writes of "the *co-evolution* of the human being *with* – and unlike those of all other primates, *with it alone* – the emergent faculties of language, storytelling."[46] This is a focus on human particularity, to be sure, but one that sees the human as an effect not of biological evolution as that has been understood by post-Darwinian eugenicist thinkers but of a hybrid bios/mythos evolutionary process that surrounds the human and conditions any particular entity's phenotypical (and affective) emergence. It might offer a conception of the human close to what Samantha Frost has called "biocultural creatures."[47] I recall that for Wynter it is "we who are the function" of literature: stories, scripts, narratives, descriptive statements are part of the evolutionary patterning that constitutes humans in their praxis.

Tensions between Wynter's and Norris's conception of biocentrism arise in part from different ways of valuing the adjective "biocentric," but it also importantly modifies different objects (or better "stories") for each: for Norris a relatively minor, and now largely "repressed," tradition that is synecdochally linked to a small number of white artists in the late nineteenth and early twentieth centuries; for Wynter the globally domi-nant – and so dominant as to have become an unremarkable part of (colonialist) common sense – descriptive statement of the human-as-Man. Over and against these two massive disagreements about the scope and political valence of biocentrism, I'm trying to also note a diffuse and sometimes vague sharing between Norris and Wynter that is most legible in their desires to rethink the human in relation to something called "nature" or "the animal," a rethinking that seems to necessarily engage not just Darwin and his specific claims about selection (sexual and other-wise) but also the entire problematic of "evolution" as a conception of how worlds unfold in their unceasing (and often surprising) particularities.

Becoming Human and the Futures of Literary Animal Studies

Zakiyyah Iman Jackson's *Becoming Human: Matter and Meaning in an Antiblack World* is explicitly an elaboration of Wynter's decolonial critique of humanism, and it builds from Wynter's critique of the biocentric descriptive statement to argue, directly, that the more-than-scientific con-cept of "the animal" is, like gender and sexuality, inseparable from racial-izing – or, as she puts it, *humanizing* – assemblages. Humanizing, for her, names the violent plasticization of black life such that it can form the outermost limits of "the human" precisely because it is figured as an *animal* humanity. As she puts it in her reading of Toni Morrison's *Beloved*, "the slave's humanity [...] is not denied or excluded but manipulated and prefigured as animal whereby black(ened) humanity is understood, para-digmatically, as a state of abject *human* animality."[48] Jackson's readings are attentive to precisely the ways that the biological knowledges produced in the nineteenth century that spoke to and about "animal" life were always already part of a broader discourse about race as a structuring principle of a world globalizing around Man: "anxieties about conquest, slavery, and colonial expansionism provided the historical context for the emergence of a developmental mode of 'universal humanity' and a newly consolidated generic 'animal' that would be defined in nonhuman *and* human terms."[49]

Jackson notes that "these subjects – 'animal' as a generic term and the racialized masculine figure of Caliban [in Shakespeare's *The Tempest*] – are intertwined and that their interrelation is ordered through the absent presence of the material metaphor of the black female as matrix-figure."[50] At stake here is a double reconfiguration, whereby what we call "the animal" and the grammars that subtend gendered and sexed legibility are both reconceived as parts of the racializing assemblages that order the world around Man as the human's overrepresentation. Jackson attends to what Spillers has called the "ungendering" of slavery – where black flesh is consigned to a "vestibulary" space at the border of "culture" and "humanity," and where the kin relations that undergird sex and gender categories in the modern biopolitical mode don't obtain because they "*can be invaded at any given and arbitrary moment by the property relations.*"[51] Arguing that "a critical engagement with gender and sexuality must be coincident to our interrogation of both dominant and emergent *praxes* of being," Jackson theorizes "ontologized" plasticity in which black flesh *is made to be* the morphologically plastic "outside" of Man's proper, "full" humanity.[52]

This biopolitical interpretation foregrounds antiblack coloniality as the milieu in which purportedly scientific concepts like "animal," "sexuality," and even "sex difference" emerge. This science is a story that the storytellers tell to make the world seem *as if* these were merely things that exist, not the results of production in humanizing assemblages. The still dominant form of the human – Man – requires those who seek even the most marginal or minimal recognition as "human" to "have" a sex, a gender, a race. One cannot be legible in Man's grammars without such demarcation, which is why for Jackson the task is "a disruption of the prevailing grammar of gender, knowledge, and being."[53]

Jackson pushes us to consider how the very terms "human" and "animal" presume this grammar, which means that to speak and think in those terms is already to fit the limits of thought within particular conceptual and ontological bounds shaped by antiblack coloniality. This allows her to focus on moments where distinctions between humans and nonhuman animals (for instance, her reading of the rooster Mister's interactions with Paul D. in *Beloved*) blur, and the capacities that we have been taught to associate with each circulate in ways that disrupt the violence of ontologized plasticity (being forcibly rendered humanization's interior "constitutive outside") with a different kind of plasticity, one that is demanding, not demanded; one that opens onto otherwise worlds: "*Becoming Human* furthers black studies' interrogation of humanism by identifying our shared being with the nonhuman without suggesting that some members of humanity bear the burden of 'the animal.'"[54]

The most obvious question that arises here – one that I think is worth raising not to answer it now but to suggest that this question is unavoidable moving forward – concerns the very concepts of "human" and "animal" that mark the intersection of literature and animal studies around and within the posthumanities. It is also to ask what we mean by "life" to the extent that "bios" can be thus translated, and to ask how and why when the human thinks life the term that mediates is always "animal," which is in turn in intimate, indissociable entanglement with "sex," "gender," and "sexuality."

Against this interrogative horizon, I want to note that all of the thinkers I've been engaging – Norris, Grosz, Massumi, Wynter, and Jackson – are attempting to think about how the practices we call "literature" (or, more broadly, "art" and "language") arise from something in "the human" that exceeds how that concept has been operationalized during colonial modernity. There is something vital here – in a sense of livingness I explicitly want to mark as more than "life" according to scientific reason's coloniality – that makes "literature" not something humans create as independent agents so much as something they participate in. Literature doesn't arise from "the human," and indeed the human, or particular genres of performing it, is an effect of this more diffuse thing called "literature." I think about this as anima-literature, where the hyphen marks the space where an inaudible *and* all-too-audible "L" separates an indication of liveliness – one that adheres across materialities without respect to being "alive": all matter is vital – and the trace of the "animal."[55] If matter as such is vital and agential – if distributed along colonial animacy scales[56] – then we might think of "the study of literature as a subset of more-than-human literacy practices, where humans are entangled with a whole host of other agencies that animate literacy situations."[57] What I'm trying to think through here is what happens if we let "the animal" be a kind of threshold sound, one we attune to precisely because it arises at the borders of the humanizing assemblages of Man. But in our patient listening to the sound of "the animal," we might begin to hear past it something on the horizon that exceeds the capture of colonial grammars, a kind of force that registers in language as its "immanent outside."[58] This is to learn to hear, to feel, to touch, and be touched by what Ashon Crawley calls "otherwise possibilities," to processually enact what Weheliye calls "the abolition of Man."[59] And it just might mean to follow Jayna Brown when she says, "We move from Wynter's call for a new genre of the human to new genres of *existence*, entirely different modes of material being and becoming."[60] What we call literature or storytelling is a constitutive part of that becoming. The concept of "biocentrism" has been one way that becoming has been articulated. What I've tried to call attention to here is both the necessity of this question and the urgency of its stakes for the possibility of decolonial and queer futures, but also the limitations on our questioning when our terminology and grammars are presumptively colonial.

One possible way forward through these more-than-human genres of existence is to foreground Audre Lorde's more-than-sexual concept of the erotic, which indexes a field of joyful, haptic (and happy in the sense of "hap")[61] encounters within which subjects are emergent and durative.[62] Working against the enclosure of what Foucault has called "bodies and pleasures" within the field of the pornographic, Lorde turns to the erotic as a source of power, of joy, and of worldmaking (it always seeks to become shared). Anima-literature is erotic without being (necessarily) sexual. If Norris's conception of biocentrism gets mired in coloniality and eugenics, and if Grosz winds up articulating a version of binary sexual essentialism, this may turn out to be because of an unwillingness to move outside sexuality as a colonial construct, an inability to notice that once you tap into erotics you can remember that most reproduction of living creatures, and the forms of temporal endurance that we might call geological, aren't sexual in even the narrow sense. If this chapter has tried to feel out a realm of potentiality that exceeds the human, a realm that is the very plenum from which literature (or story) arises and *in turn* sociogenically produces the human, then Lorde's erotic helps us understand some of those pleasures we habitually conceive though "sexuality" as something else. If colonialist biopolitics require human persons to "have" a sexuality, erotics adhere in a more-than-human situation: they speak to intimate contact, more-than-human tactility, and affects that circulate in and around those literacy events we are talking about when we say "literature."

Notes

1 Michel Foucault, *A History of Sexuality, vol. 1: An Introduction* (London: Vintage, 1978).
2 Ann Laura Stoler, *Race and the Education of Desire* (Durham, NC: Duke University Press, 1995), 3.

3 Following Wynter, I use "coloniality" as a frame that includes antiblackness and anti-indigeneity. Sylvia Wynter, "1492: A New World View," in Vera Lawrence Hyatt and Rex Nettleford (eds.), *Race, Discourse, and the Origin of the Americas* (Washington, DC: Smithsonian Institution Press, 1995); Hortense Spillers, *Black, White, and in Color* (Chicago: University of Chicago Press, 2003); Jacques Derrida, *The Animal That Therefore I Am* (New York: Fordham University Press, 2008).

4 Alexander G. Weheliye, *Habeas Viscus* (Durham, NC: Duke University Press, 2014), 43.

5 Judith Butler, *Bodies That Matter* (New York: Routledge, 1993), 8.

6 Sylvia Wynter and Katherine McKittrick, "Unparalleled Catastrophe for Our Species? Or, to Give Humanness a Different Future: A Conversation," in Katherine McKittrick (ed.), *Sylvia Wynter: On Being Human as Praxis* (Durham, NC: Duke University Press, 2015), 9–89, 33.

7 Sylvia Wynter, "The Ceremony Must Be Found: After Humanism," *boundary2* 12.3 (1984), 19–70, 50.

8 Sylvia Wynter, "Towards the Sociogenic Principle: Fanon, Identity, the Puzzle of Conscious Experience, and What It Is like to Be 'Black'," in Mercedes F. Durán-Cogan and Antonio Gómez-Mariana (eds.), *National Identities and Sociopolitical Changes in Latin America* (New York: Routledge, 2001), 30–66.

9 Jayna Brown, *Black Utopias: Speculative Life and the Music of Other Worlds* (Durham, NC: Duke University Press, 2021); Ashon T. Crawley, *Blackpentecostal Breath: the Aesthetics of Possibility* (New York: Fordham University Press, 2017).

10 Margot Norris, *Beasts of the Modern Imagination* (Baltimore, MD: Johns Hopkins University Press, 1985), 1.

11 Ibid., 2.

12 Ibid., 1

13 Norris thinks of this as a project of "rebiologizing" literature in a moment – marked by the cultural or linguistic turn that is part of the long wake of structuralist thought – where the "critical" mood is assumed to involve debiologizing.

14 Norris, *Beasts*, 1.

15 Ibid., 4.

16 Ibid., 19–20.

17 Ibid., 10.

18 Ibid., 9.

19 Ibid., 12.

20 Ibid., 101.

21 Ibid., 23.

22 Klaus Theweleit, *Male Fantasies*, vols. 1 and 2 (Minneapolis: University of Minnesota Press, 1987).

23 Donna J. Haraway, *Primate Visions: Gender, Race, and Nature in the World of Modern Science* (New York: Routledge, 1989).

24 Elizabeth Grosz, *The Nick of Time: Politics, Evolution and the Untimely* (Durham, NC: Duke University Press, 2004), 62–3.

25 Ibid., 14.

26 Ibid., 10.

27 Donovan Schaefer argues that Grosz's reading risks "reducing desire to a monoculture." See "Darwin's Orchids: Queerness, Natural Law, and the Diversity of Desire," *GLQ* 27.4 (2021), 525–50, 544.

28 Grosz, *Nick*, 29.

29 Ibid., 59.

30 Brian Massumi, *What Animals Teach Us about Politics* (Durham, NC: Duke University Press, 2014), 8.

31 Ibid., *Animals*, 8.

32 Ibid., 22.

33 Ibid., 91.

34 Ibid., 93.

35 Wynter, "1492."

36 Sylvia Wynter, "Unsettling the Coloniality of Being/Power/Truth/Freedom: Towards the Human, after Man, Its Overrepresentation – An Argument," *CR: The New Centennial Review* 3.3 (2003), 257–337, 260.

37 Ibid., 264.

38 Ibid., 267.

39 Denise Ferreira da Silva, *Towards a Global Idea of Race* (Minneapolis: University of Minnesota Press, 2007).

40 Spillers, *Black, White and in Color*; da Silva, *Global Idea*.

41 Wynter, "Towards the Sociogenic Principle," 31.

42 Wynter, "Unsettling," 267.

43 Wynter, "'No Humans Involved': An Open Letter to My Colleagues," *Knowledge on Trial* 1.1 (1994), 42–73, 50.

44 Wynter and McKittrick, "Unparalleled Catastrophe," 11.

45 Wynter, "Towards the Sociogenic Principle," 48.

46 Wynter and McKittrick, "Unparalleled Catastrophe," 25.

47 Samantha Frost, *Biocultural Creatures: Towards a New Theory of the Human* (Durham, NC: Duke University Press, 2016).

48 Zakiyyah Iman Jackson, *Becoming Human: Matter and Meaning in an Antiblack World* (New York: New York University Press, 2020), 47.

49 Ibid., 14.

50 Ibid., 13.

51 Spillers, *Black, White, and in Color*, 218.

52 Jackson, *Becoming Human*, 10.

53 Ibid., 61.

54 Ibid., 12.

55 Jane Bennett, *Vibrant Matter: A Political Ecology of Things* (Durham, NC: Duke University Press, 2009).

56 Mel Y. Chen, *Animacies: Biopolitics, Racial Mattering, and Queer Affect* (Durham, NC: Duke University Press, 2012).

57 Nathan Snaza, *Animate Literacies: Literature, Affect, and the Politics of Humanism* (Durham, NC: Duke University Press, 2019), 155.

58 Brian Massumi, *99 Theses on the Revaluation of Value* (Minneapolis: University of Minnesota Press, 2018).

59 Crawley, *Blackpentecostal Breath*, 2; Weheliye, *Habeas Viscus*, 4.

60 Brown, *Black Utopias*, 9.

61 Sara Ahmed, *Living a Feminist Life* (Durham, NC: Duke University Press, 2017); Audre Lorde, *Sister Outsider* (Trumansburg, NY: Crossing Press, 2007).

62 I elaborate this account of erotics in more detail in *Animate Literacies*.

CHAPTER 14

Health
Zoonotic Disease and the Medical Posthumanities
Lucinda Cole

From the early modern period to well into the twentieth century, until germ theory became widespread, most epidemics were explained as environmental problems. According to Christopher Loar, bubonic plague was understood as "produced by the weather (unfavorable winds or stagnant air), swarms of microscopic animals or particles, or some combination of the two."[1] The literature of the early modern period is rife with references to infections arising from putrefying wetlands. Caliban curses Prospero in *The Tempest* (1611) by invoking miasma theory: "All the infections that the sun sucks up/ From bogs, fens, flats, on Prosper fall, and make him by inch-meal a disease."[2] At a time when the Crown and investors were financing campaigns to drain the fens in the east of England, Caliban's lines invoke a causal mechanism familiar to seventeenth-century audiences: low-lying wetlands were breeding grounds for infectious diseases, both because they gave rise to venomous creatures – snakes, frogs, rats, and so on – and because they were perceived as sinkholes for organic matter that rotted and gave off noxious fumes.[3] Although writers disagreed about the nature and transmission of the plague, they acknowledged that the human body is *in some sense* vulnerable to both human and nonhuman environments: to the effluvia of human and animal others, to invisible animalcula, to earthly exhalations, deadly putrefactions, and *fomites* on traded goods. In early disease ecology, the human body is what Stacy Alaimo has identified as transcorporeal: far from being distinct from the built environment and the natural world, the body is embedded in it.[4] Within this context, two related aspects of disease transmission were hotly debated: the possibility of cross-species infection and the spread of diseases across national borders.

The most telling and widely discussed evidence in the sixteenth and seventeenth centuries for cross-species contagion was rabies. Although the term "zoonotic disease" – bacterial or viral illnesses transmitted from animals to humans, often through disease vectors – was not coined until the nineteenth century, the recognition that dogs, cats, and other creatures could carry and convey diseases goes back for centuries. Rabies was often described as "an ungovernable fury," and, before 1700, no clear distinction existed between the psychological state of being furious and the medical diagnosis of rabid, bodily infection. In fact, the term "rabies" (from the Latin *rabere*, "be mad, rave") was applied primarily to humans and only secondarily to dogs.[5] Rabies presented early modern readers and writers the clearest evidence of how humans and animals are vulnerable to the same neurological disorders, even as rabid dogs mark the limits of human knowledge about madness and disease.

The second transmission question is equally critical: How could epidemics spread from place to place? In urban London, admittedly, disease transmission could be attributed to everyone breathing bad air. A popular plague book reprinted in 1603 advocates that people "keep their houses, street, yards, and sinks, and ditches sweet and clean from all standing puddles, dunghills, and corrupt moistures" in order to prevent outbreaks; most importantly, they should not let dogs run in the house, since these "will be most apt cattle [. . .] to carry the infection."[6] In this case, humans fear the capacity of dogs to expose them (through touch or air) to "putrefactions," "corruptions," and "effluvia" – what we call bacteria – from standing water and waste. Consequently, dogs (and sometimes cats) were subject to extermination in plague-ridden London, at least through 1665. In 1636, London exterminated 3,720 dogs, roaming animals that, according to Mark Jenner, were perceived as "visible sources of disorder, out of control and unsanitary."[7] A common complaint was that dogs ate carrion, itself a possible source of contagion, and by the early eighteenth century, city dogs (at least) had been forced into regimes of containment, hygiene, and control.[8]

While miasma theory could explain site-based infection, it could not explain how some (multispecies) diseases spread across regions, countries, and even continents with markedly different ecologies. Here, as I shall argue, theology rather than science offered models of understanding. Biblical stories like the ten plagues of Egypt described infestations and infection as being so closely related as to be almost indistinguishable: the plagues included hordes of frogs, lice, and flies; pestilential livestock; boils; and – significantly – locust swarms. In the first section of this essay, I focus on insects, and especially locusts because they serve as powerful models of ecological connections between famine and pestilence in agricultural societies and, in their transcontinental flights, provide a way of imagining disease transmission across land and water. In the second section, I discuss rats, shipboard stowaways that posed recurring threats to human health and vulnerable food stores. Although rats were generally unrecognized as what we would now call disease vectors, they, like locusts, were often represented as harbingers of dearth and therefore human plague. In the final section, I turn from verminous creatures to domesticated livestock, calling attention to the underappreciated consequences of cattle plague for literary and cultural history. Between the Middle Ages and the nineteenth century, outbreaks of rinderpest and other livestock diseases disrupted trade, meat production, and food supplies in a series of epidemics so devastating that they led to international series of local and national policies – slaughtering stricken animals, quarantining herds, and banning food and hide imports – and ultimately to international cooperation. In the years between 1500 and 1900, as both zoonotic and enzootic diseases became increasingly global problems – exacerbated by European colonialism and a transnational trade in livestock, hides, and furs – animals were central to the discipline we now recognize as epidemiology.

Swarms and the Four Horsemen

Before germ theory, there was no real sense that insects such as fleas and mosquitos were causal agents in plague, malaria, and other infectious diseases; insects nevertheless figured as the source of usually providentially inflected epidemics. In one of the major sources about antiquity for Renaissance writers, Paulus Orosius's *History against the Pagans* tells the story of "an horrible and extraordinarie destruction" visited on Africa.[9] To punish nonbelievers for their rejection of Christianity, God sent locusts that devoured corn, bark, and even the wood of the trees. Although a "violent and sudden winde" bore them aloft and out to sea, where they drowned, their "lothsome and putrified carcases" were cast back onto shore, where "an incredible stinking & infectious smell" first killed birds and beasts, then men by the thousands.[10] The idea that the Christian faith offers protection against infestation, disease, and death is reinforced in countless early modern texts, including Frances Alvarez's 1540 description of several locust swarms. First, Alvarez reports on a swarm in India that covered twenty-four miles and made the people "halfe dead for sorrow."[11] The Indigenous people implored the Portuguese to help.[12] As Alvarez and the Portuguese ambassador marched through fields of wheat, cross in hand, the Portuguese singing the litany, Alvarez then performed an excommunication, "a certaine conjuration," by which he enjoined the locusts "within the space of three howers to depart towards the sea, or to the land of the Moores, or the desert mountaines, and to let the Christians alone"; seeing no progress, he "summoned and charged the birdes of heaven, the beasts of the earth, and all sorts of tempests, to scatter, destroy, and eate up their bodies."[13] This second effort, he claims, successfully drove the locusts out to sea, where a "great cloud" and thunder "met them full in the teeth." Three hours of rain later, thousands of locust bodies lay in "mightie heapes" on the shore, and the next morning, not one locust could be "found alive upon the earth."[14] Stories of this triumph spread so quickly that, presumably, in a different town three days later, the Portuguese were again enjoined to drive out the locusts, they again formed a procession, and again cleared the ground and sky of insect swarms.

John Pory collected these accounts in his English translation of John Leo Africanus's *A Geographical Historie of Africa* (1600). In Pory's view, they demonstrate how God uses locusts "as a most sharp scourge between times to discipline all the nations of Africa."[15] For us, they help explain how and why, in early plague discourse, infestation and infection were so closely related. First, and most obviously, great numbers of dead and dying insects were easily enfolded into theories of miasma as a source of infection: "an incredible stinking & infectious smell," writes Orosius, "brought about a general pestilence" killing birds, beasts, then men.[16] Second, insects are critical to Christianity's scourge logic. Within the Christian tradition, the Four Horsemen of the Apocalypse – sometimes identified as Conquest, War, Famine, and Death – are "given power," according to Revelations 6.7–8, "to kill with sword, and with hunger, and with death, and with the beasts of the earth."[17] "Scourges" function, paradoxically, as both punishment and purification. Insects in the Bible similarly often appear as part of God's militia, as "war horses" (Joel 2.4–5) or as a "great army." Even in early modern natural histories, locust swarms are cast as flying "armies" sent by God to scourge sinful populations. In his *Theater of Insects, or Lesser Living Creatures* (1658), Thomas Moffet writes that insects "are not the smallest amongst the Armies of the Lord of hosts, when he pleaseth to punish the sins of men, and to revenge himself on the despisers of his Lawes."[18] Samuel Purchas uses almost identical language: we "must conclude that these small creatures have a chief place among Gods Troops and Armies."[19] Throughout the early modern period, then, the logic of the insect scourge structures biblical, natural, and medical history alike; it divides countries into "Christian" and "Pagan," distinguishes between more and less Christian nations, and provides a way to imagine the transmission of disease over long distances.

Having said that, the insect "scourge" gained much of its power from European ecological conditions. During the Little Ice Age, populations of swarming insects often meant the difference for individuals and families between life and death. Cold temperatures, rainfall shortages, and easterly winds brought with them crop failures and higher grain prices; food insecurities and nutritional deficiencies made already vulnerable populations more susceptible to disease. Europe had its share of animal plagues, even occasional plagues of grasshoppers or locusts.[20] Moffet reports on insect-induced famine events in France in 455, 874, 1337, 1353, and 1374 in which a third of the inhabitants died; in 1476 locusts "wasted almost all *Polonia*"; and in 1536 they invaded first Eastern Europe then Germany and Italy, returning in 1543, their bodies "forming heaps above a cubit high."[21] At times during the early modern period, locust-like insects devastated crops as far north as Wales and Ireland. Moffet reports that while he was drafting his chapter on locusts he "received news that the Spaniards were sorely afflicted with swarms of Locusts brought thither out of Africa":

> For they flew like Armies through the skies and darkned the air. And the people when they saw them, rang all their bels, shot off ordinance, sounded with trumpets, tinkled with brazen vessels, cast up sand, did all they could to drive them away; but they could not obtain what they desired, wherefore sparing their labour in vain, they died everywhere of hunger and contagion: as the Mariners and steer-men reported to us, who escaped very hardly from that danger themselves.[22]

As the military imagery in this passage suggests, locust infestation was more than a historical curiosity or a faraway threat. A locust swarm may extend from 150 to 400 square miles; 50 million locusts, according to one expert, can eat 100 tons of food every night.[23] Even if England – for the most part – offered a less habitable climate to these hungry insects than more southerly nations, the English were vicarious witnesses to the damage they could do, and deeply aware of the close of the mysterious relationship between infestation, famine, and infection.

That ancient and contemporary history offer so many examples of locust-driven famine, Moffet says, "should admonish us Christians [...] that the sure way to drive from us hurtful Locusts is to call upon God by prayer joyned with true repentance and unfeigned piety, without which all our force and inventions will come to nought, nor will all our devices avail at all."[24] With this theological affirmation, Moffet underscores his commitment to providentialist history, in which God, acting through Moses or other divinely inspired agents, is alone capable of controlling "God's

Armies" and of determining the successful or failure of verminous battle: "For I highly approve of that saying," he concludes, "*For all remedies without Gods assistance are idle enterprises of men, but when God is pleased, and blesseth the means, then are they remedies indeed.*"[25] Prayer, repentance, piety – in Moffet's view, these are the essential strategies to banish destructive insect swarms; without faith, the "providence and wisdom of man" are little more help than chasing after the wind. Even as such sentiments testify to conceptual struggles to imagine insect events apart from a theological framework, they simultaneously reinforce the status of insects as agents in the promotion of dearth and disease.

Repeated vermin events kept the problem of transnational infestation at the forefront of a wide range of discussions about the typological meanings of, and remedies for, swarming things that threatened individual health, food security, and often the ecological and sociopolitical stability of the state. George Wither's *Britain's Remembrancer* (1628), for example, written so that Charles I may "*Behold (without the hazard of infection / The horrid* Pestilence *in her true form,*" begins with a description of how Famine follows the devastation of crops by vermin:[26]

> The crawling *Caterpillars*, wastfull *Flyes*,
> The skipping *Locust* (that in winter dies)
> *Floods, Frosts, & Mildewes, Blastings, Windes, & Stormes,*
> *Drough, rav'nous Fowles, & Vermine, Weedes, & Wormes:*
> *Sloth, Evill husbandry*, and such as those,
> Which make a scarcenesse where most pleanty grows.[27]

Acknowledging the roles of bad weather and poor farming, Wither devotes most of his energy to personifying Famine as a kind of general, commanding a host of "Troupes" that include caterpillars, locusts, birds, and worms.

Wither wrote *Britain's Remembrancer* shortly after one of the century's worst food crises – England's bad harvest year of 1622–3 – followed by a severe outbreak of the plague in 1625. The title is intended to function prophetically, to remind the English of the torments they will face if they do not amend their behavior. After reminding his readers that they had experienced dearth before the coming of the plague, he uses the situation on the Continent, where dearth had turned to famine, as a cautionary tale: famine had forced those of "dainty pallats" to feed "on moldy scraps," "old shoes," "Carrion, Rats, and Mice," and, in some cases, one another: "with humane flesh, the hungry men hath fed."[28] The end point in Wither's apocalyptic vision is Canto Eight, when God eventually visits plague "on each person, place, and ev'ry thing."[29] At this point, the natural order has collapsed, or more precisely, the reign of vermin is ushered in: God, unleashing a horde of prickling insects, will

> Scourge thee with Scorpions, Serpents, Cocatrices,
> And other such; whose tails with stings are armed,
> That neither can be plucked forth, nor charmed.[30]

The result will be a fallen world no longer fit for humans, where the climate and the "tem'prate ayre" shall "lose their wholsomnesses," now breeding "hot *Fevers, Murraines, Pesilences,* / And all diseases."[31] In Wither's theopolitical view, infestation breeds famine, which breeds disgusting dietary practice, which breeds diseases that, as in the ten plagues of Egypt narrative, afflict humans and nonhumans alike.

Wither's *Britain's Remembrancer* blurs differences among religious, medical, and ecological devastation. Weaving together biblical narratives and contemporary accounts of starving peoples, mothers eating babies, and epidemic disease, the poem depends on both naturalistic and allegorical readings of vermin: "All those Plagues shall fall on thee," he continues, "According as the Letter doth imply, / Or, as in mystick sense they signifie."[32] Although insects have both theological and ecological agency in explaining how epidemics start, and how they continue, Wither tends to allegorize natural phenomena; his poem demonstrates a causal relationship between infestation and infection, even as it demonstrates the entangled logics of symbol, allegorical interpretation, and observational specifics. The logic of the insect scourge, however, remains stable across all three registers. His connections among traveling disease, "the crawling *Caterpillars*," the "wastfull *Flyes*," and the "skipping *Locust*" resonate with contemporary husbandry manuals, national policies to control disease outbreaks, and ecclesiastical interventions. While pigs, dogs, and other mammals were sometimes exterminated in urban plague outbreaks, and while governments frequently passed antivermin legislation requiring citizens to set snares or nets to trap animals that could feed on vulnerable crops, insects – arguably the greatest enemies to agriculture – were a perennial problem not easily subject to secular control.

Rats, Dearth, Ecological Release

To look back on these poems, anatomies, medical treatises, and universal histories is to witness not only historical (mis)understandings of disease, but the complexities of efforts to comprehend zoonotic transmission. We are well aware of how smallpox devasted Indigenous populations during the colonial period, but the equally important histories of how zoonotic diseases – yellow fever, Ebola, Spanish flu, anthrax, and so on – proliferated are only now beginning to be told. In the words of Charles C. Mann, after 1492, "the world's ecosystems collided and mixed as European vessels carried thousands of species to new homes over the ocean."[33] Because these new species found no natural enemies in their new homes, their numbers "often exploded," writes Mann, in a "phenomenon known to science as 'ecological release.'"[34] Sometimes the introduced creatures simply destroyed food supplies. When Spanish colonists brought African plantains to Hispaniola, for example, they probably also imported some scale insects and fire ants, who were following their food supply. In Hispaniola, the scale insects destroyed orchards, "as though flames had fallen from the sky and burned them," while the fire ants multiplied into what was described as an "infinite number."[35] According to the missionary priest Bartolome de Las Casas, these biting ants "could not be stopped in any way nor by human means."[36] The Spaniards abandoned their new homes until, after a series of religious interventions, the plague diminished. In other cases, though, the animals brought disease. In 1826, Michel-Placide Justin describes what appears to have been an anthrax outbreak that occurred in 1770, after an earthquake devastated Port-au-Prince and other settlements in the French colony of Saint-Domingue. Damaged port towns were unable to supply plantations owners with codfish, the major food staple for the many Africans enslaved on the sugar plantations. At the same time, Spanish cattle rangers, experiencing what Justin calls an *epizootie*, salted, sold, and distributed meat from the infected cattle, thereby, according to Justin, spreading the "*germe*" of the disease.[37] Over the next six weeks, more than 15,000 people, white and Black, died – in the largest anthrax epidemic ever recorded – before colonial administrators belatedly halted distribution of the infected meat. But without beef or cod, the colony was devastated by famine, and another 15,000 people starved to death.

Rats, however, offer the most interesting – and still controversial – case of actual and imagined disease transmission. In 1894, Alexander Emile Jean Yersin isolated and identified *Yersinia pestis* as the bacterial contagious agent in a Hong Kong plague outbreak; four year later, the rat flea (*Xenopsylla cheopsis*) was pinpointed as the disease vector, passing the plague from rats to humans. Today, there is an ongoing debate about whether rat fleas or human fleas (and lice) were responsible for the medieval plague outbreaks, but for early modern Europeans, rats functioned much as insects did in narratives of transmission.[38] English texts tend to treat rats in one of two ways: either as the emissaries of spiritual contagion sent by Satan or as the vehicle of a God-given pestilence associated with famine. The former figure in William Drage's 1665 treatise *Daimonomageia*, which describes witches sending their "Imps, or young Spirits, [...] sometimes in the form of Mice, sometimes of Flies" into cattle, men, "Plants and Fruits of the Earth."[39] Such descriptions figure prominently in early modern travel writing, often restaging the metaphysical ravages of traditional plague literature in a barely more secular key. Garcilaso de la Vega, for example, describes "the incredible multitudes of Rats and Mice" brought to Peru by the Spaniards; "Swarming all over the Land," these voracious rodents ate seeds and killed fruit trees, nearly forcing the colonists to "abandon Dwellings" had not "God in mercy caused that Plague to cease on a sudden."[40] Samuel Clarke, similarly, recounts the history of a "great Plague" of rats, born from a few stowaways, that multiplied and ravaged the first English plantation in Bermuda; despite cats, dogs, ratsbane, trapping, and even setting the woods on fire – the rats took over the island, "eating all up," and thereby precipitating a disease called "the Feagues."[41] Suddenly, however, "it pleased God to take [the rats] away."[42] Competing with humans for food supplies and capable of traveling long distances, rats, like insects, are the early modern companion animals of global disease.

Although rats often were not described explicitly as disease vectors, they dominated narratives about dearth and famine, especially on ships. In William Dampier's accounts of his circumnavigations in the 1690s and early 1700s, rodents pose a dire threat to shipboard provisions. Leaving Cape Corrientes on the west coast of Mexico to sail across the Pacific to the East Indies, Dampier describes the crew's fear at having their meager provisions ravaged by shipboard rats: "we had not 60 days Provision, at a little more than half a pint of Maiz a day for each man, [...] and we had a great many Rats aboard, which we could not hinder from eating part of our Maiz."[43] Dampier's fellow buccaneer, Woodes Rogers, preyed on Spanish shipping along the coasts of Peru and Chile in 1708–9 and found that even when he stole grain, it was quickly "much damag'd by the [shipboard] Rats."[44] Given the absence of grain and the ability of rats to multiply quickly, island ecologies could be quickly overrun with rodents. After Rogers rescued the Scots sailor Alexander Selkirk, marooned for three years on the island of Juan Fernandez off the Chilean coast, he described the living conditions that Defoe fictionalized in *Robinson Crusoe* (1719). Selkirk, according to Rogers, was

> much pester'd with Cats and Rats, that had bred in great numbers from some of each Species which had got ashore from Ships that put in there to wood and water. The Rats gnaw'd his Feet and Clothes while asleep, which

oblig'd him to cherish the Cats with his Goats-flesh; by which many of them became so tame, that they would lie about him in hundreds, and soon deliver'd him from the Rats.[45]

Selkirk's term "pester'd" is derived from the "pest," an alternate term for the bubonic plague, but here is used in the general sense of pestilence. Before Selkirk semi-domesticates the cats, rats – reproducing, like the cats, "in great numbers" – literally threaten to eat him alive.

As I have argued elsewhere, Daniel Defoe's *Robinson Crusoe* transforms rats and other vermin from the ubiquitous threats that slither and crawl through seventeenth-century travel writing to controllable populations; rats, birds, wolves, and hostile indigenes fall victim to the same violent technologies: traps, toxicants, repellants, barriers, and banishment. Indeed, the enduring popularity of *Robinson Crusoe* – it went through about 1,000 editions and adaptations before World War I – partially depends on Defoe's narrative sleight of hand in banishing rats from Crusoe's island: the rats that plagued Selkirk and devastated Rogers's pirated grain are, like pestiferous insects, almost completely exiled from the novel. Defoe mentions rats only three times in *Robinson Crusoe*, all of them in relation to a single bag of grain. Scavenging on his shipwrecked vessel for provisions, he finds "a little Remainder of *European* Corn" that had been "laid by" for some now-deceased "Fowls": "there had been some Barley and Wheat together, but, to my great Disappointment, I found afterwards that the Rats had eaten or spoil'd it all."[46] Later, Crusoe discovers the bag of barley and wheat, and then decides to take the nearly empty bag of corn that, he supposed, "was all devour'd with Rats." Seeing "nothing in the Bag but Husks and Dust," he shakes it out once he returns to the island. A month later, miraculously, Crusoe sees "a few Stalks of something green shooting out of the Ground."[47] The providential preservation of grain against the threat of hungry rats leads to his meditation on the nature of this agricultural miracle: "for it was really the Work of Providence as to me, that should order or appoint, that 10 or 12 Grains of Corn should remain unspoil'd (when the Rats had destroy'd all the rest,) as if it had been dropt from Heaven."[48] Because grain seeds quickly succumb to moisture, whether rain or rodent urine, Crusoe attributes the fact that a few seeds remained "unspoil'd" to divine intervention. The "Work of Providence" in securing a suitable ecological niche for the seeds, protected from the effects of the tropical sun, reaffirms the values and assumptions of a colonial food system. Strangely, however, the rats that helped themselves to the poultry feed have disappeared. Unlike Selkirk, then, Crusoe is not "pester'd with" rats, and although he is prone to occasional fevers, he attributes them not to the absence of disease vectors but to divine punishment for his imagined sins.

The island's imagined environment is less an open, dynamic ecosystem than a closed zoomorphic world in which Crusoe hunts, gathers, farms, and stores under metaphysically secured conditions. This point is critical to understanding the ways that rats, like insects, figure in seventeenth- and eighteenth-century literature and its depictions of what we now would call ecology. The agricultural economy of Crusoe's island depends not simply on the providential *presence* of European corn but on the *absence* of the rats and other vermin that plagued European colonists, struggling to protect their grain supplies against rodent and insect infestations. Unable to imagine a successful agricultural colony that accommodates vermin, Defoe simply banishes them from the island, a form of magical thinking not far removed from efforts on the part of the medieval Catholic Church to anathematize vermin by cursing them. In short, he stops their motion, their mobility, in the only way available to him – through his imagination. In so doing, he imagines an island free of dearth and disease.

Agriculture and the Fifth Plague

So far, I have focused on insects and rats as perceived emissaries of disease mediated by famine and regulated by God. Paradoxically, however, sick livestock, rather than insects or rats – and in ways I can only gesture toward here – generated the most debate about the course and nature of epidemic illnesses. Between 1470 and 1570, a new system emerged in the marketing of livestock, partly prompted by the increased cultivation of arable land; by the early modern period, regional marketing systems had given way to an international cattle trade that brought with it epidemic disease and mass mortality events.[49] John Fitzherbert's *The Boke of Husbandry* (1540) was the first text to deal with murrains, or mass animal die-offs; it was followed by Girolamo Fracastoro's comparative treatise on human and animal diseases in 1546, and Leonard Mascall's *The First Booke of Cattell* in 1587.[50] By the time Shakespeare wrote his early plays, at the end of the sixteenth century, Europe had suffered at least nine major cattle plagues since 1500 – roughly one per decade – and had recorded at least 300 years of organized efforts to understand and manage murrains.

If dog bites were the clearest instance of cross- or multispecies infection, cattle plague raised more urgent questions, and perhaps sharper fear. Clive Spinage describes a fourteenth-century British epizootic after which "panic stricken" shepherds, fearing the Black Death, fled from their herds.[51]

A few surviving animals then roamed the countryside, spreading disease, but, because people feared the contagion, no one would chase down the creatures and contain or kill them. Other responses to outbreaks included a variety of local and often occult remedies: cutting off the head of a live two year-old animal and hanging it up in the house with the eyes facing east (Northern Germany), hiding a skull under the ridge of a house (Northern Europe), hanging the head of a horse in a stall (Wales).[52] Together, sermons and animal husbandry manuals record a history of large mass animal die-offs that parallel and sometimes, it was thought, serve as a frightening prelude to human plague in ways that would reinforce biblical accounts of providential punishment, as in the ten plagues of Egypt narrative. Thomas Brooks, a popular seventeenth-century Puritan divine who stayed in London during the plague to look after his flocks, demonstrates this strategy. Dismissing physicians and prophets who ascribe plague "to the heat of the Air," "driness," "corruption" of the air, "mens blood," "Satan," or the "malignancy of the Planets," he insists one must look beyond these "second causes, to the First Cause," to *"the wheel within the wheel"*:

> The Plague is a hidden thing, a secret thing; it is a sickness, a disease, that more immediately comes from God, than any other sickness or disease doth. *Behold the hand of the Lord is upon thy cattel which is in the field, upon the horses, upon the asses, upon the camels, upon the oxen, and upon the sheep, there shall be a very grievous murrain.*[53]

For Brooks, as for many others, etiological differences between human and animal plagues, murrains, and epidemics collapse under the rubric of "First Causes," or divine retributions and biblical interpretations. "The word here [in Exodus 9.3]," he continues, "translated *murrain*, is in *chap. 5. v. 3.* termed *pestilence*; and it is one and the same disease, though when it is applied to cattel, it be usually rendred by murrain, yet when 'tis applied to men, as in the Scripture last cited, it is commonly called the pestilence."[54] Zoonotic diseases crossed species boundaries; outbreaks among livestock were associated with the same rhetoric of punishment and divine retribution that accompanied the human epidemics during the early modern period.

Fearing both cross-species contagion and the dearth murrains engendered, governments mounted strict and sometimes coordinated public health responses, designed to stop the movement of cattle, and thus the spread of disease. Spinage discusses what probably was a zoonotic outbreak in or around 1514 in Venice and the surrounding areas. Around this time, he reports, people in Padua and Venice were "afflicted" by an "epidemic dysentery" after eating diseased cattle flesh – "flesh from cadavers" – imported from Hungary, a trade that sometimes reached as many as 7,418 head in one day.[55] A similar outbreak, this one in oxen, occurred in 1590, when the Council of Venice once again outlawed beef, cheese, butter, and milk. In 1598, rinderpest erupted in Germany and the next year spread to Italy where 13,000 cattle died. When human dysentery followed, the Venetian state ordered the destruction of infected animals. The plague nevertheless spread to France where, in 1604, the health department in Lyon commanded that any cattle intended for slaughter be inspected by "a master butcher in the presence of a commissioner of health" and that infected bodies be buried two meters deep and covered with quicklime.[56] What made public health responses imperative was the *scale* of death and disease. During the first year of a rinderpest or anthrax outbreak, some 70 percent of cattle were usually lost, often tens and even hundreds of thousands, a mortality rate that outstrips those reported for human plague.[57] And in the sixteenth and seventeenth centuries, "great mortalities" or "pestilences" of cattle were reported throughout Germany, the Netherlands, Italy, and Great Britain.

The fact of widespread murrain in the early modern period affects – or should affect – how we interpret its literature. The year Shakespeare wrote *Troilus and Cressida*, 1609, and the year Shakespeare died, 1616, were markedly infectious for Eastern and Central Europe, with veal and beef once again prohibited; in Italy, beef and oxen stocks were nearly depleted through disease and extensive herd culling.[58] (The traditional protocol was to cull, kill, and bury diseased or contaminated cattle deep enough so that effluvia would stay contained.) In *Troilus and Cressida*, which Jonathan Gil Harris has called Shakespeare's most "disease-ridden" play, Ajax and Thersites insult each other in imagery rife with the language of multispecies disease:[59] the venom-tongued Thersites invokes running boils, the "plague of Greece," horses, dogs, scabs, itches, porcupines, witches, scurvy, asses, and "draught-oxen" to characterize Ajax, a "mongrel beef-witted lord."[60] When the exasperated Ajax starts beating Thersites, the latter curses him with "[a] red murrain on o' thy jade's tricks" (2.1.19). But what is this bloody murrain? It is not simply a metaphor for bubonic plague. Placed within the context of mass animal die-offs that I have outlined, Thersites's curse is redolent of a neglected history of multispecies affliction, and of the associations between disease and livestock that form the substratum of his insults.

The Merchant of Venice similarly invokes the international livestock trade and the diseases that it spread. The most important lines in *The*

Merchant of Venice, in this context, are Antonio's. At the trial for defaulting on his debt, as he patiently awaits Shylock to exact his "pound of flesh," he encourages Bassiano to leave him. "I am a tainted wether of the flock," he says, "Meetest for death" (4.1. 113–14).[61] Greenblatt's edition defines "tainted" as "castrated," although the more common definition is "corrupted," "stained," or "infected"; "wether" refers to a sheep or ram; and "meetest for death" reflects the necessity of culling this diseased animal before the rest of the herd becomes afflicted. Antonio's identification with a sacrificial animal, in one respect, points to the moral and sacrificial economies of Christianity; in another, his identification with *infected cattle* points to the commercial, environmental, agricultural, and medical economies in which humans and animals are equally vulnerable to zoonotic disease.

Epilogue

If, over the centuries, humanists have lost the context for appreciating imagery embedded in the more-than-human plague discourse, that loss may partially be attributed – again – to Daniel Defoe, whose *Journal of the Plague Year* (1722) is the foundational text for early modern and eighteenth-century understandings of plague.[62] Not only does his fictionalized account of the 1665 outbreak of bubonic plague focus almost exclusively on humans, but it actively erases the preoccupation with cattle plague and the possibility of multispecies infection that characterized some of Defoe's source texts. Briefly, in 1720 cattle plague returned to northeast Germany, Italy, and parts of Switzerland and France. The cattle murrain around Marseilles was followed by an epidemic so severe that many people considered setting the town, stinking of human and animal remains, on fire. The French government eventually built a wall to isolate the Mediterranean city from the rest of Provence. The return of bubonic plague produced general alarm and a rash of texts in England about the last visitation. Nathaniel Hodges's *Loimologia, or an Historical Account of the Plague in 1665* was translated into English and republished in 1720, along with John Quincy's remarks on the plague.[63] Defoe relied on both in the crafting of *Journal of the Plague Year* but glosses the idea – shared by both authors – that cattle suffer from diseases that may or may not be transmitted to humans.

Although rinderpest, we now know, is *not* zoonotic, some 80 percent of diseases are: rabies and bubonic plague, most obviously, but also malaria, brucellosis, avian flu, swine flu, SARS, MERS, Ebola, HIV/AIDS, Lyme disease – the list is long and growing. Human economic activities, disruptions to the wildlife habitat, and intensive livestock farming have contributed to the problem. But in *Journal of the Plague Year*, as in *Robinson Crusoe*, Defoe focuses on the values and assumptions of human exceptionalism and consequently on theologically inflected views of dearth and disease as the counterpart of divinely sanctioned spiritual contagion. *Journal of the Plague Year* praises sustained efforts by the municipal authorities in London to restrict *human* mobility to halt the advance of the plague, but Defoe mentions cattle only twice in passing, and cattle plague not at all.[64] This apparently insignificant difference, arguably, is symptomatic: Defoe's narrow, anthropocentric focus has remained the norm for medical historians, and for the literary critics who rely on them. As One Health advocate Abigail Woods writes, most scholars "have not significantly revised their perceptions of what constitutes medical history."[65] Our most recent, zoonotically induced pandemic could help shake us loose from the false sense that humans exist apart from "nature," perceived largely as a vast warehouse whose stores are there for the taking, but only if we look beyond our own afflictions to the historical economic and agricultural practices increasingly responsible for them. We share a teeming zoosphere with many other creatures; a medical *post*humanities could enable us to acknowledge our multispecies existence, while taking seriously the extent to which the mass transport of animals – intentionally, as in the cattle trade, or unintentionally, as in rats hitching rides on ships – has reshaped our microbiotic and pathogenic world.

Notes

1 Christopher F. Loar, "Plague's Ecologies: Daniel Defoe and the Epidemic Constitution," *Eighteenth-Century Fiction* 2 (2019), 31–53, 37.

2 William Shakespeare, *The Tempest*, in Stephen Greenblatt et al. (eds.), *The Norton Shakespeare* (London: Norton, 2008), 2.2.1–5.

3 See Eric H. Ash, *The Draining of the Fens: Projectors, Popular Politics, and State Building in Early Modern England* (Baltimore, MD: Johns Hopkins University Press, 2017).

4 Stacy Alaimo first outlines this concept in *Bodily Natures: Science, Environment, and the Material Self* (Bloomington: Indiana University Press, 2010).

5 Historical accounts of rabies include John Blaisdell, "Rabies in Shakespeare's England," *Historia Medicinae Veterinariae* 16 (1991), 22–3; and Neil

Pemberton and Michael Warboys, *Dogs, Diseases and Culture, 1830–2000* (Basingstoke: Palgrave Macmillan, 2007).

6 Cited in Charles F. Mullett, "Some Neglected Aspects of Plague Medicine in Sixteenth-Century England," *The Scientific Monthly* 44.4 (1937), 325–37.

7 Mark Jenner, "The Great Dog Massacre," in William G. Naphy and Penny Roberts (eds.), *Fear in Early Modern Society* (Manchester: St. Martin's Press, 1997), 44–61.

8 See Lucinda Cole, *Imperfect Creatures: Vermin, Literature, and the Science of Life 1600–1740* (Ann Arbor: University of Michigan Press, 2016), 136–8.

9 Leo Africanus, *A Geographical Historie of Africa, written in Arabicke and Italian by Iohn Leo a More, borne in Granada, and brought vp in Barbarie*, trans. John Pory (London: George Bishop, 1600), 350. This edition includes accounts by Orosius and Alvarez.

10 Ibid., 350.

11 Ibid., 352.

12 On insect excommunication, see E. P. Evans, *The Criminal Prosecution and Capital Punishment of Animals* (London: Heinemann, 1906), 5.

13 Africanus, *Geographical Historie*, 352.

14 Ibid., 353.

15 Ibid., 958.

16 Ibid., 350.

17 Cole, *Imperfect Creatures*, 49–80.

18 For Moffett, I use Edward Topsell, *The history of four-footed beasts and serpents … whereunto is now added, The theater of insects, or, Lesser living creatures … by T. Muffet* (London: E. Cotes, 1658), 987.

19 Samuel Purchas, *A theater of politicall flying-insects* (London: R.I. for Thomas Parkhurst, 1657), 201.

20 There were ongoing debates about the differences between locusts and grass-hoppers. On insect infestation in Ireland and Wales, see David E. Thornton, "Locusts in Ireland? A Problem in the Welsh and Frankish Annals," *Cambrian Medieval Celtic Studies* 31 (1996), 37–53; see also Lucinda Cole, "Swift among the Locusts: Vermin, Infestation, and Natural Philosophy in the Eighteenth Century," in Bruce Boehrer, Molly Hand, and Brian Massumi (eds.), *Animals, Animality, and Literature* (Cambridge: Cambridge University Press, 2018), 136–55.

21 Topsell, *History of four-footed beasts*, 987.

22 Ibid., 987.

23 Uli Schmetzer, "'Worst Locust Plague in History' Threatens Europe," *Chicago Tribune*, May 2, 1988, http://articles.chicagotribune.com/1988-05-02/news/8803130590_1_swarms-desert-locust-locust-larvae, accessed March 2, 2017.

24 Topsell, *History of four-footed beasts*, 989.

25 Ibid.

26 George Wither, *Britain's Remembrancer* (Manchester: Charles Simms for the Spencer Society, 1880), 19.
27 Ibid., 41.
28 Ibid., 42.
29 Ibid., 513.
30 Ibid., 51.
31 Ibid., 255.
32 Ibid., 517.
33 Charles C. Mann, *1493: Uncovering the New World Columbus Created* (New York: Vintage, 2012), 7.
34 Ibid., 13.
35 Ibid.
36 Quoted in ibid., 13.
37 Justin's description can be found in David M. Morens, "Epidemic Anthrax in the Eighteenth Century, the Americas," *Emerging Infectious Diseases* 8.10 (2002), 1160–2.
38 See Katherine R. Dean et al., "Human Ectoparasites and the Spread of Plague in Europe during the Second Pandemic," *PNAS* 115.6 (2018), 1304–9.
39 William Drage, *Daimonomageia: A Small Treatise of Sicknesses and Diseases from Witchcraft, and Supernatural Causes* (London, 1665), 15, 16.
40 Garcilaso de la Vega, *The Royal Commentaries of Peru in Two Parts*, trans. Sir Paul Rycaut (London, 1688), 385.
41 Samuel Clarke, *A True and Faithfull Account of the Four Chiefest Plantations of the English in America* (London, 1670), 28.
42 Ibid., 28.
43 William Dampier, *A New Voyage around the World* (London: Printed for James Knapton, 1703), 281.
44 Woodes Rogers, *A Cruising Voyage round the World* (London: A. Bell and B. Lintot, 1712), 220.
45 Ibid., 128.
46 Daniel Defoe, *The Life and Strange Surprizing Adventures of Robinson Crusoe*, ed. W. R. Owens (London: Pickering & Chatto, 2008), 94.
47 Ibid., 114.
48 Ibid., 115.
49 For a succinct overview of international trade routes, see Ian Blanchard, "The Continental European Cattle Trades," *Economic History Review* 39 (1986), 427–60.
50 John Fitzherbert (attributed), *The Boke of Husbandry* (London, 1540); Girolamo Fracastoro, *De contagione et contagiosis morbis* (Rome, 1646); Leonard Mascall, *The First Book of Cattel* (London, 1587).
51 C. A. Spinage, *Cattle Plague: A History* (New York: Kluwer Academic/Plenum Publishers, 2003), 5.
52 Ibid., 96.
53 Thomas Brooks, *A Heavenly Cordial for all those Servants of the Lord that have had the Plague* (London, 1666), 4–5.

54 Ibid., 6

55 Spinage, *Cattle Plague*, 97

56 Ibid., 98.

57 The Netherlands, in particular, was devastated by cattle plagues in astonishing numbers. See J. A. Faber, *Cattle Plague in the Netherlands during the Eighteenth Century* (Amsterdam: Veenman-Zonen, 1962).

58 Spinage, *Cattle Plague*, 98–9.

59 Jonathan Gil Harris, "'The Enterprise Is Sick': Pathologies of Value and Transnationality in *Troilus and Cressida*," *Renaissance Drama* 29 (1998), 3–37, 4.

60 William Shakespeare, *Troilus and Cressida*, in *The Norton Shakespeare*, 2.1.1–12.

61 William Shakespeare, *The Comical History of the Merchant of Venice*, in *The Norton Shakespeare*.

62 Daniel Defoe, *A Journal of the Plague Year; Being Observations or Memorials, of the Most Remarkable Occurrenenes ... Which happened in London During the Last Great Visitation in 1665* (London: Printed for E. Nutt, A. Dodd, and J. Graves, 1722).

63 Nathanial Hodges, *Loimologia, or an Historical Account of the Plague in 1665*, 2nd ed. (London: Printed for E. Bell and J. Osborne, 1720).

64 For a longer version of this argument, see Lucinda Cole, "What Is an Animal? Contagion and Being Human in a Multispecies World," *Lumen* 40 (2021), 35–53.

65 See Abigail Woods, Michael Bresalier, Angelo Cassidy, and Rachel Mason Dentiger (eds.), *Animals and the Shaping of Modern Medicine: One Health and Its Histories* (Basingstoke: Palgrave Macmillan, 2018), 12.

Select Bibliography

Literary Texts

Baker, J. A., *The Peregrine* (New York: New York Review of Books, 2005).

Barbauld, Anna Letitia, *The Poems of Anna Letitia Barbauld*, ed. William McCarthy and Elizabeth Kraft (Athens: University of Georgia Press, 1994).

Barnes, Djuna, *Creatures in an Alphabet* (New York: Dial Press, 1982).

Nightwood (London: Faber and Faber, 2001).

Ryder (New York: St. Martin's Press, 1956).

Black, Joseph L. (ed.), *The Martin Marprelate Tracts: A Modernized and Annotated Edition* (Cambridge: Cambridge University Press, 2008).

Blake, William, *Blake: The Complete Poems*, eds. W. H. Stevenson and David V. Erdman (New York: Longman, 1971).

Brontë, Charlotte, *Jane Eyre* (London: Penguin, 2006).

Bunt, G. H. V. (ed.), *William of Palerne: An Alliterative Romance* (Groningen: Bouma, 1985).

Byron, *Poetical Works*, ed. Frederick Page, corr. John Jump (London: Oxford University Press, 1970).

Clare, John, *Major Works* (Oxford: Oxford University Press, 2004).

Poems of the Middle Period, 1822–1837, vol. 5, ed. Eric Robinson, David Powell and P. M. S. Dawson (Oxford: Clarendon, 2003).

Cortázar, Julio, *Blow-Up: And Other Stories*, trans. Paul Blackburn (New York: Pantheon Books, 1985).

Defoe, Daniel, *A Journal of the Plague Year; Being Observations or Memorials, of the Most Remarkable Occurrences . . . Which Happened in London During the Last Great Visitation in 1665* (London: Printed for E. Nutt, A. Dodd, and J. Graves, 1722).

The Life and Strange Surprizing Adventures of Robinson Crusoe, ed. W. R. Owens (London: Pickering & Chatto, 2008).

Dickens, Charles, *Barnaby Rudge* (Oxford: Oxford University Press, 2013).

Bleak House (London: Penguin, 2003).

Oliver Twist (London: Penguin, 2008).

Eliot, T. S. *Collected Poems 1909–1962* (London: Faber and Faber, 1974).

Inventions of the March Hare: Poems 1909–1917, ed. Christopher Ricks (New York: Harcourt Brace & Company, 1996).

Old Possum's Book of Practical Cats (London: Faber and Faber, 2001).

Elwes, Alfred, *The Adventures of a Bear, and a Great Bear Too!* (London: Addey and Co., 1853).

The Adventures of a Dog, and a Good Dog Too! (London: Addey and Co., 1854).

Evliya Çelebi, *An Ottoman Traveller: Selections from the Book of Travels of Evliya Çelebi*, ed. and trans. Robert Dankoff and Sooyong Kim (London: Eland, 2010).

Gowdy, Barbara, *The White Bone* (New York: Metropolitan Books, 1998).

Granta 142: Animalia (Winter 2018).

Hardy, Thomas, *Far from the Madding Crowd* (London: Penguin, 2003).

Isidore, *The Etymologies of Isidore of Seville*, ed. Stephen A. Barney et al. (Cambridge: Cambridge University Press, 2006).

Joyce, James, *Ulysses* (London: Penguin, 1992).

Kafka, Franz, *Collected Stories*, ed. Gabriel Josipovici (New York: Knopf, 1993).

Kingsley, Mary, *Travels in West Africa* (London: Phoenix Press, 2000).

Lawrence, D. H., *The Complete Poems*, ed. Vivian de Sola Pinto and F. Warren Roberts (Harmondsworth: Penguin, 1977).

Lispector, Clarice, "The Hen," trans. Elizabeth Bishop, *Kenyon Review* 26 (1964), 507–9.

MacNeice, Louis, *Zoo* (London: Faber and Faber, 1996).

McAdams, Janet, *Feral* (Norfolk: Salt Publishing, 2007).

Seven Boxes for the Country After (Kent, OH: Kent State University Press, 2016).

Melville, Herman, *Moby-Dick*, ed. Hershel Parker (New York: W. W. Norton, 2018).

Micha, Alexandre (ed.), *Guillaume de Palerne: Roman du XIIIe siècle* (Geneva: Droz, 1990).

Millet, Lydia, *I'm with the Bears: Short Stories from a Damaged Planet*, ed. Mark Martin (New York: Verso, 2011).

Nabokov, Vladimir, *The Annotated Lolita*, ed. Alfred Appel (New York: Vintage, 1991).

NDiaye, Marie, *La Naufragée – J. M. W. Turner* (Paris: Le Flohic, 1999).

Orwell, George, *Animal Farm* (Harmondsworth: Penguin, 1951).

Physiologus: A Medieval Book of Nature Lore, trans. Michael J. Curley (Chicago: University of Chicago Press, 2009).

Pico, Tommy, *Nature Poem* (Portland: Tin House Books, 2017).

Poe, Edgar Allan, *Poetry and Tales* (New York: Library of America, 1984).

Pope, Alexander, *The Poems of Alexander Pope: A One-Volume Edition of the Twickenham Text with Selected Annotations*, ed. John Butt (London: Methuen, 1963).

Rilke, Rainer Maria, *The Selected Poetry of Rainer Maria Rilke*, ed. and trans. Stephen Mitchell (New York: Vintage, 1982).

Schreiner, Olive, *The Story of an African Farm* (Peterborough: Broadview Press, 2003).

Sewell, Anna, *Black Beauty* (London: Penguin, 2008).

Shakespeare, William, *Hamlet*, ed. Ann Thompson and Neil Taylor (London: Arden, 2016).

The Norton Shakespeare, ed. Stephen Greenblatt et al. (London: Norton, 2008).

Swift, Jonathan, *Gulliver's Travels*, ed. Claude Rawson and Ian Higgins (Oxford: Oxford University Press, 2005).

Thomson, James, *The Complete Poetical Works of James Thomson*, ed. J. Logie Robertson (Oxford: Henry Frowde/Oxford University Press, 1908).

Topsell, Edward, *The History of Four-Footed Beasts and Serpents and Insects* (London, 1658).

White, Gilbert, *The Natural History and Antiquities of Selborne, in the County of Southampton* [1789] (Menston: Scholar Press, 1970).

White, T. H. (ed. and trans.), *The Book of Beasts* (London: Jonathan Cape, 1954).

Wither, George, *Britain's Remembrancer* (Manchester: Charles Simms for the Spencer Society, 1880).

Woolf, Virginia, *Flush: A Biography* (London: Hogarth Press, 1963).

Mrs. Dalloway (London: Penguin, 1992).

Wordsworth, William, *William Wordsworth: The Major Works*, ed. Stephen Gill, rev. ed. (Oxford: Oxford University Press, 2008).

Wordsworth, William, and Samuel Taylor Coleridge, *Lyrical Ballads*, ed. R. L. Brett and A. R. Jones (London: Methuen, 1968).

Yeats, W. B., *The Poems*, ed. Daniel Albright (London: Everyman, 1992).

Further Critical Reading

Adkins, Peter, *The Modernist Anthropocene: Nonhuman Life and Planetary Change in James Joyce, Virginia Woolf and Djuna Barnes* (Edinburgh: Edinburgh University Press, 2022).

Agamben, Giorgio, *Homo Sacer: Sovereign Power and Bare Life*, trans. Daniel Heller Roazen (Stanford, CA: Stanford University Press, 1998).

The Open: Man and Animal (Stanford, CA: Stanford University Press, 2004).

Alaimo, Stacey, *Bodily Natures: Science, Environment, and the Material Self* (Bloomington: Indiana University Press, 2010).

Albala, Ken, *Eating Right in the Renaissance* (Berkeley: University of California Press, 2002).

Alkemeyer, Bryan, "The Natural History of the Houyhnhnms: Noble Horses in *Gulliver's Travels*," *The Eighteenth Century* 57.1 (Spring 2016): 23–37.

Aravamudan, Srinivas, *Enlightenment Orientalism: Resisting the Rise of the Novel* (Chicago: University of Chicago Press, 2012).

Aristotle, *Nicomachean Ethics*, trans. C. D. C. Reeve (Indianapolis, IN: Hackett, 2014).

Armstrong, Philip, *What Animals Mean in the Fiction of Modernity* (London: Routledge, 2008).

Ballaster, Ros, *Fabulous Orients: Fictions of the East in England 1662–1785* (Oxford: Oxford University Press, 2005).

Baratay, Eric, and Elizabeth Hardouin-Fugier, *Zoo: A History of Zoological Gardens in the West* (London: Reaktion, 2002).

Barrell, John, *The Idea of Landscape and the Sense of Place 1730–1840* (Cambridge: Cambridge University Press, 1972).

Bate, Jonathan, *Romantic Ecology: Wordsworth and the Environmental Tradition* (London: Routledge, 2013).

Bennett, Jane, *Vibrant Matter: A Political Ecology of Things* (Durham, NC: Duke University Press, 2009).

Berger, John, "Why Look at Animals?," in *About Looking* (London: Bloomsbury, 2009).

Bisgould, Lesli, *Animals and the Law* (Toronto: Irwin Law, 2011).

Boehrer, Bruce Thomas, *Animal Characters: Nonhuman Beings in Early Modern Literature* (Philadelphia: University of Pennsylvania Press, 2010).

Boehrer, Bruce, Molly Hand, and Brian Massumi (eds.), *Animals, Animality, and Literature* (Cambridge: Cambridge University Press, 2018).

Boisseron, Bénédicte, *Afro-Dog: Blackness and the Animal Question* (New York: Columbia University Press, 2018).

Borlik, Todd A., *Ecocriticism and Early Modern English Literature: Green Pastures* (London: Routledge, 2011).

Brown, Jayna, *Black Utopias: Speculative Life and the Music of Other Worlds* (Durham, NC: Duke University Press, 2021).

Brown, Laura, *Homeless Dogs and Melancholy Apes: Humans and Other Animals in the Modern Literary Imagination* (Ithaca, NY: Cornell University Press, 2010).

Browne, Thomas, *Pseudodoxia Epidemica*, 2 vols., ed. Robin Robbins (Oxford: Clarendon, 1981).

Butler, Judith, *Bodies That Matter* (New York: Routledge, 1993).

Calarco, Matthew, *Beyond the Anthropological Difference* (Cambridge: Cambridge University Press, 2018).

Chen, Mel Y., *Animacies: Biopolitics, Racial Mattering, and Queer Affect* (Durham, NC: Duke University Press, 2012).

Chez, Keridiana, *Victorian Dogs, Victorian Men: Affect and Animals in Nineteenth-Century Literature and Culture* (Columbus: Ohio State University Press, 2017).

Cole, Lucinda, *Imperfect Creatures: Vermin, Literature, and the Science of Life 1600–1740* (Ann Arbor: University of Michigan Press, 2016).

Cosslett, Tess, *Talking Animals in British Children's Fiction, 1786–1914* (Aldershot: Ashgate, 2006).

Coulthard, Glen Sean, *Red Skin, White Masks: Rejecting the Colonial Politics of Recognition* (Minneapolis: University of Minnesota Press, 2014).

Crane, Susan, *Animal Encounters: Contacts and Concepts in Medieval Britain* (Philadelphia: University of Pennsylvania Press, 2013).

Crawley, Ashon T., *Blackpentecostal Breath: The Aesthetics of Possibility* (New York: Fordham University Press, 2017).

Crist, Eileen, *Abundant Earth: Toward an Ecological Civilization* (Chicago: University of Chicago Press, 2019).

Images of Animals: Anthropomorphism and Animal Mind (Philadelphia: Temple University Press, 1999).

Darwin, Charles, *The Expression of the Emotions in Man and Animal* (London: Penguin, 2009).

da Silva, Denise Ferreira, *Towards a Global Idea of Race* (Minneapolis: University of Minnesota Press, 2007).

Daston, Lorraine, and Gregg Mitman (eds.), *Thinking with Animals: New Perspectives on Anthropomorphism* (New York: Columbia University Press, 2005).

Davies, Jeremy, *The Birth of the Anthropocene* (Oakland: University of California Press, 2016).

Derrida, Jacques, *The Animal That Therefore I Am*, trans. David Wills (New York: Fordham University Press, 2008).

The Beast and the Sovereign, vol. 1, trans. Geoffrey Bennington (Chicago: University of Chicago Press, 2009).

Despret, Vinciane, *What Would Animals Say If We Asked the Right Questions?*, trans. Brett Buchanan (Minneapolis: University of Minnesota Press, 2016).

Driscoll, Kári, and Eva Hoffmann (eds.), *What Is Zoopoetics?: Texts, Bodies, Entanglement* (Cham: Palgrave Macmillan, 2018).

Edwards, Karen L., Derek Ryan, and Jane Spencer (eds.), *Reading Literary Animals: Medieval to Modern* (London: Routledge, 2019).

Evans, Edward Payson, *The Criminal Prosecution and Capital Punishment of Animals* (London: William Heinemann, 1906).

Farrier, David, *Anthropocene Poetics: Deep Time, Sacrifice Zones, and Extinction* (Minneapolis: University of Minnesota Press, 2019).

Feerik, Jean E., and Vin Nardizzi (eds.), *The Indistinct Human in Renaissance Literature* (Basingstoke: Palgrave Macmillan, 2012).

Feuerstein, Anna, *The Political Lives of Victorian Animals: Liberal Creatures in Literature and Culture* (Cambridge: Cambridge University Press, 2019).

Flegel, Monica, *Pets and Domesticity in Victorian Literature and Culture: Animality, Queer Relations, and the Victorian Family* (New York: Routledge, 2015).

Frost, Samantha, *Biocultural Creatures: Towards a New Theory of the Human* (Durham, NC: Duke University Press, 2016).

Fudge, Erica, *Brutal Reasoning: Animals, Rationality and Humanity in Early Modern England* (Ithaca, NY: Cornell University Press, 2006).

Quick Cattle and Dying Wishes: People and Their Animals in Early Modern England (Ithaca, NY: Cornell University Press, 2018).

Fudge, Erica (ed.), *Renaissance Beasts: Of Animals, Humans and Other Wonderful Creatures* (Urbana: University of Illinois Press, 2004).

Govindrajan, Radhika, *Animal Intimacies: Interspecies Relatedness in India's Central Himalayas* (Chicago: University of Chicago Press, 2018).

Greenberg, Jonathan, "Introduction: Darwin and Literary Studies," *Twentieth-Century Literature* 55.4 (Winter 2009), 423–44.

Griffin, Miranda, *Transforming Tales: Rewriting Metamorphosis in Medieval French Literature* (Oxford: Oxford University Press, 2015).

Grosz, Elizabeth, *The Nick of Time: Politics, Evolution and the Untimely* (Durham, NC: Duke University Press, 2004).

Gruen, Lori (ed.), *Critical Terms for Animal Studies* (Chicago: University of Chicago Press, 2018).

Haraway, Donna J., *Primate Visions: Gender, Race, and Nature in the World of Modern Science* (New York: Routledge, 1989).

    Staying with the Trouble: Making Kin in the Chthulucene (Durham, NC: Duke University Press, 2016).

    When Species Meet (Minneapolis: University of Minnesota Press, 2008).

Heidegger, Martin, *The Fundamental Concepts of Metaphysics: World, Finitude, Solitude*, trans. William McNeill and Nicholas Walker (Bloomington: Indiana University Press, 1995).

Herman, David, *Narratology beyond the Human: Storytelling and Animal Life* (Oxford: Oxford University Press, 2018).

Herman, David (ed.), "Special Issue: Animal Worlds in Modern Fiction," *Modern Fiction Studies* 60.3 (Fall 2014).

Heymans, Peter, *Animality in British Romanticism: The Aesthetic of Species* (New York: Routledge, 2012).

Höfele, Andreas, *Stake, Stage and Scaffold: Humans and Animals in Shakespeare's Theatre* (Oxford: Oxford University Press, 2011).

Hovanec, Caroline, *Animal Subjects: Literature, Zoology, and British Modernism* (Cambridge: Cambridge University Press, 2018).

Howell, Philip, *At Home and Astray: The Domestic Dog in Victorian Britain* (Charlottesville: University of Virginia Press, 2015).

Hunter, Lynette, Elisabeth Krimmer, and Peter Lichtenfels (eds.), *Sentient Performativities of Embodiment: Thinking Alongside the Human* (Lanham, MD: Lexington Books, 2016).

Jackson, Zakiyyah Iman, *Becoming Human: Matter and Meaning in an Antiblack World* (New York: New York University Press, 2020).

Kalof, Linda (ed.), *The Oxford Handbook of Animal Studies* (Oxford: Oxford University Press, 2017).

Kay, Sarah, *Animal Skins and the Reading Self in Medieval Latin and French Bestiaries* (Chicago: Chicago University Press, 2017).

    "Before the *animot*: *Bêtise* and the Zoological Machine in Medieval Latin and French Bestiaries," *Yale French Studies* 127 (2015), 34–51.

Kean, Hilda, *Animal Rights: Political and Social Change in Britain since 1800* (London: Reaktion, 1998).

Keenleyside, Heather, *Animals and Other People: Literary Forms and Living Beings in the Long Eighteenth Century* (Philadelphia: University of Pennsylvania Press, 2016).

Kendall-Morwick, Karalyn, *Canis Modernis: Human/Dog Coevolution in Modernist Literature* (University Park: Pennsylvania State University Press, 2020).

Kenyon-Jones, Christine, *Kindred Brutes: Animals in Romantic-Period Writing* (Aldershot: Ashgate, 2001).

Kete, Kathleen (ed.), *A Cultural History of Animals in the Age of Empire* (New York: Berg, 2007).

Kövesi, Simon, *John Clare: Nature, Criticism and History* (London: Palgrave Macmillan, 2017).

Kreilkamp, Ivan, *Minor Creatures: Persons, Animals, and the Victorian Novel* (Chicago: University of Chicago Press, 2018).

Lundblad, Michael (ed.), *Animalities: Literary and Cultural Studies beyond the Human* (Edinburgh: Edinburgh University Press, 2017).

Lundblad, Michael, and Marianne DeKoven (eds.), *Species Matters: Humane Advocacy and Cultural Theory* (New York: Columbia University Press, 2011).

Martin, Randall, *Shakespeare and Ecology* (Oxford: Oxford University Press, 2015).

Marvin, Garry, and Susan McHugh, *Routledge Handbook of Human-Animal Studies* (London: Routledge, 2014).

Massumi, Brian, *What Animals Teach Us about Politics* (Durham, NC: Duke University Press, 2014).

McCance, Dawne (ed.), "Special Issue: The Animal," *Mosaic* 39.4/40.1 (2006/7).

McCracken, Peggy, *In the Skin of a Beast: Sovereignty and Animality in Medieval France* (Chicago: Chicago University Press, 2017).

McHugh, Susan, "*Animal Farm*'s Lessons for Literary Animal Studies," *Humanimalia* 1.1 (2009), 25–39.

McHugh, Susan, Robert McKay, and John Miller (eds.), *The Palgrave Handbook of Animals and Literature* (Cham: Palgrave Macmillan, 2021).

McKittrick, Katherine (ed.), *Sylvia Wynter: On Being Human as Praxis* (Durham, NC: Duke University Press, 2015).

McKusick, James, *Green Writing: Romanticism and Ecology* (New York: Palgrave Macmillan, 2010).

Meighoo, Sean, "The Function of HumAnimAllegory," *Humanities* 6.2 (2017).

Menely, Tobias, *The Animal Claim: Sensibility and the Creaturely Voice* (Chicago: University of Chicago Press, 2015).

Climate and the Making of Worlds: Toward a Geohistorical Poetics (Chicago: University of Chicago Press, 2021).

Miller, John, *Empire and the Animal Body: Violence, Identity and Ecology in Victorian Adventure Fiction* (London: Anthem, 2012).

Morton, Timothy, *Humankind: Solidarity with Non-Human People* (London: Verso, 2017)

Moss, Arthur, *Valiant Crusade: The History of the R.S.P.C.A.* (London: Cassell, 1961).

Murray, Rachel, *The Modernist Exoskeleton: Insects, War, Literary Form* (Edinburgh: Edinburgh University Press, 2020).

Nagai, Kaori, *Imperial Beast Fables: Animals, Cosmopolitanism, and the British Empire* (Cham: Palgrave Macmillan/Springer Nature, 2020).

Ng, Zhao, "After *Physiologus*: Post-Medieval Subjectivity and the Modernist Bestiaries of Guillaume Apollinaire and Djuna Barnes," *symploke* 29.1–2 (2021), 401–29.

Nietzsche, Friedrich, *Untimely Mediations*, trans. R. J. Hollingdale, ed. Daniel Breakzeale (Cambridge: Cambridge University Press, 1997).

Norris, Margot, *Beasts of the Modern Imagination: Darwin, Nietzsche, Kafka, Ernst, and Lawrence* (Baltimore, MD: Johns Hopkins University Press, 1985).

Oerlemans, Onno, *Poetry and Animals: Blurring the Boundaries of the Human* (New York: Columbia University, 2018).

Payne, Mark, *The Animal Part: Human and Other Animals in the Poetic Imagination* (Oxford: Oxford University Press, 2010).

Pemberton, Neil, and Michael Warboys, *Dogs, Diseases and Culture, 1830–2000* (Basingstoke: Palgrave Macmillan, 2007).

Perkins, David, *Romanticism and Animal Rights* (Cambridge: Cambridge University Press, 1993).

Pick, Anat, *Creaturely Poetics: Animality and Vulnerability in Literature and Film* (New York: Columbia University Press, 2011).

Quinsey, Katherine M. (ed.), *Animals and Humans: Sensibility and Representation, 1650–1820* (Oxford: Voltaire Foundation, 2017).

Raber, Karen, and Monica Mattfeld (eds.), *Performing Animals: History, Agency, Theater* (University Park: Pennsylvania State University Press, 2017).

Rajamannar, Shefali, *Reading the Animal in the Literature of the British Raj* (New York: Palgrave, 2012).

Ravindranathan, Thangam, *Behold an Animal: Four Exorbitant Readings* (Chicago: Northwestern University Press, 2020).

Ritvo, Harriet, *The Animal Estate: The English and Other Creatures in the Victorian Age* (Cambridge, MA: Harvard University Press, 1987).

Robinson, Eric, and Richard Fitter (eds.), *John Clare's Birds* (Oxford: Oxford University Press, 1982).

Robles, Mario Ortiz, *Literature and Animal Studies* (London: Routledge, 2016).

Rohman, Carrie, *Stalking the Subject: Modernism and the Animal* (New York: Columbia University Press, 2009).

Ryan, Derek, *Animal Theory: A Critical Introduction* (Edinburgh: Edinburgh University Press, 2015).

  Bloomsbury, Beasts and British Modernist Literature (Cambridge: Cambridge University Press, 2022).

Scholtmeijer, Marian, *Animal Victims in Modern Fiction: From Sanctity to Sacrifice* (Toronto: University of Toronto Press, 1993).

Setz, Cathryn, *Primordial Modernism: Animals, Ideas,* transition *(1927–1938)* (Edinburgh: Edinburgh University Press, 2019).

Shaefer, Donovan O., *Religious Affects: Animality, Evolution, and Power* (Durham, NC: Duke University Press, 2015).

Shannon, Laurie, *The Accommodated Animal: Cosmopolity in Shakespearean Locales* (Chicago: University of Chicago Press, 2013).

  "The Eight Animals in Shakespeare; or, Before the Human," *Publications of the Modern Language Society of America* 124.2 (2009), 472–9.

Simons, John, *Animal Rights and the Politics of Literary Representation* (London: Palgrave, 2002).

Simpson, Leanne Betasamosake, *As We Have Always Done: Indigenous Freedom through Radical Resistance* (Minneapolis: University of Minnesota Press, 2017).

Snaza, Nathan, *Animate Literacies: Literature, Affect, and the Politics of Humanism* (Durham, NC: Duke University Press, 2019).

Spencer, Jane, *Writing about Animals in the Age of Revolution* (Oxford: Oxford University Press, 2020).

Spillers, Hortense, *Black, White, and in Color* (Chicago: University of Chicago Press, 2003).

Spinage, C. A., *Cattle Plague: A History* (New York: Kluwer Academic/Plenum Publishers, 2003).

Steel, Karl, *How Not to Make a Human: Pets, Feral Children, Worms, Sky Burial, Oysters* (Minneapolis: University of Minnesota Press, 2019).

Theweleit, Klaus, *Male Fantasies*, vols. 1 and 2 (Minneapolis: University of Minnesota Press, 1987).

Thomas, Keith, *Man and the Natural World: A History of the Modern Sensibility* (New York: Pantheon, 1983).

Tlili, Sarra, *Animals in the Qur'an* (Cambridge: Cambridge University Press, 2012).

Traisnel, Antoine, *Capture: American Pursuits and the Making of a New Animal Condition* (Minneapolis: University of Minnesota Press, 2020).

Tsing, Anna Lowenhaupt, Heather Anne Swanson, Elaine Gan, and Nils Bubandt (eds.), *Arts of Living on a Damaged Planet: Ghosts of the Anthropocene; Monsters of the Anthropocene* (Minneapolis: University of Minnesota Press, 2017).

Turner, Lynn, Undine Sellbach, and Ron Broglio (eds.), *The Edinburgh Companion to Animal Studies* (Edinburgh: Edinburgh University Press, 2020).

Tyler, Tom, *Game: Animals, Video Games, and Humanity* (Minneapolis: University of Minnesota Press, 2022).

Van Dooren, Thom, *The Wake of Crows: Living and Dying in Shared Worlds* (New York: Columbia University Press, 2019).

von Uexküll, Jakob, *A Foray into the Worlds of Animals and Humans*, trans. Joseph D. O'Neil (Minneapolis: University of Minnesota Press, 2010).
  Theoretical Biology (New York: Harcourt, Brace & Co, 1926).

Vint, Sherryl (ed.), *After the Human: Culture, Theory, and Criticism in the 21st Century* (Cambridge: Cambridge University Press, 2020).

Weheliye, Alexander G., *Habeas Viscus* (Durham, NC: Duke University Press, 2014).

Wei, Ian P., *Thinking about Animals in Thirteenth-Century Paris: Theologians on the Boundary between Humans and Animals* (Cambridge: Cambridge University Press, 2020).

West, Anna, *Thomas Hardy and Animals* (Cambridge: Cambridge University Press, 2017).

Whyte, Kyle, "Indigenous Climate Change Studies: Indigenizing Futures, Decolonizing the Anthropocene," *English Language Notes* 55.1–2 (2017), 153–62.

Wolfe, Cary, *Before the Law: Humans and Other Animals in a Biopolitical Frame* (Chicago: University of Chicago Press, 2011).

What Is Posthumanism? (Minneapolis: University of Minnesota Press, 2010).

(ed.), *Zoontologies: The Question of the Animal* (Minneapolis: University of Minnesota Press, 2003).

Woods, Abigail, Michael Bresalier, Angelo Cassidy, and Rachel Mason Dentiger (eds.), *Animals and the Shaping of Modern Medicine: One Health and Its Histories* (Basingstoke: Palgrave Macmillan, 2018).

Wynter, Sylvia, "The Ceremony Must Be Found: After Humanism," *boundary2* 12.3 (1984), 19–70.

"Unsettling the Coloniality of Being/Power/Truth/Freedom: Towards the Human, after Man, Its Overrepresentation – An Argument," *CR: The New Centennial Review* 3.3 (Fall 2003), 257–337.

Yusoff, Katherine, *A Billion Black Anthropocenes or None* (Minneapolis: University Minnesota Press, 2018).

Index

Cambridge Companions To ...

AUTHORS

Edward Albee edited by Stephen J. Bottoms

Margaret Atwood edited by Coral Ann Howells (second edition)

W. H. Auden edited by Stan Smith

Jane Austen edited by Edward Copeland and Juliet McMaster (second edition)

James Baldwin edited by Michele Elam

Balzac edited by Owen Heathcote and Andrew Watts

Beckett edited by John Pilling

Bede edited by Scott DeGregorio

Aphra Behn edited by Derek Hughes and Janet Todd

Saul Bellow edited by Victoria Aarons

Walter Benjamin edited by David S. Ferris

William Blake edited by Morris Eaves

Boccaccio edited by Guyda Armstrong, Rhiannon Daniels, and Stephen J. Milner

Jorge Luis Borges edited by Edwin Williamson

Brecht edited by Peter Thomson and Glendyr Sacks (second edition)

The Brontës edited by Heather Glen

Bunyan edited by Anne Dunan-Page

Frances Burney edited by Peter Sabor

Byron edited by Drummond Bone

Albert Camus edited by Edward J. Hughes

Willa Cather edited by Marilee Lindemann

Catullus edited by Ian Du Quesnay and Tony Woodman

Cervantes edited by Anthony J. Cascardi

Chaucer edited by Piero Boitani and Jill Mann (second edition)

Chekhov edited by Vera Gottlieb and Paul Allain

Kate Chopin edited by Janet Beer

Caryl Churchill edited by Elaine Aston and Elin Diamond

Cicero edited by Catherine Steel

J. M. Coetzee edited by Jarad Zimbler

Coleridge edited by Lucy Newlyn

Coleridge edited by Tim Fulford (new edition)

Wilkie Collins edited by Jenny Bourne Taylor

Joseph Conrad edited by J. H. Stape

H. D. edited by Nephie J. Christodoulides and Polina Mackay

Dante edited by Rachel Jacoff (second edition)

Daniel Defoe edited by John Richetti

Don DeLillo edited by John N. Duvall

Charles Dickens edited by John O. Jordan

Emily Dickinson edited by Wendy Martin

John Donne edited by Achsah Guibbory

Dostoevskii edited by W. J. Leatherbarrow

Theodore Dreiser edited by Leonard Cassuto and Claire Virginia Eby

John Dryden edited by Steven N. Zwicker

W. E. B. Du Bois edited by Shamoon Zamir

George Eliot edited by George Levine and Nancy Henry (second edition)

T. S. Eliot edited by A. David Moody

Ralph Ellison edited by Ross Posnock

Ralph Waldo Emerson edited by Joel Porte and Saundra Morris

William Faulkner edited by Philip M. Weinstein

Henry Fielding edited by Claude Rawson

F. Scott Fitzgerald edited by Ruth Prigozy

F. Scott Fitzgerald edited by Michael Nowlin (second edition)

Flaubert edited by Timothy Unwin

E. M. Forster edited by David Bradshaw

Benjamin Franklin edited by Carla Mulford

Brian Friel edited by Anthony Roche

Robert Frost edited by Robert Faggen

Gabriel García Márquez edited by Philip Swanson

Elizabeth Gaskell edited by Jill L. Matus

Edward Gibbon edited by Karen O'Brien and Brian Young

Goethe edited by Lesley Sharpe

Günter Grass edited by Stuart Taberner

Thomas Hardy edited by Dale Kramer

David Hare edited by Richard Boon

Nathaniel Hawthorne edited by Richard Millington

Seamus Heaney edited by Bernard O'Donoghue

Ernest Hemingway edited by Scott Donaldson

Hildegard of Bingen edited by Jennifer Bain

Homer edited by Robert Fowler

Horace edited by Stephen Harrison

Ted Hughes edited by Terry Gifford

Ibsen edited by James McFarlane

Henry James edited by Jonathan Freedman

Samuel Johnson edited by Greg Clingham

TOPICS

The Actress edited by Maggie B. Gale and John Stokes

The African American Novel edited by Maryemma Graham

The African American Slave Narrative edited by Audrey A. Fisch

African American Theatre by Harvey Young

Allegory edited by Rita Copeland and Peter Struck

American Crime Fiction edited by Catherine Ross Nickerson

American Gothic edited by Jeffrey Andrew Weinstock

The American Graphic Novel edited by Jan Baetens, Hugo Frey and Fabrice Leroy

American Horror edited by Stephen Shapiro and Mark Storey

American Literature and the Body by Travis M. Foster

American Literature and the Environment edited by Sarah Ensor and Susan Scott Parrish

American Literature of the 1930s edited by William Solomon

American Modernism edited by Walter Kalaidjian

American Poetry since 1945 edited by Jennifer Ashton

American Realism and Naturalism edited by Donald Pizer

American Short Story edited by Michael J. Collins and Gavin Jones

American Travel Writing edited by Alfred Bendixen and Judith Hamera

American Women Playwrights edited by Brenda Murphy

Ancient Rhetoric edited by Erik Gunderson

Arthurian Legend edited by Elizabeth Archibald and Ad Putter

Australian Literature edited by Elizabeth Webby

The Australian Novel edited by Nicholas Birns and Louis Klee

The Beats edited by Stephen Belletto

Boxing edited by Gerald Early

British Black and Asian Literature (1945–2010) edited by Deirdre Osborne

British Fiction: 1980–2018 edited by Peter Boxall

British Fiction since 1945 edited by David James

British Literature of the 1930s edited by James Smith

British Literature of the French Revolution edited by Pamela Clemit

British Romantic Poetry edited by James Chandler and Maureen N. McLane

British Romanticism edited by Stuart Curran (second edition)

British Romanticism and Religion edited by Jeffrey Barbeau

British Theatre, 1730–1830, edited by Jane Moody and Daniel O'Quinn

Canadian Literature edited by Eva-Marie Kröller (second edition)

The Canterbury Tales edited by Frank Grady

The City in World Literature edited by Ato Quayson and Jini Kim Watson

Children's Literature edited by M. O. Grenby and Andrea Immel

The Classic Russian Novel edited by Malcolm V. Jones and Robin Feuer Miller

Comics edited by Maaheen Ahmed

Contemporary Irish Poetry edited by Matthew Campbell

Creative Writing edited by David Morley and Philip Neilsen

Crime Fiction edited by Martin Priestman

Dante's 'Commedia' edited by Zygmunt G. Barański and Simon Gilson

Dracula edited by Roger Luckhurst

Early American Literature edited by Bryce Traister

Early Modern Women's Writing edited by Laura Lunger Knoppers

The Eighteenth-Century Novel edited by John Richetti

Eighteenth-Century Poetry edited by John Sitter

Eighteenth-Century Thought edited by Frans De Bruyn

Emma edited by Peter Sabor

English Dictionaries edited by Sarah Ogilvie

English Literature, 1500–1600 edited by Arthur F. Kinney

English Literature, 1650–1740 edited by Steven N. Zwicker

English Literature, 1740–1830 edited by Thomas Keymer and Jon Mee

English Literature, 1830–1914 edited by Joanne Shattock

English Melodrama edited by Carolyn Williams

English Novelists edited by Adrian Poole

English Poetry, Donne to Marvell edited by Thomas N. Corns

English Poets edited by Claude Rawson

English Renaissance Drama edited by A. R. Braunmuller and Michael Hattaway (second edition)

For EU product safety concerns, contact us at Calle de José Abascal, 56–1°, 28003 Madrid, Spain or eugpsr@cambridge.org.

www.ingramcontent.com/pod-product-compliance
Ingram Content Group UK Ltd.
Pitfield, Milton Keynes, MK11 3LW, UK
UKHW042154130625
459647UK00011B/1321